STILL MOVING

STILL MOVING

Recent Jewish Migration
in Comparative Perspective

Daniel J. Elazar
Morton Weinfeld
editors

Routledge
Taylor & Francis Group

LONDON AND NEW YORK

First published 2000 by Transaction Publishers

2 Park Square, Milton Park, Abingdon, Oxfordshire OX14 4RN
711 Third Avenue, New York, NY 10017

Routledge is an imprint of the Taylor & Francis Group, an informa business

First issued in paperback 2017

Preparation of this book for publication was made possible in part through the Milken Library of Jewish Public Affairs of the Jerusalem Center for Public Affairs, funded by the Milken Family Foundation.
Managing Editor: Mark Ami-El
Typesetting: Andrea S. Arbel, Jerusalem

Library of Congress Catalog Number: 99-16634

Library of Congress Cataloging-in-Publication Data

Still moving: Jewish migration in comperative perspective / Daniel Elazar & Morton Weinfeld, editors.
    p. cm.
    ISBN 1-56000-428-2 (alk. paper)
    1. Jews—Migrations. 2. Jewish diaspora. 3. Israel—Emigration and immigration. 4. Jews—Canada—Emigration and immigration. 5. Israel and the diaspora. 6. Immigrants—Israel. I. Elazar, Daniel Judah. II. Weinfeld, M. (Morton)
DS134.S75   1999
304.8 ' 095694—dc21

99-16634
CIP

ISBN 13: 978-1-56000-428-8 (hbk)
ISBN 13: 978-1-138-51500-0 (pbk)

Contents

Part V: Freedom of Movement:
Should There Be a Right of Free International Migration?

Tables and Figures

Preface

In the aftermath of World War II millions of Jews migrated from their original places of residence to new ones. More than a million came to settle in the new State of Israel either from the displaced persons camps of continental Europe or from long-established Jewish communities in West Asia and North Africa. Hundreds of thousands of Jews from those countries also went to North America, Australia, and France, and tens of thousands resettled themselves elsewhere in Europe and the world. Meanwhile, other millions who themselves, or whose parents, had emigrated from Old World countries to the new worlds a generation or two earlier, moved from areas of first or second settlement in the great urban centers of the United States, Canada, Australia, and South Africa, to the suburbs. By the end of the 1950s not only had Jewish geodemographics been transformed the world over, but among the Jews who had made those moves, there was a sense that the Jewish people had reached various points of final settlement; in the words of the Bible, had reached a situation of rest and landed inheritance.

Now, approximately forty years later, we look around at a world in which the Jews are still moving. Probably one-tenth of all Jews in the world have moved from one country to another in the past fifteen years, mostly from the former Soviet Union to Israel and the West. Hundreds of thousands of others have moved from colder to warmer climates in Europe and the Americas or from threatening to calmer locations, particularly from the Southern Hemisphere.

Finally, hundreds of thousands of Jews in Israel and other countries where the Jews see themselves as permanently settled have migrated internally or emigrated in search of opportunity or simply to improve their living conditions. Thus the Jewish people, known in history as one of the greatest migrating peoples of all time, are still moving, only now they are moving less because they are compelled to by external forces, particularly persecution, and more because they are motivated to do so by personal needs and experiences.

In this respect they are not unlike other new-style migrants in the contemporary world where migration has become an aspect of globalization, often international in character, involving every strata and all groups in society, and moving in an unceasing and never-ending flow. While there are certain resemblances between patterns of migration, integration, and absorption today and those in the past, in general we must recognize that the new forms of migration in an increasingly globalized world, tied together by inexpensive means of transportation and communication, are quite different from those in the past and require study in their own right to be properly understood, and for the development of proper migration policies to deal with them.

The Jerusalem Center for Public Affairs was recently invited to be the Israel research arm of an international project on "Immigration and the Metropolis: Centres of Excellence for Research on Immigration and Integration." The international project on migration is the joint initiative of the Canadian government's Department of Citizenship and Immigration, and its Social Science and Humanities Research Council. The Israeli Ministry of Absorption has also become an active partner in this international effort. Then Absorption Minister Yair Tsaban sent a ministry representative to the first planning meeting which was held in Belgium in October 1995, and the Minister himself signed an agreement with his Canadian counterpart in April 1996.

The Jerusalem Center for Public Affairs was approached through Professor Weinfeld of the Jerusalem Center's branch in Canada, the Canadian Centre for Jewish Community Studies, who is also a consultant on the Canadian Project.

The "Metropolis" project has been designed to stimulate interdisciplinary research on the effects of international migration on urban centers. Indeed, an extraordinary challenge confronts the world today as millions of people move from one country to another, in what is, in effect, a continuous stream, in most cases settling in urban centers. This migration is driven by numerous social, economic, and political factors that are increasingly beyond the ability of individual states to influence effectively, and which in contemporary times have become powerful agents of social change. Contemporary migration is also distinguished by its multicultural and ethnic (unlike in the past), religious and social diversity, which produces extremely complex interactions between and among newcomers and established communities in the large urban centers where they concentrate.

Issues to be Addressed

Participating scholars are being asked to present policy solutions to questions such as: Does immigration accelerate or retard the ability of cities and countries to restructure economically? How does greater ethnic diversity affect the social and cultural life of cities? What factors help immigrants integrate into the wider community? Does immigration contribute to the creation of a marginalized underclass?

The researchers are also being asked to identify national differences within their own countries. This will provide an inventory of "best practices" upon which decision-makers can anchor their policy ideas, as well as enable them to better integrate research more systematically into policy development. The project will feature a series of major, annual conferences to be hosted by partner countries, such as one held in Belgium. The conferences will focus on distinct policy themes and challenges requiring management. They will provide a focal point for the discussion of existing research and a venue for unveiling new "state of the art" work, commissioned expressly for the Metropolis Project.

Ultimately, a broader understanding of immigration will be available to policy-makers which will naturally lend a better understanding of these interactions as well as provide the tools for more effective policy decisions and management.

This book represents a first comprehensive examination of Israel and the Jewish people in light of this new-style migration. It is the product of a conference-workshop held at the Jerusalem Center for Public Affairs in July 1996 to begin the Israel aspect of the "Metropolis" project.

The Jerusalem Center would like to express its appreciation and gratitude to the Israel Ministry of Immigrant Absorption, in particular, Director of the Ministry's Planning and Research Division Mr. Shmuel Adler, Mr. Irwin Hochberg of New York, Mr. H. Irwin Levy of Florida, and the Government of Canada whose generosity enabled us to undertake the conference-workshop and, as such, contribute to the understanding of this important topic. We would also like to thank the staff of the Jerusalem Center for the successful undertaking of the workshop, in particular Andrea S. Arbel who organized the conference, as well as Rachel Elrom and Suzanna Cohen. Finally, we would also like to thank Yael Ami-El for skillfully copyediting the papers and preparing them for publication.

Daniel J. Elazar
Jerusalem
Elul 5758, August 1998

I

Setting the Context

1

Israel, the Jewish People, and the New World of Migration

Daniel J. Elazar and Morton Weinfeld

The Unique Experience of Israel and the Jewish People

The Jewish people have great experience with migration, perhaps more than any other people, and certainly more than any other that has positioned itself in the mainstream or center of many civilizations. Jews have always been on the move. Jewish communities have been found on every continent, and often in the most exotic locales. Jewish mass migrations have also shaped Jewish and world history. One thinks of the movement of Jews throughout the Roman Empire, the consequences of the Inquisition in Spain and Portugal, the movements of Jews from Western and Central to Eastern Europe, the migrations to the New World of Sephardic, German, and later Eastern European Jews, the post-war movement of Holocaust survivors and North African Jews to Israel, France, the Americas, Australia, and South Africa.

Because of the diasporic experience, Jewish communities worldwide have developed networks of institutions designed to meet communal needs. This has certainly been the case regarding the integration of Jewish immigrants. On the one hand, diaspora organizations and institutions like the Hebrew Immigrant Aid Society (HIAS) or Jewish Immigrant Aid Services (JIAS), as well as the early *lansdsmanschaften* and communal social welfare agencies have helped ease the integration of Jewish immigrants, and of course this is supremely true for Israel, where immigrant absorption has been a founding ethos of the state. *Aliya* (immigration) is the major responsibility of the Jewish Agency for Israel and the government has a cabinet Ministry of Absorption.

On the other hand, each wave of immigration has been met by certain feelings of resentment or condescension by the preceding waves, even as help was being extended by other communal institutions. These cases include attitudes of German Jews towards Russian Jews, Ashkenazi Jews towards recent Sephardic immigrants, old timers towards post-Holocaust "greeners," and even more recently veteran Israelis towards Russians, Georgians, or Ethiopians. Despite these initial and in some cases persisting antipathies, the integration processes proceeded.

Modern Israel has a particularly important experience in reestablishing the Jewish national home by absorbing millions of Jews within its borders. Conversely, the Jewish state has significant experience with out-migration. The first experiences were forced departures following the destructions of the First and Second Temples — the foundation of the *galut* (diaspora). In our day, modern Israel has been wrestling with *yerida* — voluntary emigration from Israel.

In addition to the waves of immigration which helped establish the Jewish state during its first 40 years of existence, since 1989 Israel has absorbed some 800,000 immigrants, the two most dominant groups being from the former Soviet Union and Ethiopia. Despite the experience gained from previous waves of immigration, Israel is still grappling with the subsequent social, economic, and political consequences. Even though more than 500,000 of these immigrants originate from the Commonwealth of Independent States, they represent a vast mix of ethnic, cultural, and academic backgrounds. Due to their strikingly different background, the approximate 20,000 Ethiopians who have arrived since May 1991 present the most formidable absorption challenge. (Interestingly, both of these immigrant groups raised once again the persistent problem of "Who is a Jew?") The Jerusalem Center is interested in bringing Israel's experience into the world's mainstream, but is also interested in the larger question of migration due to the fact that Israel is also caught in the world tide.

These recent tides of immigration can be viewed as a continuation of a trend which began more than 40 years ago. In addition, the State of Israel is grappling with a new set of problems, almost all of which are commonly found in the Western world. Some of these new challenges are directly related to the most recent wave of immigration while others are not. Moreover, migration to Israel from the former Soviet Union in particular has also changed. Migrating to Israel no longer means that one has to cut all ties with one's native country, and thus there are naturally new types of relations and opportunities tied to the migrants' native land. Also for the first time, a segment of the migrants from the former USSR and elsewhere are migrating to Israel to enjoy aspects of the Jewish state that are not Jewish per se.

In terms of developments not related to immigration, for example, extended closures on the entrance of workers from Judea, Samaria, and Gaza have resulted in Israel importing foreign workers to meet agricultural and construction needs. Not unlike other countries with guest workers, Israel now has to effectively and efficiently face the challenges that this growing sector brings with it. Israel has no experience in this area and can surely learn from more experienced countries. The response which will emerge will likely blend self-interest with a compassion nurtured by the biblical injunction to be kind to the strangers in your midst, and the memory of the mistreatment of Jewish refugees in the pre-Holocaust and immediate post-Holocaust periods.

The peace process may present another sensitive and formidable problem — an unknown number of returning Palestinians. A significant wave of Palestinians coming into Israel and/or the administered territories will present highly sensitive problems. Israel can also learn from the experience of other countries which have faced comparable challenges.

In terms of diasporas, Israel and the Jewish people have also attained unique experience and perspective. For more than 2,000 years, the Jewish people have been dispersed throughout the world, experiencing migration and absorption under a long list of countries and conditions. Since the establishment of the State of Israel, either parts or all of these diaspora communities have resettled in Israel, yet the vast majority of world Jewry lives in the diaspora. Today the existence of diasporas is no longer unique to the Jewish people. Indeed, due to this growing worldwide phenomenon there is new interest in diasporas in general, as other peoples are organizing communally and politically. Automatically, these groups are turning to the Jewish people and Israel because they have the greatest experience. New diasporas include traditional groups like the Chinese, some among *gastarbeiter* groups like the Turkish and the North African Arabs, some among retirees as Americans in Latin America and the Caribbean, and some for purposes of commerce such as the large communities of expatriates that the British have established all over the world because of their business interests.

The entire paradigm of migration has indeed shifted dramatically in the second half, and even faster in the second quarter, of the twentieth century. The mass migrations at the turn of the century were essentially one way. To be sure, return migration was not uncommon, though less so among Jews. But these return migrations often represented a failure of adjustment, or a return (with earnings) that had been planned in advance.

In most cases, once the immigrant arrived, contact with the old country and the old culture began an inexorable process of attenuation and dilution. There were usually no return visits or few visits from old country relatives. Immigrants were generally ready to give up their Old World loyalties and become citizens of their new country.

Today much of this has changed. Immigrants can remain in constant touch with all aspects of their country of origin through regular return visits to and from the old country, frequent telephone and e-mail contacts, and up-to-date radio and television shows dealing with the homeland. The ease of movement within the European Community has also lessened the salience of specific national boundaries. In short, there is greater fluidity in the movement of peoples, and less certainty that processes like integration can mean what they once did. Thus diaspora communities can be created and sustained with greater efficacy than ever.

Indeed, diasporas, along with sub-national and supra-national regions, weaken the centrality of nation-states. There is a growing recognition of the commonalities among mega-cities throughout the globe. The fact that these cities are also the magnets attracting large migrant flows means that Toronto or Los Angeles or London or Tel Aviv may have more in common with each other in part because of the strains of immigrant integration, than they do with smaller cities and regions within their respective countries.

The direction of population flows is also reversible. The number of Canadians migrating from Canada to Italy is greater than the number from Italy to Canada. Changing flows also affect Israel, long understood only as an immigrant receiving country.

Israel has also been grappling with the issue of *yerida,* with hundreds of thousands of Israelis having resettled mainly in the United States and Canada. Israel's attitude toward their out-migrating brethren has transformed over the years from one of disdain to one of neutrality and, in some cases, pride, particularly in the instances of those Israelis who have "made it." Today, due to the fact that there are first and even second generation Israeli descendants living abroad, Israelis are now realizing that they need to build ties with these populations. Again, Israel can learn from those countries which have long accepted "out-migration" and developed ways in which to benefit from the existence of those populations.

The Jerusalem Center has been among the first to research and publish on the subject of diasporas and the Jewish people as the model of a classic diaspora. Over the past 25 years, the JCPA has published books and/or monographs on practically every known Jewish community throughout the world (see Appendix). Today the subject has become so mainstream in its importance that there is a scholarly journal devoted to the subject and a Penguin *Atlas of Diasporas*.

We have identified the following eighteen topics as ones that are of particular relevance for Israel to explore:

1. The Jewish experience with migration
2. Israel's experience with migration
3. Diasporas
4. Refugees
5. Absorption of immigrants
6. Coping with continuing migration
7. Constitutional and institutional arrangements for handling migration — domestic, international, and multinational
8. Migration and multiculturalism
9. Integration and segregation of migrants
10. Stresses between locals and migrants
11. Competition between locals and migrants

12. The political impacts of migration
13. Frontiers and migration
14. Overpopulation and migration
15. The literature of migration
16. Language and migration
17. Religion and migration
18. Cultural transformations caused or shaped by migration

Five specific topics have been identified as particularly appropriate for the Jerusalem Center:

1. The contemporary Israel-Jewish diaspora experience as a model for other state-diaspora relationships.
2. Survey of Israeli literature on immigration and absorption since the beginning of the Zionist enterprise.
3. The role and problematics of guest workers in Israel.
4. Relations between Israelis and Palestinians in light of Palestinians being daily migrants.
5. Relations between *yordim* and Israelis.

This volume has tried to explore a wide range of migration topics as they relate to Jewish migrants in Israel and throughout the diaspora. These include:

- Issues of ideology, such as the difference between migrants and *olim* in Israel or equivalent differences in other countries.
- Public policies in various domains toward migrants, migration, and integration.
- Institutions and services.
- Ethnic communities and organizations.
- International law.
- Non-governmental organization (NGOs) and migration.
- Personal experiences.
- The experience of immigration and integration.
- New and old conceptions of diaspora.
- Migrations from the former Soviet Union to Israel, the United States, Canada, and elsewhere.
- Families and migration.
- Identity or identities of migrants.

We have raised the question of migration and frontier societies as more in need of and more open to immigrants. We have raised questions about the differences among Jews where Jewish identity is their first identity and where it is not, and concluded that the difference is not only great but also changes the terms of migrant connection and absorption. The issues of guest workers and partial migrants were touched on minimally; that is to say, those people who maintain homes in more than one country or place and rotate among them during the course of the year.

We have looked at how to combine the unique aspects of Jewish migration in a larger comparative and global perspective and have agreed that the larger perspectives are necessary. At times we have seen how clashes between the historic Jewish political tradition and modern Jewish liberalism affect our attitudes on migration, particularly when it comes to issues of Jewish survival and continuity, both in Israel and the diaspora.

We have used a number of Canadian models and once again have seen how Canada, because of its positioning between the especially different United States and the Old World, or at least its European models, often serves as a bridge between the two. We have noticed this in other areas of Jewish concern, especially in the work of the organizations that comprise the world Jewish polity such as the Jewish Agency, the World Zionist Organization, and the World Jewish Congress.

We have periodically touched on the existence of a Jewish polity that organizes Jews wherever they are and keeps Jewish life going and coherent. We have also raised questions as to whether the postmodern world is not bringing about a new model of the Jewish polity because of its technological advances, particularly in transportation and communication, and because of new patterns of state-diaspora relationships.

We have repeatedly made reference to the three critical concerns of migrants as well as real estate: location, location, and location. We would suggest that the three uses of the term "location" can be understood as referring to the three dimensions of location: in space, in time, and in culture, and that as any or all of these change, an individual's location changes.

Perhaps the major item that has not been discussed in our focusing on migration and the migrants themselves is what are the rights of the host cultures or countries which receive migration and migrants, with regard to the preservation of their own culture even at what is seemingly a disadvantage to the migrants. In frontier societies, especially in the nineteenth century when limited host populations sought to augment their numbers by bringing in or encouraging people from abroad to come to settle for the sake of economic development, the very fact that the matter was somewhat in the nature of a commercial transaction, with immigrants needed for development of the frontier, may have given the migrants a certain legitimate right to alter the local culture to suit their needs. Ironically, that was the period when the host cultures were strongest in insisting upon migrant assimilation to what already existed, although the results were distinctly mixed. On the other hand, since the end of World War II, many of the major host countries have taken in migrants less for local need than for humanitarian reasons to help refugees or people seeking greater opportunity than is available in their places of origin. Do these host countries have an obligation to sacrifice their way of life because of their humanitarianism?

Put another way, countries are grappling with the question of the mutual obligations which immigrants and host societies have toward each other and how immigrants may have changed the dominant culture of the majority group, even as they may have assimilated. This has been true in the United States, where mass migrations transformed a predominantly Anglo-Protestant culture of the founding fathers. A similar process occurred in Canada. This has also been the case in Israel, where the characteristics of the succeeding waves of immigration have impacted on Israeli society and culture. But these impacts have generally been minimized by the overarching pressures for conformity on the part of the host society.

To what extent will the new culture of multi-culturalism, or cultural pluralism recognized legally and in policy, transform the bargain? Canadian policy-makers have talked about establishing a type of "moral contract" recognizing these mutual obligations. It is not clear if or how institutionalized cultural pluralism will become established in Israel, but these are questions that need serious consideration.

While the Metropolis Project is formally directed toward the impact of migration on cities, in a rapidly urbanizing world in which migrants to all the major countries are overwhelmingly attracted to cities and even in less developed countries move from rural to urban areas, creating huge urban agglomerations, this definition may involve a distinction without a difference. In a country the size of Canada, where its population is heavily urbanized and migrants overwhelmingly tend to move to cities, there is still so much land in between the major metropolitan concentrations that it is possible to talk about migration to cities as a separate phenomenon, even though in fact it may be the only significant phenomenon in the relocation of migrants. In a country like Israel in which even in the few formally designated non-urban settlements the rural character has disappeared and they have become "rurban," so that Israel in a certain sense is one big city, the distinction really has no difference. Indeed, Israeli political scientist Ira Sharkansky has suggested that all of Israel can be seen as a single metropolitan region or megalopolis. Hence, all of Israel fits the formal criteria of the project and we can pursue it on a countrywide basis as we have begun doing. In that respect, we intend to continue our activities in this project, both for Israel's needs and as part of the worldwide effort.

2

The Global Context of
Migration to Israel

Sergio DellaPergola

Between the beginning of 1989 and the end of 1996, more than one million Jews and non-Jewish family members emigrated from the former Soviet Union. Of these, nearly 670,000 went to Israel, nearly 270,000 to the United States, over 50,000 to Germany, and about 40,000 to other countries. This chapter aims to provide a general background to the demographic and sociological analyses of recent immigration to Israel. It reviews several aspects of immigration to Israel (usually addressed with the Hebrew term *aliya*, "ascent"), in the context of a broader overview of modern and contemporary Jewish international migrations, and provides some more specific observations on the main aggregate and compositional characteristics of migrants. It addresses countries of origin and destination, volume and timing of migration streams, selectivity of migrants relative to population stocks in the countries of origin, and features associated with the split of migration from one given place of origin to different places of destination. While description of major trends and patterns is the main goal, the historical and comparative perspective presented is bound to raise issues whose analytical relevance transcends the specific case-study considered here.

Sources and Definitions

The following analysis is based on a compilation, critical evaluation, and integration of many different sources of data and estimates of varying quality, yet of sufficient coherence (see detailed references in Sicron, 1957; Lestschinsky, 1960; Schmelz, 1971; Schmelz and DellaPergola, 1991-1996; DellaPergola, 1984, 1986, 1989, 1991, 1993b, 1997). The main body of data emanates from the State of Israel Central Bureau of Statistics (CBS). Several national censuses and Jewish population surveys conducted in recent years, as well as data compiled by international organizations involved with assisting Jewish migrations, provide retrospective information on the situation in other countries, and allow for reconstructing a synoptic picture.

Migrations of Jews represent a specific case of sociodemographic change among a minority, or subpopulation. Attention should be paid to the problem of definition of that population, and of Jews specifically (DellaPergola, 1993c, 1997; Goldstein and Kosmin, 1992). Before the spread of modernization and secularization trends, religious, ethnic, national or cultural boundaries were clearly perceived both from within and from outside the relevant groups and communities. More recently, the specific definitions and contents of ethno-religious identifications tend to become blurred in a context of increasing intermarriage and other cultural changes. Self-definitions given by respondents about their identity provide the basis for the current analysis of Jewish, as well as other, subpopulations.

In this general context, a meaningful distinction to be kept in mind, and of increasing relevance in the study of Jewish migrations and other social trends, is between:

1. *The core Jewish population:* all those individuals and household members who identify as belonging to the given group. It includes all cases of joiners or accessions to the group, either through formal procedures or informally through simple self-definition. It also includes those descendants of intermarriages who identify themselves or are described as identifying with the given group. It excludes those of a given descent who formally adopted a different group identity, or disclaim belonging to their group of origin. By such definition, the core population includes a large variety of types

regarding the adherence to Jewish normative cultural or religious patterns, and the amount of Jewish community activism.

2. *The enlarged Jewish population:* besides the core, also includes people who report a Jewish origin but currently proclaim a different identification. These also include quitters, or secessions, their direct descendants, and those descendants of intermarriages who do not identify as Jews. Also included are any further mates in the respective households (spouses, in-laws, etc.) who personally or by ancestry never belonged to the Jewish group. Some households in the enlarged definition may be totally composed of non-Jews, some of whom are of Jewish origin.

These definitions, while affecting the sociological boundaries and quantitative assessment of Jewish populations, involve a measure of fluidity, as some individuals may change their identification according to the circumstances of the moment. On the other hand, Israel's Law of Return (*Hok hashvut*) creates a legal definitional framework even broader than the enlarged Jewish population, as it grants Israeli citizenship immediately upon immigration to Jews, children and grandchildren of Jews, and their nuclear families (no matter if not Jewish). Decisions concerning eligibility for the Law of Return are usually made based on written documentary evidence or legal testimony.

General Features of Jewish and Israeli Migrations

World Jewish Population Distribution

Jewish migrations, in the first place, should be assessed in relation to the changing geographical distribution of the world Jewish population, which they crucially affect, and by which they are much affected. The Holocaust (Shoah), in which about six million Jews perished during World War II, destroyed the main centers of Jewish life in Eastern and Central Europe and dramatically changed the geographical distribution of world Jewry. The center of gravity shifted to the West, with the United States as the largest and most dynamic community. Israel's independence in

1948 was the other major turning point in modern Jewish history. Independence generated, or at least made possible, a major immigration wave. Israel absorbed the remnant Jewish communities of Eastern Europe and the Balkans (with the initial exception of the Soviet Union), largely composed of refugees and displaced persons, as well as entire Jewish communities from Arab countries in the Middle East and North Africa, whose existence had become precarious. In a few decades continuing immigration, as well as steady natural increase, made Israel the second largest Jewish population center in the world (see Table 2.1).

Since the 1970s, the size of world Jewry has been overall quite static, approaching zero population growth, but important geographical changes occurred. Under the impact of continuing international migration, and of the internal balance of vital and identificational changes, Jewish population increase in Israel occurred simultaneously with declines throughout most of the diaspora. Recent trends in emigration effected especially sharp declines in Asia, Africa, and Eastern Europe. In some cases, only tiny and aging remnants were left of once ancient and thriving Jewish communities. The size of Jewish population in Western Europe and North America has been overall quite stable. The leading process is one of polarization between the two major Jewish centers in the United States and Israel. In 1995, these two countries alone included 78 percent of the total Jewish population worldwide (DellaPergola, 1997).

Jewish world population distribution has tended to converge toward the economically more developed and politically more stable societies. Around 1990, before the major emigration wave from the former Soviet Union, about 55 percent of world Jewry lived in the highest quintile of countries (out of 160 nations) ranked according to a pool of major economic and social indicators, against 14 percent of total world population. Another 42 percent of world Jewry lived in the second highest quintile of countries, against 12 percent of total population. The top quintile included the United States, and the second included Israel (DellaPergola, 1992). Since 1990, while these two countries absorbed large numbers of new Jewish immigrants, Israel's improved standing on the global socioeconomic scene brought about its joining the quintile of most developed nations. Consequently, the percentage of Jews living in such countries rose to about 90 percent of the world total. Interna-

TABLE 2.1
World Jewish Population By Continents and Major Regions, Core
Definition — Absolute Numbers and Percent Distribution,
1948-1995

Continent/region	1948	1970	1995	1948	1970	1995
	Absolute n. (thousands)			*Percentages*[a]		
Total world	11,500	12,643	13,059	100	100	100
Europe	3,700	3,093	1,741	32	25	13
West	1,035	1,124	1,037	9	9	8
Former USSR in Europe[b]	2,000	1,757	601	17	14	5
East and Balkan[b]	665	212	103	6	2	1
Asia	1,300	3,080	4,629	12	25	35
Israel	650	2,582	4,549	6	21	35
Former USSR in Asia	375	394	59	3	3	1
Rest	275	104	21	3	1	0
Africa	700	195	106	6	1	1
North[c]	595	71	9	5	0	0
Central and South	105	124	97	1	1	1
America	5,760	6,205	6,486	50	49	50
North	5,235	5,686	6,052	45	45	46
Central and South	525	519	434	5	4	3
Oceania	40	70	97	0	0	1

a. Minor discrepancies due to rounding.
b. Including Asian territories of Russian Republic and Turkey.
c. Including Ethiopia.
Sources: adapted from DellaPergola (1993b), DellaPergola (1997).

tional migration, when not hampered by political obstacles, has obviously been a powerful mechanism in the inherently rational readjusting of Jewish geography worldwide.

World Jewish Migration Perspective

In historical perspective, the overall profile of the changing volume of Jewish international migration between 1880 and 1996 is presented in Figure 2.1. Yearly estimates and five-year moving averages were computed from available migration data to each of the main countries of destination. Overall, the movement of over eight million persons is described in Figure 2.1. Of these, 2.4

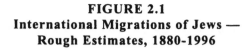

FIGURE 2.1
International Migrations of Jews —
Rough Estimates, 1880-1996

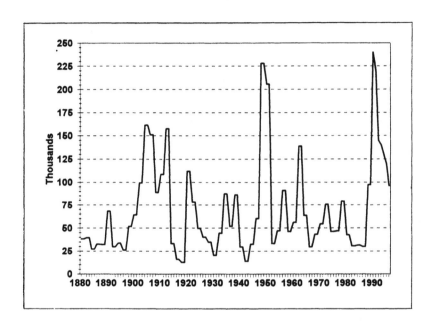

million migrated between 1880 and 1918, 1.6 million between 1919 and 1948, over 1.3 million between 1948 and 1960, about 1.6 million between 1961 and 1988, and about 1.1 million between 1989 and 1996.

The graphical evidence of continuous ups and downs in the volume of Jewish migrations effectively demonstrates the recurrence of crises affecting the position of Jewish communities in different parts of the world, and the consequent need for prompt relocation. Such wave-like patterns suggest consistent instability in the Jewish migration experience, which in turn raises disquieting questions about the apparent vulnerability of the Jewish presence in the diaspora. Some of the factors which stimulate large scale emigration appeared to operate in recent years in essentially the same way as they did a century ago, in spite of the basic sociopolitical changes among contemporary Jewish communities versus those in the past.

The long-term cyclical pattern includes three major waves among several minor ones: (a) the pre-World War I mass migration from Eastern Europe to North America, peaking in fiscal years 1905/06 and 1913/14; (b) the massive migration wave to Israel between 1948 and 1951; and (c) the more recent exodus from the former Soviet Union. These major moments of international crisis and adaptation within the Jewish world, much in response to major events in the global polity, have occurred at comparable intervals of about 40-45 years. No mechanical or deterministic assumption is suggested about the alignment of global geo-political forces under-lying such major cycles. Nevertheless, the possible existence of long-term economic cycles, their impact on socio-political systems generally, and on specific social groups particularly — hence their influence on mass migration — have been discussed by economists and demographers (Kuznets, 1958; Thomas, 1972). The possible existence of recurring, if not truly cyclical, conjunctures should be carefully considered when examining Jewish migrations. Mass international migration has represented a major mechanism of adjustment for Jewish communities endangered by the disruption of the orderly relationship with the surrounding society and the severe worsening of economic opportunities.

One important factor in shaping the frequency of international migration was the availability of alternative destinations. Legal limitations of the possibility to leave major countries of Jewish settlement and to access major countries of immigration signifi-cantly shaped the profile of Jewish international migrations, espe-cially during the period between the two world wars. Jewish mi-grants were therefore extremely dependent on options and con-straints that were beyond their control. This situation was radically transformed after the independence of Israel, the opening of its doors to Jewish migration, and the establishing of the special legal framework provided by the Law of Return in 1950. This substantial migration incentive came together with a modicum of socioeco-nomic help aimed at easing the initial integration of new immi-grants and their households. The resulting package in Israel of fundamentally unrestricted and unselective Jewish immigration being awarded civil rights and material help stands out when compared to the restrictive immigration policies that persist in most other countries.

Competing Areas of Origin and Destination

Global Jewish international migration trends are better understood in the framework of an integrated system of competing areas of origin and destination. The term "system" is appropriate as it implies that at any given point in time the likelihood for change, in this case further migration, is contingent on the equilibrium situation reached, specifically geographical distribution, which in turn reflects past migratory changes (Kritz, Lim, Zlotnik, 1991). A simple typology distinguishes among two major reservoirs of Jewish emigration, (a) Eastern Europe, and (b) countries in North Africa and Northwestern Asia; and two major and competing areas of destination, (a) North America, West Europe and other Western countries, and (b) the State of Israel. Jewish migrations from countries where a situation of stress prevailed for Jewish communities were significantly assisted by various Jewish international organizations, often involving the transfer of whole households. Migrations between Western countries and Israel, and vice versa, were sparser, more voluntaristic and individualistic. The concept of Western countries in this scheme obviously includes a variety of situations, as some have shifted periodically from receivers to senders of Jewish international migration.

Table 2.2 presents data and estimates on the volume of Jewish intercontinental migration between 1948 and 1995, according to the schematic geographical classification now described. For each of six major migration streams, including emigration from Israel, absolute numbers and percentage distributions of migrants, and yearly emigration rates per 1,000 Jews in the countries of origin are presented.

Between 1948 and 1995, an estimated four million Jews migrated internationally. Of these, about 2.5 million (63 percent) went to Israel. Significant shifts occurred over time in the intensity and preferred direction of Jewish migrations worldwide. As against a yearly average of 84,000 migrants for the whole period, one observes peaks of 190,000 migrants, on the average, between 1948

TABLE 2.2

Major Jewish International Migration Flows, By Areas of Origin and Destination — Absolute Numbers, Percent Distribution and Rates per 1,000 Jewish Population in Countries of Origin, 1948-1995

Areas of origin and destination	1948[a]-1952	1953-1960	1961-1968	1969-1976	1977-1982	1983-1988	1989-1992	1993-1995	Total
Absolute numbers (thousands)									
Grand total	855	460	565	445	320	250	705	390	3,990
Yearly average	190	58	71	56	53	42	176	130	84
Percent distributions									
Grand total	100	100	100	100	100	100	100	100	100
From East Europe[b]	45	27	20	40	44	41	83	74	48
To Israel	37	20	17	32	17	7	60	48	33
To West countries	8	7	3	8	27	34	23	26	15
From Asia-Africa	46	55	59	14	16	13	6	3	29
To Israel	42	36	30	9	6	10	5	2	20
To West countries	4	19	29	5	10	3	1	1	9
From Israel									
To West countries[c]	4	15	14	20	22	29	8	18[d]	14
From West countries									
To Israel	5	3	7	26	18	17	3	5	9
Regional subtotals									
To Israel	84	59	54	67	41	34	68	55	62
To West countries	16	41	46	33	59	66	32	45	38
Yearly emigration rates per 1,000 Jews in countries of origin									
Grand total	17	5	6	4	4	3	14	10	7
From East Europe[b]	31	7	6	10	13	11	115	115	22
To Israel	25	5	5	8	5	2	83	75	9
To West countries	6	2	1	2	8	9	32	40	13
From Asia-Africa	109	43	108	44	66	79	146	147	83
To Israel	100	28	56	30	21	60	128	94	56
To West countries	9	15	52	14	45	19	18	53	27
From Israel									
To West countries[c]	6	6	4	4	3	3	4	5[d]	4
From West countries									
To Israel	1	0	1	2	1	1	1	1	1

a. May 15.
b. Including Former Soviet republics in Asia.
c. All emigration from Israel included here.
d. Provisional.
Source: DellaPergola (1986), and author's estimates.

and 1952, and 176,000 between 1989 and 1992; and a low average of 42,000 migrants between 1983 and 1988.

The single largest migration flow, out of the six outlined in Table 2.2, involved migrants from Eastern Europe to Israel, which comprised 33 percent of total Jewish migrants between 1948 and 1995. Jews moving from Asia and Africa to Israel included 21 percent of the total migrants; from Eastern Europe to Western countries, 15 percent; from Israel to Western countries, 13 percent; from Asia and Africa to Western countries, 9 percent; and from Western countries to Israel, roughly the same amount. Between 1948 and 1968, the single largest flow was from countries in Asia and Africa to Israel; between 1969 and 1976, and again between 1988 and 1995 it was from countries in Eastern Europe to Israel; and between 1977 and 1988 it was from East Europe to Western countries. The latter alternative to *aliya* was defined in Israel as *neshira* (drop-out).

Overall, Israel was the leading country of destination, receiving 84 percent of world Jewish migrants in 1948-52 and 67 percent in 1969-76, but that tendency steadily declined between 1977 and 1988. Since the renewal in late 1989 of the current migration wave from the former Soviet Union, Israel recovered a role of primacy as the major recipient of Jewish international migration. Judging on the basis of regional migration propensities (see the rates per 1,000 resident Jews in the bottom part of Table 2.2), the area with the highest relative frequency of emigration was the complex of Muslim countries in Asia and Africa, where only tiny residuals of the preexisting Jewish populations have remained (these data include Ethiopia). Over the whole period considered here, an average of 83 Jews per 1,000 living in Asian and African countries left each year. Eastern Europe produced a greater volume of Jewish emigration, but consistently lower emigration rates than Near Eastern countries, as shown by a yearly average of 27 migrants per 1,000 Jewish population in the countries of origin.

The absolute number of Jewish emigrants from Israel tended to increase over time, and was especially noteworthy in the early 1980s and again in the early 1990s. Israel's net migration balance with the Western countries was consistently negative. However, emigration from Israel tended to be comparatively low and stable, around an average rate of 4 per 1,000 inhabitants, in spite of the periodical security and economic difficulties faced by the country.

Jewish emigration from the Western countries was the lowest, around a yearly average of 1 per 1,000, as appropriate to the West's position at the core of the world socio-economic and political system, and to their role of a shelter to immigrants from other parts of the world.

Timing of Emigration and the Choice of Destination: Recurring Patterns

Table 2.3 presents in greater detail four cases of large scale migration of Jews from one country of origin, splitting among two or more destinations: the Western societies and Israel. Such comparison relates to the Jews of Egypt, Morocco and Tunisia, Algeria, and the Soviet Union over the forty-year period 1948-88. The cases examined range from the complete exodus of a community to the departure of a relatively small and highly selective minority within it. Several interesting parallelisms emerge from these data. In each instance, the first to leave were those harboring the strongest propensity to go to Israel (see bottom panel in Table 2.3). The second stage saw the departure of the largest numbers of emigrants (intermediate panels in Table 2.3), with a parallel falloff in the proportion of those going to Israel. Emigrants who left last, sometimes under the worst conditions, included Jewish population strata that were more solidly established economically, were more culturally assimilated in the framework of host societies, and had the least inclination for *aliya*. In each case, immigration to Israel gradually gave way to a growing tendency to seek alternative destinations in the West.

Similar patterns were observed in recent years, albeit on a smaller scale, among Jews who emigrated from Iran or from less stable Western countries such as South Africa or Argentina, where shifting local circumstances generated relatively important emigration. Relevant trends in the choice of country of destination emerging from the ongoing emigration wave from the former Soviet Union are discussed later, in the section on personal characteristics of migrants.

TABLE 2.3
Selected Examples of Jewish Mass Migration — Period,
Volume, and Percent Migrating to Israel, 1948-1988

Phase	Egypt	Morocco Tunisia	Algeria	USSR
		Years		
Total	1948-66	1950-79	1950-79	1968-88
1	1948-55	1950-59	1950-59	1968-75
2	1956-59	1960-69	1960-69	1976-80
3	1960-66	1970-79	1970-79	1981-88
		Total number of migrants^a		
Total	63,000	393,000	137,000	295,000
1	23,000	176,000	38,000	118,000
2	34000	192,000	98,000	133,000
3	6,000	25000	1,000	44,000
		Average yearly migrants		
Total	3,300	13,100	4,550	14,050
1	2,900	17,600	3,800	14,750
2	8,500	19,200	9,800	26,600
3	8,50	2,500	100	5,500
		Percent migrating to Israel		
Total	48	72	8	57
1	61	77	11	91
2	44	72	7	40
3	25	40	0	18

a. Rough estimates.
Sources: adapted from Bensimon and DellaPergola (1984), DellaPergola (1989),
Florsheim (1990), Prital (1987), Israel CBS.

Recent Migration from the Former Soviet Union: Some Lessons

The most significant recent development in the world Jewish migration system is the exodus from the former Soviet Union. Emigration from Eastern Europe, besides its deep roots in modern Jewish history, was a long-standing item on the Jewish and international public agenda (Brym, 1988; Gitelman, 1996). Yet, its sudden large-scale renewal caught many observers by surprise, which raises the question: To what extent are large Jewish migration waves, particularly *aliya* to Israel, predictable? In trying to answer this question, one should assess the different factors that act in concert in such circumstances, the possible independent impact of each factor, and the final outcome due to the interplay of all factors. Specifically, the main factors playing were:

1. *The intensity of pro-migration forces in response to the socioeconomic and political situation within the country of origin.* These forces gained momentum since the late 1980s but could, theoretically, dissipate over time.
2. *The actual possibility to leave the country of origin.* Since the late 1960s, and especially since the late 1980s, this was affected by changing political considerations and decisions by the Communist party and government in the former Soviet Union.
3. *The availability of alternative destinations for Jewish migration.* The American policy of immigration quotas was especially significant in this regard since the early 1920s, during the immediate pre- and post-World War II period, and until the more recent changes in immigration regulations. After several years of a sustained "drop-out" of Jewish migrants who supposedly had left the Soviet Union directed to Israel, in 1989 the U.S.A. stopped granting automatic refugee status to Soviet nationals and a yearly quota of 40-50,000 was established for Jewish immigrants (Heitman, 1991); in 1996 that quota was reduced to 20,000, reflecting a general reduction in the refugees quota. Emerging German and Canadian immigration policies also played a significant role in this respect.
4. *The extent of involvement and the nature of the assistance provided by Israeli and international agencies.* Different bodies promoted, directed and supported Jewish migration, such as the Jewish Agency for Israel, the American Jewish Joint Distribution Committee (JDC), the Hebrew Immigrant Aid Society (HIAS), and Nativ, the "Liaison Bureau" of Israel's government in the former Soviet Union (popularly known as Lishkat Kesher).
5. *The demographic, socioeconomic, and sociocultural characteristics of the Jewish population.* These tended to affect

differently the propensity to emigrate, and the choice of country of destination (see below for details).

6. *The quality of absorption and feedback by recent migrants.* Information sent back by immigrants from Israel, the U.S.A., and other countries to families and other social networks in the former Soviet Union about the absorption process significantly affected the latter's decision-making about possible migration.

7. *Finally, from the point of view of recipient countries, what counts is the number of immigrants who stay for good.* Net immigration is the total number of immigrants minus remigrants or return migrants. In the case of the former Soviet Union, the latter are likely to constitute a small share of total migrants. Those who return supposedly display socio-demographic characteristics different from those who settle permanently.

Over the 1970s, 1980s and 1990s, Jewish migration rates from the (former) Soviet Union fluctuated vigorously. The role of emigration/immigration laws in the countries involved was significant. Some amendments to the U.S. Immigration Act in 1990 temporarily increased the prospects of entry by Soviet Jews, whose numbers had been hitherto limited to 40,000 a year. The preference of migrants for Israel versus alternative Western destinations varied quite sharply over time. While Israel received a clear majority of the migrants of the 1970s, during the 1980s most of them preferred the United States. On the other hand, of those who went to Israel, only a modest fraction estimated at 5 to 7 percent remigrated during the first years after immigration (Israel CBS).

Even if these and other demographic parameters could allow for a reasonable assessment of future developments in Jewish emigration, no one imagined the degree of transformation that would overtake and eventually cause the Soviet political system to crumble in the late 1980s and early 1990s, with the result of extreme changes in emigration policy. This should be borne in mind by anyone who attempts to predict sociodemographic developments (in the former Soviet Union or elsewhere) in light of the routine assumption that "existing trends will continue." Emigration of Jews and their households, including *aliya*, from the former Soviet Union and other countries with similar sociopolitical configurations will presumably continue, and migrants will seek shelter in places they deem stable and secure, and where adequate opportunities and networks for social and economic absorption can develop. However, one should be especially wary of forecasting that postulates gradual, smooth developments, such as a fixed number of migrants or stable migration rates across several years, the logistic-curve model, or Markov-type matrixes.

Global Migration Perspective

Israeli immigration occurred at a far less even pace in comparison to the other four countries. The variation ratio, a simple measure based on the means and standard deviations of absolute numbers of immigrants, shows a much higher value — hence a more variable intensity — for Israel. The characteristic wave-like pattern of Israeli immigration is confirmed in the bottom part of Table 2.4, showing rates of immigration per 1,000 inhabitants in each of the five countries compared. Between 1960 and 1994, five-year average immigration rates for Israel ranged between a low of 3.2 and a high of 23.7 per 1,000, against a range of 1.5-3.5 per 1,000 for the U.S.A., 4.4-8.8 for Canada, 5.1-12.7 for Australia, and 8.2-14.7 for West Germany.

The product of such exceptionally high-scale migration clearly reflects on Israel's population composition by countries of birth. Based on data compiled for 1990 (United Nations, 1996b), at the beginning of the last major wave of Jewish migration Israel's total population included 31 percent foreign-born. Worldwide, such a percentage was then surpassed only by countries in the Persian Gulf, such as the United Arab Emirates (90 percent), Kuwait (72 percent), Qatar (63 percent), Bahrain (35 percent) and Oman (34 percent). Political developments in the latter countries since 1990 must have led to a decline in the percentage of foreign-born. Other major countries of immigration had relatively much smaller stocks of foreign-born, namely Australia (23 percent), Canada (16 percent), the United States (8 percent), France (10 percent), and Germany (6 percent).

Following the renewal of large-scale immigration in the 1990s, but also reflecting the ceaseless process of structural transformation toward a growing proportion of people born in Israel (due to the

TABLE 2.4
Immigrants to Israel, United States, Canada, Australia, West Germany
— Average Yearly Number and Rate per 1,000 Population, 1960-1994

Year	Israel	U.S.A.	Canada	Australia	West Germany
		Thousands			
1960-64	50.7	283.8	88.0	115.0	576.2
1965-69	24.1	358.9	182.0	147.2	706.1
1970-74	44.3	422.2	158.9	141.6	873.1
1975-79	25.0	628.4	130.1	70.6	527.5
1980-84	16.7	801.2	114.1	94.3	502.2
1985-89	14.0	692.3	137.9	114.5	817.8
1990-94[a]	121.9	680.1	211.9	121.5	–
Mean	42.4	552.4	146.1	115.0	667.1
Standard deviation	37.6	195.8	41.8	26.4	142.4
Variation ratio	0.888	0.354	0.286	0.230	0.213
	Average Yearly Rate of Immigrants per 1,000 Population				
1960-64	22.2	1.5	4.4	11.0	10.0
1965-69	8.9	1.8	8.8	12.7	12.1
1970-74	14.0	2.0	7.4	11.1	14.7
1975-79	6.9	2.9	5.7	5.1	8.7
1980-84	4.1	3.5	4.7	6.3	8.2
1985-89	3.2	2.8	5.3	7.0	13.4
1990-94	23.7	2.6	7.6	6.8	–
Mean[b]	11.9	2.4	6.3	8.6	11.2

a. U.S.A. and Australia: 1990-1991; Canada: 1990.
b. Unweighted.
Source: Israel CBS; Zlotnik (1994).

death of elderly foreign-born and the birth of a new generation locally), at the end of 1995 the foreign-born constituted 31 percent of Israel's total population including non-Jews, and 39 percent of Israel's Jewish population. The truly unique impact of immigration should be kept in mind when studying Israeli society in comparative perspective.

A further aspect of migration to Israel, which cannot be adequately dealt with here, is the recent arrival of large numbers of (partially undocumented) workers from less developed countries. In November 1996, according to data of Israel's Employment

Service, there were 103,000 foreign workers holding an employment permit (*Ha'aretz*, 1996), but including also unlisted workers, their numbers were roughly evaluated at between 200,000 and 300,000. Such immigration, stimulated by the rapid growth of the Israeli economy, labor-oriented, and often aimed at relatively short periods of stay, has long prevailed in many other developed or rapidly developing countries. The respective data are not included in any of our analyses. Yet, this "new" or "dual" migration to Israel, conceptually different from the typical, long-term inflow of Jewish aliya, should not be ignored when assessing the role of international migrations in shaping Israeli society. It is a further indicator of the globalization of economic and social processes, and of Israel's full integration and rising position in the framework of the world system.

Migration To and From Israel: Major Patterns

Overall Profile

As already noted, since independence in 1948, Israel became the main recipient of Jewish international migrations. The net migration balance constituted about 42 percent of Israel's total population growth, and nearly 50 percent of total Jewish population growth between 1948 and 1995 (Israel CBS). The respective figures for 1948-1961 were 65 percent and 69 percent, respectively.

A profile of the yearly volume of *aliya* is presented in Figure 2.2, which shows absolute numbers of immigrants and the respective rates per 1,000 Jewish inhabitants. The predominant characteristic of migration to Israel was its wave-like profile, namely, a recurring pattern of several consecutive years of increase followed by several years of decrease. While each wave was dominated by immigrants from a different pool of countries of origin, the underlying determinants and motivations appeared to be similar. The first and most significant wave included large numbers of newcomers from a heterogeneous set of Jewish communities in Eastern Europe, the Near East, and North Africa. These mostly impoverished immigrants produced a doubling of Israeli Jewish population within three years since independence in 1948 and constituted the backbone of the ensuing development of Israeli society. In subsequent

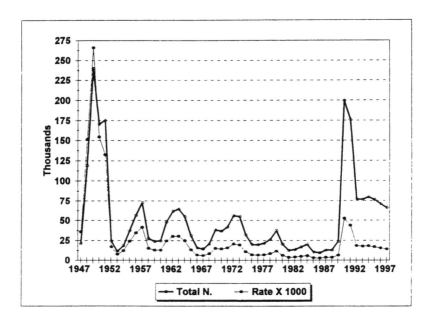

FIGURE 2.2
Immigrants to Israel: Number (thousands) and
Rate Per 1000 Jewish Population, 1947-1997

years, despite a slow-down in immigration, Israel consistently kept a clearly positive international migration balance.

After the 1967 Six-Day War, immigration from Western countries became more visible, soon followed by the first wave of immigrants from the USSR during the early 1970s. Immigration was closely matched by emigration during the 1980s which were years of economic stress. The declining trend in migration to Israel shown by the data was reversed dramatically by the developments in Eastern Europe since the end of the 1980s. In absolute numbers, immigration in the early 1990s was roughly comparable with the major migration wave of 1948-1951. In relative terms, though, because of the much increased receiving population, the impact was much less, and immigration rates per 1,000 inhabitants in Israel in the early 1990s resembled those of the mid-1950s.

Country Profiles

At first sight, the wave-like pattern of Jewish immigration to Israel suggests the existence of components of stress in the process of decision-making associated with the timing of migration (this assumption is tested below). An alternative assumption would be that immigration to Israel is fundamentally driven by changes occurring in Israeli society, especially on the economic scene (see discussion of these different approaches in Bachi, 1977; Friedlander and Goldscheider, 1979; Ben-Porath, 1986). While these hypotheses apply to *aliya* in general, the fact that Israel absorbed immigrants from so many different countries makes it imperative to look at trends based on more disaggregated data. Indeed, the total immigration trends could be an artifact of quite different developments independently occurring in each country of origin and only by chance generating the observed periodical immigration waves. Is the predominant push or, respectively, pull pattern of *aliya*, or a combination of both, supported once the evidence is examined for each country of origin separately?

At the descriptive level, if one examines detailed year-by-year profiles of the number of immigrants to Israel from each of over 50 main countries of origin, four leading and quite different model situations emerge:

1. Near complete transfer of a community to Israel soon after independence in 1948, as demonstrated by the cases of Iraq, Yemen, Bulgaria, and a few other mostly Near Eastern and Balkan countries.
2. Extreme fluctuations between virtually zero and very sizable migration, reflecting the shifting emigration policies of the respective countries of origin, as in the cases of the Maghreb, Ethiopia, the (former) Soviet Union, and most other East European countries.
3. Comparatively significant migration with continuous and sharp fluctuations, in response to local economic and political crises, as featured by Argentina, most other countries in Latin America, and South Africa.
4. Generally scarce migration, except for a more intense period following the 1967 Six-Day War in Israel, as typical of most

countries in Western Europe and North America, including the United States.

The yearly *aliya* profiles of some other countries were intermediate between the extreme cases mentioned here. It is from the weighted average of these very different patterns that the overall rhythm and geographical composition of total migration to Israel were decisively effected. It is therefore at the disaggregated country level rather than with reference to total *aliya* that one would seek an explanation of the observed trends. The interplay of socioeconomic and cultural determinants behind these data is discussed in greater detail in the next section.

Multivariate Analysis: Toward a Causal Explanation of Aliya *Differentials*

As already noted, most Jewish migration to Israel from countries in Eastern Europe, Asia, and Africa reflected a set of hostile, unattractive, or push conditions for Jewish communities there, conducive to a high propensity to emigrate. In contrast, a broader set of assumptions can be expressed about *aliya* from Western countries. It can be mostly, or a combination of:

1. Factors (positive or negative) related to the general characteristics of the society in the countries of residence.
2. Factors (stimulating or hampering) related to the characteristics of Jewish communities in each country.
3. Values and norms related to the ideological pull of Israel toward committed members of Jewish diaspora communities. In popular perceptions, this third alternative is probably considered the most likely determinant of *aliya* from Western countries.

To verify these hypotheses, we analyzed migration patterns to Israel from about 20 Western countries with Jewish populations of at least 10,000 over the period 1961-1986. One significant and necessary common ground among these countries was the opportunity for free emigration allowed to citizens. By comparing the intensity of emigration from each country, the general characteristics of each society and of the respective Jewish community, and the additional effects produced by the changing characteristics of Israeli society over time, insights may be provided about the mechanisms conducive to more or less *aliya* under conditions of freedom of movement.

Remarkable variation appears in the absolute figures and in the corresponding average yearly rates of migration to Israel from each country (not reported here; see Israel CBS; DellaPergola 1984, 1989). In recent years, with regard to countries with a consistent record of free emigration, the lowest emigration rates were observed for the United States and Canada (down to a yearly minimum of 0.6 emigrants per 1,000 Jewish population), and the highest for Turkey and Uruguay (up to a yearly maximum of 22.6 emigrants per 1,000). Along with inter-country variation, significant variation also appeared within each country over time. Table 2.5 summarizes the results of a multivariate analysis of Western migration to Israel based on detailed country-by-country data for the period 1961-1986.

The dependent variable in this multiple regression analysis was the rate of migration to Israel per 1,000 Jews in each country. Several major types of explanatory factors operating in the countries of origin were considered. They included:

1. Major indicators of general socioeconomic and political trends.
2. Indicators of the characteristics of the Jewish communities in the respective countries.

Moreover, different ways in which the Jewish community in each country of origin is related to the country of destination, Israel, were incorporated in the explanatory model by observing:

3. The amount of response to changes in Israeli society shown by yearly changes in the number of immigrants from each country.
4. The amount of satisfaction or dissatisfaction experienced by immigrants from each country in the course of their absorption in Israel (for a brief description of variables, see the footnotes to Table 2.5).

TABLE 2.5

Contribution of Major Groups of Variables to Variation in Migration from Free-Migration Countries to Israel — Coefficients of Determination and Percent of Explained Variance, 1961-1986

Major group of variables	R^2 due to group of variables alone		% distribution of explained variance (R^2) (all inclusive)	
Model 1: 1961-1976[a]				
	1961-68	1969-76	1961-68	1969-76
General society abroad:			(74)	(83)
Societal hold[c]	.585	.266	68	31
Societal push[d]	.290	.622	6	52
Jewish community abroad[e]	.258	.129	9	12
Immigration feedback[f]	.332	.169	14	2
Immigration cost[g]	.009	.010	3	3
Total R^2 (all inclusive)[h]	.715	.716	100	100

Migrants per 1,000 Jews in country of origin

Total world	3.7	3.6		
Free-emigration countries	0.7	1.8		

	Model 2: 1973-1986[b]					
	1973-77	1978-82	1983-86	1973-77	1978-82	1983-86
General society abroad[i]	.465	.284	.327	63	38	53
Jewish community abroad[j]	.412	.297	.345	11	16	14
Immigration feedback[k]	.182	.283	.239	5	32	6
Israeli society[l]	.457	.242	.314	20	14	27
Total R^2 (all inclusive)[m]	.727	.547	.611	100	100	100

Migrants per 1,000 Jews in country of origin

Total world	2.3	1.7	1.1			
Free-migration countries	1.4	1.2	1.1			

a. N of countries = 21. b. N of countries = 20. c. 1. Country's energy consumption per capita; 2. Political freedom index. d. 1. Consumer price increase; 2. Political violence index. e. 1. Jewish population size; 2. percent Jewish education; 3. percent Jewish intermarriage. f. 1. Years of seniority in Israel; 2. Frequency of remigration from Israel. g. 1. Country's distance from Israel. h. 10 variables overall; adjusted for degrees of freedom. i. 1. Country's energy consumption per capita; 2. Political freedom index. j. 1. Jewish population growth; 2. percent Jewish day-school education. k. 1. Years of seniority in Israel; 2. Country's distance from Israel. l. 1. Reaction to wars in Israel; 2. Reaction to unemployment in Israel. m. 4 variables overall (n. 1 in notes i.-l.); adjusted for degrees of freedom. For sources of data and detailed descriptions of variables, see: DellaPergola (1984; 1989).

In the following analysis, two somewhat different but basically comparable models were tested for the period 1961-1976 and for the period 1973-1986. The earlier period included the significant historical divide of the 1967 Six-Day War, after which Western migration to Israel increased substantially for a few years. To find out whether factors of push in the countries of origin added to the expectedly increased pull of Israel in the aftermath of the Six-Day War, migration rates were compared for the years 1961-1968 and 1969-1976 (the pre- and post-war periods, allowing for a moderate time lag). A multivariate model, comprising ten variables representing each of the major types of factors specified above, provided high percentages of explained variance (R^2), around 72 percent in each period (see upper half of Table 2.5). However, regarding the internal composition of explained variance (right hand columns in the upper part of Table 2.5), by far the better predictor during the earlier and less intensive migration years (1961-1968) was the variable hold (attractiveness) of the countries of origin, negatively related to *aliya* frequencies. For the later and more intensive migration years (1969-1976) the focus of explanation shifted to push variables, positively related to *aliya*, indicating the emergence of elements of economic and political stress in Western societies, in spite of the generally stable and attractive conditions that prevail there.

With regard to the years 1973-1986, two variables were designated for each of the major types of explanatory factors indicated above. Regressions were initially run to ascertain how much of the overall variation in *aliya* frequencies could be explained by one type of variables alone. These simple models appear in the first four lines of the left columns in the bottom half of Table 2.5, respectively, for 1973-1977, 1978-1982, and 1983-1986. Each of these four single-cause models provided statistical measures of explained variance (R^2) in the range of 20 percent to 45 percent. The best predictor was then selected from each of the preceding four models, and run together in an all-inclusive model.

The respective four predicting variables were:

1. Energy consumption per capita, an indicator of a country's economic development and modernization (negatively related to *aliya*).

2. Jewish population growth in country of origin, an indicator of the strength and autonomy of the respective Jewish community (also negatively related).
3. Response to wars in Israel, an indicator of the measure of emotional solidarity of diaspora communities toward Israel in moments of crisis (positively related).
4. Recency of immigration to Israel among the pool of immigrants from a given country, an indicator of (temporary) lack of satisfaction among migrants, and seemingly connected with the nature of feed-back to other Jews in the country of origin (negatively related to *aliya*).

The more comprehensive, four-variable model again provided high amounts of explained variance of the observed differences in frequencies of migration to Israel from free societies. The amount of variance explained for each of the three periods examined was: 73 percent (1973-1977), 55 percent (1978-1982), and 61 percent (1983-1986). Three variables out of four — energy consumption abroad, Jewish population growth abroad, and response to Israeli military crises — proved statistically highly significant.

Variables related to general society in the country of origin provided most of the explained variance in inter-country variation in migration rates to Israel (right hand columns in the lower half of Table 2.5). The immigrants' feedback (as operationalized here) seemed to play an important role only once, in the aftermath of the years of augmented *aliya* that followed the Six-Day War. It should be noted that numerous other key Israeli social indicators that were tested as possible determinants of the changing levels of *aliya* proved to be statistically not significant.

The preceding analysis substantially emphasized determinants of migration to Israel related to the life and experience of Jews in the countries of residence before migration, rather than in Israel. Israel's appeal evidently was an important element in the choice of Jews who decided to emigrate there rather than to alternative destinations. This was reflected in the personal characteristics of migrants, which were generally skewed toward higher levels of Jewish religious commitment, knowledge, and communal activism. However, non-ideological factors of a general nature, in particular, temporary or permanent economic and political instability in the countries of origin, appeared to play a more significant role in the timing and size of *aliya*. This was obviously true in the case of countries where Jews had a prolonged experience with duress, but a similar finding emerged for the pool of free-emigration and apparently more attractive societies in the Western world. Replication of a similar procedure with more detailed data for individual countries, such as the United States or Mexico (not reported here), strikingly confirmed the main results of this analysis.

Emigration from Israel

Between 1948 and 1994, the ratio between Israel's net international migration balance and the total size of immigration was 80 percent, pointing to a missing share, i.e., a ratio of emigrants to immigrants, of 20 percent. International comparisons show that countries receiving large masses of immigrants typically experience significant amounts of remigration or even plain emigration. For example, at the peak of immigration between the mid-nineteenth and twentieth centuries, no country receiving large-scale immigration, such as the United States, Argentina and Brazil, retained all of its immigrants, and in some cases, such as Australia and New Zealand, not even a majority of them. Therefore, the net contribution of international migration to total population growth in such countries tended to be much less than the total volume of immigration. The erosion of immigration due to emigration was actually lowest in the case of Jewish migration to the United States at the turn of the century: the ratio of Jewish remigrants to immigrants was then as low as 5 percent (Hersch, 1931). However, Israel's long-term migration retention ratio (80 percent) was comparatively higher than in the case of each of the countries just mentioned. Limited to the years 1960-1989, when immigration to Israel was comparatively low, the migration retention ratio was 65 percent (Israel CBS). In the same years, migration retention ratios for some other countries that received significant numbers of immigrants were as follows: Belgium, 18 percent; New Zealand, 26 percent; Germany, 28 percent; Netherlands, 29 percent; Sweden, 52 percent; Australia, 86 percent (i.e., higher than Israel) (Zlotnik, 1994).

Two related factors played a major role in Israel's comparatively high migration retention performance. The first was the significantly family transfer character of *aliya*. Relocation of entire households, including women, children and the elderly, implied a choice of definitive abandonment of the place of origin. Elsewhere, economically motivated, hence demographically selective, migrations dominated by young adult males tended to be less permanent and more prone to remigration. The second factor, often implicit in Jewish emigration, was the impossibility to return to countries of origin where perceived discrimination or actual persecutions were among the main motivating factors for leaving (Schmelz, 1993).

The annual profile of emigration from Israel is completely different from that of immigration (compare Figure 2.3 with Figure 2.2). The data refer to all emigrants, including Jews and non-Jews, but Jews constitute the predominant component. Israeli emigration data are in fact estimates based on a cohort follow-up of residents who did not return at the end of a designated number of years of stay abroad. The data reported here refer to residents who did not return after four uninterrupted years of stay abroad (but might have returned subsequently) (Israel CBS), which is an admittedly rough but reasonable proxy for the purpose of assessing emigration trends.

Keeping in mind the much smaller numerical scale of the figures on emigration, as compared to immigration, no major waves spanning over several consecutive years appeared to reflect a major crisis that might have occurred in Israel. A more limited range of variation obtained for percentages of change in the yearly number of emigrants than of immigrants. The profile of Israeli emigration was characterized rather by frequent and short term ups and downs, broadly comparable to those of the typical business cycle. Indeed, the relationship between socioeconomic and labor-market indicators and emigration routinely found in developed countries appeared to be a leading explanatory factor in the changing numbers of emigrants from Israel (Lamdany, 1982). Another main determinant was the variable pool of very recent immigrants, many of whom were not yet adjusted and satisfied in their new environment. As expected in any context of large scale immigration, each major immigration wave stimulated a smaller wave of emigration shortly after. Such a feature clearly developed following the more recent immigration wave from the former Soviet Union. In the long run, absolute numbers of emigrants actually tended to increase over time. However, once adjusted for the rapidly growing size of the

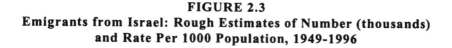

FIGURE 2.3
Emigrants from Israel: Rough Estimates of Number (thousands)
and Rate Per 1000 Population, 1949-1996

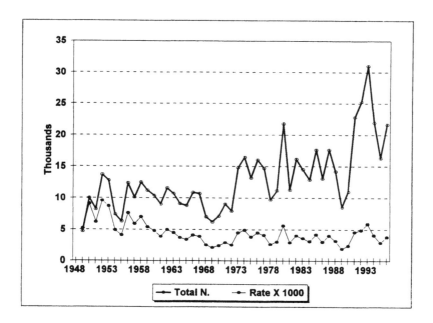

Israeli population, annual emigration rates were substantially stable, or even somewhat declining, between 3 and 5 per 1,000 inhabitants.

Propensities to emigrate from Israel also displayed significant internal demographic variation. Remigration was generally greater among the relatively few Jewish immigrants from North America and Western Europe than for immigrants from Asia, Africa, and Eastern Europe, or for the Israeli-born. Table 2.6 illustrates these differences with regard to remigration of immigrants who arrived between 1969 and 1987 who left during their first three years of stay in Israel. Moreover, controlling for country of origin, remigration was slightly more frequent for those entering the country as potential immigrants versus those entering as immigrants. The latter category reflects a greater initial commitment to stay on the part of newcomers, but also less economic independence and the need to rely on public assistance in the initial stages of absorption.

During the 1970s and 1980s, remigration of new immigrants from the USSR was notably low, between 3 and 7 percent over the first three years from arrival. Preliminary evidence for the immigration wave of the 1990s indicates substantially similar and low remigration propensities (Damian and Rosenbaum-Tamari, 1996).

TABLE 2.6
Percent of Immigrants Who Left Israel within the First Three Years Since Arrival, by Country of Origin — Immigrants of 1969/70 to 1987

Country of origin	Year of migration to Israel				
	1969/70- 1970/71	1971/72- 1974/75	1978/79- 1979/80	1984- 1985[a]	1986- 1987[a]
	Total immigrants				
Total	16	13	12	16	22
North America	}	32	24	27	34
	} 29				
South America	}	17	22	22	25
Western Europe	29	26	29	30	38
Eastern Europe	5	7	3	6	7
Asia-Africa	8	9	15	2	7
	Thereof: Potential immigrants				
Total	30	28	25	29	34
North America	}	33	24	29	34
	} 32				
South America	}	21	25	23	27
Western Europe	31	28	32	34	41
Eastern Europe[b]	–	–	–	–	–
Asia-Africa	28	19	16	19	20

a. Unweighted two-year averages.
b. Few cases.
Source: adapted from Israel CBS.

Characteristics of Jewish Migrants from the Former Soviet Union

Background

Viewed in historical perspective, minority status which prevailed in the diaspora exposed Jewish populations to manifold legal, political, economic, and cultural influences. These enhanced the emergence of considerable sociodemographic diversity between the Jewish communities of different countries and regions in the world. Heterogeneity became a crucial factor when, at a much later stage in history, mass migration began to flow to Israel. Diversity in levels of modernization and socioeconomic development attained by various Jewish communities worldwide quickly translated into internal social gaps within the new framework of Israeli society. The targets of "ingathering of the exiles," "fusion of the diasporas," and "closing the gaps" thus became, in due course, central tenets of Israeli social policies (Schmelz, DellaPergola, Avner, 1991).

Looking at the characteristics of migrants, the split that occurred among the migrants from each given country of origin when they chose different countries of destination reflected significant patterns of sociodemographic self-selection. In broad aggregate generalization, since 1948 more of the culturally traditional and socially lower strata emigrated to Israel, while more of the better educated, entrepreneurial and professional strata preferred France, the United States and other Western countries. Near Eastern Jewish immigrants to Western countries generally displayed comparatively good human capital characteristics, in spite of the relatively backward status of their countries of origin. In contrast, Israel had to absorb, train and equip large strata of immigrants with poorer personal socioeconomic characteristics, and much heavier demographic dependency ratios. Compositional differences among migrants from Eastern Europe to Israel and to the Western countries were less sharp, but broadly went in the same direction. These compositional differences deeply affected the speed of mobility processes of immigrants in their new countries. In turn, the respective absorption experiences of migrants to different countries of destination may have fed back to some extent into the migration propensities of subsequent migrants from the same countries of origin (Leshem, Rosenbaum, Kahanov, 1979; DellaPergola, 1986).

Characteristics of Migrants, 1989-1996

In this section some of the main compositional differences that emerged among Jewish migrants from the former Soviet Union to Israel and to the United States over the period 1990-95 are reviewed. Emigration patterns in relation to demographic changes that occurred among Jews in the former Soviet Union in recent decades are examined (Tolts, 1993a). Migration to the U.S.A. refers to migration assisted by HIAS. Not included are a small number of migrants (possibly a few hundred each year) who do not need resettlement assistance, or are assisted by non-Jewish agencies. Table 2.7 reports the yearly numbers of former Soviet Union Jewish migrants, including non-Jewish relatives, to the two principal countries of destination, as well as yearly rates of emigration (according to the enlarged definition) per 1,000 Jews (according to the core definition) remaining in the former Soviet Union.

Of the over 930,000 migrants who went either to Israel or to the U.S.A. between 1989 and 1996, nearly 670,000, or 71.5 percent, migrated to Israel. It should be recalled that over the period 1971-1989, 49 percent of total former Soviet Union migrants went to Israel and 51 percent dropped out in Vienna (Rosenbaum-Tamari and Damian, 1991). If the more recent picture is rounded off by incorporating migrants who reached other countries during the same years — Germany in first place, followed by Canada — Israel still can be estimated to have attracted slightly less than two-thirds of the total migrants from the former Soviet Union in 1989-96. The percentage of migrants preferring Israel over the U.S.A. jumped to 85 percent in 1990, declined to 58.5 percent in 1992, and rose again to 74 percent in 1996.

Migration rates were computed by comparing the known numbers of migrants (including non-Jews) with year-by-year revised estimates of Jewish population in the former Soviet Union which, besides migration itself, also take into account Jewish births, deaths, and identificational changes (Schmelz and DellaPergola, 1991-1996). The eight-year average yearly migration rate to Israel and the United States combined was 118 per 1,000 Jews in the

TABLE 2.7

Migrants from the Former Soviet Union to Israel and the United States — Number and Rate per 1,000 Jews in the Country of Origin, 1989-1996

Year of arrival[a]	FSU Jewish population, beginning of year	Number of migrants to:			Migrants per 1,000 Jews in Former Soviet Union[b]			% to Israel
		Israel	U.S.A.	Total	Israel	U.S.A.	Total	
Total		669,040	267,046	936,086	84.1[c]	34.1[c]	118.2[c]	71.5
1989	1,450,500	12,932	38,395	51,327	8.9	26.5	35.4	25.2
1990	1,370,000	185,227	32,714	217,941	135.2	23.7	157.9	85.0
1991	1,150,000	147,839	35,568	183,407	128.6	30.9	159.5	80.6
1992	990,000	65,093	46,083	111,176	65.8	46.5	112.3	58.5
1993	890,000	66,145	35,928	102,073	74.3	40.4	114.7	64.8
1994	817,000	68,079	32,906	100,985	83.3	40.3	123.6	67.7
1995	739,000	64,847	24,765	89,612	87.8	33.5	121.3	72.4
1996	660,000	58,878	20,687	79,565	89.2	31.3	120.6	74.0

a. Israel: calendar year; U.S.A.: fiscal year.
b. Jewish migrants, including non-Jewish relatives, per 1,000 Jewish population at beginning of year.
c. Unweighted average of eight-year migration rates.
Sources: Israel CBS; HIAS; Schmelz and DellaPergola (1991-1996), DellaPergola (1997).

country of origin. Migration rates to Israel reached a peak of 135 per 1,000 in 1990, declined to 66 per 1,000 in 1992, and then gradually rose again to 89 per 1,000 in 1996. A different trend occurred in emigration rates to the United States which reached a maximum of 46 per 1,000 in 1992, and subsequently declined to 31 per 1,000 in 1996. The main notion conveyed by these data is that over the eight-year period examined here, while the Jewish population in the former Soviet Union was steadily shrinking, emigration rates remained remarkably high and steady.

Republic of Origin

Table 2.8 describes the composition of migrants between 1990 and 1995, by republic of origin. The table compares the distributions by country of destination, and hints at the impact of emigration on the geographical structure of Jews still remaining in the

TABLE 2.8
Republic of Origin of Immigrants from the Former Soviet Union
to Israel and the U.S.A., 1990-1995

Republic	Jewish population 1989 thousands	Migrants				Migrants[b] as % of Jewish population 1989
		N(thousands)		Percentages		%Ratio Israel /USA[a]
		Israel	USA	Israel	USA	
Total	1,450.5	597.2[c]	208.0[c]	100.0	100.0	100	55.6
Baltic[d]	39.9	15.7	5.5	2.7	2.6	102	53.0
Belarus	112.0	52.2	23.2	8.9	11.2	80	67.4
Moldova	65.8	40.8	12.0	7.0	5.8	120	80.3
Russia	551.0	175.2	48.1	29.9	23.1	129	40.5
Ukraine	487.3	171.9	87.7	29.3	42.2	69	53.3
Uzbekistan	94.9	61.6	19.3	10.5	9.3	113	85.3
Caucasus[e]	56.3	42.0	7.1	7.2	3.4	210	87.1
Other Asia[f]	43.3	26.8	4.8	4.6	2.3	197	72.9
Europe	1,256.0	455.9	176.5	77.7	84.9	91	50.3
Asia	194.5	130.4	31.2	22.3	15.0	148	83.1

a. Percent ratio of percentages in two preceding columns.
b. Emigrants to Israel and the U.S.A., including non-Jewish family members.
c. Including Republic unknown or not reported.
d. Estonia, Latvia, Lithuania.
e. Armenia, Azerbaijan, Georgia.
f. Kazakhstan, Kirgizstan, Turkmenistan, Tajikistan.
Sources: Israel CBS; HIAS.

former Soviet Union. The fifteen republics were regrouped into eight major divisions, five in Europe and three in Asia. The geographical composition of the two migration streams to Israel and the United States was quite different. The percentage of all emigrants coming from Asian republics to Israel was 22 percent, versus 15 percent to the U.S.A. Migration to the U.S.A. hence drew more heavily from the European republics. Within the European origin, migrants to Israel included nearly equal shares from Russia and from Ukraine, while those preferring the U.S.A. included a predominant stock from Ukraine. It should be noted that *aliya* from Russia disproportionately came from the Russian Caucasus area whose Jewish population is sociologically more similar to that of the Asian republics than to that of the large cities in northwestern

Russia. Ratios between numbers of migrants to Israel and the U.S.A. show the highest propensity toward Israel among migrants from the Caucasus republics, and the lowest among those from Ukraine (for more disaggregated data on past emigration propensities, see Riss, 1990).

Emigration figures over the years 1990-95, including non-Jewish household members, were compared with the 1989 Jewish population distribution by republics (excluding non-Jews), to provide a very rough indicator of emigration propensities (last column of Table 2.8). The highest propensity to leave appeared in the Caucasus republics, followed by Uzbekistan, Moldova, and the pool of other Central Asian republics, each with a ratio of emigrants to initial Jewish population of more than 70 percent. Each of these areas experienced severe political and military disturbances over the years considered here. Declining emigration propensities were found in Belarus, Ukraine, the Baltic republics, and, prominently last with a ratio of 40 percent, the Russian republic. The resulting effect of emigration on the Jewish population remaining in the former Soviet Union was a growing concentration in Russia (particularly in the largest and more developed urban areas), and the quick emptying of the peripheral, less secure, and economically less developed regions.

More detailed year-by-year data, not reported here, demonstrate interesting changes in the propensity to prefer Israel over the United States for each republic or group of republics. A declining tendency to migrate to Israel appeared between 1991 and 1993. It was not synchronized across the different regions of the former Soviet Union, confirming the relevance of local determinants in migration decisions already discussed above. While in the first year of mass migration, 1990, 80-90 percent of migrants from all republics of origin went to Israel, by 1992-93 Israel received less than half of all migrants from Belarus and Ukraine, and about half of those from the Baltic republics and Moldova. Propensities to prefer Israel were consistently high among migrants from the Caucasus republics and other central Asian republics, and, in declining order, from Russia, Moldova, and Uzbekistan. Between 1993 and 1995 propensities to prefer Israel over the U.S. tended to increase or remained generally stable, thus reversing the trend to "drop out" that, based on the experience of the 1970s and 1980s, could be inferred to gain momentum. However, migration to other countries of destination was increasing, too, so that Israel's primacy as a country of destination declined in comparison to the two peak years 1990 and 1991.

The fact that the U.S. quota for 40,000 immigrants from the former Soviet Union was not filled in 1993, 1994, and 1995 is possibly explained by difficulties experienced by immigrants in finding employment in America. According to 1990 U.S. census data, people born in the former Soviet Union had the highest percent on welfare among immigrants from any European country (Borjas, 1993). True, an alternative explanation for the latter fact would be that Jews who knew in advance that their opportunities for employment would be limited, e.g., because of their relatively older age (see below), deliberately preferred to emigrate to the United States and to rely on the comparatively liberal welfare provisions available there. One may also speculate that the sharp decline in immigration to the U.S. in 1995 reflected an early enforcement by the immigration authorities of a smaller quota, although the latter was to be started in 1996. On the other hand, evidence exists that notwithstanding difficulties and initial unemployment, the economic absorption of immigrants in Israel was more successful than in the United States (Klinov, 1991; Hercovitz and Meridor, 1991). This may have set a favorable mood toward migrating to Israel.

Age

Table 2.9 shows the differential composition by age of emigrants versus the total Jewish population in the former Soviet Union, and of emigrants to Israel versus the U.S.A. One should pay attention in the first place to the quite overaged composition of Jews in the country of origin in 1989. Keeping in mind the distorted characteristics of population structure, the general tendency to emigrate tended to be negatively correlated with age. The very rough ratios of emigrants (including non-Jewish relatives, see last column of Table 2.9) to initial Jewish population for major age groups sharply declined from over 95 percent among the younger population segment up to age 20, to close to 75 percent for the 21-40 age-group, about 40 percent for the 41-65 age-group, and about 33 percent for those aged 65 and over in 1989.

TABLE 2.9
Age Distribution of Immigrants from the Former Soviet Union
to Israel and the U.S.A., 1990-1995

Age	Jewish population 1989 thousands	Migrants				%Ratio Israel /USA[a]	Migrants[b] as % of Jewish population 1989
		N(thousands)		Percentages			
		Israel	USA	Israel	USA		
Total	1,450.5[c]	597.2	208.0[c]	100.0	100.0	100	55.6
0-5	54.2	37.4	12.1	6.3	5.9	107	91.7
6-10	56.5	45.8	13.6	7.7	6.6	117	105.6
11-20	113.7	85.7	25.3	14.3	12.2	117	97.4
21-30	131.9	88.1	26.1	14.8	12.6	117	86.8
31-40	188.6	95.5	29.8	16.0	14.4	111	66.7
41-50	185.5	71.3	25.8	11.9	12.4	96	52.3
51-60	244.0	59.9	28.1	9.9	13.5	73	36.0
61-64	133.8	33.3	11.8	5.6	5.7	98	33.9
65-70	107.9	33.8	17.3	5.7	8.3	69	47.7
71+	233.9	46.5	17.5	7.8	8.4	93	27.5
0-20	224.4	168.9	51.0	28.3	24.6	115	98.1
21-40	320.5	183.6	55.9	30.8	26.9	114	75.0
41-64	563.3	164.5	65.7	27.4	31.7	86	40.9
65+	341.8	80.3	34.8	13.5	16.8	80	33.9

a. Percent ratio of percentages in two preceding columns.
b. Emigrants to Israel and the U.S.A., including non-Jewish family members.
c. Including age not stated.
Sources: Israel CBS; HIAS.

Age 40 seems to constitute a sharp dividing point in the choice whether to stay or leave, as well as in choosing a country of destination. Such significant self-selection of migrants by age reflects not only the usual greater propensity to leave among younger adults, but also the substantial weight of nuclear families of parents and their children among the emigrants. It is also the artifact of a greater proportion of non-Jews among younger house-hold members such as children and younger adults. This is clearly demonstrated by an "emigration ratio" of over 100 percent for the 6-10 age group (non-Jews are included in the numerator but not in the denominator).

Comparing the age distributions of migrants to Israel and to the U.S.A. does not reveal extreme differences. Yet, Israel on balance absorbed a younger population. The percentage of migrants up to 20 was 28 percent to Israel and 25 percent to the U.S.A., while the percentages of migrants aged 65 and over were 13 percent and 17 percent, respectively. Migration from the former Soviet Union produced some aging effect on the Jewish and total population in Israel, which is comparatively young for a developed society, but it produced even more significant aging effects on the non-migrant population stock, by subtracting from it most of its younger cohorts. Only minor age-structural effects were produced by migration on the composition of American Jewry, which in recent years was quite similar to that of migrants from the former Soviet Union.

Gender and Marital Status

The overall composition of Jewish migrants to Israel and the U.S.A by gender was nearly identical. In both cases it included about 47 percent of males and 53 percent of females. This excess of females among migrants is noteworthy. Because of better survivorship rates, women generally predominate among older age-groups, and indeed Jewish population in general and migrants in particular display a rather elderly age composition. However, females also regularly predominated among Jewish migrants at young and intermediate adult ages (20-50), whereas data on Jewish population composition in the former Soviet Union showed a clear excess of males (Tolts, 1995). This inconsistency appears to be related to the marital status and household composition of migrants, which included comparatively high percentages of divorced women and of one-parent households headed by women. Such evidence stresses the strong role of women in decision-making related to emigration and *aliya*.

Occupation

The socioeconomic stratification of Jews in the USSR was shaped over the decades by the complex interplay between the general trends and effects of Soviet policies on society, and unique adaptation processes within the Jewish minority (Altshuler, 1987). The perhaps unexpected product was a Jewish occupational structure extremely similar in many respects to that of Jews in advanced capitalist societies, with a predominant emphasis on white-collar occupations contingent upon high educational attainment. We do not have published data on the occupational stratification of the Jewish population for the former Soviet Union as a whole. It should also be noted that occupational classifications adopted in the past under the Soviet regime did not conform with the standards routinely used in Western countries. However, 1989 census data for the Russian Republic show that 52 percent of Jews aged 15 and over had attained higher education, while 79 percent were employed in white-collar jobs (Tolts, 1996). It can be assumed that parallel trends prevailed in other republics.

The occupational composition of migrants is a crucial element in their adaptation to the new environment in the countries of destination. High levels of education and occupational skills were instrumental in socioeconomic absorption in the past (Chiswick, 1991; Ofer et al., 1991). On the other hand, the overwhelming concentration of Jews who left the former Soviet Union in relatively few occupational strata and branches produced an excess of certain skills, such as in the medical professions, in engineering, or the performing arts, with the consequence of strong competition both with the established labor markets in the countries of immigration, and within the immigrant group itself (Shuval, 1983). The initial consequence was relatively high unemployment, or at least forced, and usually downward, occupational mobility (Sabatello, 1992).

Table 2.10 provides a broad illustration of the occupational characteristics of migrants from the former Soviet Union to Israel (1990-1995) and to the United States (1993-1995). Overall, in both cases the occupational distribution was extremely skewed toward white-collar occupations. Among those who reported an occupation in the country of origin, blue-collar occupations roughly corresponding to the three bottom lines in Table 2.10 (services, skilled, and unskilled), included 25 percent of migrants to Israel, and 21 percent of migrants to the U.S.A.

Occupational differences between migrants to Israel and the U.S.A should be cautiously considered, as they may derive from different classification criteria by the organizations handling new immigrants in Israel and in the U.S.A. In the U.S. data classifica-

TABLE 2.10
Occupation Abroad of Immigrants from the Former Soviet Union
to Israel and the U.S.A., 1990-1995

Occupation before migration	Migrants		
	Israel 1990-1995	U.S.A. 1993-1995	% Ratio Israel/U.S.A.[a]
Total N., thousands	315.9	51.2	
Total %	100.0	100.0	100
Scientific, academic	33.9	32.6	104
Professional, technical	33.7	15.7	215
Managerial, clerical, sales	7.3	30.7	24
Services	4.0	6.3	64
Skilled	16.1[b]	11.4	141
Unskilled	5.0	3.3	152
White-collar	74.9	79.0	95
Blue-collar	25.1	21.0	120

a. Percent ratio of percentages in two preceding columns.
b. Including 0.1 in agriculture.
Sources: Israel CBS; HIAS.

tion, all engineers were included in the higher-status scientific and academic occupational group, while in Israel practical and other lower-status engineers were included among professionals and technicians. On the face of available data, around one-third of the labor force within each migration stream reported a scientific and academic occupation in the country of origin, including professions in medicine, engineering, law, the natural sciences, the social sciences, and the humanities. The major difference concerned the distribution between the next two major occupational groups, the professional and technical, and the managerial and clerical (including sales). The professional and technical category, including mostly teachers, social workers, accountants, technicians and practical engineers, was comparatively much more visible among migrants to Israel. On the other hand, the managerial and clerical category, including managers and office workers, and sales persons, was comparatively more visible among migrants to the United States.

From a broader aggregation of all cases into two occupational groups of white- and blue-collars, which possibly compensates for classification inconsistencies, it appears that Israel tended to draw somewhat more from the (relatively small) lower occupational strata, while more of the occupational higher strata went to the U.S.A. (see last column of Table 2.10). A similar conclusion most likely applies with regard to the top occupational elite, more of whom would find immediate placement in the American context than in the much more limited Israeli one. These trends appear to be quite closely related to the patterns of geographical selectivity of migrants already noted above, namely, the greater propensity to migrate to America among Jews from the Slavic republics of the former Soviet Union among whom higher levels of education and more widespread professionalization prevail.

Ethno-Religious Identification

One final compositional aspect concerns the ethno-religious identification of migrants. While the general definition of Jewish migration applies to the whole of the observed migration flow, the fact that not all of the migrants are actually Jewish carries significant implications for their final social integration. Intensive assimilation experienced by Jews in the former Soviet Union in recent decades determined high percentages of mixed marriage, and an enlarged Jewish population probably close to twice the size of the core Jewish population (Tolts, 1993b). In other words, the number of people entitled to emigrate under special provisions for Jewish migrants that exist in Israel, the United States, and Germany tends to be double or greater than the estimated size of the Jewish population.

There is little documentary evidence on the ethno-religious composition of migrants from the former Soviet Union. The better information stems from Israeli authorities, whose findings, however, are not fully consistent. Since 1985, religion is recorded only after immigrants apply to the bureau of the Population Register of the Ministry of Interior in order to obtain an identity card. Before application, religion appears as "not recorded." After application to the bureau, religion is recorded as Jewish or otherwise, according to the documentation presented. For that minority of all immigrants for whom religion cannot be ascertained, the record is changed from "not recorded" to "no religion." Data processed by Israel

CBS, the authoritative central institution in charge of handling all statistical information in Israel, indicate the following percentages of non-Jews (including persons with no religion) among immigrants whose religion was ascertained, by year of arrival:

1985-89	1990	1991	1992	1993	1994
4.8	3.8	8.2	14.2	15.9	28.4

Source: adapted from Israel CBS, *Immigration to Israel, 1995.*
Data refer to all countries of origin.

There is a clear increasing trend in the percentage on non-Jews among new immigrants to Israel. Data directly processed by the Population Register of Israel's Ministry of Interior on apparently the same database actually indicated higher percentages of non-Jews among immigrants whose religion was ascertained, as follows: October 1989-end 1990: 5.4 percent; 1991: 13.3 percent; January-August 1992: 20.5 percent (DellaPergola, 1993b). Percentages based on statistical sources and definitions of the Russian and other republics would probably be even higher. In any event, it stands to reason that the more the continuing emigration from the former Soviet Union will come to approach the maximum emigration potential, i.e., the total enlarged Jewish population remaining there, the proportion of non-Jews among the migrants will tend to rise. This aspect should be considered in formulating expectations and programs concerning the successful absorption of immigrants in Israel.

As to the share of non-Jews among migrants to other countries, the partial available evidence is that it tends to be higher than among migrants to Israel. Data released by the German Federal immigration authorities (Polian and Teschemacher, 1995; Jewish Agency, 1996) indicate that between 1990 and 1995, 118,000 admission requests were submitted by people in the former Soviet Union in the framework of the Jewish quota. Of these, 90,000 were accepted, and out of these, 44,000 people actually migrated to Germany. Of the latter, 26,000 registered as members of the local Jewish community organization, the Zentralwohlfahrtsstelle der Juden in Deutschland, whose admission criteria are based on *halakhah* (Jewish law). It can thus be inferred that the remaining 18,000 immigrants (41 percent) were not Jewish.

Summary and Conclusions

The recent migration wave from the former Soviet Union represents a major stage of the broad international migration movement which has been one of the major social forces shaping the Jewish population and society over the last century. Selected aspects of these more recent migrations were examined here in the context of a survey of major trends and determinants of change within the global Jewish migration system, with special regard to migration to Israel. A number of major patterns clearly emerged, rationally tying international migrations of Jews to socioeconomic and cultural forces which operate both in society in general, and within Jewish communities in particular. A good understanding of the forces and processes emerging in the intense migration experience of Jews worldwide may usefully serve in handling the current continuing wave, monitoring and assisting similar migrations in the future, and drawing lessons for other migrant groups as well.

Viewed cross-culturally and in historical perspective, a unique interplay of economic and cultural factors governed the Jewish migration experience. The primary force operating behind the intensive geographical redistribution related to the complex of negative conditions, generally described as push factors. In different ways, but quite consistently across time and space, material elements of socioeconomic dislocation and more symbolic components of religious intolerance and anti-Semitism negatively affected the relationship between different Jewish communities and the total society. Often such a relationship was completely disrupted, leading to the unavoidable choice of mass emigration.

While ideal perceptions of countries of destination, in particular Israel, played an important role in the process of decision-making, ideologies were necessary but not sufficient to generate large-scale migration. The principal stimulus to leave came from the experience of personal insecurity and economic stress of Jews in the countries of origin. The somewhat intriguing conclusion is that migration to Israel, although supposedly motivated by the Israeli pull, was very little connected with what was actually occurring in Israeli society.

In the process, significant differentiation intervened among migrants versus non-migrants, and between migrants to different countries of destination. This very deeply affected Israeli society and Jewish communities, and to a lesser extent, the general society of other countries demographically, socially, economically, and culturally. Migration generally stimulated significant socioeconomic development, although the immigrants themselves often had to suffer serious personal stress during the first years after migration and resettlement. Regarding the more recent experience of the early 1990s, migration from the former Soviet Union to Israel persisted at significant levels in spite of the economic hardships experienced by new immigrants. This again points to the predominant consideration of actual or expected push factors in migration decisions.

Facing the odds of relocation, Jews, not unlike other migrants, were naturally oriented toward the more attractive destinations, mostly represented by economically affluent and politically free societies in the Western countries. Since 1948, the State of Israel represented a unique outlet, combining ideological appeal with the decisive advantage of an open-door immigration policy. But in the course of time, Israel also emerged globally as a fairly developed and democratic society, hence becoming more attractive also on non-ideological grounds for migrants coming from comparatively less developed societies. This was translated into comparatively high immigrant retention rates. Economic prosperity related to the incipient peace process in the Middle East strengthened these patterns.

Israel's paramount interest in continuing to attract immigration, besides its being one of the declared existential tenets of the country, is rooted in the favorable impact on constructing the demographic bases of society and on promoting economic growth in the country. This logically led to policies of encouragement to immigration primarily directed toward the Jewish diaspora. However, the pace of immigration itself appeared to be largely out of the control of Israeli government and society, and rather reflected economic, political, and cultural trends which operated on the general world scene and within the respective Jewish communities in each country. Moreover, favorable economic conditions in Israel eventually stimulated large-scale additional immigration of non-Jewish workers, unrelated to the basic Jewish premises of Israeli society.

Looking prospectively at the world Jewish migration system, the traditional reservoirs of emigration — Muslim countries in North Africa and the Near East, and Eastern Europe, namely the former Soviet Union — have become or in the longer term will become virtually emptied, mostly because of large scale emigration but also because of the aging and assimilation of those Jews who choose to remain. On the other hand, the traditional receiving areas of Jewish migration, the Western countries and Israel, where nowadays most of world Jewry live, generally were characterized by rather low emigration propensities. This would suggest a future stabilization of Jewish international migration, including *aliya*, at low levels of mobility, unlike most of the past experience.

The problem with such an assumption is that it views the world-system as static according to its present configuration, which stands contrary to the long-term historical experience. Indeed, large-scale Jewish migrations often reflected important transformations in the mutual economic and political relationships between nations and societies globally. It is reasonable to assume that changes in the world-system, specifically regarding Israel's position within it and the development of peace and other political processes in the Middle East, will continue to affect the pace and direction of international migration in general, and of Jewish migration in particular. But to predict what those global changes could be is far beyond the scope of this review.

Acknowledgments

This chapter reflects prolonged research activities undertaken at the Division of Jewish Demography and Statistics of the A. Harman Institute of Contemporary Jewry, the Hebrew University of Jerusalem. Portions were presented at the International Conference on Human Migration in a Global Framework, University of Calgary, Alberta, Canada, June 1994; and at the Conference on Jewish Migration, Jerusalem Center for Public Affairs, Jerusalem, June 1996. Judith Shuval, Eli Leshem, Mark Tolts, and Judith Even provided useful remarks to a draft. The author wishes to thank Yoel Florsheim, Dorit Tal, Carol Bines, and Yifat Klopstock of the Population and Demography Division at Israel Central Bureau of Statistics in Jerusalem, and Norman Levine and Lisa Habersham of the Hebrew Immigrant Aid Society (HIAS) in New York, for kindly facilitating access to published and unpublished statistical materials.

References

Altshuler, M. 1987. *Soviet Jewry Since the Second World War: Population and Social Structure.* Westport: Greenwood Press.

Bachi, R. 1977. *The Population of Israel.* Jerusalem: Hebrew University.

Ben-Porath, Y. 1986. "The Entwined Growth of Population and Product, 1922-1982." Ed. Y. Ben-Porath, *The Economy of Israel: Maturing through Crises.* Cambridge, Mass.: Harvard University Press, pp. 27-41.

Bensimon, D. and S. DellaPergola. 1984. *La population juive de France: sociodmographie et identit.* Jerusalem: The Hebrew University, and Paris: Centre National de la Recherche Scientifique.

Borjas, G.J. 1993. "Immigration and Welfare, 1970-1990." Paper presented at Department of Sociology, University of California, Los Angeles.

Brym, R.J. 1988. "Soviet Jewish Emigration: A Statistical Test of Two Theories." *Soviet Jewish Affairs* 18(3):15-23.

Chiswick, B. 1991. "Soviet Jews in the United States: A Preliminary Analysis of their Linguistic and Economic Adjustment." *The Economic Quarterly* 148:188-210 (Hebrew).

Damian, N. and Y. Rosenbaum-Tamari. 1996. *Immigrants from the Commonwealth of Independent States after Five Years in the Country.* Jerusalem: Ministry of Immigrant Absorption, Planning and Research Branch (Hebrew).

DellaPergola, S. 1984. "On the Differential Frequency of Western Migration to Israel." *Studies in Contemporary Jewry* 1:292-315. Bloomington: Indiana University Press.

DellaPergola, S. 1986. "Aliya and Other Jewish Migrations: Toward an Integrated Perspective." Ed. U.O. Schmelz and G. Nathan, *Studies in the Population of Israel in Honor of Roberto Bachi, Scripta Hierosolymitana,* vol. 30:172-209. Jerusalem: Magnes Press.

DellaPergola, S. 1989. "Mass *Aliyah* — A Thing of the Past?" *Jerusalem Quarterly* 51:96-114.

DellaPergola, S. 1991. "The Demographic Context of the Soviet Aliya." *Jews and Jewish Topics in the Soviet Union and Eastern Europe* 16:41-56.

DellaPergola, S. 1992. "Israel and World Jewish Population: A Core-Periphery Perspective." Ed. C. Goldscheider, *Population and Social Change in Israel.* Boulder, Co.: Westview Press, pp. 39-63.

DellaPergola, S. 1993a. "Sociodemographic Surveys of World Jewry in the 1990s: Aims, Techniques, Implications." Ed. U.O. Schmelz and S. DellaPergola, *Papers in Jewish Demography 1989*. Jerusalem: Hebrew University, pp. 14-23.

DellaPergola, S. 1993b. "Demographic Changes in Israel in the Early 1990s." Ed. Y. Kop, *Israel Social Services 1992-93*. Jerusalem: Center for Social Policy Studies in Israel, pp. 57-115.

DellaPergola, S. 1993c. "Demographic Processes and Their Impact on the Identity and Survival of Minorities." *International Population Conference*. Montreal: International Union for the Scientific Study of Population. Vol. 3, pp. 89-98.

DellaPergola, S. 1997. "World Jewish Population, 1995." *American Jewish Year Book*. Vol. 97.

Eisenstadt, S.N. 1954. *The Absorption of Immigrants*. London: Routledge and Kegan Paul.

Florsheim, J. 1990. "The Emigration of Soviet Jews, 1979-1988, and Its Influence on Soviet Jewry." *Yahadut Zemanenu* (Contemporary Jewry) 6:305-321 (Hebrew).

Friedlander, D. and C. Goldscheider. 1979. *The Population of Israel*. New York: Columbia University Press.

Gitelman, Z. 1996. "From a Northern Country: Russian and Soviet Jewish Immigration to America and to Israel in Historical Perspective." Ed. N. Lewin-Epstein, Y. Ro'i, and P. Ritterband, *Russian Jews on Three Continents*. London: Cass, pp. 21-41.

Goldstein, S. and B. Kosmin. 1992. "Religious and Ethnic Self-Identification in the United States 1989-90: A Case Study of the Jewish Population." *Ethnic Groups* 9:219-245.

Ha'aretz. 1996. "Some 300,000 Foreigners Work in Israel; Some 100,000 are Staying Legally." November 14 (Hebrew).

Heitman, S. 1991. "Soviet Emigration in 1990: A New 'Fourth Wave.'" Ed. T. Basok and R. Brym, *Soviet-Jewish Emigration and Resettlement in the 1990s*. Toronto: York Lanes Press.

Hercovitz, Z. and L. Meridor. 1991. "The Macro-Economic Implications of Mass Immigration into Israel." *Economic Quarterly* 148:236-261 (Hebrew).

Hersch, L. 1931. "International Migration of the Jews." Ed. W. Wilcox, *International Migration*, Vol. 2. New York: National Bureau of Economic Research, pp. 471-520.

HIAS. *Statistical Report*. New York: Hebrew Immigrant Aid Society (annual publication and unpublished materials).

Israel Central Bureau of Statistics. *Immigration to Israel*. Jerusalem (annual publication).

Israel Central Bureau of Statistics. *Statistical Abstract of Israel*. Jerusalem (annual publication).

Jewish Agency for Israel. 1996. *Internal Report*. Jerusalem: Division for Immigrant Absorption (Hebrew).

Klinov, R. 1991. "Migrants from the Soviet Union to the United States and to Israel — Initial Comparison Following Barry Chiswick's Article." *Economic Quarterly* 148:225-231 (Hebrew).

Kritz, M.M., L.L. Lim and H. Zlotnik. 1991. *International Migration Systems: A Global Approach*. Oxford: Oxford University Press.

Kuznets, S. 1958. "Long Swings in the Growth of Population and in Related Economic Variables." *Proceedings of the American Philosophical Society*, Vol. 102, 1:25-52.

Lamdany, R. 1982. *Emigration from Israel*. Jerusalem: Maurice Falk Institute for Economic Research in Israel, Discussion Paper No. 82.08.

Leshem, E., Y. Rosenbaum and O. Kahanov. 1979. "The 'Drop-Out' Phenomenon among Soviet Jews: Main Findings and Recommendations." Jerusalem: Hebrew University, Center for Research and Documentation of Eastern European Jews.

Lestschinsky, J. 1960. "Jewish Migrations, 1840-1956." Ed. L. Finkelstein, *The Jews: Their History, Culture and Religion*, 3rd ed., Vol. 2. New York: Harper, pp. 1536-1596.

Ofer, G., K. Flug and N. Kassir. 1991. "The Absorption in Employment of the Immigrants from the Soviet Union: 1990 and Beyond." *Economic Quarterly* 148:135-179 (Hebrew).

Polian, P. and K. Teschemacher. 1995. "Jewish Emigration from the Commonwealth of Independent States to Germany." Paper presented at 3rd European Population Conference. Milan: European Association for Population Studies.

Prital, D. 1987. *The Jews of the Soviet Union*, Vol. 10. Jerusalem: Public Council for Soviet Jewry, p. 315 (Hebrew).

Riss, E. 1990. "Spatial Patterns of Jewish Emigration from the USSR, 1976-1988." *Jews and Jewish Topics in the Soviet Union* 13:5-16.

Rosenbaum-Tamari, Y. and N. Damian. 1991. *Two Waves of Aliyah: USSR Immigrants in the 1970s and at the Beginning of the 1990s — Demographic and Socio-economic Aspects*. Jerusalem: Ministry of Immigrant Absorption, Planning and Research Branch (Hebrew).

Sabatello, E.F. 1992. "Migrants from the USSR to Israel in the 1990s: Socio-demographic Background and First-Year Occupational Trends." Paper presented at Conference on Mass Migration, International Institute for Applied Systems Analysis, Vienna.

Schmelz, U.O. 1971. "Migrations." *Encyclopaedia Judaica*, Vol. 16, cols. 1518-1529.

Schmelz, U.O. 1993. *Jewish Refugee Immigrants in Israel*. Occasional Paper, Jerusalem: Hebrew University, Institute of Contemporary Jewry.

Schmelz, U.O. and S. DellaPergola. 1991-1996. "World Jewish Population." *American Jewish Year Book,* Vols. 91-96.

Schmelz, U.O., S. DellaPergola and U. Avner. 1991. *Ethnic Differences among Israeli Jews: A New Look.* Jerusalem: Hebrew University, and American Jewish Committee, Jewish Population Studies, no. 22.

Shuval, J. 1983. *Newcomers and Colleagues: Soviet Immigrant Physicians in Israel.* Houston: Cap and Gown Press.

Sicron, M. 1957. *Immigration to Israel, 1948-1953.* Jerusalem: Falk Project for Economic Research in Israel and Israel Central Bureau of Statistics, Special Series, no. 60.

Thomas, B. 1972. *Migration and Urban Development: A Reappraisal of British and American Long Cycles.* London: Allen Unwin.

Tolts, M. 1993a. "Some Basic Trends in Soviet Jewish Demography." Ed. U.O. Schmelz and S. DellaPergola, *Papers in Jewish Demography 1989.* Jerusalem: Hebrew University, Jewish Population Studies, no. 25, pp. 237-243.

Tolts, M. 1993b. "Jews in the Russian Republic since the Second World War: The Dynamics of Demographic Erosion." *International Population Conference.* Montreal: International Union for the Scientific Study of Population. Vol. 3, pp. 99-111.

Tolts, M. 1995. "Trends in Soviet Jewish Demography since the Second World War." Ed. Y. Ro'i, *Jews and Jewish Life in Russia and the Soviet Union.* London: Cass, pp. 365-382.

Tolts, M. 1996. "The Interrelationship between Emigration and the Socio-Demographic Profile of Russian Jewry." Ed. N. Lewin-Epstein, Y. Ro'i and P.Ritterband, *Russian Jews on Three Continents.* London: Cass, pp. 147-176.

United Nations. 1996a. *World Population Monitoring 1993, With a Special Report on Refugees.* New York: United Nations, Department for Economic and Social Information and Policy Analysis, Population Division.

United Nations. 1996b. *International Migration Policies 1995.* New York: United Nations, Department for Economic and Social Information and Policy Analysis, Population Division.

Zlotnik, H. 1994. "Migration to and from Developing Regions: A Review of Past Trends." Ed. W. Lutz, *The Future Population of the World: What Can We Assume Today?* London: Earthscan, pp. 321-360.

3

Israel, Democracy, the Law, and the Protection of Citizens and Minorities

Irwin Cotler

In August 1994, the Canadian Immigration and Refugee Board (IRB) sponsored one of its regular "Country Conditions" hearings on "refugee producing countries" — in this instance, Israel. The purpose of the hearing was to hear witness testimony and receive documentary evidence that would assist the IRB in its adjudication of refugee claims from Israel, particularly those emanating from the class of immigrants from the former Soviet Union to Israel. These were now seeking "asylum" in Canada on the grounds that they had a "well-founded fear of persecution" were they to be returned to Israel.

In this chapter I describe a set of questions or criteria that might assist a refugee determination process in determining whether a particular country has an "ability to protect" its citizens, the basic criterion established by the Supreme Court of Canada in the *Ward* case for the determination of refugee status;[1] and second, seek to apply these criteria to the country under discussion at the hearing — Israel — in order that adjudicators could best determine whether claimants from Israel met the definition of "Convention Refugee." Again, the *Ward* case sets out the basic principles and presumptions to be applied.[2]

In setting before the IRB a set of criteria designed to determine whether a state has "an ability to protect" its citizens, and in applying these criteria to Israel, I anchored my testimony in, first, my own experience as a scholar/advocate in the matter of the international protection of human rights, including the case of Soviet Jews; second, my involvement as scholar/advocate respecting the situation of human rights in the State of Israel and the administered territories, and which has been the focus, *inter alia*, of my academic work in comparative human rights law; and third, my involvement as international legal counsel to a number of human rights non-governmental organizations, including those concerned, *inter alia*, with refugee rights.

Indeed, these criteria were advanced as "generic" or basic "testing" criteria applicable to any refugee determination process, and to any state which is the subject of that process; they are intended to be read cumulatively rather than separately; they are to serve as testing criteria to assess a state's "ability to protect" its citizens; and they are to be read and applied in the light of the basic principles of Canadian Refugee law, which are themselves inspired by Canada's 1969 signing of the United Nations Convention Relating to the Status of Refugees[3] and its Protocol,[4] and which signified Canada's commitment to the principle of *non-refoulement*, or non-return, the Convention's main obligation;[5] while the definition of "Convention Refugee" in Canada's Immigration Act[6] is itself taken directly from the Refugee Convention itself.

These principles include, *inter alia*, that the IRB must distinguish between democratic and non-democratic countries; it must presume that the government of any country is able and willing to protect its citizens; in particular, it must presume that, if the claimant comes from a country with a democratic government and an independent judiciary, then evidence to counter this presumption would only be forthcoming in exceptional cases. Indeed, Canadian courts have accepted the principle that no democratic country can guarantee the protection of its citizens at all times.[7] If, then, a democratic government is in effective control of its territory, and makes serious efforts to protect its citizens, then the mere fact that it is not always successful in doing so will not justify a claim of refugee status.

Admittedly, Canada has left open the possibility that refugee status may be conferred on claimants from a democratic country, though this would appear to be an "exceptional" determination, but thus far this "exceptional" determination appears to have been limited in its application to Israel. This invites one of two responses: first, either refugee claimants from Israel have a seemingly preferred or privileged status, and Israel appears to be singled out for differential and discriminatory treatment among democratic countries, or Israel itself is not, in fact, counted among the world's democracies, which appears to be at variance with Canadian public policy and diplomatic discourse.

Accordingly, with these principles and presumptions in mind, the following testing criteria for refugee determination status are offered in the form of a series of ten questions; and, in accordance with these "Country Conditions" hearings, these testing criteria or questions will be applied to Israel, which emerges, therefore, not only as the subject of a "Country Condition" hearing to facilitate adjudication of refugee claims from Israel, but as a case study for the invocation and application of criteria for the determination of refugee status.

Is There a Democratically Elected Government and Parliament That One Can Petition for Redress of Grievance?

Admittedly, the mere assertion that a state is a parliamentary democracy — or the ritualistic holding of elections every four years, or the existence of the trappings of democracy — do not alone warrant an "ability to protect"; indeed, the assertion, or ritual, or trappings of democracy may even mask something very sinister — a state's unwillingness as well as "inability to protect its citizens" — and where such citizens may indeed have a "well-founded fear of persecution." Here are some examples:

- Pre-apartheid South Africa claimed it was a parliamentary democracy; but it was a parliamentary democracy for "whites only." There was no universal franchise, no one person-one vote. Indeed, apartheid was not only a racist philosophy, but a racist legal regime. It was racism institutionalized as law, and it used the notion of a parliamentary democracy as a legal cover for institutionalized racism.
- The Soviet Union had a universal franchise — and a ritual of parliamentary elections, but it was a single party system. Everyone had the right to vote — and was free to vote in regularly scheduled elections

— but you could vote only for the Communist party, and you risked imprisonment or exile for just criticizing the party, let alone advocating any other option.

• Other states, particularly in Latin America, Africa, Asia, or the Middle East, have allowed for universal franchise and permitted opposition parties; but the elections, and subsequent governance, were controlled by the military; dissenters ran the risk of imprisonment, "disappearances," extra judicial executions and the like; judiciaries were neither independent nor protective of rights, while the "independent" press was controlled, and "independent" NGOs effectively prohibited.

With respect to Israel, it can be said that it is an effective parliamentary democracy: there is a universal franchise based on one person-one vote; a vigorous multi-party system, such that the criticism is not that there are too few parties but that there are too many; the regular holding of elections that are open and freely contested; a free and robust media in many languages; an independent judiciary with the broadest principles of standing and justiciability of any democracy; and a dynamic, if often cantankerous, civil society, the whole as will be seen more fully below.

Indeed, the most recent elections of 1992 and 1996 reflect the political leverage — as distinct from political marginalization — of two of Israel's distinct minorities. First, newly arrived immigrants from the former Soviet Union, far from being politically expendable, were in fact credited with having given the Labor government its margin of victory in the 1992 elections; while in the 1996 elections, a newly formed political party organized around immigrants from the former Soviet Union — the Yisrael B'Aliya party — garnered seven seats and significant political leverage in the Israeli political system. Second, just as Israeli Arab parties were regarded as being crucial to maintaining the Labor government's majority in the last Knesset so that if the Israel Arab parties were to withdraw their support, the government would have fallen, so are Israeli Arabs a potent political force under the new election law mandating the "direct election" of the prime minister.

In a word, Israel's two distinct minorities — Jews from the former Soviet Union and Israeli Arabs — now exercise a distinct, if not arguably disproportionate, political influence in Israel's increasingly "tribalized," and overheated, democracy.

Is the Country in Question — Israel — Not Only a Parliamentary Democracy, But a Constitutional Democracy?

This question is not only of academic interest but goes to the heart of whether there is a state "ability to protect" its citizens. For the "Constitutionalization of Rights" — as evidenced by the Canadian Charter of Rights and Freedoms and the Quebec Charter of Human Rights and Freedoms — has been a transformative, indeed, revolutionary act in the protection of human rights in Canada and in the provision of remedies for that protection.

For example, any inquiry into the first 115 years of Canadian constitutional history would reveal a constitutional process preoccupied with the division of powers between the federal and provincial governments rather than limitations on the exercise of power regardless of government. The constitutional question, as former Chief Justice Bora Laskin put it, was "which of the two levels of government has the power to work the injustice — not whether the injustice itself should be prohibited."[8] With the advent of the Charter of Rights, Canada moved from the sovereignty of Parliament to the sovereignty of the constitution, from a "powers process" to a "rights process." In the words of Chief Justice Antonio Lamer of the Supreme Court of Canada, the enactment of the Charter — the "constitutionalization of rights" — was as revolutionary an act as the discoveries of Pasteur in science.[9]

It is a little known but enormously important and parallel revolutionary development that Israel embarked upon the "constitutionalization of rights" in 1992 with the enactment of two Basic Laws — Basic Law: Human Dignity and Liberty and Basic Law: Freedom of Occupation.

Moreover, and no less important or revolutionary — though even less well-known — is that the Israeli Basic Laws on Human Dignity and Liberty and Freedom of Occupation were amended in 1994 to include express reference to basic principles of human dignity as constitutional norms; and they incorporated by reference the basic principles set out in the Declaration of the Establishment of the State of Israel. Indeed, given the revolutionary importance of this amendment to the constitutionalization and protection of rights in Israel — and the importance of the incorporation in the Basic Laws of the principles of the Declaration of Independence — both the amendment containing the "basic principles" and the principles of the Declaration will now be set forth in full.

The "basic principles" underlying the fundamental rights, as set forth in both Basic Laws enacted in 1992, read as follows:

> Fundamental rights of a person in Israel are grounded on the recognition of the value of human beings, on the sanctity of life and of their freedom, and they will be honored in the spirit of the principles set out in the Declaration of the Establishment of the State of Israel.

The Basic Law: Human Dignity and Liberty incorporates a balancing test along the lines of section 1 of the Canadian Charter of Rights and Freedoms. Section 8 of the Basic Law states:

> The rights according to this Basic Law shall not be infringed except by a statute that befits the values of the State of Israel and is directed toward a worthy purpose, and then only to an extent that does not exceed what is necessary, or by a regulation promulgated by virtue of express authorization in such a statute.

An explanatory section was added to this Basic Law in 1994 to guide the courts in determining what are "the values of the State of Israel." Section 1A of the Basic Law now states that "[t]he purpose of this Basic Law is to protect human dignity and liberty, in order to anchor in a Basic Law the values of the State of Israel as a Jewish and democratic state."

Finally, the Basic Laws were further amended in 1994 to constitutionally entrench the basic principles of the Declaration of the Establishment of the State of Israel which reads as follows:

> The Declaration of the Establishment of the State of Israel (14th May 1948), proclaims, *inter alia*, that "The State of Israel...will foster the development of the country for the benefit of all its inhabitants; it will be based on freedom, justice and peace as envisaged by the prophets of Israel; it will ensure complete equality of social and political rights to all its inhabitants irrespective of religion, race or sex; it will guarantee freedom or religion, conscience, language, education and culture."

In the words of Chief Justice Aharon Barak, as President of the Supreme Court of Israel, as part of a lecture to a Canada-Israel Law Conference on "Chartering Human Rights" held in Israel in December 1992 in the immediate aftermath of the enactment of the Basic Laws:

> This conference is taking place at the outset of a new legal and political era in Israel. Two recently enacted laws — Basic Law: Human Dignity and Liberty, and Basic Law: Freedom of Occupation — have brought about nothing less than a revolution in the Israeli legal system. These new laws give the courts, and the Supreme Court foremost, the power not only to give meaning to statutes, but also to determine their validity in light of the higher norms enshrined in the new Basic Laws.

Indeed, this mini-Israeli Bill of Rights is very much modelled upon — and inspired by — the Canadian Charter of Rights and Freedoms. Again, to quote Justice Barak: "Israel in 1992 is where Canada was in 1982, and Canada will be the single most important legal repository for Israel in the next decade."

Accordingly, with the advent of an Israeli Charter of Rights — modelled on Canada's Charter of Rights and having regard to the importance for Israel of the Canadian experience under the Charter, jurists from Canada and Israel established in 1992 the Canada-Israel Legal Cooperation Programme — the first joint venture in human rights and law reform between the two countries, and whose honorary co-chairs are the Chief Justice of the Supreme Court of Canada, Antonio Lamer, and the President of the Supreme Court of Israel, Aharon Barak.

It should be noted, however, that the absence of a comprehensive constitutional bill of rights in Israel does not mean — any more than its absence meant for Canada — that Israel is without a constitution, or does not qualify as a constitutional democracy. In the words of Justice Haim Cohn, former Deputy President of the Israeli Supreme Court and a distinguished international human rights jurist,

> it makes no difference whether we will have a written bill of rights or we continue living without it....Even without a statute defining and laying down the various human rights, all those rights which could possibly or foreseeably be so defined and laid down are in actual practice legally recognized, protected and enforced. We derive these fundamental rights and freedoms not only from the constitutional conventions which form part of the common law of England, and are thus, *mutatis mutandis*, the residuary law applied here as long as no

other law has been enacted on the subject-matter; but it has been held time and again that the State of Israel, as a modern parliamentary democracy, will uphold and protect all those individual liberties that are of the essence of the rule of law and which may now be regarded as forming a part of universally recognized principles of international law.[10]

or as former Chief Justice Meir Shamgar put it:

The new draft Basic Law: Human Rights is designed to consolidate certain principles and mark their boundaries. Its central function is to enshrine these in an enacted law in order to protect them from the dangers that come with the various crises that arise from time to time. Its purpose is to serve as an expression of those values by which the citizen may be guided and to block in advance those who would trespass on their rights. But even now...basic freedoms are enshrined in the foundation of our legal system and form an intrinsic part of the law in Israel.[11]

Is the Country in Question a State Party to Major International Human Rights Treaties?

Admittedly, the fact that a state is a party to international human rights treaties is not conclusive or even probative of its ability to protect its citizens. But it is clearly demonstrative of an intent to subject its citizens to international human rights norms, and to provide them with another "rights-protection" medium; this is particularly the case when the state enacts domestic legislation to implement its international obligations, and/or when the courts of that state invoke and apply the international human rights treaties in domestic litigation.

At present, Israel is a state party to all the major international human rights covenants, including the International Covenant on Civil and Political Rights; the International Covenant on Economic, Social, and Cultural Rights; the International Covenant on the Elimination of All Forms of Racial Discrimination; the International Covenant on the Elimination of All Forms of Discrimination against Women; and the International Covenant on the Rights of the Child.

Moreover, the application of international law to domestic law by the Israeli courts very much parallels the Canadian judicial experience where, for example, customary international law is automatically part of Israeli law; while international treaty law is invoked as "a relevant and persuasive authority" in the interpretation of the Israeli Basic Laws on human rights, as well as being part of Israeli law itself when domestic legislation is enacted to implement an international treaty.

In a word, international human rights law is another source of human rights norms, and a rights-protecting instrument in Israel, while the application of international human rights law to Israeli law, and the resulting jurisprudence, is of increasing interest and value to the international and Canadian human rights community.

Is There an Independent Judiciary that One Can Petition for Relief?

The compelling role played by the Israeli judiciary in the enforcement of the rule of law and the protection of human rights is rooted largely in the independence and method of appointment of the Israeli judges. The judges enjoy both substantive and personal independence. Substantive independence is set out in Section 2 of Basic Law: The Judiciary: "[a] person in whom judicial power is vested shall, in judicial matters, be subject to no authority but that of the law."

In Israel, judges are selected by a special Judges' Selection Committee, designed to minimize political influence on the selection of judges and maximize the integrity and impact of the judiciary. The committee is composed of the Chief Justice (the President of the Supreme Court) and two other supreme court justices; the Minister of Justice and one other minister, elected by the government; two members of the legislative branch, elected by the Knesset; and two members of the Chamber of Advocates. There is also a tradition that the members of the Knesset and the government's representatives are jurists by training. Indeed, Madame Justice Claire L'Heuvre-Dube of the Canadian Supreme Court has commended the Israeli method of judicial appointment as a model that Canada might well emulate to ensure the independence, integrity, and quality of the Canadian judiciary. Moreover, apart from this independence that has reserved for the Israeli judiciary a special place as the custodian of the rule of law and protector of human rights in Israel, there are several "rights-protecting" features of the Israeli judiciary that are unique to Israel, and which distinguish it among free and democratic societies.

First, the Israeli Supreme Court operates also as a "High Court of Justice" with general and open jurisdiction "to grant relief in the interests of justice." In the words of a commentator on the Supreme Court:[12]

> It thus has power to make the following orders: orders for the release of persons detained or imprisoned unlawfully; orders directed to the State authority, local authorities and their officials, and to other bodies and persons performing public functions under the law, requiring them to do or refrain from doing, any act in the performance of their functions according to law, and if they were unlawfully elected or appointed, to refrain from acting; orders directed at courts, tribunals and other bodies and persons having judicial or quasi-judicial powers.

In a word, all the authorities of the state and all public authorities are subject to the jurisdiction of the High Court, there being no difference if these should be carrying out legislative, executive, or judicial functions.

Secondly, petitions may be submitted by citizens directly to the Supreme Court sitting as the High Court of Justice, as a court of first and sole instance, and upon which there is no appeal. This procedure opens the gates of the High Court to grant a remedy to those injured by the acts of the governing authorities. The procedure is simple, cheap and flexible, and legal representation is not mandatory. It is a procedure which enables every citizen to bring their disputes with the authorities before the High Court of Justice. The procedure, known as *"bagatz"* — which is the Hebrew shorthand for "High Court of Justice" — is actually invoked as a verb, "to petition the High Court of Justice," rather than the noun which it is, thereby signifying the dynamic nature of this remedy. It has resulted in the Supreme Court of Israel being characterized as "the Guardian of Civil Liberties."

Finally, as a corollary, Israel may be said to have the broadest law of "standing" — of access to the courts — of any comparable democratic society; and it may also be said to have the broadest principle of "justiciability" — of the scope of the issues that are subject to judicial review — of any democracy; for there is scarcely an issue that will not be heard by the High Court of Justice, including sensitive matters relating to foreign policy and national security, and domestic political questions such as the legitimacy of coalition agreements, issues which would clearly be non-justiciable in a democracy like Canada.

Is There an Independent Press that Monitors/Exposes Human Rights Violations?

The Israeli press has emerged as an important crucible for the protection of human rights in Israel, and this for the following reasons:

First, Israel has more newspapers per capita than almost any other free and democratic society. Moreover, discussion and debate in the pages of these newspapers is "uninhibited, robust, and wide open," to borrow language expressive of the First Amendment doctrines and as befits a free press; indeed, if there is one thing upon which there is general agreement among Israeli civil libertarians, it is that there is a free and open press in Israel.

Second, this debate takes place not only in the Hebrew language, but in English, French, Yiddish, and particularly Russian. In fact, there are more Russian language newspapers than there are newspapers in any language other than Hebrew.

Third, there is no difficulty accessing an Israeli newspaper, particularly a Russian language newspaper, to report upon alleged violations of the rights of Jews from the former Soviet Union. Indeed, many of the allegations brought by claimants for refugee status before the Canadian Immigration and Refugee Appeal Board were reported in Israeli newspapers; in fact, the articles were submitted as "supporting evidence" for these allegations in many of the hearings, even though the reporting of these allegations in the Israeli press is more indicative of the role of a free press in monitoring and exposing these allegations — and providing them with a press forum — then it is necessarily of the validity of the allegations themselves; and even if valid, it demonstrates the importance and role of the free press in Israel rather than, as the allegations suggested, of the press as an agent of Israeli censorship. Quite the contrary.

Fourth, Israeli newspapers themselves have ombudspersons to whom complaints may be made if there is any attempt at suppression or misrepresentation of information; as well, there is an Israeli Press Council which itself exercises an oversight review of the Israeli press.

Finally, where there have been attempts at censorship in the interest of "national security" — which attempted censorship in any case has not involved the allegations of press censorship that are at the basis of a claim for refugee status — this "national security" claim has itself been subject to parliamentary oversight and judicial review. Indeed, in recent years, the Israeli Supreme Court has judicially reviewed national security claims and the "reasonableness" of the censorship decisions. For example, in 1989, even before the enactment of the two Basic Laws and Israel's "constitutional revolution," the Supreme Court allowed publication of an article that had initially been suppressed by the Military Censor on grounds of national security, thereby indicating the importance of freedom of the press as a fundamental principle of Israeli society.

Is There Religious Pluralism in Israel — Is There Protection for Freedom of Religion?

From a variety of perspectives, Israel may be regarded as a pluralistic society. The country is inhabited by people from over seventy nations, professing different religions, belonging to various ethnic groups, speaking different languages, and possessing different cultural and social traditions as well as having different political allegiances and ideologies. These manifold sources of pluralism make it somewhat difficult to single out the element of religious pluralism in particular, since in Israel religious affiliation is itself often bound up with nationality, ethnic origin, language, culture, and political allegiance; nor do these intersecting components permit easy appreciation to determine to what extent religious pluralism, in general, and freedom of religion, in particular, is protected. Accordingly, what follows is a summary of the essential components of religious pluralism in Israel, with particular references to the protective regime for the exercise of freedom of religion.

1. Not only is Israel inhabited by adherents of various religions, it also holy to four major faiths: Judaism, Christianity, Islam, and Bahai. For Judaism the country itself is holy; for Christianity and Islam many places in the country have a special religious significance, with Muslim religiosity increasingly imbued by nationalistic ideology; and for the Bahais it is not only the site of various holy places, but it is also their spiritual and world center.

2. Israeli policy toward religion and state can only be understood in its historical context of the Ottoman "millet" system for "religions of the book," which accorded them organizational autonomy and exclusive jurisdiction in matters of personal studies. The Ottoman structure of "church-state" relations was largely preserved under the British mandate, with the Palestine Order-in-Council of 1922 granting eleven communities autonomy in matters of personal law and communal jurisdiction — Muslims, Jews, and nine Christian churches.[13]

Upon its establishment in 1948, the State of Israel adopted this Mandatory law, save for modifications resulting from the establishment of the state.[14] The entire traditional system of personal law and religious jurisdiction was retained. The most important change, however, related to the Jewish community. Rabbinical courts now operated not only over those who voluntarily accepted their jurisdiction, but over all those who belonged to the Jewish people. In 1957, the Druze community was recognized; under a 1962 statute, the same jurisdictional principle relating to rabbinical courts applied to their religious courts.[15] At present, all religious courts have exclusive jurisdiction over members of their respective communities in matters of marriage and divorce.

3. The basic attitude of Israel towards religious pluralism is reflected in the Declaration of Independence of 1948; "It [i.e., the state] will guarantee freedom of religion and conscience, of language, education, and culture. It will safeguard the Holy Places of all religions." Indeed, even before the incorporation in 1994 of this Declaration into Israel's Basic Laws on Human Dignity and Liberty and Freedom of Occupation, as set forth above, the Supreme Court had already decided that the Declaration "expresses the aspirations of the people and their basic credo," and "should be taken into consideration when the courts attempt to interpret or clarify the laws of the state."[16] In this context, one may also refer to a legislative text enacted at the time of the British Mandate in 1922,

and which is still part of the protective legal regime in Israel respecting freedom of religion:

> All persons in Palestine shall enjoy full liberty of conscience, and the free exercise of their forms of worship subject only to the maintenance of public order and morals. Each religious community shall enjoy autonomy for the internal affairs of the community subject to the provisions of any Ordinance or Order issued by the High Commission.[17]

4. Since the principles respecting freedom of religion in the Declaration of Independence have been incorporated into the recent Basic Laws on human rights, they can now be said to enjoy entrenched constitutional status. Moreover, the Basic Laws themselves provide a protective basis for freedom of religion, with provisions of the Basic Law on Human Dignity and Liberty lending themselves to a broad and liberal protective interpretation. In particular, Sections 2, 4, and 7 of this law specifically protect human dignity, privacy, and personal confidentiality; the provisions respecting freedom of occupation in the other Basic Law buttress this protection, while the "purposive" principle in each of the Basic Laws — that their purpose is to entrench "the values of the State of Israel as a Jewish and democratic state" — can be used and has been used to support both freedom of religion and freedom from religion.

Indeed, judicial intervention in support of religious freedom has increased with the enactment of the Basic Laws. For example, the Israeli Supreme Court has held that legislation that prohibited the import of non-kosher meat violated the provisions of the Basic Law on Freedom of Occupation; it has rejected "religiously motivated" activities of the government and thereby reduced state intervention with freedom of religion; and while the legacy of the "millet" system, as we have seen, is that marriage in Israel must take place according to religious law, the Supreme Court has recently limited the scope of religious law and enlarged the application of civil law in matters connected with marriage.[18]

5. This is not to suggest that the religious autonomy of the "millet" system has not prejudiced the rights of the non-observers. Clearly, as the religious communities enjoy special legal status, and their jurisdiction, *inter alia*, in matters of marriage and divorce extends to observers and non-observers alike, the protection of

freedom from religion emerges as weaker than the protection of freedom of religion. For example, not only is jurisdiction over matters of marriage and divorce vested in the religious community, but for Jews this autonomy is vested in the Orthodox Jewish community, with the Jewish religion in Israel effectively identified with Orthodoxy. The result is not only that the rights of non-observers are affected, but the rights of different denominations within Judaism are also prejudicially affected, as exemplified in the unsuccessful attempt to have the Minister of Religious Affairs authorize the performance of marriages by Reform rabbis.[19]

6. It should be noted, however, that the Supreme Court has increasingly intervened to mitigate the discriminatory impacts of the "millet" legacy. For example, the court ruled that a person who underwent conversion "in any Jewish community abroad" will qualify for registration as Jewish under the Population and Registration Law.[20] This decision opened the way for Reform and Conservative converts to immigrate to Israel and register as Jews. The court also ruled that Reform and Conservative members cannot be disqualified from being appointed to religious councils,[21] and ordered a local council to make a public hall available for Reform community services during the High Holidays.[22] The court also ordered that state funding be accorded applicable religious institutions of both the Reform and Conservative movements.[23]

Finally, the entire operation and decisions of these religious bodies are subject to judicial review, mainly by the Supreme Court of Israel. A case in point is *Raskin v. Jerusalem Religious Council and the Chief Rabbis of Jerusalem*.[24] The Chief Rabbinate of Jerusalem granted a *kashrut* certificate to wedding halls, only if such weddings did not include "immoral performances" such as belly dancing. Admittedly, this condition was not without *halakhic* basis; yet the Supreme Court of Israel declared the Chief Rabbinate's demand to be illegal, and ordered it to grant an unconditional certificate. The court reasoned that the rabbinate went beyond the authority conferred upon it in the 1983 *Kashrut* (Prohibition of Deceit) Law, which provided that "in issuing a *kashrut* certificate, the rabbi shall have regard to the *kashrut* laws only."

7. Freedom of religion — including the right to manifest one's belief — has been granted to members of all religions, and enjoys specific statutory protection in addition to the constitutional one. More particularly, it is protected by the Penal Law of 5737-1977

which has made it a punishable offense to violate religious sentiments, to disturb worship, and to desecrate holy places; by the
Protection of Holy Places Law of 5727-1967; as well as by the
Basic Law: Jerusalem Capital of Israel of 5740-1980. These rights
— and the protection of the criminal law — have been granted to
"all religions," without distinction.

8. Indeed, another feature of the legal status of religious pluralism is not only the question of the civil and political rights of the
members of the various religious communities, but the equality of
status as between religious communities. Again, the Declaration of
Independence of 1948 — now "constitu-tionalized" through its
incorporation into the Basic Laws — proclaims that "It [i.e., the
State of Israel] will maintain complete equality of social and
political rights for all its citizens, without distinction of creed, race,
or sex." An interesting example of this equality principle is the
provision in the Basic Law on the President of the State, which lays
down only two conditions for a person to qualify as a candidate for
this office: that person must be a citizen and a resident of Israel. An
amendment proposed at the time which would have reserved this
office for Jews was not adopted by the Knesset.

As well, among the specific provisions of Israel's laws which
are intended to guarantee equality and protection to members of
various religions, reference should also be made to the Law on the
Prevention and Punishment of the Crime of Genocide, 5711-1951;
the Employment Service Law, 5719-1959; the Succession Law,
5725-1965; the rules on recognition of institutions of higher education made in 1964 under the Council for Higher Education Laws,
5718-1958; and the Defamation [Prohibition] Law, 5725-1965.

9. It has been alleged that discrimination exists against non-
Jews in the areas of immigration and nationality. For example, the
Declaration of Independence states that "The State of Israel will be
open for Jewish immigration and for the ingathering of exiles"; as
well the Law of Return of 5710-1950 provides that "every Jew has
the right to come to this country as an immigrant"; while, according
to the Nationality Law, 5712-1952, every Jew automatically ac-
quires Israeli nationality unless he/she does not wish to.

However, as international law experts such as Professor Ruth
Lapidoth have pointed out, this preference should not be characterized as involving an improper discrimination on religious grounds
for several reasons. In the words of Professor Lapidoth:[25]

(1) When a people attains statehood in fulfillment of its aspirations for national liberation, it is common and natural that all members of that people be permitted and invited to come and live in that country. From this point of view, Israel is no more discriminatory than most new states. In fact, many states, new and old, grant preference, for the purpose of bestowing nationality, to persons who have close social, cultural, or ethnic links with the nation, e.g., Greece, the Federal Republic of Germany, the USSR, Italy, Czechoslovakia, Denmark, El Salvador, Guatemala, Honduras, Liberia, Mexico, Nicaragua, Poland, Venezuela, and Jordan.

(2) In 1965, the United Nations adopted the International Convention on the Elimination of All Forms of Racial Discrimination, which is now in force among more than 100 states. Although this document deals with racial discrimination, it seems that by analogy one can draw some important conclusions with regard to restrictions or preferences on religious grounds as well. The International Convention has laid down that, in matters of nationality, citizenship, and naturalization, states are free to prefer certain groups, on condition that there is no discrimination against any particular group (Article 1[4]). Since Israeli legislation does not impose any restriction on any particular group, it is within the letter and the spirit of the International Convention.

(3) Moreover, the International Convention permits the granting of preferences if necessary to undo the effects of prior discrimination, i.e., affirmative action (Article 1[4]). In the case of Israel, one has to remember that since 1939 the gates of Mandatory Palestine had been closed to Jewish immigration, thus contributing to the perishing of millions of Jews in Europe during World War II. The opening of the gates on the occasion of the establishment of Israel can thus be considered a lawful case of affirmative action.

(4) It should be emphasized that the law does not close the state's doors to anyone but creates a preference in favor of Jews. With regard to non-Jews, the applicable rules on immigration are quite similar to those that exist in other states. Everyone, including non-Jews, may apply for permission to enter Israel and for naturalization. It is only the automatic right to enter and the automatic acquisition of nationality that is reserved for Jews.

(5) Moreover, not only the Jew enjoys these automatic rights, but also members of his family, whether they are Jewish or not.

In this matter of immigration and nationality, the dual nature of Judaism as a religion and as a people is of particular relevance. Despite the semi-religious definition of Jew, the relevant laws are basically concerned with the return of members of the Jewish people to their homeland, in accordance with the principle of self-determination.

Is There a Protective Legal Regime Specifically Developed Against Racism, Discrimination, and Harassment of Identifiable Groups?

It should not be surprising that in a state born of a history of persecution — and where Judaic sources of human rights evince a particular sensibility to matters of discrimination — that Israeli doctrine, legislation, and decisions by the High Court of Justice should have developed one of the more comprehensive legal regimes to combat discrimination of any free and democratic society. But it should also not be surprising that, despite the development of a comprehensive legal regime — including specific remedies to protect victims from discrimination — such discrimination does in fact exist; and that, in particular, violations of the human rights of minorities, new immigrants, and that of Arabs and other groups of non-Jews continue to persist. The question, however, from the point of view of the conferral of refugee status under international and Canadian law, is not whether incidences of racism, discrimination, and harassment exist — they do; the question is whether there exists a protective legal regime against such racism, harassment, and discrimination. What follows is an enumeration of the elements of this protective legal regime which, for reasons of brevity, will not be elaborated upon.

The Role of the Supreme Court of Israel

In the absence of a written constitution and a comprehensive and entrenched bill of rights, the Israeli Supreme Court has emerged, as we have seen, not only as the custodian of the rule of law, but as the judge-made protector of human rights. Indeed, the principle of the rule of law was defined early by the Israeli Supreme Court as a "guarantee of a democratic system"; as well, the Israeli Supreme Court developed a "Background Understanding Model" of judicial review — a model of principles of interpretation — which recognized a whole array of "unwritten rights," such as freedom of religion, freedom of speech, freedom of association, freedom of movement, and the like; also, the "Background Understanding Model" incorporated into Israeli constitutional law a number of basic principles including equality before the law, human dignity, due process of law, the right to a fair trial, and other rights and principles that underlie a written bill of rights in a democracy.[26]

Basic Laws

Again, while Israel as yet has no written constitution, it has enacted a series of Basic Laws which together form the core of such a constitution; moreover, the two recently enacted Basic Laws on Human Dignity and Freedom, and Freedom of Occupation not only are at the core of the prospective Israeli written constitution, but are themselves the basis for an entrenched bill of rights. Indeed, even as a mini-bill of rights, as we have seen, they constitute a veritable human rights "revolution" in Israel.[27]

Freedom of Religion

Freedom of religion is not just another of a series of rights, but in Israel is regarded as a "core" and "fundamental" right. Whether one speaks of the express reference to freedom of religion in the Declaration of Independence, or to its sanctioning in Israeli criminal law, or to the basic principles of human dignity that are now part of the Basic Law — and which incorporate freedom of religion by reference or the express protection of freedom of religion in the decisions of the Israeli Supreme Court, one thing is clear: freedom of religion emerges as a kind of domestic *jus cogens* in the Israeli protective legal regime, however much it may still be breached in practice.

The Combatting of Racism and Racial Incitement

Israel has developed one of the more comprehensive legal regimes to combat racism and racial incitement, the whole expressive of a fundamental concern with human dignity. For example, reference may be made to the Political Parties Law, 5752-1992, enacted on March 8, 1992, under which political parties must register with the Register of Parties. Section 5 of the law states that, "A party will not be registered if there is on its aims or actions, explicitly or implicitly, one of the following: ...(2) incitement to racism."

Freedom of the Press

The Israeli media, both print and electronic, not only engage in the most robust of critiques, but their increasing culture of investigative inquiry — which some critics have characterized as a culture of inquisition — has emerged as an important component of the protection of the legal regime against racism, harassment, and discrimination of any kind. Indeed, the very intimacy of the Israeli kinship culture has resulted in exposures of human rights violators — and demands for redress — appearing first in the Israeli media, which then triggers the invocation of the varying juridical and oversight mechanisms such as the *"bagatz,"* judicial review of administrative action, and the like.

The Israeli NGO Human Rights Community

It is somewhat ironic that while the Israeli government is somewhat insensitive to the work and impact of the international NGO human rights culture, a flourishing NGO human rights community has developed in Israel itself; indeed, questions of equality, non-discrimination, and the protection of human dignity are the *raison d'etre* of their work. Some of them, like the Israeli Association for Civil Rights, have a broad-based human rights agenda; others are increasingly "single-issue" or "special interest" groups, organized around a particular issue, e.g., women's rights or children's rights;

or organized around a particular claimant group, e.g., the Association for Ethiopian Jewry, Forum for Soviet Jewry, etc. Similarly, there are an increasing number of "peace" groups devoted to securing Israeli-Palestinian peace, with still others are working toward Jewish-Arab coexistence within Israel itself.

Finally, there are a host of groups monitoring the rule of law, abuse of the administrative process, government corruption and the like, and where concerns of equality, non-discrimination, and the protection of human dignity underpin their work.

What is the Status of — and the Protection for — the Rights of Women?

From the beginning of the 1980s, and particularly in the past ten years, there has been a considerable breakthrough in the Israeli legal system on issues of equality for women. Gains have been made through legislation and court decisions in a wide variety of areas, as set forth below.

1. As regards women's entitlement to human dignity and bodily integrity, the law was reformed in a number of ways. First, in matters of sexual assault, including rape, the Law of Evidence was amended in 1982 to abolish the requirement for corroborative evidence, while leaving in its stead a requirement that a judge who convicts on the evidence of the rape victim alone must give his/her reasons for doing so; second, as a result of a 1988 amendment to the Criminal Law (Amendment No. 22), evidence of a rape victim's past sexual experience was made inadmissible unless its exclusion would cause a miscarriage of justice; and third, the definition of what constitutes sexual assault was expanded, and the prohibition of rape within marriage, already established by case law, was confirmed.

2. In the matter of domestic violence, an important Law on Prevention of Violence in the Family was enacted; this allowed for a new independent remedy, which made it possible for victims of family violence to have a violent spouse removed from the home.

3. In the economic arena, a series of equal opportunity measures were enacted. First, the Equal Retirement Age Act for female and male employees was passed; second, the Equal Employment Opportunities Law was enacted in 1988; indeed, there have been some

50 employment discrimination actions in the labor courts in the last eight years alone, an amount which constitutes a veritable flood of litigation in comparison with the sum total of four such actions brought in all the years prior to 1988; third, an amendment was made to the Property Relations Between Spouses Law in 1990, extending the definition of matrimonial property subject to division in a balancing of resources to include non-transferable property; fourth, a further gain was made in 1992 when, after six years of lobbying by women's organizations, the Tax Ordinance was amended putting an end to attribution of a married woman's income to her husband's for income tax purposes; rather, a sex neutral test was introduced under which the higher income spouse is the family representative for tax purposes.

4.   In 1990, in *Nevo v. The National Labor Court*, the Supreme Court introduced, for the first time, a concept of heightened scrutiny for group discrimination, in the context of a petition to achieve equal retirement age for women. In reversing the order of the National Labor Court, Justice Bach held that the imposition of early retirement age on women in an Employees' Pension Code was discriminatory and void. More important, Justice Bach, in his reasons for judgement, said that Israeli law and policy — and the public generally — is not sufficiently aware of discrimination against women; that such discrimination is the result of gender prejudice; that it undermines the motivation of women to participate actively in society; and that the courts must "scrutinize with seven eyes" provisions which restrict the opportunity of women as a group.

5.   In a continuation of this line of reasoning, but also in what might be the beginning of a more radical interventionist and superintending role of the Supreme Court over the rabbinical courts, the High Court of Justice recently held in the *Bavli*[28] case that civil law notions of equality must be applied by the rabbinical courts in adjudication of matrimonial property rights. In the past, the Women's Equal Rights Law, 1951, although binding on the rabbinical courts in matters of matrimonial property, had not been interpreted as requiring these courts to apply the civil law presumption of joint ownership of property acquired during marriage rather than the Jewish law concept of separation of spousal property rights. However, in *Bavli*, Justice Barak held as follows:

Every religious law which is applied by the rabbinical courts must conform with the principle of equality (laid down in Section 1 of the Woman's Equal Rights Law). The Rabbinical Court is, hence, not authorized to establish a law of joint ownership — or a law of non-joint ownership — which rests on discrimination against women.

Admittedly, as Professor Frances Raday has put it, "the regulatory norms of the recognized religious communities are blatantly patriarchal,"[29] a fact not unrelated to the "millet" legacy referred to above. Indeed, in their areas of autonomy and jurisdiction, as in matters of marriage and divorce, the religious communities have not been subject to the principle of equality as set forth in the Women's Equal Rights Law, 1951, which "expressly provides that women's rights to equality under the law would not apply to the determination of status in marriage and divorce." At the same time, gender discrimination continues to obtain even apart from the religious-based dimension.

Nevertheless, as set forth above, the plethora of legislation mandating gender equality in employment; the advent of the Basic Laws on human rights; the increasing interventionist role of the High Court of Justice; and a growing "gender sensibility" — anchored in the work of the NGO culture — are transforming women's rights in Israel.

It is clear, of course, that the combatting of discrimination, and protection of equality, cannot be measured by reference only to the substantive legal system, and that inequality on the social level still persists, despite the law. Moreover, the prohibition of discrimination may not be sanctioned by appropriate remedies, and there may be — and in Israel this is still the case — a lack of institutional mechanisms to combat private discrimination. As well, the lack of social and gender equality is probably compounded by the political element; most of Israel's non-Jews are ethnically Arabs, and some suspicion or distrust may well persist, however unwarranted, given the perceived — and understandable — affinity of Palestinian Arabs with Arab and Palestinian peoples in historically hostile neighboring states. This is not intended to condone, let alone justify, such discrimination; it is only to identify the context in which it takes place; and it makes the need for protective legal remedies — as distinct from the protective substantive law which was the subject of this criterion, all the more necessary. That is the subject of the next question, or criterion, to be addressed.

Are There Protective Legal Remedies Available to Members of "Identifiable Groups" Who are Victims of Discrimination?

While Israel has developed a comprehensive legal regime to combat discrimination — as set forth above — the incidence of discrimination, as the evidence will show, still persists; indeed, it may well raise for some members of "identifiable groups" — or groups identifiable by reason of their color (e.g., Ethiopian Jews), ethnic origin (Russians), gender (Russian women) — a question of the state's "ability to protect" them, an issue which is at the core of the allegations made by the claimants for refugee status.

Indeed, a typical claimant tends to be a recent immigrant to Israel, Jewish or non-Jewish, from the former Soviet Union. On leaving the Soviet Union he or she may have claimed to be Jewish, or to be married to or the child or grandchild of a Jew, in order to take advantage of Israel's Law of Return. After some time in Israel, and in an application for refugee status in Canada, he or she may acknowledge that they are not Jewish, indeed, that their non-Jewishness is the very source of the discrimination practiced against them. Finally, the typical and particular grounds for claiming refugee status from Israel, especially as it involves women claimants from the former Soviet Union, are that the immigrant was a victim of violence such as beating or rape, and the police and law enforcement authorities showed indifference to the crime.

Accordingly, it might be appropriate to conclude this examination of the testing criteria by looking at the remedies available to protect victims of discrimination, which include the following:

"Bagatz" — Petition to the Supreme Court of Israel Sitting as a High Court of Justice

Reference has already been made to this distinct remedy, which is unique among parliamentary and constitutional democracies;

more particularly, any person who believes that his or her right has been violated by any governmental or public authority — by their act or failure to act — may petition the Supreme Court *directly* and seek relief and redress for the violation.

As set forth earlier, the broad, almost open-ended principles respecting "standing" to bring this petition; the broad, almost open-ended principle of justiciability respecting the subject matter of the petition; and the court's "Background Understanding Model" of human rights, have resulted in the "*bagatz*" emerging as an enormously powerful remedy that has been used with distinct success by "the disadvantaged" in the Israeli legal system.

The Constitutionalization and Internationalization of Human Rights

The "revolution" in the Israeli legal system occasioned by the enactment of the two Basic Laws regarding Human Dignity and Freedom and Freedom of Occupation, and the ratification by Israel of the major international human rights treaties, have given the prospective Israeli victim of discrimination, racism, or any other human rights violation a "right and remedy" not hitherto available in Israeli law. In a word, the Israeli "human rights revolution" — not unlike the Canadian one — has reinforced the "states's ability to protect," and added another major support system to the already comprehensive legal and statutory — let alone judicial — regime for the protection of rights.

The Israeli Knesset (Parliament)

The historical antecedents of the Israeli parliament — and its historical role in the establishment of the State of Israel and Israeli democracy — have secured for it a significant protective and remedial role as the elected "house of representatives of the people," as the people's "constituent assembly." As the expression and embodiment of the "people's sovereignty" — as it was originally characterized — its authority precedes and prevails over the branches of the state. On the legislative level this supremacy means that the will of the Knesset, pursuant to the rule of law, obligates all other authorities of the state, and that the source of power of the other branches stems, directly or indirectly, from the Knesset.[30]

Admittedly, the nature of the Israeli "administrative state," and the preemptive capacity of cabinet government, have diminished somewhat the salience and significance of the Israeli Knesset; but the development of viable parliamentary oversight committees, the culture of inquiry, and the increasing Knesset-NGO connection have maintained it as an instrument for the promotion and protection of human rights.

The Attorney General

The office of the Attorney General in Israel has developed into a unique one in comparison with that of other countries, and a crucial one with respect to the protection of human rights in Israel. In a word, the Attorney General is a guardian of the rule of law, serving not only as the government's lawyer but also as a "watchdog" over government activities. In this sense, as Alan Zysblatt has put it,

> he is not only the government's lawyer but the people's lawyer. He regularly attends all Cabinet meetings, not only to advise on legal questions, but also to see to it that the Cabinet acts within its powers. Nor is this power merely theoretical: as has been mentioned, it is the rule that the government may not pursue a course of action which in the opinion of the Attorney-General is unlawful; and if the government should nonetheless choose to act against his opinion, and the act is then challenged in court, he may refuse to defend it, thus leaving the government with no legal defence whatsoever.[31]

It is a long-standing tradition that the Attorney General must be a jurist of high repute who is not affiliated with political circles, and who, upon appointment, is not a member of the cabinet, nor a member of the Knesset. The Minister of Justice, to whom the Attorney General administratively reports, has stressed the fact that the Attorney General, and the state attorneys serving under him, "are and should be wholly independent of the government in the exercising of their discretion in criminal matters."[32]

The State Comptroller — The Israeli Ombudsperson

One of the more recent Basic Laws deals with the office of the State Comptroller, who is elected by the Knesset, is wholly independent from the executive branch, and is accountable only to the legislature. The State Comptroller serves as the "long arm" of the Knesset, and his or her function is, *inter alia*, to supervise the executive branch of government. Although the office of the State Comptroller is not unique to Israel, the breadth of the mandate — and the centrality of this institution in Israeli law and public life — makes its role a clearly distinguishable one.

The Basic Law: State Comptroller (1988) charges the Comptroller with the duty to carry out the inspection of "assets, finances, undertakings, and administration of the Government's departments, of every institution, enterprise or public agency, and local authorities." According to the law, the Comptroller is empowered to request information, documents, or any other materials necessary for a full review. The Comptroller is required to present reports to the Knesset, and these reports are discussed by the Knesset's State Comptroller Committee. The State Comptroller also serves as an ombudsman (public complaints commissioner), empowered to examine complaints of the public regarding the functioning of public bodies. The centrality of its role — and the high visibility of its reports — ensure that the State Comptroller exercises a significant remedial role in the Israeli polity.

Commissions of Inquiry

The public's right to receive information regarding matters of vital public importance, or "the right to be informed," has resulted in the establishment of a governmental mechanism designed to expose the truth on matters of public importance. Indeed, the apprehension in Israel that an inquiry by politicians might be influenced by political considerations has led to the establishment of a special judicial and inquisitorial mechanism to be used whenever a matter of vital public importance requires clarification. Accordingly, an independent, quasi-judicial mechanism known as the Commission of Inquiry was established by a law of the Knesset in 1968, with the authority to appoint its members entrusted to the

Chief Justice in order to avoid the appearance of a possible political bias; and with the position of chairman of the commission to be held by a high judicial official in order to ensure that the inquiry is conducted judicially and impartially, without causing unnecessary harm and injustice to persons involved in the inquiry.

The Commission of Inquiry, the Supreme Court has said, is "to be an objective, professional body. The Commission's recommendations must be viewed in light of the depth of investigation, the fairness of the Commission's deliberations, and the Commission's impartiality. As a result, the recommendations of the Commission will normally be acted upon even though they are not directly binding upon the Executive."

Finally, reference to the protective legal remedies available would be incomplete without incorporating by reference discussion in the earlier sections of this chapter including the viability of the democratic process; the independence of the judiciary and its general superintending role as the "guardian of civil liberties"; the remedial role of the fiercely independent Israeli media; the critical mass of NGO human rights groups; and the presence of an engaged — albeit cantankerous — civil society.

Conclusion

In conclusion, this chapter not only proposes a framework of inquiry for a state's "ability to protect" its citizens — the normative referent for a refugee determination process and involving a set of "testing" criteria for this purpose — it is also a case-study both of Israel's "ability to protect" its inhabitants, and the integrity of the Canadian IRB's refugee determination process.

It is hoped, then, that this study will contribute to a necessary introspection by both Canada and Israel of their understanding of the "other" as well as themselves, including the dynamics and dialectics involved — both for world Jewry and the world community — in Israel's development as a "Jewish and democratic state," and that it will contribute to a reform and refinement of the refugee determination process as a whole.

Notes

1. *Canada (A.G.) v. Ward* [1993] 2 S.C.R.689.
2. The Court held that "asylum denotes surrogate protection" and is only available when no national protection is available elsewhere. At p. 709, the Court stated:

   International refugee law was formulated to serve as a back-up to the protection one expects from the state of which one is a national. It was meant to come into play only in situations where that protection is unavailable and then only in certain situations. The international community intended that persecuted individuals be required to approach their home state for protection before the responsibility of other states became engaged.

3. 28 July 1951, 189 U.N.T.S. 150, U.K.T.S. 39 (1954) (entered into force 22 April 1954) [hereinafter Convention].
4. Protocol Relating to the Status of Refugees, 31 January 1967, 606 U.N.T.S. 267, 6 I.L.M. 78 (entered into force 4 October 1967).
5. The Convention states:

   No Contracting State shall expel or return [*"refouler"*] a refugee in any manner whatsoever to the frontiers of territories where his life or freedom would be threatened on account of his race, religion, nationality, membership in any particular social group or political opinion (*supra* note 2 at art. 33. s. 1).

6. Canada's Immigration Act, R.S.C. 1985, c. I-2, as am. by R.S.C. 1985 (4th Supp.), c. 28, s. 1, provides that:

   "Convention refugee" means any person who
   a) by reason of a well-founded fear of persecution for reasons of race, religion, nationality, membership in a particular social group or political opinion,
     (i) is outside the country of the person's nationality and is unable or, by reason of such fear, is unwilling to avail himself of the protection of that country, or
     (ii) not having a country of nationality, is outside the country of the person's former habitual residence and is unable or, by reason of such fear, is unwilling to return to that country, and
   (b) has not ceased to be a Convention refugee... (Immigration Act, *ibid*. at s. 2 (1)).

7. See, for example, the *Ward* case, *supra*, note 2, at 709.

8. B. Laskin, *Canadian Constitutional Law*, 2nd ed. (Toronto: Carswell, 1960), at 939.

9. A. Lamer, "Introduction," in G.-A. Beaudoin, ed., *The Charter — Ten Years Later* (Cowansville: Les Editions Yvon Blais, 1992).

10. Justice Haim Cohn, "The Spirit of Israel Law," 9 *Is.LR.* (1974), 456 at 459.

11. *Ha'aretz v. Electricity Company* (1977) 31(2) PD 281, 294-5.

12. Yaacov S. Zemach, *The Judiciary of Israel*, 2nd ed. (Jerusalem: Institute for Judicial Training, 1998), p. 71.

13. These are the Eastern Orthodox, Roman Catholic, Gregorian Armenian, Armenian Catholic, Syrian Catholic, Chaldean Uniate, Greek Catholic Melkite, Maronite, and Syrian Orthodox.

14. See section 11 of the Law and Administration Ordinance, 1948.

15. Druze Religious Courts Law, 1962.

16. *Yardor v. Knesset Central Election Committee* (1965) 19 (3) *Piskey Din* (Law Reports of the Supreme Court of Israel) 365 (Hebrew).

17. The Palestine Order in Council of 1922; in 1948 the State of Israel adopted this Mandatory law, save for modifications resulting from the establishment of the state. See section 11 of the Law and Administration Ordinance, 5708-1948.

18. See, for example, the landmark ruling in *Bavli v. Bavli* discussed more fully below.

19. See *Progressive Judaism Movement v. Minister of Religious Affairs* (1989) 43 (2) *Piskey Din* 661, abridged in *Israel Law Review* 25 (1991):110.

20. See *Shas Movement v. Minister of Interior*, 40 (4) *Piskey Din* 436. See also *Miller v. Minister of Interior*, 1986 40 (40) *Piskey Din* 436. A petition to recognize the legal effect of Reform conversion performed in Israel is pending before the Supreme Court.

21. See *Hoffman v. The City Council of Jerusalem*, not yet published.

22. *Peretz v. Head of Local Council of Kfar Shmaryahu*, 17 *Piskey Din* 2101.

23. See *Hebrew Union College v. Minister of Religious Affairs*, not yet published.

24. 44 (2) *Piskey Din* 673; abridged in *Israel Law Review* 26 (1992):77. See also A. Maoz, "State and Religion in Israel," in Menachem Mor, ed., *International Perspectives of Church and State* (Omaha, 1993), p. 239.

25. Ruth Lapidot, "Freedom of Religion and Conscience in Israel," 47 *Catholic University Law Review* (Winter 1998):458-459

26. For further elaboration on this point, see B. Bracha, "The Protection of Human Rights in Israel," 12 *Is.YB on HR* (1982):110; A. Shapira, "The Status of Fundamental Individual Rights in the Absence of a Written Constitution," 9 *Is.LR* (1974):497; G. Hausner, "The Right of

the Individual in Court," 9 *Is.LR* (1974):477; J. Albert, "Constitutional Adjudication Without a Constitution: The Case of Israel," 82 *Harvard LRev* (1969):1245; S. Shetreet, "Reflections on the Protection of the Rights of the Individual: Form and Substance," 12 *Is.LR* (1977):32; I. Zamir, "Rule of Law and Civil Liberties in Israel," 7 *CJQ* (1988):64; A. Maoz, "Defending Civil Liberties Without a Constitution — The Israeli Experience," 16 *Melbourne University LR* (1988):815.

27. D. Kretzmer, "The New Basic Laws on Human Rights: A Mini-Revolution in Israeli Constitutional Law," 26 *Is. LR* (1992):238.

28. H.C. 1000/92, *Bavli v. The Great Rabbinical Court*, Jerusalem, et al. 48(2) P.D. 221.

29. F. Raday, "Religion, Multiculturalism and Equality: The Israeli Case," *Israel Yearbook on Human Rights* (1996), 193 at 230.

30. A. Zysblatt, "The System of Government," I. Zamir and A. Zysblatt, eds., *Public Law in Israel* (Oxford: Clarendon Press, 1996).

31. *Ibid.*

32. *Ibid.*

4

Comparing Recent Multi-Ethnic Immigration to Canada and to Israel: Impact on Social Cohesion and Approaches to Integration

Alti Rodal

Introduction

Does growing ethnic and racial diversity arising from immigration inevitably generate conflict, aggravate existing schisms and reduce social cohesion? Is it divisive and fragmenting, or a potential source for a renewed sense of nationhood, strengthened by cross-cultural enrichment and opportunities to institute and affirm principles of equality and justice? Canada and Israel, two very different societies in some fundamental respects, are both preoccupied by the project of nation-building, at the same time as they are trying to adapt to the reality of increasingly assertive ethno-racial diversity.

The first part of this chapter compares recent experiences in Canada and in Israel in integrating new immigrant groups that are too distinctive or too large and self-contained to be assimilated. To illustrate points of comparison for integration challenges and approaches in the two countries, the discussion draws from the experience of the following groups of immigrants in each country:

for Israel, immigrants from the former Soviet Union and Ethiopia; and for Canada, the "visible minorities" which include immigrants from the West Indies, Africa, Asia, and Latin America.

A challenge for the discussion is taking into account the diversity within these groups. There are important differences between the different waves of immigrants to Israel from the former Soviet Union and Ethiopia which give rise to different integration challenges. Even more striking is the diversity within Canada's "visible minorities" community: one cannot lump together the impact and experience of, and attitudes towards, newly arrived Chinese, Jamaicans, and refugees from Central America or Somalia. In addition to some fundamental differences in the nature of the receiving countries, there is the inherent difficulty of comparing experiences with very different groups of immigrants, motivated to immigrate for very different reasons, and drawn from different social and economic backgrounds.

The focus is on the impact of multi-ethnic immigration on social cohesion — understood as a society's capacity to maintain order, stability, cooperation, and a common sense of belonging among its citizens. The impact on social cohesion may be gauged both in attitudes towards and on the part of immigrants, and actual behavior between immigrants and the veteran population. While resentment of immigrants for factual or perceived reasons may indeed undermine social cohesion at the level of sentiment and symbols, negative behavior in the form of discrimination or violent conflict can be socially explosive.

The key indicators used here to assess the impact of immigration on social cohesion are: (i) public attitudes to immigration in general; (ii) the prevalence of negative perceptions and stereotypes of particular groups of immigrants; (iii) attitudes of the immigrants towards the host society, including the degree of alienation from or sense of "belonging" in the society on the part of the immigrants; (iv) discriminatory practices towards immigrants in employment or education, or other barriers to full participation; (v) incidents of conflict — violent or non-violent; and (vi) emerging views and existing mythologies about the nature and purpose of the national collectivity, which may be either rigidly defined and exclusive or accommodating and inclusive of diverse minority groups.

Findings relating to the last-mentioned indicator will likely correlate to findings for the other indicators. Those who see the growing diversity resulting from immigration as a threat to social cohesion and valued traditions will likely have negative attitudes towards immigrants, and in some instances express such attitudes in discriminatory behavior or violence. Those who see diversity as a key to building a dynamic, pluralist society will likely manifest positive attitudes and assessments of the contribution of immigrants and act to support their integration. Both sides are likely to exaggerate or oversimplify the social and economic impacts of immigration, often on the basis of insufficient evidence, in order to support predetermined views. Immigrants, for their part, will react to how they are perceived and received.

The second part of this chapter describes the evolution over the last two decades of the concept and policy of multiculturalism in Canada as an approach to promoting the integration of minority and immigrant groups of diverse backgrounds. Reference is then made to developments in Israel which reflect that society's growing concern — beyond the primary preoccupation of "absorption" in terms of employment, housing, health and social services — about the cultural and social integration of new groups of immigrants. Experience in both countries is then discussed in the context of the broader debate on assimilation and pluralism as approaches to the integration of diverse minority and immigrant groups.

There are clearly pitfalls in comparing immigration and integration issues for such radically different contexts as Israel and Canada. A fundamental difference is in the understanding of the term "ethno-racial." In Israel, all these diverse groups have a common base rooted in their identification as Jews, and they are being integrated into a Jewish state ready to accommodate Jews of any ethno-racial background. The common ground for the diverse immigrant groups in Canada is that they have come together in this country and are participating in building a multi-ethnic state, which in principle is completely neutral with regard to their ethno-racial background.

However, there is a parallel between Quebec and Israel: Neither are "neutral" in assessing the desirability of immigrants of diverse backgrounds. Both societies are concerned with survival, and in both cases, there is a sense that the national purpose of the place would be lost if large numbers of people came in who did not care about that purpose. A key determinant of Israel's immigration policy is Jewish identification; a key determinant in Quebec's immigration policy is the capacity and preparedness of immigrants to integrate into a French Quebecois culture — at least linguistically, and to contribute to the flourishing of the Quebecois nation. In comparing immigrant integration and social cohesion issues in Canada and Israel, a separate comparison of Quebec and Israel is warranted.

Despite the differences in the national contexts and the nature of the immigrant groups received, there is scope for a valuable exchange of lessons regarding the common challenge both countries face in integrating ethnically and racially diverse groups, against a backdrop of existing internal schisms and tensions, and current aspirations to promote a cohesive society. At a practical level, the comparison may shed light both on common fault lines in host societies which tend to undermine social cohesion in the presence of multi-ethnic immigration, and approaches which are conducive to social cohesion and fuller integration of immigrants.

Comparing Contexts and Integration Challenges

National Identity, Immigration Policies, and Demographic Transformation: Implications for Social Cohesion

Israel, geographically a very small country, has a unique national identity and stance towards immigration. Traditionally, for most Jews, immigration to Israel is spiritually and nationalistically a "coming home" — in some instances raising expectations which it may not be possible to meet. If such immigrants are disappointed or feel that they are treated unfairly, their sense of betrayal is all the more intense (as has been the case for some Ethiopian immigrants). Conversely, immigrants who come to Israel primarily for economic reasons, or who see their move as a stepping stone for migration to other countries, may encounter resentment and criticism (for example, a component of immigrants from the former Soviet Union). With its strongly ideological character and subject both to significant societal rifts as well as powerful forces for cohesion, Israel is a land of immigration like no other.

Canada, endowed with large land areas occupied by a relatively small population, is a federal state with a history of French coloni-

zation and British association and institutional inheritance, many
different aboriginal peoples, and many other well-established ethnic groups and more recent groups of immigrants. In 1967, Canada
adopted a new immigrant selection system based on the perceived
needs of the Canadian labor market, without regard to ethnic origin,
color or religion. Over the following three decades, a substantial
influx of immigrants of diverse ethno-racial background has been
superimposed on the ongoing search for national identity and
cohesion — a quest for "unity" challenged by Quebec nationalists'
demand for special political status or separation from the rest of
Canada, regional self-assertiveness in other parts of the country,
and aboriginal peoples' demands to be recognized as distinct societies and to be granted the right of self-government.

Demographic Transformation

Something which the two countries have in common is the
radical pace and scope of demographic change over only a few
decades. Considering its very small geographic size and population, Israel has been absorbing immigrants from diverse backgrounds at a remarkable rate. Established after the Holocaust as a
state where all Jews can find refuge, Israel has a unique immigration policy unlike that of any other modern state, even those which
welcome immigration. This policy is based on the Law of Return,
enacted in 1950 as a cornerstone of the state's vision of itself as the
Jewish homeland. This law grants automatic citizenship to any Jew,
including anyone who has at least one Jewish grandparent or who
has converted to Judaism, except those who pose a threat to public
safety. Spouses and children are also allowed in, even if they are not
Jewish.

The Law of Return has enabled 2.3 million immigrants of very
diverse backgrounds to come to Israel since its establishment. From
1989 to 1995, Israel absorbed 710,000 immigrants, boosting its
population by 14 percent. The equivalent for Canada would be to
take in some four million immigrants. Some 610,000 of these recent
immigrants have come from various republics of the former Soviet
Union. Together with an earlier wave of 137,000 immigrants in the
1970s, ex-Soviet Jews now surpass immigrants from Morocco as
the country's largest single Jewish ethnic group and have changed

the face of the nation. There are also now approximately 57,000 Ethiopian Jews in Israel. Most came in two waves: Operation Moses brought in 8,000 in the early and mid-1980s, and Operation Solomon airlifted 14,400 in 36 hours in 1991. Others came before and after these two waves, and some 10,500 were born in Israel.[1] It is perhaps not surprising, given the challenges of integrating these new groups, that there has been a decline from 1973 to 1994 in the opinion that immigration to Israel is imperative for the state — from 87 percent to 67 percent.[2]

Canada, too, has changed radically since World War II in its fundamental make-up, largely but not only because of immigration. In 1939, when Canada entered the war, it was a country with clear affiliation to Britain, a largely rural population, an Anglo-Protestant majority and a defensive French Catholic minority centered in Quebec. By the 1960s, Canada was heavily urbanized, with a Catholic majority, and had a growing immigrant population, including about half a million people of Italian origin residing in Toronto.

In recent years, the annual immigration intake in Canada relative to its population has been small, particularly in comparison to Israel.[3] However, over the last two decades, there has been a highly noticeable demographic change, particularly manifest in the main urban centers, as Canada's prime source of immigration shifted from European countries and the United States to Asia, Central and South America, the West Indies, and Africa. Nearly 150,000 immigrants per year from these new source countries have been arriving in Canada. The term "visible minorities" has been coined to describe this growing group of Canadian residents who are distinct by virtue of their color, physical appearance, or mode of dress. They now comprise the majority of the immigrant population. Of 200,000 new residents in Canada in 1990, 140,000 or 70 percent were considered "visible minorities."[4]

To illustrate the magnitude of this change and its impact demographically: of the 25 percent of the population in 1961 whose origins were neither British nor French, only 3 percent represented visible minorities. By 1991, 45 percent of Canadians reported at least one origin other than British or French, and approximately 10 percent were defined as members of visible minorities. The proportion is now closer to 20 percent in the largest urban areas.[5]

The recent immigrants have significantly reenforced the multi-ethnic, multi-racial, and multi-religious character of Canada, particularly in the large urban centers. There are now five Chinatowns in Toronto; 90 percent of immigrants to Quebec settle in Montreal where several neighborhoods are now predominantly non-white; and visible minorities constitute significant proportions of the student body in many schools in Vancouver, Montreal, and Toronto. The issues raised by this new demographic reality have a direct bearing on social cohesion, particularly in urban centers where most of the Canadian population is concentrated, and have shaped approaches to the integration of newcomers and minority groups.

Selective Versus Non-Selective Immigration Policies

While both Israel and Canada are among the handful of countries which encourage permanent settlement, there is a fundamental difference in the key determinants of immigration policy for the two countries, which has some bearing on attitudes towards them.

Apart from criteria set by the Law of Return, Israel has an essentially non-selective immigration policy and, despite its small size, places no limits on the numbers that will be accepted for permanent settlement. Dedicated to the principle of immigration as rescue, it cannot control or plan sudden influxes of large numbers of people, nor can it select immigrants for the potential economic benefits they might bring. Instead, it has to try to accommodate all who come into its economy as best it can and carry the burden of supporting those unable to contribute. This means that regardless of the potential impact on the economy or the health and welfare system, the settlement/absorption process has to gear itself to address the special challenges of each new immigration wave (such as that of the Ethiopian Jews) and the needs of large groups of immigrants who arrive within a brief space of time (such as the massive immigration wave from the former Soviet Union after 1989). The potential for resentment and the manifestation of negative attitudes towards immigrants is therefore considerable, but often offset by nation-building considerations and sentiments.

In contrast, Canada, with a relatively small population for its geographic size, has been following an increasingly rigorous selective immigration policy which permits it to choose immigrants likely to contribute to the economy (i.e., immigrants able to invest, of working age, or with desired skills) and who will not be a financial burden on the system. In addition to this "economic immigration," which constitutes about half of the immigrants to Canada, there are two other categories: Family Class immigration permits reunification with a close family relation who is already a permanent resident in the country — arrivals under this category declined from about 45 percent in the early 1980s to about 35 percent.[6] Refugee Class immigration, under Canada's Humanitarian Mission, which has increased to an average of about 15 percent, presents integration challenges comparable with those of immigrants coming to Israel under the Law of Return, though within a much more controlled framework and on a far smaller scale.

Again, the province of Quebec is a case apart. Under the Canada-Quebec Accord (1991), Quebec can formulate and implement its own immigration policy. A key thrust of Quebec's policy has been a clear preference for French-speaking immigrants. This concern with the "French" factor in accepting immigrants in a way parallels the importance Israel attaches to the Jewish background of immigrants. In its aspiration to accommodate Quebec within a truly bilingual Canada, the federal government too has placed greater emphasis than in the past on immigrants' ability to speak French, making it easier for Haitians and French-speaking Africans to be accepted as immigrants.

Profiles of Immigrant Groups: Integration Challenges and Host Society Attitudes

Ex-Soviet Immigrants in Israel

The approximately 750,000 ex-Soviets who now live in Israel have changed the face of the nation. They have more than tripled the number of engineers in the country, and doubled the ranks of medical doctors. Some 14,000 musicians, artists, actors, directors, choreographers, and dancers have made an impressive contribution to Israeli culture. They have become the nation's most prominent and politically and socially influential "ethnic" group.

They are a very diversified group which includes people of different backgrounds and levels of Jewish identification, who have come to Israel for very different reasons. About one-third are from Leningrad and Moscow, and there are large groups from Ukraine, the Baltic republics, and the Moslem-dominated Asian republics. These diverse groups have little more than the Russian language in common. In Israel, they have come together and are recreating themselves as a community for the first time.

There are important differences in the motivation and composition of the two main waves of ex-Soviet immigrants. The earlier 1970s wave included the "refuseniks," who were in a sense already a community of people, having participated in the underground struggle to assert their Jewish identity in the urban centers of Leningrad and Moscow. The 1970s wave also included people from the Baltic and Asiatic republics, who had maintained a stronger Jewish and Zionist background. The immigrants coming since 1989 have little attachment to Jewish tradition and a problematic Jewish identification, having lived for three generations under a Communist regime which suppressed Jewish religious and ethnic identity. Their main motivation for emigrating was not so much the desire to come to Israel, but fear of political and economic instability in the post-Soviet era; dismay with the corruption and malfunctioning of most major social institutions, including government, the army, and the health care system; ecological hazards; and some anti-Semitism.[7]

The earlier immigrants have served as a significant reference group for the 1990s immigrants, providing them with social support, guidance, and the precedent of their relatively successful experience in social and economic integration. The newer wave of immigrants is integrating more slowly, partly because of its sheer mass, and partly because of a lack of desire to identify with Israeli culture, particularly among those who have come from the large urban centers of Russia.[8]

Though deeply dismayed with life under Communism and with the instability which followed the demise of Communism, the ex-Soviets in Israel take great pride in, and have maintained a strong attachment to, the culture of their country of origin. They have established a far-reaching Russian-speaking subculture in enclaves across Israel. This subculture — which includes a score of newspapers and journals, radio and television programs, bookstores, supplementary education programs, specialty food shops, Russian-language video outlets, a Russian theater company, and several orchestras, tour agencies, real estate agencies, moving companies, and other services catering to their needs and tastes — has reduced their incentive to study more than basic Hebrew or to venture out to interact with other Israelis.

The ex-Soviet community poses a number of significant integration challenges: In the first place, there is the culture shock experienced by people "emigrating from a formerly totalitarian society and a command economy to a modern 'capitalist' democracy, and from minority ethnic status to life in a Jewish state."[9] There are challenges arising from the demographic composition of the immigrants — the large proportion of elderly and one-parent families, whose health care and social needs have to be accommodated.

There is also the challenge of economic integration of such a large, highly educated group, top-heavy with professionals — doctors, scientists, and engineers. Some 60 percent have worked in academic, scientific, or free professions — compared to 28 percent of the veteran Israeli population. The task of finding work for them is daunting, particularly in their own fields, and many have expressed frustration and discontent with the downgrading of their professional status in Israel.

A major challenge is addressing the needs of immigrant children — in particular, the large number of high school dropouts among the immigrant youth, many of whom are drawn to crime. Editorials have drawn attention to the problem and have called for training Israeli teachers and bringing in many more Russian-speaking counsellors to the schools to deal with immigrant problems.

Another major challenge, with strong implications for social cohesion, is the "un-Jewishness" of the newer wave of immigrants. In contrast with the Ethiopian Jews who preserved their communal identity and leadership in transition to Israel, the ex-Soviet Jews are overwhelmingly secular and by and large ignorant of, and alienated from, Jewish tradition and customs. Many are in fact non-Jews according to rabbinical criteria. While most estimates vary from 20 to 30 percent, the Central Bureau of Statistics made known its much lower estimate of 8.3 percent in 1995, asserting that immigration will not change the Jewish character of the country.

Some observers anticipate that the presence of this very large, highly secular group, with a substantial sub-group of non-Jews in its midst, will in fact have far reaching impacts on Israeli society, particularly in adding momentum to the push for separation of state and religion. As stated in a plea by the former Minister of Absorption: "The religious authorities must stop opposing civil marriages, at least for those who are prevented from marrying by Jewish law. Conversion to Judaism should be made readily available, and more flexibility should be shown in matters of secular burials."[10] Such developments would of course be strongly opposed by Orthodox groups in Israel.

Considering the strain that the absorption of this massive migration has put on Israel's infrastructure, it is noteworthy that resentment of tax-subsidized benefits accorded to new immigrants has been minimal and readily countered by arguments relating to nation-building. A former government minister, critical of the number of elderly Russian Jews arriving without families and in need of massive assistance, made the statement that "one third of the immigrants are social cases, one third are handicapped, and the remaining third are single-parent families." While her stance prompted many supportive phone calls, she was also sharply criticized for undermining the state's foundation, sowing discord between veteran Israelis and newcomers, and hurting the delicate process of nation-building.[11] Her call for selective immigration was publicly rebuked by fellow cabinet ministers and Prime Minister Rabin, who said "Aliyah (Hebrew for immigration) is the soul, the raison d'etre of the state. There is no such thing as selective aliya, and God help us if we get to that."

Nonetheless, these new immigrants have to contend with the prevalence of negative attitudes and stereotyping, including some resentment based on the same ideological, "nation-building" grounds. There is resentment of non-Jews who have passed themselves off as Jews in order to escape instability and poverty in the Soviet Union, and there is resentment of Jews who came not because they felt strongly about Israel but because they could not go anywhere else. There is also ambivalence about a group which has insulated itself with such pride and determination in its own subculture, about immigrants who are not trying to emulate and become "Israelis."

Integration of this group into Israeli society may exacerbate existing social tensions — between the secular and religious camps, as noted above, and in relation to Israelis of Sephardi background. It has been observed that the 1980s, which was a decade of low immigration, allowed Israel's ethnically heterogeneous society to begin to coalesce. It was during this period that the Sephardi population found its place in the political, economic and cultural mainstream, causing the growing Sephardi-Ashkenazi schism of preceding years to recede. The arrival of the large numbers of Soviet immigrants — some 75 percent of whom are professionals or trained technicians — has raised fears of renewed ethnic tensions as Sephardim, "who have just crossed the middle-class threshold, are in danger of being pushed back to the end of the line by the new immigrants."[12]

A disturbing aspect of the new immigration wave is that it has been accompanied by a significant rise in crime in Israel (20 percent according to a 1993 account), particularly crimes of fraud and forgery. Reports about ex-Soviet immigrants engaging in money laundering, fraud and forgeries, and prostitution, alongside reports about the culture of alcoholism and violence in their former homeland, have reenforced stereotypes which label immigrants as criminals and operatives of the Russian mafia, Russian women as prostitutes, and immigrant youths as corrupt drop-outs and drug dealers. As in other immigrant-receiving countries, there is a sense within the ex-Soviet community that the media has a tendency to pounce on stories of crime, corruption, and chicanery involving immigrants.

A survey of immigrants from the CIS released in January 1994 by the Jewish Agency, which examined social integration rather than economic status, showed that the majority of recent immigrants "feel like outsiders," not particularly welcomed in Israeli society. Only one-fifth of the immigrants surveyed felt that Israeli attitudes toward them are what they should be.

Offsetting the negative stereotyping is the focus on the tremendous contribution the immigrants are making to Israeli society. Editorials have referred to this immigration as one of the greatest boons to befall Israel since its founding. They highlight the remarkable educational and occupational level of the immigrants, the unprecedented number of scientists and engineers, and the contribution they are making to Israel's economy, its educational level, its culture, and its prospects of becoming a leading industrial, technological country as it enters the twenty-first century.

Ethiopian Immigrants in Israel

For Ethiopian Jews, who had maintained strong Jewish identification and traditions and a longing for Jerusalem for millennia, immigration to Israel was the fulfillment of a dream. In Ethiopia they lived mostly in small villages in mountainous regions, as subsistence farmers with a close-knit social structure and family life. In sharp contrast with the highly educated ex-Soviet immigrants, most of the immigrants were either illiterate or had very little education. As a result of the move to Israel, many families were divided, village communities broken up, and traditional hierarchies destroyed. Men who had been masters of their houses — self-sufficient farmers, blacksmiths, and weavers — were reduced to idleness or dependency.

The group that arrived in the early 1980s was smaller and arrived over a number of years, mostly as families, during a period when immigration was low. They had suffered greatly both before and during their difficult journey to Israel, and their dramatic story of persistence and survival aroused compassion and was an inspiration to other Jews. The much larger second group came over a single weekend, at a time when the massive immigration wave from the former Soviet Union was at its peak, and when unemployment in the country was also at a peak of 11 percent. In the later wave, there were many cases of family members being left behind in Ethiopia and of children arriving without their parents.

When they first arrived, they were received with warmth and emotion by the Israeli public, and the government poured large resources into housing and education for them. Public attitudes toward them were very positive and Israelis took pride in the belief that racism was not a problem. Integration problems were often dismissed as inevitable glitches in the transition of a people from subsistence in Africa to a modern society.

However, among the immigrants there was disappointment and frustration, and they have made themselves heard. The world media has focussed attention on the difficulties Ethiopian Jews were having in integrating into Israeli society:[13] they were housed in grim trailer parks (or "caravans") or in distant "development towns"; unemployed, they were becoming idle and losing their pride; there were racially-tinged fights with Soviet immigrants in crowded absorption centers; their children were concentrated in a number of religious schools, which was perceived to be a kind of segregation; their teenagers were placed in boarding schools designed for tough welfare cases and streamed for "vocational studies" which were regarded as offering little chance of higher education or rewarding jobs; and they have experienced very high divorce and suicide rates since their arrival. After more than a decade in Israel, many of the Ethiopian Jews feel they are at the bottom of the social and economic ladder.

These grievances express real discontent with aspects of their integration, aspects which by and large can be (and have been) addressed through appropriate programs and measures (as discussed below). More painful and alienating, and with serious implications for social cohesion, has been their sense that there has been little respect for them at the fundamental level of ethnic identity. They felt humiliated when their religious leaders were de-legitimized and the Judaism they had proudly sustained for centuries was questioned by the Orthodox rabbinical establishment. When the rabbinate finally agreed to accept them as Jews, it was on the condition that they undergo a symbolic conversion, which they found degrading.

A last straw, which raised the specter of racism and hit hard at a symbolic level, was the revelation in January 1996 that the country's blood banks were routinely discarding blood donated by Ethiopians because of a purportedly high incidence of the AIDS virus among them. This revelation evoked strong emotions, as it was seen by the Ethiopians as a powerful symbol of rejection and stigmatization of the community by Israeli society. A violent protest followed. More than 15,000 people turned up outside the prime minister's office in January 1996 and clashed with police, leaving some 70 injured. The appearance of racism and the demarcation of the group as a racial underclass was disturbing. It is noteworthy that the Israeli government promptly distanced itself from the blood banks' decision, apologized to the Ethiopian community and appointed a commission of inquiry into the affair. Also, a public poll showed 68 percent unequivocal support for the Ethiopians in their protest.[14]

The Ethiopian Jews have succeeded in politicizing their discontent. From the government's perspective, there is a sense that, though some mistakes were made, a great deal of effort and resources have been put into integrating this group. A policy of affirmative action had been implemented in various facets of their absorption. A special mortgage program since 1993 has helped most families purchase housing in the center of Israel, so that 90 percent of residents of the caravan sites have now been moved to permanent housing.[15] In 1995, only 5 percent of the community's children were in separate classes, compared to 70 percent in 1991.

Despite these supportive measures, and despite the group's strong sense of identification with the Jewish people, a report released in 1995 by the Israel Association for Ethiopian Jews — "Creating an Underclass" — indicates that they still have some strong grievances, and still do not feel to be part of Israeli mainstream society. Only 7 percent of Ethiopian immigrants (in contrast to 60 percent of the overall population) who graduated from high school in 1995 received a matriculation certificate — the key to getting into good army units and university. There is a burgeoning high school drop-out rate and growing juvenile delinquency, and some say they have difficulty integrating in the army, considered to be Israel's "melting pot."

Advocates on behalf of the group are calling for better strategies to overcome educational gaps and to heal their wounded self-respect. In its response, the government has stated that it will be guided by the following five principles: (i) strengthening the policy of preferential treatment or affirmative action for the Ethiopian population with regard to housing, education, and integration into employment; (ii) supporting actions which promote integration rather than segregation; (iii) allocating special resources, currently 75 percent higher than for other immigrants; (iv) developing leadership within the Ethiopian community and involving immigrants from earlier waves in decision-making; and (v) promoting the preservation of Ethiopian Jewish culture and its contribution to "the mosaic of Israeli life."[16] In a number of practical measures, absorption programs have been designed for communities in various municipalities, at the local level, in the following areas: educational enrichment to students studying in the schools; employment programs for adults and women; upgrading language skills; and, to promote "mutual integration," cooperative programs between the general Israeli population and the Ethiopian immigrants in the community.[17]

These actions appear to have had an impact. A 1995 study on integration of Ethiopian immigrants who live in permanent housing (carried out by the Brookdale Institute and the Ministry of Immigrant Absorption) showed that 76 to 96 percent viewed the relationships with their non-Ethiopian neighbors as positive, 77-97 percent feel well-treated, and their children play with non-Ethiopian children in the community.

While there are no formal barriers preventing Ethiopian Jews from living wherever they want, getting work, or marrying whomever they want, older Ethiopians often prefer to live among other Ethiopians, and youngsters often still find they have more in common with others of the same cultural background. The same may be said about immigrants from the United States or from the CIS. However, as dark-skinned East Africans, with religious customs developed in centuries of isolation from mainstream Judaism, they feel that they have often been treated like primitives, condescendingly, with some discrimination. Such feelings, whether based on reality or not, can stand in the way of full integration.

Attitudes in Israel toward Immigration and Immigrants Overall

Attitudes in Israel seem divided between viewing the recent newcomers as a source of demographic, economic and cultural strength, and fears that they will erode Israel's hard-won sense of social cohesion.

A 1991 poll showed very positive attitudes towards immigration and immigrants among the Israeli population: 85 percent of Israelis answered that they would take a drop in living standards to help absorb immigrants; 93 percent had a "favorable impression" of the Ethiopians; and 76 percent were favorably impressed by the Russian immigrants.[18]

The majority of Israelis believe that accepting Jewish immigrants is the country's raison d'etre. There is therefore general affirmation of open doors, wide endorsement of continued benefits for immigrants, and no major conflicts. Though the country's infrastructure has been highly stressed by the arrival of large numbers of new immigrants in recent years, most Israelis have faith that the country will muddle through the resulting economic problems.

However, there is also an undercurrent of discontent and some concern about "how the influx may affect the country's delicate social balance and evolving national identity."[19] As noted above, apart from some grievances relating to practical issues (such as housing and economic integration), many of the Ethiopian and ex-Soviet immigrants feel alienated or ethnically stereotyped. They also feel that the secular and religious establishments do not accept them for what they are, that the effort to make them over in the image of the "Israeli" is both offensive and impossible. Many are resigned to being the "generation of the desert," placing hopes for real integration on their children.

"Visible Minorities" in Canada

Visible minorities represented only 3 percent of the Canadian population in 1961; by 1986 they were 6.3 percent; in 1991, 9.6 percent, and the percentage is rising quickly. The proportion is now closer to 20 percent in the largest urban areas. Some predict that by 2001 half of the population of Toronto will be from this group. The substantial numbers of immigrants from the Caribbean, India, Pakistan, Vietnam, Korea, Hong Kong, the Philippines, and Africa have indeed changed the complexion of the Canadian urban landscape culturally and socially. Their concentration in the main urban centers has resulted in daily contact with the mainstream population. Some who came with high qualifications and job skills have moved into employment and housing which in the past had been populated largely by the white community.

Media reports and public consultations undertaken in the late 1980s and early 1990s indicated that there was public concern about immigrants changing the demographic face of Canadian cities. A 1991 study by the Economic Council of Canada posed the question: Does the changing population mix brought about by increasing immigration from Asia, Africa, and the Caribbean carry the risk of greater social frictions and racial conflict? The Council reviewed surveys and studies of attitudes towards immigrants and visible minorities, and concluded that tolerance among native-born Canadians towards immigrants was reasonably high and rising, particularly in urban areas where there was greater contact between people of different ethnic origins. However, the Council did suggest the likelihood of social friction should there be high unemployment, together with a rapid increase of visible minority immigrants.

Other sources point to a contrary finding — that resentment of immigrants in urban centers where there are high concentrations of newly established "visible" minorities is prevalent. Immigrants have been blamed for exacerbating levels of concentration in certain centers; their habits of consumption or waste disposal have been criticized; and concerns voiced about the implications of their arrival for real estate or urban planning. For example, in Vancouver, some claim that immigrants are bidding housing prices up or creating urban sprawl, perhaps overlooking other factors also responsible for these developments such as the movement of internal migrants from rural areas or from other parts of the country. Hong Kong immigrants in Vancouver have aroused resentment because of their wealth, because they are perceived as builders of "monster" homes, as lacking commitment to Canada, and as only wanting a Canadian passport.

Discrimination, Inter-Racial Tensions, and Government Responses

Expressions of concern that the sudden presence of large numbers of "visible minorities" in the main urban centers was generating negative reactions and biases in the mainstream community were in fact accompanied by a number of disturbing racial incidents in the 1970s and 1980s. In response, the federal and Ontario governments established task forces and conducted surveys of racial attitudes. They found evidence of serious problems. Briefs from racial minorities across the country described the existence and effects of discrimination in major sectors — including unfair treatment in the educational system, discriminatory barriers in housing, bias in the media, discriminatory treatment by law enforcement agencies and the justice system, and discrimination in the workplace in relation to recruitment, hiring, promotion, training, and termination practices. This stock-taking resulted in several reports calling for immediate implementation of concrete measures to combat discrimination and increase equity for disadvantaged groups, including legislation on employment equity.[20]

Further investigation highlighted discrimination in the educational system, which relied on a curriculum consisting of "Eurocentric" textbooks and focussed only on Christian holidays, Anglo culture, and white faces. These criticisms and a number of racial incidents in the schools prompted boards of education in several provinces (Ontario, in particular) to take the lead in developing policies to promote equality and better race relations. The initiative soon broadened to a national scale when the Canadian Council for Multicultural and Intercultural Education met in Winnipeg in 1981, and provincial multicultural councils and educational associations came into being with the goal of building coalitions and developing curriculum materials and programs that were inclusive of all groups, including aboriginal peoples.

The approach gradually extended to other institutions affected by the demographic changes. In response to racial incidents involving the police, an Ontario Government Task Force recommended increasing representation of minorities on police forces, a province-wide civilian-headed unit to investigate complaints against the police, and training and educating the police on race relations.

In the late 1980s and early 1990s, there was an increase in ethnic tensions and some violent incidents. In Montreal, fights erupted between white and black youth gangs and there were many allegations and some confirmed instances of police harassment of non-Caucasians. In Toronto, there was also escalating tension between police and minority groups, reported instances of racism including differential treatment, verbal abuse, excessive, sometimes lethal use of force, and a resulting sense of alienation, distrust, and hostility. A violent peak was reached in a 1,000-person race riot in Toronto in 1992, which involved considerable vandalizing of property. In Vancouver and Toronto, there were also cases of racial murders of young South Asians.

These incidents and their high profile media coverage have raised fears that ethno-racial diversity arising from immigration will inevitably generate conflict and reduce social cohesion. These fears have been reinforced by parallel examples of anti-immigrant sentiment in Western Europe in this decade, where there were attacks on immigrants, foreign workers, and asylum seekers.

However, such conflicts must be assessed and addressed in context. Considering the marked and rapid demographic transformation of Canada's major cities in recent years, it is noteworthy that there have been so few incidents of overt hostility and conflict. Anti-racist legislation and public education seem to have had an impact. Public authorities and the media in particular have been trained to address issues in their own right without racist overtones. For example, Toronto police are expected to treat murders in Chinatown as crimes pure and simple, not as "Asian crime." Considerable emphasis has been placed on the role which educational institutions and non-governmental organizations can play in disseminating the ideal of cultural diversity. Observers also point to the role and impact which government has had, through a range of policies and activities at both the federal and provincial levels over a twenty-five year period, in promoting social cohesion and in shaping public attitudes towards immigrants.

The Evolution of Multiculturalism in Canada[21]

Official and community receptiveness towards immigrants of diverse ethnic backgrounds in Canada has been conditioned by an official government policy and social ideology called "multiculturalism." Though it came into being for very different reasons, multiculturalism policy, as it has evolved over the last few years, is widely perceived as a strategy and mechanism for managing the challenges of ethno-racial diversity in Canada, with potentially far-reaching influence if implemented in various spheres of society, such as education, the mass media, and enforcement agencies. Positive assessments of the success of this approach state that "the entrenchment of multiculturalism at constitutional and statutory levels has catapulted Canada to the front ranks of countries in the field of managing diversity."[22]

The government's multiculturalism policy was announced in 1971. While there were some concerns about the integration of immigrants and relations between cultural groups at the time, the concept was coined and gained prominence in the context of the debate in the late 1960s on bilingualism and biculturalism, which seemed to relegate cultural communities other than the French and English to second-class citizenship. Leaders of these other communities — some of which could claim centuries of settlement in Canada, such as the Germans, Italians, Ukrainians, and Jews — protested and eventually prompted the federal government to announce its policy of "Multiculturalism within a Bilingual Framework."

Concrete expression was soon given to this policy. A small Multiculturalism Directorate was created within the federal Department of the Secretary of State in 1972, with a broad mandate to support heritage languages, ethnic studies, and cultural activities, mostly through funding made available to voluntary ethnic associations. The emphasis of programs under this mandate was on cultural retention and cultural sharing — "Celebrating Our Differences" — with the initiative for the direction of programs coming from the groups themselves.

Once programs were established and funds generated, multiculturalism became politicized and acquired a momentum of its own. Agents of the Multiculturalism Directorate were posted in many Canadian cities to assist the population in dealing with multiculturalism policies. Several provinces (notably Ontario and Quebec) eventually established their own agencies to promote multiculturalism.

Multiculturalism as government policy was soon to be subjected to a range of criticisms. A key criticism was that such a policy tends to generate psychological ghettos because it leads people to identify themselves as members of specific ethnic groups rather than as ordinary Canadians, that it was a divisive policy producing "hyphenated Canadians." Others were critical of the fact that public funds were used to support these programs; that the emphasis on folklore trivialized ethnocultures, reducing them to "song and dance" affairs; that the policy was a political device used by the government to buy votes through grants; and that through allocation of subsidies, government officials risked being drawn into the internal politics of ethnic communities.

In Quebec, multiculturalism policy was perceived as serving to dilute the special status of French Canadians deriving from the original pact between the "two founding peoples" by turning them into merely another ethnic group in Canada, albeit a larger one. Based on a very different concept of citizenship than that which Quebec was promoting, multiculturalism was viewed as a threat, as a kind of Trojan horse which would prevent the Quebecois from defending their specificity as a state. Aboriginal peoples too have felt that multiculturalism does not respond to their particular needs and aspirations.

By the 1980s, multicultural policy shifted from group maintenance toward intergroup communications, community participation, and integration, with an added mandate for race relations.
These revisions of multiculturalism policy were prompted by a
number of developments, including the fact that second-generation
members of ethnic communities were more interested in integration
than in preserving ethnicity. The most compelling factor, however,
was the increase in the size of the "visible minorities" population
as a result of immigration. Ethnic differentiation was increasingly
based on race and color, not only on culture and language. For
members of visible minorities, the problems of maintaining ancestral languages and cultures was far less important than being
discriminated against by judges, police, teachers, employers, land-
lords, neighbors, and fellow-citizens.

Another important influence in the reorientation of policy was
the creation of a "rights-based society" — the surge in advocacy
action and pronouncements in the 1970s and 1980s, in Canada and
internationally, regarding the elimination of racial discrimination,
the promotion of employment equity, and the protection of minority
rights and human rights more generally. In 1982, the Canadian
Charter of Rights and Freedoms entrenched multiculturalism and
equality rights in the constitution. This was followed by amendments to various human rights codes which empowered commissions to monitor and enforce such rights, and, as noted above, a
number of task forces and reports which called for the implementation of measures to combat discrimination and increase equity for
disadvantaged groups.

However, attempts to implement these policies and recommended measures met with some resistance, and backlogs of complaints were piling up at Human Rights Commissions. Effective
race relations training was still clearly lacking in the key sectors —
education, media, policing, and health. Recognition that the problems stemmed from systemic inequalities, which were beyond the
capability of individuals or communities to resolve, led to lobbying
for a new approach. The view was that to achieve such goals as
employment equity and full acceptance, not merely tolerance, of all
communities as part of Canadian society, the cooperation and
active involvement of government and mainstream institutions was
essential.

This concept is at the core of the 1988 Multiculturalism Act, which emphasized equality of opportunities and full social, economic, and political integration — with a focus on the role and responsibility of mainstream institutions to remove barriers and reduce discrimination, in contrast to the earlier almost exclusive focus on the ethnocultural communities themselves. The Act gave government the responsibility of providing programming not just for community groups but for the mainstream institutions — including police, health care facilities, education, social services, and the arts.

The revised approach bears more directly on the needs of immigrants, as is evident in the key current thrusts of multiculturalism programs (delivered since 1993 through the Department of Canadian Heritage):

> Eliminating racial and ethnic discrimination through public education and institutional change, in collaboration with the educational system, other levels of government, communities, business, labour and other key players in Canadian society;
>
> Helping first-generation Canadians with the longer term process of adjusting to Canada, and acting to remove barriers and address such issues as cross-generational conflicts, mental health problems of immigrants and refugees, and problems faced by immigrant and minority youth;
>
> Promoting mutual integration as a two-way process which highlights the obligations of both immigrants and native-born Canadians — by funding activities for institutions to make newcomers feel at home, while sponsoring projects to help newcomers appreciate Canadian values and take an active part in society; and
>
> Promoting social equality and cultural diversity as fundamental Canadian values.

The public education effort to advance these goals is two-pronged: addressing the needs of the minority communities to ensure social justice, occupational mobility, and educational equity for them; and educating the rest of society in the value of social pluralism and the richness of cultural diversity.

A 1995 review of multiculturalism programs again emphasized intergroup relations, integration of communities, and breaking down barriers to equality — in particular, racism and discrimination. The stated aim is to ensure that everyone can participate fully and with respect in the Canadian mainstream; and that the mainstream does not exclude people because they do not conform to some narrow stereotypical image of what a Canadian should be.

The bulk of multiculturalism programs now target the long-term integration of immigrants and their children into Canadian society. (Short-term settlement and integration programs, including language instruction for adults, are handled by the Department of Citizenship and Immigration.) For example, key areas on which multiculturalism program officers are currently concentrating include building awareness among primary and secondary-school students of the importance of eliminating racial discrimination; sponsoring projects, such as race-relations training packages for municipalities, school boards, community colleges, universities, business and labor, police forces, and hospitals; and encouraging Canada's institutions — in particular, the media, business, health services, and the police — to be accessible to, and inclusive of, Canadians of diverse origins.

Another current thrust — facilitated by the government but usually initiated by ethnic community organizations — is to implement the multicultural ideal by developing coalitions among different groups to address issues relating to social cohesion in such areas as education and legislation. Such coalitions, it is believed, would encourage groups to work together in the common interest instead of being pitted one against the other for scarce resources; they would also provide a forum for resolving issues as they arise in the absence of an incident or crisis, and would constitute a grassroots effort to bind the country together.

From its inception, multiculturalism in Canada has been linked to the country's preoccupation with issues of national cohesion and unity. The 1988 Multiculturalism Act, explicit in its application to all Canadians, entrenched multiculturalism as a fundamental principle of Canadian society, thereby formally recognizing cultural and racial diversity as "a fundamental characteristic of the Canadian heritage and identity" and a force for national unity. At play is a bold initiative to forge both political unity and social equality from the dynamics of ethno-racial diversity.

This position stands in contrast to that which sees multiculturalism policy as discouraging the evolution of a common Canadian identity, as exacerbating the fault lines of Canadian society. It also bypasses more reserved assessments which express concern about how far the Canadian state can take its accommodation of diversity without becoming fragmented.[23]

It has been observed that multiculturalism has provided the concept, terminology, and perspective for discussing ethnocultural diversity, immigration policy, racism, and the future of Canada, all potentially socially explosive topics. It has provided "both a unique flavour to the debate and a set of terms for discussing awkward and contentious problems. Above all, it has encouraged an atmosphere of tolerance and accommodation that extends into the fabric of all Canadian communities."[24]

While multiculturalism emerged for very different reasons, it has become a determining feature in policies for managing immigrant settlement and inter-ethnic tensions. Recent reformulations of the policy and the fact that it has been given formal, concrete, institutionalized expression in legislation, a federal minister, and Offices of Multicultural Affairs at federal and provincial levels has helped in the integration of newcomers to Canada, even while holding out promise for a country still groping for national unity and identity.

Assimilation, Pluralism, and the Integration of Immigrants

Strategies or approaches which a host society can adopt towards immigrants or minority groups include segregation, marginalization, assimilation, and integration in a pluralistic context. Neither of the first two would be acceptable in a just and democratic society. However, there is a history of segregation and marginalization of aboriginal peoples in Canada which the government has been trying to address in recent years; and despite its good intentions, a number of measures taken by the Israeli government in integrating Ethiopian immigrants have been criticized for the effect they had in segregating and marginalizing this group. The real choice and debate, both in Israel and in Canada, is between assimilation and pluralism.

Studies on the American experience in seeking an ultimately desirable relationship between "the political one and the cultural many" have focussed on these two broad categories.[25] Assimilation presumes the disappearance of minority cultural differences as a result of the absorption of minority ethnicity into the dominant ethnicity, or the fusion of diverse groups (according to the "melting pot" concept) into a new creation with its own ethnic culture, structure, and identity. Both of these assimilationist options imply a move towards cultural homogeneity. Cultural pluralism, on the other hand, is based on the view that specific ethnic components do not have to disappear and assimilate, that there is value in differentiation, and that a nation which is a "mosaic" of different, harmoniously co-existing cultures can be built and sustained.

The pluralistic vision may be limited to the idea of tolerance of different ethnic cultures co-existing within a larger framework, or it may see the virtue of such diversity as the very essence of national identity, or as offering a unique opportunity for cultural enrichment of the society.[26]

Until the 1960s, the Canadian government had implicitly promoted assimilation of immigrants into the Anglo-Canadian majority culture. However, many of the larger ethnic groups maintained strong ties to their cultural heritages and affiliated with ethnic institutional structures in Canada. Since the late 1960s, as discussed above, the government has favored a policy of integration in the context of pluralism, as expressed in the concepts of multiculturalism and the "Canadian mosaic."

It has been observed that Canada is one of the most "pluralist" countries in the world.[27] Differentiation among ethnic groups composed of immigrants and their descendents, and between them and the "mainstream" population, has been superimposed on historic cleavages between native peoples and Europeans, between the English-speaking and French-speaking collectivities, as well as on religious cleavages and regional differences. While parallel cleavages exist in the United States, they are given greater official recognition in Canada. Canada has proportionately more native people, more of whom have legal status; more official languages and overarching official languages communities; more official recognition of immigrant ethnicity; and more pronounced regionalism.

As noted above, the strategy of integration, as opposed to assimilation, of ethno-racial groups has become a central ideal of Canadian nation-building, directed specifically toward immigrant groups. As stated in the 1991 study of the Economic Council of Canada, integration permits members of different groups to meet on equal terms; it promotes the distinctiveness of groups as something to be valued and appreciated by other segments of the society; and it gives newcomers more readily accessible role models, as they are not pressured to relinquish their identity. Discussions now bear on the need to promote mutual integration as a two-way process which highlights the obligations of both immigrants and members of the host society.

The Canadian public has, by and large, embraced the ideal of multiculturalism and its central place in nation-building. However, as noted above, the concept and the policy has had its critics, and an anti-pluralist sentiment has become more manifest in recent years. According to one report published in 1995, "Back in 1985, 56 percent of Canadians supported the mosaic and only 28 percent the melting pot. But in 1995, 44 percent supported the mosaic and 40 percent the melting pot — almost equal."[28] One may draw the conclusion that the public can approve of the ideal of multiculturalism, but have difficulty in accepting the reality of, and living in harmony with, sizable diverse ethnic-racial groups, with equal rights and privileges.[29]

Pluralism has much less of a hold in the province of Quebec, where there is a sharp division between the French-Canadian majority and the ethno-cultural and mostly English-speaking minority. The former remains one of the most homogeneous communities in North America, having fostered either isolationist or assimilationist policies to protect its French culture. In the 1970s, Quebec's Ministry of Immigration stressed the importance of assimilating immigrants into French-Canadian society. In the 1980s, Quebec government policies were moving, at least in principle, toward an integrationist rather than assimilationist approach to absorbing immigrants. In practice, immigrants in Quebec continued to be coerced into the French-speaking educational system and culture.

Nonetheless, acknowledgement of the presence and importance of diverse ethnic groups has led the provincial government to promote its own multiculturalism policy — referred to as "interculturelle" rather than "multiculturelle" in order to underline the predominance of the majority French society and its position as the "host culture" prepared to tolerate minority ethnic groups. The stated policy is to encourage the preservation of various cultural identities provided French is confirmed as the common language. However, the question remains: Can a non-white person of Haitian or Vietnamese ancestry, born in Quebec, ever become a "Quebecois," even if they speak French fluently. The vast majority of immigrants and minority groups in Quebec do not think that they or their children will ever feel fully at home in Quebec and have not supported the "sovereigntist" project, which they regard as exclusivist and ethnically-based. Statements made by Quebec nationalist political leaders over the last few years have confirmed them in this view.

Israel, too, is a land of cleavages. It has faced the challenge of integrating successive waves of immigrants from very diverse national backgrounds into a society marked by divisions between Ashkenazim and Sephardim, between the religious and secular, all against the backdrop of the historic conflict-ridden cleavage between Jews and Palestinians. In recent years, the term "pluralism" has come to be associated in some circles with greater representation and accommodation not only of Jews of diverse ethnic backgrounds, but also of the diverse branches of contemporary Judaism (i.e., Conservative, Reform), particularly in relation to demands for official recognition of conversions, marriages, and divorces conducted by Conservative and Reform rabbis. Some advocates of pluralism extend the concept to apply to greater "democratic rights" for non-Jews, including Israeli Arabs. The overwhelming response has been that Israel was founded as a homeland for the Jewish people, and that maintaining the "Jewish" character of the state is, by and large, a predominant concern, viewed as integral to the raison d'etre of the state and a precondition for any pluralist initiatives.

With regard to policies and practices in relation to the integration of immigrants, the approach adopted by the Israeli government in the 1950s was mainly assimilationist. Immigrants from Morocco, Egypt, Syria, Iraq, Iran, Yemen, and other parts of the Mediterranean region were lumped together as a group (referred to as the "eastern communities"), despite their very different backgrounds and levels of sophistication. They were to be refashioned, along with all the European Jews, in the Israeli Labor Zionist image as quickly as possible. Since the 1970s, this approach has increasingly been regarded as a mistake in the past, and certainly as not desirable or workable for the present.

The large number of immigrants who arrived since 1989 have proven more resistant to being integrated into Israeli society. The ex-Soviets in particular constitute too large and culturally assertive a group to assimilate. Ethiopian Jews — as a racially distinctive group adhering to a unique version of Judaism which has evolved in isolation for several thousand years — also call for a more tailored approach and recognition of their distinctive heritage. Integration of these immigrants means acknowledgement of their status as members of a particular group, not only as individuals. The challenge they pose for integration into Israeli society has inspired a more pluralistic outlook in government circles.[30] One might note in this regard the observation that the greater the number of subpopulations to be incorporated as collectivities rather than as individuals, the higher the level of pluralism that will result.[31]

Observations/Conclusions

Though there are fundamental differences between Canada and Israel relating to societal contexts, immigration policies, and the nature and proportional size of the groups of immigrants received, both countries face a common challenge — to promote social cohesion and build a nation which can accommodate inherent schisms and growing ethnic diversity. The comparison of recent experiences in the two countries in integrating distinctive and not easily assimilable groups of immigrants points to a number of parallel developments and opportunities for the exchange of lessons, both at the level of practical concrete measures and broader policy approaches. Some of the key areas for the exchange of lessons of particular relevance to maintaining social cohesion include the following: addressing the problem of stereotyping; promoting collaborative action at the local level and the participation of community organizations and individual citizens in the integration process; the potential of ethnic support networks in promoting social cohesion; and, in a more ambitious, far-reaching effort, promoting a pluralistic and just society in which peoples of diverse ethno-racial background can fully participate and contribute.

Stereotyping and Negative Attitudes towards Immigrant Groups

Negative attitudes towards distinctive immigrant groups, as reflected in public opinion surveys, are common in most immigrant-receiving countries. In addition to the usual paternalism and disdain which veteran populations tend to have for different customs and ways of newcomers, real concerns may be highly exaggerated, and pernicious stereotypes and myths may be created. For example, there are perceptions in Canada that immigrants take jobs away from the veteran population and that they are a drain on social services; and, as noted earlier, both in Canada and in Israel, media coverage has contributed to stereotyping particular groups of immigrants as criminals.

Some negative attitudes may be taken to indicate unfounded prejudice. Others may be explainable in terms of actual facts, or sometimes as reflecting passionately held positions on issues regarded as critical to national well-being. For example, in Israel, the impact of immigration on the religious mix of the country has aroused strong concerns about preserving the "Jewish character" of the state. In Canada, there are concerns about the impact of new immigrants on social cohesion. Such free-floating anxieties may be quick to fasten on negative stereotypes of newcomers

As a first step, such myths and perceptions need to be researched and, where warranted, dispelled or properly addressed. Studies on the Canadian experience have helped to put some of these myths into perspective.[32] An appropriate response, suggested in the Canadian experience, to counter negative stereotyping of particular immigrant groups is to research and document such stereotyping and to present it in context; to educate the public, particularly the media, about ethnic stereotyping; and to use the education system to promote the ideal of diversity and pluralism. The aim is to come up with constructive recommendations for remedying actual problems — for example, better screening for criminal background, addressing barriers which immigrant groups face, and measures to improve intergroup relations.

The Value of Collaborative Action, Particularly at the Local Level

The scope of this chapter did not permit a substantive comparison and analysis of existing policies and practices relating to collaborative action and citizen involvement at the local level in the integration of immigrants, and the effects of such an approach on social cohesion. This is an area that merits research as it seems obvious that improving intergroup relations needs action across society by individuals, governments, voluntary organizations, the media, the private sector, and other institutions. Friction and conflict, as well as healthy intergroup relations, happen at the local, often personal, level.

The current trend, both in Canada and in Israel, is to devolve settlement and integration services to the local level and to involve all relevant government and non-governmental organizations and the public in meeting the challenges of immigrant integration. This policy thrust is very recent in Canada where the federal government has been deliberating on how to implement it through an appropriate local decision-making model. Driven by a similar policy thrust, Israel's Ministry of Absorption now has a "Division of Absorption within the Community" which facilitates and oversees collaborative programs in localities with a high proportion of immigrants. The budget of this division allocates funding to promote social and cultural activities in Hebrew language schools; cultural and social activities to preserve traditions; enrichment programs for children and youth; activities to increase interaction among immigrant and veteran youth; special activities on caravan sites housing new immigrants; and the development of integration awareness and volunteerism. Paralleling Canada's revised multiculturalism policy's new focus on "mutual integration" is the Israeli Ministry of Absorption's much emphasized policy goal of encouraging the active participation of the Israeli public in the absorption of new immigrants through cooperative programs in the community

Ethnic Support Networks

In Canada and in Israel, as in other immigrant-receiving countries, immigrants can often rely on and greatly benefit from support they receive from ethnic organizations and networks established by earlier waves of immigrants of the same origins. This has been especially true for the ex-Soviets and Ethiopian Jews in Israel, and for the Chinese in Canada. Recent Hong Kong immigrants to Canada can readily access official information printed in Chinese, get advice from well-established community organizations, and utilize a range of Chinese social institutions, including newspapers, retailers, and Chinese religious organizations.[33] Similarly, the earlier waves of ex-Soviets in Israel provided a support and access network for later immigration waves.

These earlier groups may provide culturally-sensitive mediators and social service professionals to address problems as they arise, as well as precedents and positive role models for economic and social integration. Questions to research include: Has this resource been explored and tapped as a vehicle for promoting social cohesion? Has the host society (in particular, the government) supported and encouraged community support mechanisms for these latter waves and helped to ensure that they are in fact a positive influence on social cohesion? Have social workers and mentors from the earlier waves of immigrants been called upon to help address problem areas, for example, in relation to school dropouts and juvenile delinquency?

Approaches to Integration — Assimilation Versus Pluralism

Israel faces the challenge of integrating highly assertive and distinctive groups of immigrants who have recently arrived against the backdrop of intense divisions between religious and secular groups, and between radically opposed political positions bearing on the nature and future of the state. In Canada, the recent immigration of significant numbers of "visible minorities," which has resulted in a remarkable demographic transformation particularly in the major urban centers, is superimposed on the ongoing search for a national identity and for ways to address demands for recognition of French Canada as a distinct, more autonomous society, and demands by aboriginal peoples for self-determination.

There are some major differences in the forces and incentives for social cohesion and nation-building in the two countries. In Israel, one looks to the sentiments and powerful symbols of Jewish history, destiny and identity, and external threats to survival. In answering the existential questions, "What is the fundamental purpose for which the country exists, and why keep it together?" there is still some groping in Canada. Given demographic realities in Canada, one will not point to common origins but to other bonding elements such as broad agreement across the country on values relating to political institutions and culture, representational democracy, the rule of law, commitment to collective provision for social needs, equalization of life conditions and chances across regions, and, more recently — and of particular relevance to this discussion — the ideal of pluralism, or accommodation of diversity as embodied in the notion of the "Canadian mosaic."

From the perspective of longer-term nation-building, the view which is increasingly gaining acceptance both in Canada and in Israel is that the pluralist ideal — which entails acknowledgement and respect for the particularities of ethno-racial groups and sustaining their internal communal resources while facilitating their full participation as citizens — will outweigh the merits of an assimilationist option, and that the latter option is in fact not workable given the demographic changes in both countries resulting from recent immigration. A significant and determining factor is the recent politicization of these less assimilable groups of immigrants — the "visible minorities" in Canada, and ex-Soviets and Ethiopians in Israel, as demonstrated in the role and successful showing of the new political party, Yisrael B'Aliya, representing immigrants in the 1996 Israeli election.

The Canadian experience with multiculturalism has served as a kind of testing ground for roles which government can play in accommodating the needs of immigrant and ethnic minority groups in the process of nation-building. For reasons unique to its own political and demographic situation, the Canadian government's multiculturalism policies have evolved through a number of clear phases over the last twenty-five years — from funding cultural folkloristic activities and the teaching of heritage languages, to promoting intercultural communication, to helping to eliminate discrimination and systemic barriers in economic and social spheres, to playing a facilitative role in encouraging grassroots intercultural coalitions. These different approaches to multiculturalism suggest a number of models which merit examination for possible relevance to the needs of other countries such as Israel, which are also facing the challenges of integrating diverse ethnic groups, promoting social cohesion, and forging a sense of national identity. The various approaches are not mutually exclusive; they can alternate or be cumulative and applied to address the needs of immigrant groups at any one time or over time. Different combinations of these approaches may be appropriate in addressing the needs of particular groups of immigrants at different stages of their adaptation and integration into Israeli society.

This chapter describes and raises questions about different policy responses which immigrant-receiving countries have adopted as they try to assure social cohesion in the face of growing social, religious, cultural, racial, and ethnic diversity resulting from immigration. The underlying aim is to integrate the diverse groups, to overcome barriers among them and between them and the mainstream, to build on common values in which all can share and with which they can identify. The conclusion reached, based on experience in Canada and Israel, is that successful integration begins with emphasizing the value of cultural diversity and actively promoting healthy intergroup relations — based on a pluralistic vision of the society, while balancing the merits, acceptability, and feasibility of policies and programs designed to remove barriers and differences over time. In the Israeli "mosaic," this means promoting Ethiopian Jews' sense of pride in their heritage while giving them a sense of belonging to Israeli society, and allowing the present generation of the ex-Soviet community to flourish and contribute, not only as individuals but as a community recreated in the Israeli context.

A premise on which Canada's revised multiculturalism policy rests is that ghettoization and division do not occur in a society because people are different, but because the society in question has not developed mutual respect among groups for each other's distinctiveness and has made difference a reason for divisiveness. Israel's previous Minister of Immigrant Absorption reached a similar conclusion: after expressing pride in his ministry's achievements in housing and employment for the recent massive immigration wave, he acknowledged that there were still problems of social and cultural integration whose solution was contained in one word: "I believe that the key word for successful absorption is 'respect' — respect for the immigrant, for his identity, and the heritage he represents."[34]

Integration of the recent immigration waves to Canada and to Israel involves addressing a range of issues at both the practical and symbolic levels. Policy responses at the practical level may require identifying key existing barriers to economic and social integration, or developing tailored approaches, such as the policy of "preferential treatment" for advancing the integration of Ethiopian immigrants into Israeli society in relation to housing, language instruction, education, health, and social services. At the level of symbols and identity, a range of supportive measures may be needed to enable these groups to maintain their distinctive cultural heritage; to give others in society an appreciation of, and respect for, the immigrants' unique contribution in terms of culture and values; and to give the immigrants a sense of belonging by acknowledging their heritage as an integral part of the national heritage, and allowing them to recognize themselves in the symbols of the society into which they have entered and in which they are to become full participants.

Notes

1. Facts and figures come from Ministry of Absorption reports, "The Absorption of Ethiopian Immigrants in Israel: The Present Situation and Future Objectives," January 1996; and "Situation, Challenges and Goals," April 1996.
2. Survey cited in "Situation, Challenges and Goals," p. 57.
3. Canada's average annual intake of immigrants since the mid-1980s has been about 240,000 for a population of some 29 million; *Facts and Figures: Overview of Immigration*, publication of the Department of Citizenship and Immigration, 1994. Current planning is to limit intake to 190,000-220,000, and Canada's population has reached 30 million.
4. *New Faces in the Crowd*, The Economic Council of Canada, 1991.
5. *Facts and Figures*.
6. According to recent immigration strategies, there has been a shift in focus from annual targets for each of these categories (with the possibility of increasing numbers in one category to compensate for a shortfall in another) to a focus not on numbers but on policy objectives — which currently are to decrease the numbers of immigrants likely to be a burden or not likely to contribute to the economy. Selection criteria have been tightened in a variety of ways: for skilled workers, selected according to a "points" system, the new strategy is to increase the number of points awarded for education and skill levels and to

tighten the assessment of English and French language skills. The Canadian immigration strategy for the coming years includes in its objectives continued support for family reunification for spouses and dependent children, though within an age limit and with the introduction of a separate category for parents and grandparents so that the size of that category can be more controlled — to lessen the likelihood of their use of Canada's social welfare system. *Into the 21st Century: A Strategy for Immigration and Citizenship,* publication of the Department of Citizenship and Immigration, 1994.

7. Naomi Shepherd, "Ex-Soviet Jews in Israel," *Israel Affairs,* vol. 1, no. 2 (Winter 1994).
8. "A World of Their Own," *Jerusalem Report,* 9 December 1994.
9. Naomi Shepherd, "Ex-Soviet Jews in Israel."
10. "The Aliyah Revelations," *Jerusalem Post,* 24 May 1995.
11. Natan Sharansky, "Letting the Genie Out of the Bottle," *Jerusalem Report,* 3 November 1994.
12. "Suddenly its Raining Jews," *Jerusalem Report,* 13 June 1991, citing Daniel Elazar.
13. "Exodus to Isolation: Ethiopians Endure Hardships," *New York Times,* July 1992; "Ethiopian Absorption Proving Anything but Smooth," *Canadian Jewish News,* 3 December 1992; Shula Mula, "What Happens to a Dream Deferred?" *Jerusalem Report,* 21 September 1995; "Welcoming Newcomers Isn't Always So Easy," *New York Times,* 4 February 1996.
14. "Israelis Struggle to Make a Home for Ethiopian Jews," *Christian Science Monitor,* 7 February 1996.
15. The preferential treatment has in fact upset ex-Soviet immigrants who proceeded to petition the High Court of Justice that this was a discriminatory practice. The justices defended the policy on the grounds that the Ethiopians were genuinely impoverished and faced the additional handicap of poor education and a vastly different cultural background, but agreed that classification according to country of origin is a questionable practice. *Jerusalem Post International,* 9 December 1995.
16. Ministry of Absorption report, "Situation, Challenges and Goals." The government has opened a Center for the Preservation of Ethiopian Jewish Culture in Tel Aviv. A number of cities have Ethiopian synagogues and community centers geared to the social and cultural needs of Ethiopians. The non-governmental organization JDC-Joint, which has been very involved in various aspects of the Ethiopian absorption process, has long supported the organization "Betachin" ("Our House") which has employed *kesim,* Ethiopian religious leaders and elders who work to bring about reconciliation between couples according to traditional means of "family therapy."

17. Ministry of Absorption report, "Situation, Challenges and Goals."
18. The poll was carried out for *Jerusalem Report* by the Guttman Institute of Applied Research; *Jerusalem Report,* 13 June 1991.
19. *Jerusalem Report,* 13 June 1991.
20. Equality Now! Task Force (1984) and the Employment Equity Commission (1984).
21. In addition to the wide range of government documentation reviewed for this discussion of multiculturalism in Canada, this account draws from A. Fleras and J.L. Elliot, *Multiculturalism in Canada* (Toronto: Nelson Canada, 1992); L-J. Dorais, et al., "Multiculturalism and Integration," *Immigration and Refugee Policy: Australia and Canada Compared,* ed. Howard Adelman, et al. (Toronto: University of Toronto Press, 1994); Bruce Nesbitt, "Canadian Multiculturalism in the 1990s" (unpublished paper).
22. "Multiculturalism into the Future: Changing Realities, New Directions," A. Fleras and J.L. Elliot, *Multiculturalism in Canada.*
23. Reginald Bibby, *Mosaic Madness* (Toronto: Stoddart, 1990), warns about making a national virtue out of a descriptive reality and taking pluralism to excess. He urges Canadians to discover a national vision and commitment based on interconnectedness and interdependence, rather than adversarial and random coexistence.
24. Bruce Nesbitt, "Canadian Multiculturalism in the 1990s."
25. See entries in *Harvard Encyclopedia of American Ethnic Groups,* ed. Stephan Thernstrom (Boston: Harvard University Press, 1980): Michael Novak, "Humanistic Pluralism"; Michael Walzer, "Political Pluralism"; and Harold J. Abramson, "Assimilation and Pluralism."
26. Dale Maharidge, in *The Coming of the White Minority: California's Eruptions and the Nation's Future* (New York: Times Books, 1996), tries to dispel fears of societal disintegration and violence which might accompany the establishment of substantial ethnic enclaves in California. He points to the fact that remarkably little friction has in fact occurred, and that a striking number of native Californians continue to think that immigrants reinforce rather than undermine what is best in America: "Just when the Protestant work ethic is fading, Asians are introducing a Confucian work ethic; and Latinos are reminding many whites of the virtues of family values and small businesses." Review in *The Economist,* 15 February 1997.
27. Leslie S. Laczko, "Canada's Pluralism in Comparative Perspective," *Ethnic and Racial Studies,* vol. 17, no. 1 (January 1994).
28. Reginald Bibby, *The Bibby Report* (Lethbridge: University of Lethbridge, 1995).
29. One may see a parallel in the highly positive public attitude in Israel regarding the importance of immigration, which had manifested itself at a practical level with wide participation by the Israeli population in

helping Russian immigrants with their initial resettlement needs, and the warm reception given to Ethiopian Jews when they first arrived. Nonetheless, some resentments and problems of stereotyping soon arose.

30. In addressing the conference on Jewish migration at which this review was first presented, Israeli Minister of Absorption Yuli Edelstein (himself an immigrant from the Soviet Union) emphasized the appropriateness of the "ethnic mosaic" model for Israel.

31. Laczko, "Canada's Pluralism."

32. For example, recent Canadian data indicate the proportion of the foreign-born residents for ten years or less receiving welfare assistance is below that of non-immigrants, while foreign-born persons of working age are also less likely to be in receipt of social assistance than non-immigrants of the same age. *New Faces in the Crowd,* The Economic Council of Canada, 1991. Studies of crime in Canada, Australia, and the U.S. in the early 1990s have found that immigrants were in fact under-represented in crime statistics. Allan Borowski, "Immigration and Crime," *Immigration and Refugee Policy: Australia and Canada Compared,* Adelman, et al.

33. D. Lary, C. Inglis, and Chung-Tong Wu, "Hong Kong: A Case Study of   Settlement and Immigration," *Immigration and Refugee Policy: Australia and Canada Compared,* Adelman, et al.

34. Introductory remarks to "Situation, Challenges and Goals."

II

Jewish Migration and Integration in Israel

5

The Wave of Immigration to Israel in the 1990s

Shmuel Adler

The recent wave of immigration that began in the latter half of 1989 was the largest wave of immigration to arrive in Israel (or to Palestine as this land was called until 1948). During this period (1989-May 1996) Israel's population increased by some 16 percent, with the arrival of 800,000 immigrants. The previous large wave arrived during the formative years of the State of Israel (1948-1951) when 688,000 immigrants arrived, doubling the population of the new Jewish state.

Table 5.1 shows that this period can be divided into two parts: from 1990 to 1991 when 375,000 immigrants arrived, and from 1992 to the present when annual immigration stabilized at 70,000-80,000, which is an annual rate in increase of population of some 1.5 percent.

As can be seen in Table 5.2, some 85 percent of the immigrants came from the former Soviet Union (FSU). Thirty-one percent of the immigrants from the FSU came from the Russian Republic and 30 percent from Ukraine (see Table 5.3). In 1995, Ukraine became the major republic of immigration and this trend continued through 1997. Twenty-one percent came from the Caucasian and Asiatic parts of the FSU.

Approximately two-thirds of the immigrants were employed prior to their emigration. The immigrants from the FSU are highly

TABLE 5.1
Immigration to Israel — Yearly Data, 1989-1996

	780,000 People Immigrated to Israel from 1989 to 1996							
Year	1989	1998	1991	1992	1993	1994	1995	1996
No. of immigrants[a]	24,050	199,516	176,100	77,057	76,805	79,844	76,361	70,600

[a] Including potential immigrants
Source: Central Bureau of Statistics

TABLE 5.2
Immigration to Israel by Region of Origin, 1992-1996

Year	1992	1993	1994	1995	1996
Total	77,100	76,800	79,800	76,400	70,600
Former USSR	65,100	66,100	68,100	64,800	58,900
Other Europe	3,900	4,200	4,500	4,100	4,200
North America, Oceana	2,200	2,400	2,600	2,700	2,400
Latin America	800	800	1,000	1,500	2,200
Other	5,100	3,100	3,600	3,300	2,900

Source: Central Bureau of Statistics

educated and many were in professions that demanded higher education (see Table 5.4). The percentage of these professionals has been declining since the beginning of this wave from about 65 percent of those who were employed in the FSU prior to their emigration to about 55 percent in 1996. In the Israeli work force in 1995 only 25 percent were employed in these professions. Among the FSU immigrants, 73,000 declared upon arrival in the country that they were employed as engineers prior to their immigration. In a study initiated in 1995 by the Ministry of Immigrant Absorption of the employment of FSU immigrant engineers below the age of 60 who arrived in Israel between 1989 and 1994, it was found that 97 percent held documentation that they had completed a recognized engineering school and that 93 percent in fact had been employed as engineers prior to their emigration. According to the Labor Force Survey of the Central Bureau of Statistics, there were some 30,000 employed engineers in Israel in 1989. In addition, over 15,000

TABLE 5.3
Immigration to Israel from Former Soviet Union by Republic, 1989-1996

Republic	1989	1990	1991	1992	1993	1994	1995	1996	Total
Russia	3,100	45,500	47,300	24,800	23,100	24,600	15,700	16,450	200,550
	24.0%	25.0%	32.0%	38.0%	35.0%	36.0%	24.0%	28.3%	(30.8%
Ukraine	3,600	58,900	39,800	13,100	12,800	22,700	23,600	23,400	197,900
	28.0%	32.0%	27.0%	20.0%	19.0%	33.0%	36.0%	40.3%	30.4%
Belarus	1,100	23,400	16,000	3,300	2,300	2,900	4,200	4,350	57,550
	9.0%	13.0%	11.0%	5.0%	3.0%	4.0%	6.0%	7.5%	8.8%
Moldova	1,500	11,900	15,400	4,300	2,200	1,900	2,400	2,000	41,600
	12.0%	6.0%	10.0%	7.0%	3.0%	3.0%	4.0%	3.4%	6.4%
Baltic Republics	600	7,400	3,100	1,300	1,800	1,200	1,000	1,150	17,550
	5.0%	4.0%	2.0%	2.0%	3.0%	2.0%	2.0%	2.0%	2.7%
Central Asia, Azerbaijan, Georgia, Armenia	2,800	34,800	25,800	14,000	18,400	14,100	15,500	10,750	136,150
	22.0%	19.0%	17.0%	22.0%	28.0%	21.0%	24.0%	18.5%	20.9%
Unknown	100	3,300	400	4,300	5,500	700	2,400	800	16,700
Total	12,800	185,200	147,800	65,100	66,100	68,100	64,800	58,900	668,000
	100.0%	100.0%	100.0%	100.0%	100.0%	100.0%	100.0%	100.0%	100.0%

Source: Central Bureau of Statistics
Note: percentage frequency does not include "unknown"

TABLE 5.4
Immigrants to Israel from Former Soviet Union by Occupation, 1989-1996

Occupation	1989	1990	1991	1992	1993	1994	1995	1996	Total
Engineers	1,400	24,400	18,500	6,600	5,200	6,000	6,000	5,000	73,000
	10.9%	13.3%	12.5%	10.1%	7.9%	8.8%	9.3%	8.5%	10.9%
Physicians, Dentists	500	5,900	3,500	1,200	1,100	1,000	1,100	900	15,200
	3.9%	3.2%	2.4%	1.8%	1.7%	1.5%	1.7%	1.5%	2.3%
Musicians, Artists	500	4,900	3,500	1,400	1,300	1,300	1,200	1,000	15,100
	3.8%	2.6%	2.4%	2.2%	2.0%	1.9%	1.9%	1.7%	2.3%
Nurses, Paramedical	300	4,100	3,600	1,500	1,700	1,800	1,700	1,400	16,100
	2.3%	2.2%	2.4%	2.3%	2.6%	2.6%	2.6%	2.4%	2.4%
Teachers	500	10,000	7,700	3,100	3,000	3,400	3,200	2,700	33,600
	3.9%	5.4%	5.2%	4.8%	4.5%	5.0%	4.9%	4.6%	5.0%
Total	12,800	185,200	147,800	65,100	66,100	68,100	64,800	58,900	668,000
	100.0%	100.0%	100.0%	100.0%	100.0%	100.0%	100.0%	100.0%	100.0%

Source: Central Bureau of Statistics

physicians and dentists arrived, while only some 14,000 were active in these professions in Israel in 1989.

This large number of people who joined the work force in Israel since 1990 increased the unemployment figures which were relatively high in any case (9.6 percent). Some 46 percent of immigrants above the age of 15 who arrived during 1990-1991 joined the civilian work force and in the last quarter of 1991, 38.5 percent of them were unemployed and sought work. However, by the last quarter of 1995, 52 percent of all the immigrants were in the civilian work force and unemployment among them was 9.6 percent (7 percent for the general population). During the latter half of 1996, unemployment increased in general and during the last quarter of 1996, 11 percent of the immigrants were unemployed with 8 percent unemployment among the general population.

Although unemployment among the immigrants was not much higher than among the general population, and among the more veteran immigrants — those who arrived in 1990-91 — it was a bit lower (7 percent), most of those who had worked in academic professions were not working in their fields of training. Only some 30-40 percent, depending on profession, were engaged in their professions or in fields close to their profession in the FSU. Finding means and ways to engage these people in their professions and utilize the human capital they represent is one of Israel's major challenges today.

In 1989, the median age of FSU immigrants was 32 as compared to 26 for the Israeli population. However, the immigrants to Israel are much younger than the Jewish population remaining in the FSU. It is estimated that the median age of the Jews in the FSU today is 55. Of the immigrants from the FSU, 13.4 percent were 65 or older, as compared to 9 percent among the Israeli population in 1989 (see Table 5.5). The relatively large percentage of elderly immigrants presented the absorption authorities with the challenge of finding them permanent housing solutions. Most of the immigrants, including the elderly, upon arrival in the country utilized the generous rental subsidies offered them. As time went by and the immigrants began finding jobs, they purchased apartments with the aid of government subsidized mortgages. Some bought apartments in partnership with their elderly parents, thus using two mortgages, one for the young family and one for the elderly parent or couple. About one-third of the elderly, mainly singles, found permanent

TABLE 5.5
Immigrants to Israel from Former Soviet Union by Age Group, 1989-1996

Age Group	1989	1990	1991	1992	1993	1994	1995	1996	Total
0-24	4,700	64,600	50,700	23,300	24,700	25,000	23,700	21,600	238,300
	36.7%	34.9%	34.3%	35.8%	37.4%	36.7%	36.5%	36.7%	35.6%
25-44	4,600	64,600	47,000	19,200	18,700	18,700	17,800	16,300	206,900
	35.9%	34.9%	31.8%	29.5%	28.3%	27.5%	27.5%	27.7%	30.9%
45-54	900	15,900	15,000	6,400	5,900	6,300	6,300	6,100	62,800
	7.0%	8.6%	10.1%	9.8%	8.9%	9.3%	9.7%	10.4%	9.4%
55-64	1,000	17,600	14,700	6,700	7,500	8,300	8,300	7,350	71,450
	7.8%	9.5%	9.9%	10.3%	11.3%	12.2%	12.8%	12.4%	10.7%
65+	1,600	22,500	20,400	9,500	9,300	9,800	8,800	7,550	89,450
	12.5%	12.1%	13.8%	14.6%	14.1%	14.4%	13.5%	12.8%	13.4%
Total	12,800	185,200	147,800	65,100	66,100	68,100	64,800	58,900	668,000
	100.0%	100.0%	100.0%	100.0%	100.0%	100.0%	100.0%	100.0%	100.0%

Source: Central Bureau of Statistics

housing by these means. It is estimated that another quarter of the elderly will utilize their eligibility for receiving mortgages together with their children. However for some 40 percent of the elderly the only viable solution will be to provide them with government housing at very highly subsidized rentals. Unfortunately there are very few of this type of apartments in supply. The government has decided to undertake the construction of 3,000 units in hostels over a four-year period, but this is a far cry from the needs. At present this decision is being reevaluated and alternate cheaper solutions are being sought.

There are two additional groups of newcomers in need of public housing — single-parent families and families with members with a serious handicap or who are chronically ill, whose needs cannot be fulfilled.

Will immigration to Israel continue at its present rate? Most experts agree that the present wave of immigration of 45-60,000 immigrants from the FSU and another 10-15,000 from the rest of the world will continue at least until the year 2000, providing that there are no major political, social, or economic changes in the FSU or other countries with major Jewish populations. In the FSU, however, the potential for such changes still exists (see Table 5.6). The estimated population of people who were eligible to enter Israel under the Law of Return by the end of 1996 was 1.1 million. The challenge of fully integrating the present wave of newcomers and those who will be arriving in the next few years, together with trying to attain peace with its neighbors, will be the main items on the agenda both for the Israeli government and Israeli society in the foreseeable future.

TABLE 5.6
Immigration from Former Soviet Union (FSU) — Background

Potential for immigration from FSU (Soviet census 1989)[a]	2,280,000
Thereof: Immigrated to Israel (1989-1996)	668,000
Immigrated to other countries (1989-1996)	366,000
Negative natural increase	217,000
Potential remaining in former FSU	**1,029,000**
– 31 Dec 96[b]	

Republic	Potential as of Soviet Census 1989[a]	Immigrated to Israel 1989-1995	Percent of which immigrated to Israel	Remainder in FSU (est.)[b]	Percent of remainder in FSU from potential in 1989
Russia	920,000	200,550	24.0	504,000	54.8
Ukraine	736,000	197,900	26.9	270,000	36.7
Belarus	169,000	57,550	34.1	38,500	22.8
Moldova	84,000	41,600	49.5	14,300	17.0
Baltic Republics	64,000	17,550	27.4	31,000	48.4
Central Asia, Azerbaijan, Georgia, Armenia	307,000	136,150	44.3	171,200	55.8
Unknown		16,700			
Total	2,280,000	668,000	29.3	1,029,000	45.1

Source: Liaison Office and Ministry of Immigrant Absorption. The Liaison Office data are based on estimates that are updated from time to time.
[a] Eligible for immigration in accordance with the Law of Return
[b] 1989 potential less immigrants to Israel and other countries and negative natural increase

Bibliography

Central Bureau of Statistics — State of Israel. 1990-1996. *Statistical Abstracts*. Nos. 41-46.

Ministry of Immigrant Absorption — State of Israel. April, 1996. *Immigrant Absorption — Situation, Challenges and Goals*.

Ministry of Immigrant Absorption — State of Israel. June, 1997. *Immigrant Absorption — Situation, Challenges and Goals*.

6

The Current Wave of Former Soviet Union Immigrants: Their Absorption Process in Israel — An On-Going Survey (1990-1995)*

Natalia Damian
Yehudit Rosenbaum-Tamari

Introduction

Israel's demographic make-up is virtually unique in that Israel is not only a country with immigrants, but essentially a country of immigrants.[1] Indeed, statistical evidence indicates that immigration has been, and still remains, one of the main sources of population increase in Israel, whose Jewish population grew from 649,600 upon the establishment of the state (15 May 1948) to 3,373,200 in 1982, and 4,441,100 in 1994 (*Statistical Abstract of Israel*, 1995: 43). Immigration accounted for more than 2,443,325 persons, or approximately 55 percent of this increase. In 1994, 39 percent of the Israeli population was foreign born, and 76 percent of the inhabitants were either immigrants or immigrants' children (*Statistical Abstract of Israel*, 1995:98).

The size and structure of the Soviet Jews' immigration to Israel varied over time, the yearly average for 1970-1979 being 14,794 persons, and, as a result of Soviet authorities' restrictive policy towards emigration, dropped in the years 1980-1989 to less than 3,000 persons per year (*Immigration to Israel*, 1994:32). The current wave of immigration from the former Soviet Union began by the end of 1989, and it represents the largest immigration to arrive in Israel (or the former Palestine).

In the years 1989-1996, some 730,000 immigrants arrived in the country — most of them from the former Soviet Union — increasing its total population by 15 percent (Adler, S., 1996). With the beginning of this wave of new immigrants, an on-going survey on the processes of their absorption in Israel was initiated by the Ministry of Immigrant Absorption. The survey was started in 1990, and is being carried out by the authors of this summary report.[2]

Goals and Study Design

The main goals of this research are as follows:

1. To supply a thorough comprehension of what motivated such unprecedented masses of Jews to leave their country of origin and settle in Israel.

2. To provide detailed and updated information on the extremely complex and manifold absorption process of these new immigrants in various spheres, such as housing, employment, language acquisition, social integration, etc.

3. To identify the main difficulties encountered by the new immigrants during their first years in Israel, and look for appropriate ways to meet their needs.

4. To identify the factors which are influencing the immigrants' absorption process in various spheres, as well as their general adaptation and their decision to stay in Israel or reemigrate.

5. To evaluate the "Direct Absorption Track" itself — that is, examine to what extent the main goals of this new track were achieved.[3]

The Target Population and the Samples

All immigrant families that arrived in Israel from the former Soviet Union during a given period of time (a specific month in different years), and were absorbed by the "direct absorption track," constitute the target population of this study. Four stratified samples of about 1,100 family heads each were drawn from the files of the Computer Department, Ministry of Immigrant Absorption. They represent all immigrant families that arrived in November 1989, July 1990, September 1991, and January-March 1995. The main characteristics of each sample (geographical distribution in Israel, marital status, age, sex, occupation, etc.) closely match those reported for the target population.

Procedure

Each individual in the sample is investigated at different stages of stay in Israel: during the first year after immigration (some six months in the country), after a year and a half to two years, after three and a half years, and, finally, after five years. The interviews are carried out by trained interviewers at the respondents' home with the help of questionnaires comprising closed-ended questions. All the questionnaires were translated into Russian, their identity with the Hebrew version being ascertained. Each questionnaire includes about 140 items, some of the measures being different according to the length of time in Israel, while others remaining identical in the four questionnaires. For instance, the first interview concentrates on immigrants' socio-demographic characteristics, and on the factors influencing the respondents' decision to immigrate to Israel. Also investigated is their initial process of absorption (first contacts with Israelis and the Israeli support system, first arrangements in housing, beginning of Hebrew language studies, etc.). Subsequent interviews, using mainly identical measures, follow up the process of absorption in various spheres — work, housing, command of Hebrew language, social integration, etc. Finally, the last interview (five years after immigration) is mostly dedicated to the in-depth analysis of respondents' general adaptation, their degree of commitment to Israel, and their future prospects. To assess the immigrants' Jewish and Israeli identity, the motives behind their decision to leave the former Soviet Union and settle in Israel, as well as their general adaptation, some composite measures — all based on the respondents' reports — were used (see Appendix).

To determine the similarities/differences between different groups of immigrants in the process of their absorption (starting with the second investigated group), the situation of each group at a given period of time is compared with the situation of all the other previously investigated groups at a similar length of stay in Israel (six months, one and a half to two years, three and a half years, and five years). Furthermore, to accurately examine the changes which occurred in each group of respondents' situation, those respondents who did not answer all the previous questionnaires and the last one were eliminated from the analysis. Thus, for instance, the research reports after three and a half years in Israel refer exclusively to those respondents who answered our questionnaires six months, one and a half to two years, and three and a half years after their arrival. Similarly, after five years, the data exclusively include those individuals who answered all of our questionnaires.

Whenever possible, our results were compared with general statistical data of the Central Bureau of Statistics, as well as with other current research results on similar topics. For a better understanding of the "direct absorption" track characteristics, comparisons were also made with the Soviet immigrants' absorption process in the 1970s (when almost all of them began their absorption process in absorption centers).

Results

Motivation for Migration: Jewish Identity and Immigration to Israel

The successful integration of immigrants into their new society is usually related not only to the absorption capacities of the host country, and the newcomers' demographic and socio-economic characteristics, but to their ideological motivations and willingness to integrate themselves in their new society as well. This is particularly true for immigration to Israel which, as already mentioned, is unique in that it is national in character — diaspora Jews are returning to their ancestral homeland.

However, shortly after the beginning of the current wave of immigration from the former Soviet Union,[4] the Israeli mass media, and some social scientists as well, gave voice to a different opinion, claiming that this particular case represents a type of "lack of alternative choice" emigration from an unstable society, due exclusively to "push" motives, rather than aliya. It was claimed that these new immigrants' commitment to the Jewish people and Jewish values played a negligible role, if any.[5]

With the rapid and substantial increase in the number of Soviet immigrants, by the fall of 1990 it was decided to include in our questionnaires specific measures dedicated to a thorough examination of these aspects. Starting with the first interview of immigrants who arrived in September 1991, each of our questionnaires (for six months in the country) includes a block of some 40 questions concerning respondents' economic and professional situation in their country of origin, evaluations of the intensity of anti-Semitism, degree of satisfaction with housing, work and social life, and the motives behind the Jews leaving the Soviet Union and coming to Israel. In addition, multi-item measures concentrating on respondents' ethnic and national identities were included in all of our questionnaires.

Based on the rationale delineated by Herman (1977), our attempts to measure immigrants' Jewish identity concentrated on the affective level.[6] More precisely, respondents' Jewish identity was operationally defined in terms of (a) an individual's strong positive feelings towards his/her ethnicity, and (b) his/her strong feeling of solidarity with the Jewish people. According to this definition, two composite measures were elaborated. Factor analysis ascertained that the items used in the questionnaires belonged to the same content universe (see Appendix). Survey data indicate that the respondents' global index of Jewishness, as calculated from the two multi-item measures, is quite similar for the two independent samples of immigrants, those arrived in September 1991 and those who came during January-March 1995. Furthermore, the findings indicate that there are indeed differences in the immigrants' feelings towards their Jewishness and their solidarity with the Jewish people, as compared with the overall Jewish population of Israel.[7] These differences, however, are far from being as dramatic as one would expect to find if these immigrants are not to be considered as properly *olim*. Some 44-52 percent of the immigrants were found to have a high index of commitment to their Jewishness, and 56-59 percent were characterized by a strong positive feeling of solidarity with the Jewish people.[8] Among veteran Israelis the figures were 67 percent ("Jewishness"), and 73 percent ("Solidarity") (see Table 6.1).

As we would suspect, the survey data indicate that our respondents displayed different and complex motivations for choosing to leave their country of origin and emigrate elsewhere. Furthermore, the findings suggest that, for most of them, Israel appeared to be the favored target. Some 75-80 percent of each interviewed group reported their coming to Israel out of choice. Similarly, about 70 percent declared that, when considering emigration from the former Soviet Union, they were not interested in migrating elsewhere in the West. Moreover, when asked "if you would have to decide today to immigrate to Israel, would you do so?," in 88-90 percent of cases the answer was "yes."[9]

Subsequent analysis of respondents' reasons for emigration, as reported by themselves, indicate that their decision was affected by five main categories of motives or factors: 1. the situation of Jews in the USSR; 2. the economic and political situation in the Soviet Union; 3. willingness to come to Israel; 4. concern for one's children's future; 5. interest in migrating elsewhere in the West (see Appendix).

Three of the above mentioned factors for migration (nos. 1, 3, 4) appear to be related to Jewishness and Israel, and could thus be considered as characterizing "aliya," and "immigration to Israel," while the other two (nos. 2, 5) represent reasons for any emigration. Furthermore, it was found that among all the reported motives for migration, those related to Jewishness and Israel rank higher in the respondents' hierarchy of reasons. As selected figures in Table 6.2 indicate, the three most important motives, as ranked by the respondents themselves — "concern for the welfare of one's children," "willingness to live as a Jew in a Jewish environment," and "desire to bring up one's children in Israel" — are indeed specific to immigration to Israel and not to any emigration.[10]

The study also investigated the factors influencing the respondents' motives for emigration. As figures in Table 6.3 indicate, the decision to come to Israel highly correlates with one's religiosity,

TABLE 6.1
**Feelings Towards Jewishness and Solidarity with the Jewish People:
Immigrants and the Overall Israeli Jewish Population**
(percentages)

Respondents' feelings towards their Jewishness*

Global Score Population Groups	Low (5-9)	Medium (10-15)	High (16-20)	Total
Immigrants arrived in September 1991	4	44	52	100
Immigrants arrived in July 1990	2	54	44	100
Israeli Jewish Population, 1992	4	29	67	100

Solidarity with the Jewish people**

Global Score Population Groups	Low (4-8)	Medium (9-12)	High (13-16)	Total
Immigrants arrived in September 1991	7	37	56	100
Immigrants arrived in July 1990	7	34	59	100
Israeli Jewish Population, 1992	5	22	73	100

*   Index which included 5 variables (see Appendix). Each item was scored 1 to 4 according to whether the subject agreed or disagreed. Thus, respondents' scores fall in a range from 5 to 20; the higher the score, the stronger positive Jewish feelings expressed by the respondent.

** This index included 4 variables, each of them being scored 1 to 4 according to its extent of influence as reported by the respondents. Individuals' final scores range from 4 to 16, a high score indicating a strong feeling of solidarity.

strong positive feelings toward the Jewish people, and the acknowledgment of the centrality of the State of Israel in the life of the Jews. Significant correlation was also found between the respondents' decision to choose Israel and their previous knowledge about the main specific rights provided to *olim*.

In contrast, it was found that one's desire to emigrate to Western democratic countries strongly correlates with other factors, namely, age (relatively young), education (relatively high), existence of kinsmen/friends in a Western country, and lack of previous information on immigrants' rights in Israel.

TABLE 6.2
Motivations for Emigration by their Degree of Importance
as Evaluated by the Immigrants

Motives for Emigration*	Mean Score** Immigrants	
	Sept. 1991	Jan.-March 1995
Motives Specific to Aliya		
"Push" Motives		
Discrimination against Jews in the USSR	3.50	2.89
Anti-Semitism in the USSR	2.81	1.89
"Pull" Motives		
Concern for the welfare of one's children	3.51	3.10
Desire to bring up one's children in Israel	2.87	2.64
Willingness to live as a Jew in a Jewish environment	3.00	2.87
Desire for being close to one's kinsmen/friends in Israel	2.30	2.64
Motives for Any Migration		
"Push" Motives		
Economic situation in the USSR	2.75	3.04
Political situation in the USSR	2.70	2.72
"Pull" Motives		
Lack of opportunities to emigrate elsewhere than to Israel	1.60	1.25
Willingness to live in a Western democratic society	2.83	2.58
Expectations to improve one's standard of living	2.20	2.18

*   Selected questions.
** For each motive respondents were asked to specify its degree of importance
     when deciding to emigrate. Each item was scored 1 to 4 according to its degree
     of importance as evaluated by the respondents, "4" meaning "very important,"
     and "1" "not at all important."

TABLE 6.3
Factors Influencing the Russian Jews' Motives for Aliya/Emigration*

1. Aliya – Willingness to come to Israel		
Factor	**Beta****	**Sig.T*****
Religiosity	.19	.00
Feeling Jewish rather than a son or daughter of his/her country of origin (in the former USSR)	.18	.00
Acknowledgment of the Israeli state's centrality in the life of the Jews (1)	.16	.00
Detailed information about "absorption basket" and customs grant for *olim*	.15	.00
General satisfaction (in the former Soviet Union) (2)	-.13	.00
Solidarity with the Jewish people (1)	.12	.00
	R Square Change: .30	
	Signif. F Change: .00	

2. Aliya – Willingness to bring up one's children in Israel		
Factor	**Beta**	**Sig.T**
Positive feelings towards one's Jewish ethnicity (1)	.15	.00
Religiosity	.13	.00
Acknowledgment of the Israeli state's centrality in the life of the Jews	.11	.00
Dissatisfied with the situation of the Jews in the former USSR (3)	.12	.00
Detailed information about life in Israel	.10	.00
	R Square Change: .21	
	Signif. F Change: .00	

3. Emigration – Interest in migrating elsewhere in the West		
Factor	**Beta**	**Sig.T**
Age (relatively young)	.31	.00
Lack of information on immigrants' rights in Israel	.16	.00
Education	.11	.00
Lack of information about "absorption basket" and customs grant for *olim*	.15	.00
Kinsmen/friends living in a Western country	.10	.00
	R Square Change: .24	
	Signif. T Change: .00	

*   Multiple Regression Analysis — Immigrants arrived in January-March 1995.
**   Standardized regression coefficient (indicating the relative influence of each independent variable when all the others are kept constant).
***   Degree of Significance.
(1)   See Appendix.
(2)   Multi-items measure including "Satisfaction with standard of living," "Satisfaction with income," "Satisfaction with housing," and "Satisfaction with social life."
(3)   Composite variable including "Lack of satisfaction with the opportunities of living a Jewish life," and "Lack of satisfaction with freedom of speech."

Absorption Processes: Different Periods of Arrival, Same Length of Stay in Israel

As mentioned earlier, the first interview (six months after immigration), concentrates mainly on immigrant motives for aliya, and their first steps in Israel. More precisely, the accent is on their first arrangements in housing (where did they go from the airport, how many days/weeks did they spend looking for an apartment, who helped them in finding it, etc.), their beginning of Hebrew language studies, their initial exploration of the Israeli labor market, and their first contacts with veteran Israelis. Other aspects of their absorption processes, such as finding a permanent dwelling, a suitable place of work, and an appropriate niche within their new society, are profoundly examined in subsequent interviews. However, since our survey is a longitudinal one, aiming to measure the changes occurring over time in an immigrant situation, the main indicators of the absorption process, as a whole, were included in the first questionnaire as well. The data in Table 6.4 refer exclusively to these indicators. It should also be noted that Table 6.4 does not include any inter-group comparison for five years in Israel. That is because until now, only two immigrant groups were interviewed after a five-year period, those who arrived in July 1990 and September 1991. (The data for September 1991 are currently being analyzed.)

Given the rapid and substantial increase in the number of immigrants by the beginning of 1990,[11] and the significant pressure exerted upon the absorption capacities of such a small country as Israel, we would expect to find the absorption process of the immigrants arrived in 1990, 1991, or later, much more problematic

TABLE 6.4
**Absorption Processes — Immigrants Who Arrived in November 1989,
July 1990, September 1991, January-March 1995**
(Selected Measures)

	6 Months in Israel	1.5–2 Years in Israel	3.5 Years in Israel
A. Absorption in Housing			
Permanent Dwelling*			
(Percentages)			
November 1989	1	13	**
July 1990	1	15	51
September 1991	–	24	53
January-March 1995	6	**	**
1970s Immigrants (Arrived in 1978/79)***	–	–	91
Average Density (persons per room)			
November 1989	1.3	1.1	**
July 1990	1.3	1.4	1.3
September 1991	1.5	1.4	1.2
January-March 1995	1.5	**	**
Satisfied with housing ("definitely or fairly")			
November 1989	75	80	**
July 1990	69	61	65
September 1991	43	53	68
January-March 1995	55	**	**
1970s Immigrants (Arrived in 1978/79)	–	–	81
B. Absorption at Work			
Employed persons (% from those belonging to the labor force)			
November 1989	5	76	**
July 1990	24	76	89
September 1991	27	72	90
January-March 1995	62	**	**
1970s Immigrants (Arrived in 1978/79)	–	–	87

*   Includes family-owned apartment and public housing. It is important to mention here that in the 1970s, for most of the immigrants "permanent dwelling" meant "public housing," while today it means "family-owned apartments" (see Table 6.5).

TABLE 6.4 (cont.)

	6 Months in Israel	1.5–2 Years in Israel	3.5 Years in Israel
Satisfied with work			
(% "definitely or fairly")			
November 1989	Not	64	**
July 1990	asked	61	66
September 1991	43	52	52
January-March 1995	36	**	**
1970s Immigrants	–	–	71
(Arrived in 1978/79)			
C. Hebrew Acquisition			
Studied Hebrew in Ulpan (% "Yes")			
(special courses for immigrants)			
November 1989	78	82	**
July 1990	81	84	Not
September 1991	75	78	asked
January-March 1995	67	**	**
1970s Immigrants	–	–	68
(Arrived in 1978/79)			
Speaking Ability			
(% "fluently" or "almost")			
November 1989	13	26	**
July 1990	7	47.	53
September 1991	4	45	49
January-March 1995	7	**	**
1970s Immigrants	–	–	42
(Arrived in 1978/79)			
Hebrew Usage			
(% "only" or "mainly")			
November 1989	Not asked	13	**
July 1990	4	9	13
September 1991	1	6	7
January-March 1995	3	**	**
1970s Immigrants	–	–	11
(Arrived in 1978/79)			

** Immigrants who arrived in November 1989 were interviewed only after 6 months and 1.5-2 years in Israel. For those arrived in January-March 1995, second interview completed in 1996 (research report forthcoming), and third interview planned for 1998.

TABLE 6.4 (cont.)

	6 Months in Israel	1.5–2 Years in Israel	3.5 Years in Israel
D. Social Absorption			
Frequency of meetings with immigrants of their country (% "often")			
November 1989	59	64	**
July 1990	79	61	72
September 1991	51	61	67
January-March 1995	43	**	**
1970s Immigrants (Arrived in 1978/79)	–	–	45
Frequency of meetings with veteran Israelis (% "often")			
November 1989	12	17	**
July 1990	7	11	19
September 1991	5	11	20
January-March 1995	10	**	**
1970s Immigrants (Arrived in 1978/79)	–	–	5
Satisfied with social life ("definitely or fairly")			
November 1989	82	76	**
July 1990	32	57	69
September 1991	42	59	64
January-March 1995	48	**	**
1970s Immigrants (Arrived in 1978/79)	–	–	63
Evaluating Israelis' attitudes towards new immigrants as "good" (% "really" or "quite")			
November 1989	85	79	**
July 1990	76	49	42
September 1991	42	33	40
January-March 1995	39	**	**

*** Central Bureau of Statistics, 1986.

than it was for those who came earlier (i.e., by the fall of 1989). The survey data, however, indicate that our initial assumption is somewhat questionable.

First of all, survey data examined here indicate that, with one single exception (average density of dwelling and satisfaction with housing related to it), after one and a half to two years in the country, the objective situation of the three investigated groups is quite similar, no matter when they arrived in Israel.

Secondly, the data referring exclusively to 6 months after immigration show, in addition to the gradual worsening in the immigrants' living conditions, a decrease in the percentage of persons studying Hebrew among the immigrants who arrived in 1991 and 1995, as compared with those who arrived in 1989-1990. At the same time, an increase in the percentage of employed persons (among the same immigrants) could be observed. These conjugated findings seem to stand for the assumption that the new track of "direct absorption" grants to new immigrants the freedom of choice not only to decide where to live in Israel, but also to establish their own priorities within the complex process of their absorption — in this case, to postpone their Hebrew studies and start to work as soon as possible after their arrival.[12]

Third, it could be observed that, three years after their arrival, the percentage of employed persons among the 1990s immigrants and among those arrived in the 1970s is quite similar. However, the absorption process of these two waves of immigrants appears to be different in four important ways:

(a) The proportion of immigrants living in "permanent housing" is substantially lower today than it was in the 1970s: 51-53 percent, as compared with 91 percent. As will also be seen, this difference is related to the change in government housing policies, and to the immigrants' subsequent efforts to solve this problem by themselves. More precisely, in the 1970s most of the immigrants were provided with "public housing," while today they are encouraged (by heavily subsidized mortgage) to purchase their own apartment. Among the above mentioned groups, 44 percent of the immigrants who arrived in July 1990, and 50 percent of those who arrived in September 1991, were living in family-owned apartments three and a half years after their arrival, as compared with 31 percent of the immigrants who arrived in 1978/80 (after three years in Israel). About 60 percent of the 1970s immigrants were living in public housing three years after their arrival; today, this percentage has been reduced to 3-7 percent. This situation, associated with the relatively high density of the 1990s immigrant apartments (1.2-1.3 persons per room), could explain the significant differences in immigrants' satisfaction with their housing: 65-68 percent today, as compared with 81 percent in the 1970s.

(b) In the sphere of Hebrew acquisition (formal studies and command of the Hebrew language), the situation appears to be, in a way, better today than it was in the 1970s. Some 49 to 53 percent of our respondents, as compared with 42 percent of the 1970s immigrants declared that they can speak Hebrew "fluently" or "almost fluently" three and a half years after their arrival. However, the same discrepancy which was observed in the 1970s between immigrants' Hebrew-speaking ability and their daily use of this language continues to persist among the current wave of immigrants as well.

(c) The current immigrants seem to be less socially isolated than those who arrived in the 1970s, the frequency of their social encounters (with immigrants of their country of origin, and other veterans and Israeli-born as well) being substantially higher. It should also be noted that, despite the fact that the percentage of respondents stating that they meet frequently with veteran Israelis is still relatively low, 19-20 percent (in the 1970s it barely reached 5 percent), more than 90 percent of these contacts are quite close and informal ones, at the respondents' or at their friends' home.

(d) Despite the above-mentioned similarity in the rate of employment, after a three to three and a half year period in Israel, the 1990s immigrants are less satisfied with their job than those who arrived in the 1970s. This is undoubtedly due to the immigrants' occupational mobility, which today essentially means, more than in the 1970s, downward mobility (see Table 6.5).

Finally, the data in Table 6.4 indicate that, with the substantial increase in the number of immigrants after 1990, veteran Israeli attitudes toward them were perceived as being less friendly than they were at the beginning of this wave. During their first months in the country, the percentage of respondents evaluating veteran Israelis' attitudes toward the new immigrants as being "really or quite good" dropped from 85 percent among the immigrants who arrived in November 1989, to 42 percent among those who came in September 1991, and to 39 percent for those who arrived in Janu-

TABLE 6.5
Absorption Processes — Immigrants Who Arrived in July 1990
(Selected Measures)

	1.5-2 Years in Israel	3.5 Years in Israel	5 Years in Israel	1970s Immigrants*
A. Absorption in Housing				
Permanent Dwelling	15	51	79	96
(Percentages)				
Family-owned apt.	10	44	70	41
Public Housing	5	7	9	55
Average Density	1.4	1.3	1.1	–
(persons per room)				
Satisfied with housing	61	65	79	80
(% "definitely" or "fairly")				
B. Absorption at Work				
Employed persons	76	89	95	96
(% of those belonging to the labor force)				
Occupation:				
Scientific, academic	8	19	24	15
Other professional and technical	11	19	11	18
Skilled and unskilled	62	43	43	39
Other (sales, service, etc.)	19	19	22	18
DELTA Index**	–	35	30	12
Satisfied with work	61	66	67	76
(% "definitely" or "fairly")				
Evaluating economic and occupational future opportunities as "good" (% "really" or "fairly")				
For themselves	–	24	30	–
For the next generation in their family	–	66	80	–

TABLE 6.5 (cont.)

	1.5-2 Years in Israel	3.5 Years in Israel	5 Years in Israel	1970s Immigrants*
C. Hebrew Acquisition				
Speaking Ability (% fluently or almost)	47	53	64	55
Understand...(in Hebrew) (% fluently or almost)				
A simple conversation	–	–	67	65
Theater plays	–	–	43	45
Discussions on radio and television	–	–	51	46
Translations on radio/TV	–	–	40	58
Hebrew Usage (% "only" or "mainly")				
At work	52	56	63	82
With children	1	3	3	21
With spouse	1	1	1	–
Reading newspapers	2	3	4	–
Listening to radio	4	8	11	–
D. Social Absorption				
Frequency of meetings with immigrants of their country (% "often")	61	72	58	42
Frequency of meetings with veteran Israelis (% "often")	11	19	22	9
Satisfied with social life (% "definitely" or "fairly")	57	69	72	66
Evaluating Israelis' attitudes towards new immigrants as "good" (% "really" or "quite")	49	42	58	–

*　Immigrants who arrived in 1973/74, 5 Years in Israel (CBS, 1982).
**　The Delta Index of Dissimilarity indicates the differences between two occupational distributions. It is the percentage of cases in one distribution which have to be shifted to a different category so as to obtain the same distribution (Duncan, O.D., Duncan, B. 1955:494; Katz, R. 1983: 669).

ary-March 1995. Three and a half years after immigration, this proportion still remains around 40 percent (immigrants who arrived in July 1990, and September 1991). Invariably, around 40 percent of all the investigated immigrants, who came between 1990 and 1995, defined the veterans' attitudes towards the newcomers as being "cold" (six months, one and a half to two years, and three and a half years after immigration).

Absorption in Housing

The proportion of immigrants living in permanent housing rose from 15 percent, one and a half to two years after their arrival, to 50 percent in their fourth year in the country, and to almost 80 percent after five years in Israel. Although this percentage is substantially lower then it was among the 1970s immigrants, when almost all of them (96 percent) were living in permanent housing five years after their arrival, it should be pointed out that in the 1970s only 41 percent of the immigrants were living in dwellings owned by their family, while 55 percent of them were found in public housing. Today, the situation is substantially different; some 9 percent of our respondents are living in public housing, while 80 percent are in family-owned dwellings. Additional in-depth data analysis, however, revealed that some 20 percent of our respondents (most of them elderly unemployed people, arriving alone, or single-parent families) cannot solve the acute problem of their permanent housing by themselves and are still waiting for more substantial help from the Israeli authorities.

As for ownership of major durable goods, the immigrant situation five years after immigration is similar to that of the overall Israeli population: approximately 90 percent own washing machines and color televisions, and 50 percent own private cars.

Housing density has also improved over time, from an average density of 1.4 persons per room after one and a half to two years in Israel, to 1.3 persons per room after three and a half years in Israel, and to 1.1 persons per room after five years in Israel.[13] Despite the fact that present housing density for immigrants is lower than it was in their country of origin (1.3 persons per room, according to their own report), it is still slightly higher than that of the total

Jewish population of Israel: 1.0 persons per room (CBS, *Statistical Abstract of Israel*, 1995:341).

The percentage of satisfied ("definitely" or "fairly") with their housing among our July 1990 respondents increased from 61 percent after one and a half to two years in the country to 65 percent after three and a half years, and to 79 percent five years after immigration (quite similar with that found among Soviet immigrants in the 1970s five years after their arrival in Israel).

Occupational Absorption

Our findings, as well as the general statistical data of the CBS and other research findings, clearly indicate that immigrant occupational absorption, while being the area with the most spectacular achievements, is also the one associated with great hardships and frustrating difficulties. This situation may be best understood through at least two other factors: immigrant labor force characteristics versus that of veteran Israelis, and the large-scale effort on the part of Israeli authorities to absorb the new immigrants into the country's economy.

It should be noted first that the proportion of immigrants who had been working in their country of origin is substantially higher than that of veteran Israelis. Sixty-six percent of the total FSU immigrants (aged 15+) who arrived in Israel in the years between 1990 and 1994 were employed before their emigration (CBS, No. 9 1995:93).

By the end of 1989 (that is, at the beginning of the current wave of immigration), the figures for the total Israeli population (also aged 15+) were 52 percent of the civilian labor force, with 8.9 percent unemployed (CBS, *Statistical Abstract of Israel*, 1995:355).

An even more important factor, the new immigrants' occupational structure, applies significant pressure upon the Israeli economy's absorption capacities, particularly in certain specific fields such as technical and medical professions. Thus at the end of 1989 there were some 27,000 engineers and 11,000 physicians in Israel (CBS 1990:218); by the end of 1995, the new wave of immigration brought into the country an additional 68,100 engineers and 14,300 physicians and dentists (Ministry of Immigrant Absorption 1996:9). Sixty-eight percent of all the FSU immigrants (aged 15+) who arrived during the period 1990-1994 were employed abroad in the two "top" occupational categories — scientific and academic work, and other professional and technical work (CBS 1995, 9:93). The figure for the Israeli population (also aged 15+) by the end of 1989, before the present wave of immigration, was 25 percent of total employed persons (CBS, *Statistical Abstract of Israel*, 1995:380).

For the absorption authorities to ensure jobs, especially jobs that suited the skills and occupations of such an unprecedented wave of new immigrants, proved to be a most serious challenge. It should be emphasized that in Israel, as in every free-market country, employment is generally a function of supply and demand. Therefore, individual initiative in job-finding continues to play an important role, but, under the new situation, it is far from being an essential and sufficiently efficient one. Therefore, in order to assist new immigrants in finding suitable employment, the Ministry of Absorption, in conjunction with the Ministry of Labor, the local authorities, and other state or private agencies, launched a varied and complex series of programs, including professional retraining courses, in-service training programs, loans and grants for salaried and self-employed persons.

Are these programs efficacious? Can immigrant occupational absorption be summed up as a success, or at least a partial one? Our survey data (Table 6.5 above) show that the percentage of employed people, from those belonging to the labor force, rises from 76 percent after one and a half to two years in Israel, to 89 percent after three and a half years in the country.[14] Five years after their immigration, this percentage is as high as 95 percent, i.e., quite similar to that found among the 1970s immigrants (96 percent after five years), and slightly higher than that of the overall Israeli population (aged 15+) in 1995 (94 percent).

The area of immigrant occupational mobility appears to be much more problematic. It is well known that, not only in Israel but in most other contemporary societies, immigration implies, at least during the initial absorption period, a substantial shift from the occupations held abroad to other ones in the host country (Katz, R., 1983:345-356; Damian, N., 1984:338-341). However, the data in Table 6.5 indicate that for current immigrants this "shift" clearly means downward mobility and, in addition, a more drastic and lasting one than was noted among the Soviet immigrants of the 1970s.

Thus, 65 percent of the July 1990 respondents were employed abroad in academic, scientific, and other professional, technical and related works,[15] whereas only 19 percent were working in these fields after one and a half to two years in Israel. As would be expected, this percentage increases with time in Israel, but five years after immigration it did not reach more than 35 percent.[16] However, it should be noted that this proportion is higher than that found among all Israeli employed persons in 1994, which is 26 percent (CBS, *Statistical Abstract of Israel*, 1995:380).

The acute difficulties encountered by the immigrants in finding employment in their previous occupational field undoubtedly explain the relatively low percentage of July 1990 respondents satisfied with their work. Despite a slight increase with length of time in Israel (from 61 percent after one and a half to two years, to 66 percent after three and a half years, and 67 percent after five years), this percentage is significantly lower than what was found among the 1970s immigrants (76 percent "definitely" or "fairly" satisfied after five years in Israel). It should also be noted that, when compared with indicators referring to immigrant satisfaction with their housing absorption process, their satisfaction with work remains invariably lower over time.

Furthermore, and typical of any other immigration movement, the data in Table 6.5 indicate that present immigrants relate to themselves as to a "sacrificed generation," their expectations for a better future in Israel being transferred to their family offspring. Five years after their arrival, 70 percent of respondents pessimistically evaluate their own economic and professional perspectives as looking "bad" or "rather bad," while 80 percent of them appreciate the same perspectives as being "good" or "fairly good" for the next generation in the family.

Hebrew Acquisition

Almost all the immigrants who came from the FSU in the years 1989-1995 (98-99 percent) arrived in Israel without any previous knowledge of the Hebrew language. This fact, in conjunction with their rather spectacular performance in Hebrew acquisition, undoubtedly indicates the high motivation of these immigrants for acquiring the host language. These motives, however, as the selected data in Table 6.5 clearly show, appear to be rather instrumental in character, that is, intimately bound up with the newcomers' compelling urge "to manage" in their new society. More precisely, our findings indicate that there are at least two distinctive dimensions related to immigrant language performance: (a) the first dimension refers to "passive ability" (Hebrew understanding) as compared to "active ability" (Hebrew usage); (b) the second refers to the "compulsory/elementary level" of Hebrew understanding (and/or usage — such as "a simple conversation") as compared to the "higher/cultural level" ("understanding theater plays"). This holds true for the 1970s immigrants as well as for the 1990s ones. Thus, both then and now, more than 65 percent of the investigated immigrants declared, five years after their arrival, that they "can understand a simple conversation in Hebrew," while no more than 43-45 percent acknowledged their ability to accurately "understand a theater play" in this language. The same "instrumental" motives could be detected in immigrants' answers regarding the circumstances of their Hebrew usage; 82 percent of the 1970s Soviet immigrants and 63 percent of the July 1990 respondents declared that they use Hebrew ("only" or "mainly") at their place of work; with spouse, children, and friends, they continue, even after five years in Israel, to use their mother tongue.[17]

Social Integration

Social integration, by its very nature, differs from housing or employment absorption in two significant respects. It is not to be measured within the scope of a few months or years; social integration is an extended process which may last for many years, or even span several generations. Further, the principal efforts in this area cannot be exerted by absorption authorities; rather, social integration involves both the immigrants and the absorbing society. Its success is decisively contingent upon the veteran society's receptiveness towards immigrants, on the one hand, and on the development of a feeling of identification on the part of the immigrants with their new surroundings, on the other (Rosenbaum, Y., 1977:9; Gitelman, Z., 1982:151; Damian, N., 1985:514).

To assess the social integration of the current FSU immigrants, the following measures — all based on the respondents' reports — were used:

1. Frequency of social contacts with immigrants and veterans from their country, as well as with Israeli-born, and immigrants and veterans from other countries.
2. Satisfaction with social life in Israel.
3. The perceived receptiveness of veteran Israelis towards new immigrants.
4. General adaptation.

The data in Table 6.5 indicate that today, even more than in the past, most FSU immigrants interact socially mainly with other immigrants from their country of origin. However, in contrast to the 1970s USSR immigrants, our respondents do not restrict their social contacts to these encounters, and tend to meet more frequently with veteran Israelis as well. Hence, the observed differences in immigrants' satisfaction with their social life in Israel: 72 percent of the respondents, as compared with 66 percent of 1970s immigrants, reported five years after their arrival that they are definitely or fairly well satisfied with their social life in the host country. It should also be noted that, for the first time since their immigration, respondents seemed to be more satisfied with veteran Israeli attitudes toward the new immigrants. Thus, the percentage of those evaluating veterans' attitudes as "good" or "good enough" increased between their fourth year and their sixth year in the country from 40 to 60 percent. Correspondingly, the proportion of immigrants considering Israeli attitudes as being "cold" decreased during the same period from 40 to 30 percent.

Immigrants' general adaptation was assessed by three composite measures: (a) global satisfaction, (b) feeling of belonging to Israeli society, and (c) the degree of their alienation in the host country, as a negative measure of adaptation (see Appendix).

Global Satisfaction

This measure includes four items: "satisfaction with standard of living," "satisfaction with general situation," "satisfaction with social life," and "satisfaction with cultural life."

In contrast to immigrants' satisfaction with their social life (see above, Table 6.5), they appear to be relatively less satisfied with their standard of living, their cultural life, and their general situation in Israel. Five years after their arrival, only 38 percent of our respondents reported that they are satisfied ("definitely" or "fairly") with their standard of living, 47 percent expressed satisfaction with their general situation, and 49 percent declared that they are satisfied with their cultural life. At the same time, however, the immigrants' subjective evaluation of their situation in these domains tends to become more positive as the period of stay in Israel becomes longer.

Feeling of Belonging to Israeli Society

This factor includes three variables assessing the immigrants' feeling at home in Israel, their certainty of staying in the country, and their conviction that, if they could do it over again, they would decide to immigrate to Israel. It should be pointed out that our July 1990 respondents, as well as all the other investigated groups, expressed a high level of commitment to their new society. Eighty-one percent of the immigrants who arrived in July 1990 asserted, five years after their arrival, that they now feel at home in Israel; 88 percent declared that, if they could do it over again, they would decide to reimmigrate to Israel; and 91 percent are certain (definitely or fairly) that they will stay in Israel.

Multiple regression analysis revealed that the immigrants' predisposition to stay in the country, or to emigrate once again, strongly correlates with their positive feelings towards their Jewishness and towards Israel.[18] Furthermore, our data indicate that immigrants' predisposition to stay in the country does not correlate with their objective situation (permanent housing, suitable job, etc.), but it is influenced by their subjective evaluation of this situation (i.e., their "global satisfaction" with life in Israel and perceived receptiveness of the veteran population towards them; see Table 6.6).

TABLE 6.6
Factors Explaining the Immigrants' Commitment to Israel

Factor	Beta	Sig.T
The respondent's feelings towards his Israeli citizenship*	.34	.00
Positive evaluation of veteran Israelis' receptiveness toward the new immigrants	.26	.00
Immigrants' expectations for a better economic and professional situation in Israel (for themselves and for the next generation)	.21	.00
Individual's positive feelings towards his Jewishness	.15	.01
Global satisfaction	.14	.05
	R Square Change: .38	
	Signif. F Change: .00	

* Composite measure including four variables (see Appendix).

Alienation

The alienation scale (Vianello, et al., 1977) includes five statements with which the respondents were asked to agree or disagree. The five statements relate to an individual's feelings of "meaninglessness," "isolation," "powerlessness," "frustration," and "valuelessness" (see Appendix). Each item was scored 1 to 5 according to whether the subject agreed or disagreed. Thus, respondents' scores fall in a range from 5 to 25; the higher the score, the greater the alienation manifested by the respondent. Our data indicate that the degree of immigrants' social alienation diminishes with the length of stay in Israel. For example, three and a half years after their arrival, 30 percent of the immigrants who arrived in July 1990 were found in the "high alienation" group; after five years in Israel, this percentage decreased by up to 19 percent, and is quite similar to that found among the overall Jewish population (see Table 6.7).

TABLE 6.7
Alienation Score — Immigrants Who Arrived in July 1990
and the Overall Israeli Jewish Population (1992)

Alienation Score	Low (5-11)	Medium (12-18)	High (19-25)	Total
Immigrants who arrived in July 1990	12	69	19	100
The overall Jewish population (1992)*	27	55	18	100

* Source: Damian, N., Rosenbaum-Tamari, Y., *Trends in Public — Opinion on Immigration and Immigrant Absorption*, 1992.

Conclusion

1. The findings indicate that the current immigration from the former Soviet Union has, to a significant extent, the character of free choice. Indeed, among all the reported motives for migration, including "pull" and "push" factors, those related to Jewishness and Israel rank higher in the immigrants' hierarchy of reasons. Furthermore, most of our respondents declared that they were not interested in migrating elsewhere in the West, and that they intended to stay in Israel. The immigrants' predisposition to stay in the country or to emigrate elsewhere cannot be explained by their "objective" situation in Israel; it appears to be decisively contingent upon the respondents' "subjective" evaluation of their situation and the degree of their attachment to Jewish values and to the State of Israel.

2. The survey data regarding changes over time in the immigrants' situation clearly indicate that for most, the absorption process proved to be a successful one indeed.

(a) From their first year in Israel up to their sixth, the immigrants' situation in many specific fields (such as permanent housing, number of persons per room, ownership of major durable goods, unemployment rate) continuously improved, so that by the end of six years in the country they are quite similar to the overall Israeli population.

(b) The current immigrants display a high motivation for acquiring the Hebrew language and for using it as an efficacious instrument in their absorption process (mainly in the occupational sphere).

(c) The direct absorption track proved to be efficacious and appropriate for most of these immigrants, ensuring them the freedom of choice in deciding where to settle in Israel, and in establishing their own priorities among different spheres of the absorption process (for instance, to postpone for a given period their language studies, and start to work as soon as possible after their arrival).

(d) All our investigated groups displayed a high level of commitment to Israeli society, expressed in their predisposition to stay in the country and make Israel their home.

(e) Immigrants' satisfaction with their situation in different spheres of the absorption process (housing, work, social life, etc.) permanently increases with the length of stay in Israel. After five years in the country, the majority of respondents evaluated veteran Israeli attitudes towards them as "good."

All these findings corroborate those documented in an array of other studies.

3. In their social and cultural behavior, our immigrants appear to be quite similar to any other migrant population anywhere in the world. Thus, even after five years in Israel, most of them meet socially mainly with other immigrants from their country of origin, and there was a slight percentage change of those declaring that they meet frequently with veteran Israelis between their fourth year in Israel and their sixth.

As for the cultural domain, the findings indicate a clear tendency of respondents "to live simultaneously in two worlds"; on the one hand, they continue to be "faithfully attached" to their previous culture, while on the other, they manifest a given "openness" to their host country's cultural life as well. Five years after their arrival, the overwhelming majority of July 1990 immigrants continue to use their mother tongue in their private life and in fulfilling their cultural needs.

4. Finally, a significant percentage of immigrants among all our investigated groups encounter particular difficulties in two specific spheres:

(a) Some 20 percent of the respondents (mostly elderly unemployed people, arriving alone, or single-parent families) cannot solve by themselves the acute problem of their permanent housing and are still waiting for more substantial help from the Israeli authorities.

(b) The immigrants' occupational absorption implies a substantial shift from the occupations held abroad to others in Israel. For current immigrants this shift clearly means downward mobility, more drastic and lasting than in the 1970s, particularly among scientific and academically-trained professionals. As a result, the immigrants' satisfaction with work and their expectations for a better economic and professional future remain relatively low over time. From this point of view, today's immigrants relate to themselves as a "sacrificed generation," while their expectations for a better future in Israel are transferred to the next generation in the family.

APPENDIX
Selected Composite Measures
(Factor Analysis)

1. Jewish and Israeli Identity

1.1. Individual's feeling towards his Jewishness
This measure includes five statements with which the respondents were asked to agree or disagree:

	Factor Loading Immigrants*	
	Sept. 1991	Jan.-March 1995
1. I am proud of being a Jew.	.86	.81
2. If I were be given the possibility of being born once again, I would choose to be a Jew.	.86	.81
3. If a stranger tells me that I am not a Jew, I will immediately correct him, and say "I am a Jew."	.81	.81
4. In my opinion, it is indispensable to give the children Jewish education.	.70	.80
5. I consider Jews all over the world members of a unique family.	.60	.76

1.2. Solidarity with the Jewish people
Each respondent was asked to what extent his feelings of being a Jew have been influenced by the following events:

	Factor Loading Immigrants	
	Sept. 1991	Jan.-March 1995
1. Six-Day War (1967) between Israel and the Arab countries	.91	.89
2. Yom Kippur War (1973) between Israel and the Arab countries	.89	.89
3. The Gulf War (1991)	.73	.88
4. The European Jews' extermination by the Nazis	.61	.77

1.3. The respondent's feelings towards his Israeli citizenship

This measure includes four statements with which the respondents were asked to agree or disagree:

	*Factor Loading***
1. The fact that I am an Israeli citizen plays an important role in my life.	.91
2. If a stranger tell me that I am not an Israeli, I will immediately correct him, and say "I am an Israeli citizen."	.82
3. I am proud of being Israeli.	.82
4. My fate is indisputably connected with the fate of the Israeli state.	.79

1.4 Centrality of the Israeli state in the life of the Jewish people

Respondents were asked to specify their degree of agreement with the following four statements:

	*Factor Loading***
1. Israel is the unique country in the world where one can live a truly Jewish life.	.81
2. Israel represents the spiritual center of the Jewish people.	.80
3. In case of war, Jews all over the world have to support the Israeli state, even when their support is in contradiction with the interests of the state they are living in.	.79
4. The fate of the Jewish people is indissolubly connected with the fate of the Israeli state.	.78

2. Motives for Emigration/Immigration to Israel

2.1. Motives Specific to Aliya

	Factor Loading Immigrants	
	Sept. 1991	Jan.-March 1995
2.1.1. "Push" Motives: The situation of Jews in the FSU –		
Jews being discriminated against	.82	.82
Respondent felt personal discrimination being a Jew	.81	.81
Anti-Semitism in the FSU	.66	.72
2.1.2. "Pull" Motives: Israel as the target country –		
Willingness to live as a Jew in a Jewish environment	.74	.76
Desire for being close to one's kinsmen/friends in Israel	.73	.63
2.1.3. "Pull" Motives: Concern for the future of one's children –		
Concern for the welfare of one's children	.81	.91
Desire to bring up one's children in Israel	.67	.68

2.2. Motives for any Migration

2.2.1. "Push" Motives: The current situation in the FSU –

Economic situation	.87	.77
Political situation	.86	.82

2.2.2. "Pull" Motives: Willingness to go to a Western country –

Willingness to live in a Western democratic society	.68	.68
Expectations to improve one's standard of living	.68	.75

3. General Adaptation

3.1. Global Satisfaction

Variables:	Factor Loading**
1. Satisfaction with standard of living	.81
2. Satisfaction with general situation	.78
3. Satisfaction with cultural life	.62
4. Satisfaction with social life	.59

3.2. Feeling of Belonging to Israeli Society

Variables:	Factor Loading**
1. Feeling at home in Israel	.85
2. If they could do it over again, they would decide to immigrate to Israel	.80
3. Certainty to stay in Israel	.76

3.3. Alienation

   The alienation scale*** includes five statements with which the respondents were asked to agree or disagree:

	Factor Loading**
1. Sometimes politics and government seem so complicated that a person like me cannot really understand what is going on (meaninglessness).	.78
2. Life is nowadays so confusing that one does not know how to distinguish right from wrong (valuelessness).	.76
3. Today nobody can be trusted, everyone thinks only of themselves (isolation).	.75
4. A person like me cannot try to influence the course of events (powerlessness).	.73
5. I can never do what I would like because circumstances compel me to do otherwise (frustration).	.72

*   The two previous groups of immigrants (who arrived November 1989 and July 1990) were not asked these questions.
** Immigrants who arrived in July 1990, after five years in Israel.
***Vianello, et al., 1977; Seeman, 1959.

Notes

* The authors are much indebted to Shmuel Adler, Director of the Planning and Research Division, Ministry of Immigrant Absorption, for his useful advice and assistance in preparation of this paper. An earlier version of this chapter was published in 1996 by the Ministry of Immigrant Absorption.

1. According to Israeli legislation, immigration to Israel means remigration from the diaspora to the Jewish homeland. The 1950 Law of Return, Israel's fundamental statute of citizenship, declares that any Jew, from anywhere in the world, has the right to settle in Israel. Immigration to Israel is thus national in character. This unique characteristic is even reflected in the Hebrew words for "immigration" and "immigrant to Israel" — "*aliya*" and "*oleh*" (f: "*olah*"), respectively — which derive from a root meaning "ascent."

2. Between 1990 and 1996, ten detailed research reports on these topics were published (in Hebrew) by the Ministry of Immigrant Absorption, Planning and Research Department.

3. The direct absorption track was known in the 1970s as well, though its meaning was different. Then, most of the immigrants were initially sent to absorption centers, while some were provided with permanent housing on a highly subsidized rental basis by the government. The new concept of direct absorption, initiated some two years before the beginning of the current wave, essentially aimed to ensure the new immigrants freedom of choice in deciding where to settle in Israel, as well as in establishing their own priorities among different spheres of the absorption process, and in deciding how to administrate their "absorption" basket — the new, global financial help provided by the absorption authorities (Adler, S., 1997:141-142).

4. This term, or "USSR," will be used for all immigrants who arrived from the territories that comprised the Soviet Union until its breakup, as well as the term "Soviet immigrants."

5. Thus, it was claimed that the current immigrants were looking exclusively for "economic refuge," their "commitment to the Jewish community in their country of origin and to the Israeli state being rather nebulous" (Lisak, M., 1995:168). Or, similarly, "This influx is the first to be perceived by Israelis as neither traditionally Jewish nor Zionist but rather as impelled by economics and fear alone. Hebraically, these immigrants have been arriving virtually illiterate" (Glinert, L.H., 1995:353). And, consequently, "this immigration to Israel does not substantially differ from other migratory movements" (Ben-Sira, Z., 1994:64).

6. In measuring individuals' Jewish identity, one could relate to three relatively distinct levels: the cognitive, the behavioral, and the affec-

tive. Our data refer exclusively to the affective level. As stated by Herman, "the extent to which the group identity will be reflected in a particular individual will depend upon whether...on the affective level, being Jewish has high positive valence" (Herman, S.N., 1977:55). There is evidence that the affective component is also perceived by Jews still living in the FSU as the most important one when defining their ethnic identity. For instance, a survey carried out in 1993-1994 among Jews in six towns and cities in the Volga Region revealed that "Only 25.6 percent answered the question 'Who is a Jew by your definition?' by indicating 'the son or a daughter of a Jew.' For 71.7 percent, being a Jew has a broad sociocultural significance; that is, one should feel part of the Jewish people, connected to its historical memory, its fate and future" (Krapivenskii, S.,1995:56).

7. Data from a public opinion survey carried out by the authors in 1992, based on a national representative sample of the Israeli Jewish population (not including the kibbutzim). The questionnaire included the same measures used in the immigrants' survey, and the sample comprised 1,200 respondents who were interviewed in their home.

8. As stated before, our data refer exclusively to the affective component of Jewish identity. It should be pointed out that Krapivenskii's survey among the FSU Jews, relating to the behavioral and cognitive components, revealed that the percentage of respondents having a high or medium score was 53 percent (behavior), and 70 percent (knowledge).

9. Since our survey was carried out "post factum," that is, some six months after the decision was taken, and the respondents were aware that it was directed by Ministry of Immigrant Absorption representatives, there is indeed a possibility that some answered these questions the way they believed they should, by giving the "correct" responses which were supposed to be consistent with our expectations. However, three surveys carried out in 1990, 1991, and 1992 among Jews still living in the Soviet Union indicate that Israel is the favored "target" of those who intend to emigrate. The authors divided their population into three groups: those interested in migrating to Israel (40.9 percent in 1990, 43.2 percent in 1991, and 50.9 percent in 1992), those interested in migrating to other Western countries (31.5-41.8 percent), and those indicating no interest in emigrating (27.6 percent in 1990, 15.0 percent in 1991). If we eliminate those who were not considering emigration at all, the "Israel-oriented" group among the "potential emigrants" appears to be preponderant: 50.8 percent in 1990, 56.5 percent in 1991, and 68.9 percent in 1992 (Aptekman, D., 1993:29).

Another survey carried out in Israel in 1993 achieved similar results: 77.5 percent of new Soviet immigrants reported that they wanted to come to Israel, and only 13.9 percent declared that they came here because "there was nowhere else to go" (Ritsner, et al., 1993:11). Finally, more recent demographic research concluded that the "aliya from the USSR to a significant extent had the character of free choice which reflected the socio-demographic profiles of the immigrants to Israel" (Constantinov, V., 1995:5).

10. Other surveys carried out among the Jewish population in the former Soviet Union, as well as among new immigrants in Israel, though using other measures, arrived at comparable results. Thus, the results of the three above-mentioned surveys among the Jews in the USSR indicate that the three most frequent causes for emigration, as cited by the "Israel-oriented" respondents, were: "increased anti-Semitism" (70.9 percent), "instability of the political situation and aggravation of ethnic problems in general" (49.4 percent), and "desire to live in a Jewish environment," that is a Jewish state (Aptekman, D., 1993:18). Similarly, the researchers who conducted their survey in Israel found that Soviet Jews' desire to emigrate was connected with a variety of reasons, yet the primary ones were: "children's future" (74.3 percent), "economic difficulties" (39.9 percent), and "anti-Semitism" (39.9 percent) (Ritsner, et al., 1993:12, 18).

11. In 1989, a total of 12,800 immigrants arrived from the FSU. For 1990 and 1991 the figures were 185,200 and 147,800, correspondingly. During the years 1992-1995, the number of immigrants relatively stabilized at a yearly average of 66,000 persons (Ministry of Immigrant Absorption, 1996:8).

12. The findings for one and half to two years indicate that the immigrants did not abandon their language studies, they just postponed them for a while. Moreover, some 43 percent of the immigrants who arrived in July 1990, and 57 percent of those who arrived in September 1991, declared that they were continuing to learn Hebrew systematically in an institutionalized framework. That, in contrast with the 1970s when "almost no one studied Hebrew formally after the first year in the country" (Rosenbaum, Y., 1983:118).

13. In 1995, the average housing density among all FSU immigrants who arrived in 1990-1991 was the same: 1.1 persons per room (CBS 1996, 1022:44-45).

14. Among all the FSU immigrants (aged 15+) who arrived in Israel in October-December 1990, the percentage of employed, three years after immigration, was 91.3 percent (CBS 1995, 6:104).

15. The CBS figure for all the 1990s FSU immigrants (aged 15+) was even higher: 71 percent (CBS 1994, 4:231).

16. Similarly, a recent study dedicated to the absorption process of immigrant engineers (a sample of 1,432 individuals aged 20-54, representing 45,241 FSU engineers who arrived in the years 1989-1994) reveals that, after five years in Israel, 32 percent are working as

engineers, and another 8 percent are employed in related occupations (Naveh, G., 1996:5). For the immigrant physicians (a study carried out in 1994 among 6,754 doctors who arrived between 1990 and 1992), the picture is much more optimistic: 72 percent of the immigrant physicians who are licensed to work as doctors in Israel are doing so (they represent 50 percent of those who declared upon entry that they were employed abroad as physicians).

17. The difference between the two groups does not indicate a poorer language acquisition among the 1990s immigrants. It is rather related to the huge number of current immigrants, and their increasing opportunities to find compatriots everywhere, including at their place of work.

18. An earlier study of ours on emigration from Israel, using quite similar measures, indicated that the predisposition to leave the country highly correlated with a low index of commitment not only in the case of the immigrants, but in the case of the Israeli Jewish population as well (Damian, N., 1987). Our findings were further confirmed by other research dedicated to the main factors of emigration from kibbutzim (Mittelberg, D., Sobel, Z., 1993:773-782).

References

Central Bureau of Statistics. 1990. *Labor Force Surveys*. No. 912. Jerusalem: 218.

Central Bureau of Statistics. 1986. *Immigrants of the Seventies — The First Three Years in Israel*. No. 771. Jerusalem: 33, 37, 67, 69, 101, 123, 125.

Central Bureau of Statistics. 1994. *Immigrants from USSR 1990-1992, Demographic Characteristics by Last Republic of Residence*. Supplement to the *Monthly Bulletin of Statistics*. No. 4. Jerusalem.

Central Bureau of Statistics. 1995. *Employment of Immigrants from the USSR Who Arrived in Israel in October-December 1990: A Follow-up Survey, Three Years after Immigration*. Supplement to the *Monthly Bulletin of Statistics*. No. 6. Jerusalem.

Central Bureau of Statistics. 1995. *Immigrants from the Former USSR, by Last Republic of Residence and by Selected Demographic Characteristics*. Reprint from the Supplement to the *Monthly Bulletin of Statistics*. No. 9. Jerusalem.

Central Bureau of Statistics. 1995. *Immigration to Israel 1994*. No. 1005. Jerusalem.

Central Bureau of Statistics. 1995. *Statistical Abstract of Israel*. No. 46. Jerusalem.

Central Bureau of Statistics. 1996. *Average Housing Density in Israel 1995.* No. 1022. Jerusalem.

Ministry of Immigrant Absorption. 1996. *Immigrant Absorption — Situation, Challenges and Goals.* Jerusalem.

Adler, S. 1996. "The Wave of Immigration to Israel in the Nineties." Paper presented at the International Conference on Jewish Migration, Jerusalem Center for Public Affairs (forthcoming).

Adler, S. 1997. "Israel's Absorption Policies in the 1970s and the 1990s." *Russian Jews on Three Continents.* Ed. Noah Lewin-Epstein, Yaakov Ro'i and Paul Ritterband. London: Cass, pp. 135-144.

Aptekman, D. 1993. *Jewish Emigration from the USSR, 1990-1992: Trends and Motivations.* Hebrew University of Jerusalem, Center for Research and Documentation of East European Jewry. Jerusalem (Spring): 15-33.

Ben-Sira, Z. 1994. *Immigration, Integration and Readjustment.* Israel Institute of Applied Social Research. Jerusalem:63-77.

Constantinov, V. "Aliya of the 1990s from the Former Soviet Union." *Jews in Eastern Europe.* Hebrew University of Jerusalem (Fall):5-26.

Damian, N. 1984. "Immigrants and Their Occupational Absorption: The Israeli Case." *International Migration.* Vol. XXII, no. 4:334-342.

Damian, N. 1985. "Divorce and Immigration: The Social Integration of Immigrant Divorcees in Israel. *International Migration.* Vol. XXIII, no. 4:511-520.

Damian, N. 1987. *Emigration from Israel: A Public Opinion Survey.* Ministry of Immigrant Absorption, Planning and Research Division. Jerusalem (Hebrew).

Damian, N. and Y. Rosenbaum-Tamari. 1992. *Trends in Public Opinion on Immigration and Immigrant Absorption.* Ministry of Immigrant Absorption, Planning and Research Division. Jerusalem (Hebrew).

Duncan, O.D. and B. Duncan. 1995. "Residential Distribution and Occupational Stratification." *American Journal of Sociology.* 60.

Gitelman, Z. 1982. *Becoming Israelis. Political Resocialization of Soviet and American Immigrants.* New York: Praeger Publishers, pp. 150-153.

Glinert, L.H. 1995. "Inside the Language Planners' Head: Tactical Responses to a Mass Immigration." *Journal of Multilingual and Multicultural Development.* Vol. 16, no. 5:351-371.

Herman, S.N. 1977. "Jewish Identity: A Social Psychological Perspective." *Sage Library of Social Research.* Vol. 48:59-60.

Katz, R. 1983. "Occupational Mobility of Immigrants and Their Job Satisfaction: A Secondary Analysis." *International Migration.* Vol. XXI, no. 3:345-356.

Krapivenskii, S. 1995. "Jewish Identity of Russian Jews in the Volga Region: A Sociological Survey." *Jews in Eastern Europe*. Hebrew University of Jerusalem (Fall):55-59.

Lisak, M. 1995. "Immigrants from CIS Between Isolation and Integration." Israeli Center of Cultural Policies Research:167-174 (Hebrew).

Mittelberg, D., and Z. Sobel. 1993. "Commitment, Ethnicity and Class as Factors in Emigration of Kibbutz and Non-Kibbutz Population from Israel." *International Migration Review* (Spring):769-782.

Naveh, G. 1996. *Occupational Absorption of Immigrant Engineers from the FSU*. JDC — Brookdale Institute of Gerontology and Human Development. Jerusalem (Hebrew).

Nirel, N. and G. Naveh, 1996. *The Employment of Immigrant Physicians in Israel: Is it Stable? Selected Characteristics of Employment of Immigrant Physicians from the FSU*. JDC — Brookdale Institute of Gerontology and Human Development. Jerusalem (Hebrew).

Ritsner, M. (coord.). 1993. *Demoralization Among Soviet Immigrants and Zionist Forum Support: First Year Experience of Psychological Support Project*. Soviet Jewry Zionist Forum, Talbieh Mental Health Center, Jerusalem.

Rosenbaum, Y. 1977. *Social and Cultural Absorption of Immigrants in Israel,* Ministry of Immigrant Absorption, Planning and Research Division (Hebrew).

Rosenbaum, Y. 1983. "Hebrew Adoption Among New Immigrants to Israel: The First Three Years." *International Journal of Sociology of Language*. No. 41:115-130.

Rosenbaum-Tamari, Y. and N. Damian. *Absorption Processes of the Current Wave of Russian Immigrants: On-Going Research*. Ministry of Immigrant Absorption, Planning and Research Division. Jerusalem, Research Report no. 1, 1990; no. 2, 3, 1991; no. 4, 5, 1993; no. 6, 7, 8, 1995; no. 9, 1996; no. 10, 1996 (Hebrew).

Vianella, M., et al., 1977. *Fantasy and Subversion: A Study of Alternative Organizations in the Scandinavian Countries,* University of Rome, Italy.

7

Absorption Policies in Israel: The Retraining of Immigrant Scientists in an Emergency Mass Immigration

Iris Geva-May

Introduction

The wave of Russian immigration between 1989 and 1991 brought a large number of highly qualified scientists to Israel. These immigrants were faced with social and professional integration problems.

In 1989, according to publications of the Israeli Central Bureau of Statistics, the population of Israel was 4.5 million. Out of 400,000 Soviet immigrants who had come to Israel in 1989/1991, 160,000 were academics and 6,000 of these were scientists in various fields of science and technology. The majority of scientists were university professors or research engineers who could not find an academic or research position, and whose concern was to find suitable employment.

In Israel immigration is considered mainly the responsibility of the state, while employment is regarded as a major requirement for social absorption. In 1990, the Absorption Department of the Ministry of Science and Technology, in collaboration with the Ministry of Education and Culture and the Ministry of Immigration and Absorption, initiated retraining of scientists for high school teaching. Officials openly declared that "immigrant training for the teaching profession is proposed as a positive employment solution and as a way of raising the level of science and technology teaching in Israel" (Eyal, 1990). First and foremost, this policy aimed at enabling the immigrant scientists to find relatively suitable employment; second, it was supposed to facilitate immigrant absorption; at the same time it proposed to reinforce the Israeli education system with teachers of a high intellectual and academic level.

The universities commissioned to offer teacher retraining programs to immigrant scientists in the academic year 1991-1992 were: Bar-Ilan University in mathematics and physics, Ben-Gurion University of the Negev, Beer-Sheva, in mathematics, physics, and chemistry; the University of Haifa in mathematics; the Hebrew University, Jerusalem, in mathematics and physics; the Technion, Israel Institute of Technology, Haifa, in electronics and mechanics; and Tel Aviv University in mathematics. Such retraining programs had never been attempted in Israel before and were considered pilot experiments. The retraining programs were offered by the Departments of Education in each university and designed according to the academic teacher training philosophy of each individual department. Subject matter updating, first language (Hebrew), and Israeli culture were added to the usual curriculum, and varied in emphasis according to the orientation of each department. Program proposals were submitted by each university's education department to the Ministry of Science and Technology for approval and financing. At the end of these courses the scientists were expected to obtain a teaching certificate which would qualify them to teach in Israeli high schools. The certification assessment and the teaching certificates were similar to those granted to Israeli students attending the same department.

For feedback and accountability reasons the Ministry of Science and Technology, in collaboration with the other two ministries, commissioned a three-year evaluation study that looked into the extent to which this particular retraining enterprise presented a feasible absorption-policy proposition. Indicators of success were considered to be the social impact, the educational impact, and the benefit of the project in light of the aims of this policy.

Problems in the Retraining of Immigrant Scientists

Absorption and adult-retraining problems are assumed to be major potential interfering variables in an immigrant retraining context. They pertain to cultural, psychological, socio-occupational, academic, and professional aspects. The extent to which these problems were met ultimately served as our analysis criteria and determined the success of the retraining policy.

Adult Education

Despite the commonly held view that at a certain age adults reach a developmental plateau which can affect learning effectiveness, Lasker and de Windt (1976), Loevinger (1976), and Cummings and Murray (1989) point to existent developmental stages at adulthood. Loevinger's Adult Development Taxonomy acknowledges various developmental stages at the moral, personality, cognitive, and interpersonal levels. This provides a positive outlook at possibilities inherent in the retraining of adults and at the feasibility of the retraining policy.

Loevinger also points at various causes for learning in adulthood: at the self-protective level, knowledge is required for concrete ends; at the conformist level for meeting the standards of others; at the conscientious level it is needed to achieve competence and meet external standards; while at the autonomous level knowledge is required for self-development and self-knowledge. Considering the socio-economic position of the immigrant scientists, it seemed right to assume that the main reason for their joining the course would range from self-preservation to a few cases of seeking self-knowledge of an autonomous type. The effectiveness of the five retraining models was evaluated in relation to their ability to identify, acknowledge, and assist these motivations.

On the other hand, research in the field of adult education regards adult learners as a much more varied group than the traditional undergraduate or graduate students (Epstein, 1986; Verduin et al., 1986; Weathersky, 1981), and whose individual needs are more difficult to meet. Furthermore, in our case the retraining program may easily have turned into a confrontation between course teachers and scientists who may well have had a higher level of subject matter knowledge. This situation could lead to professional and personal tensions affecting the effectiveness of the retraining programs.

Socio-Occupational Implications

From the socio-occupational point of view, the retraining of scientists for the teaching profession does not follow the distinctive career patterns characteristic of the academic world. The academic world is characterized by an orderly path of upward vertical movement and stability: professors tend to move up the ladder from instructor to assistant, to associate and finally to full professor. Upward mobility also implies crossing barriers into and within status groups (Reiss, 1962), as well as discernible changes in prestige, income, power, or other rewards (Wilensky, 1962). The latter situation is in direct opposition to the horizontal movement or lack of stability which is usually identified with skilled or semi-skilled professionals (Wilensky, 1962; Form and Miller, 1962). In fact, the retraining policy required scientists to follow a downward vertical movement both in terms of professional and social status. In addition, the scientists were forced to abandon any attachment to their occupation and previously established professional networks and interests, and to adopt different orientations. Reiss presents a series of studies proving that people in established professions have a higher degree of attachment to their occupations. In the case of the immigrant scientists in our study, they were forced to go against this socio-occupational tendency.

Socio-Psychological Factors

Although this paper is not concerned with an analysis of socio-psychological aspects in an immigration context, socio-occupational success is dependent on socio-psychological factors; that is, on the attitude and willingness of the absorbing field and on positive relationships with the scientist teachers. Social psychology points at instances where social relationships are affected by the weakness, disparity, and lack of orientation of one of the parties, and which usually result in unkindness (Aaronson, 1972).

Moreover, integrating highly qualified scientists into a school system where the majority of teachers themselves are less qualified could in fact intensify the apprehension and rejection of the new immigrants.

Socialization

Another variable affecting absorption is related to immigrant socialization. For instance, a study by Horowitz (1990) shows that the impact of socialization of teachers in their country of origin can be seen while performing in another country. The immigrant teachers' philosophy, ideology, and attitudes reflect their continuous socialization in the framework of their former social system. In our study the controlled centralized Soviet system was found to deeply affect the Soviet teacher, who indicated strong custodial attitudes, as opposed, for instance, to teachers who immigrated to Israel from North or South America. Custodial orientation in this context is identified with the traditional school, which is autocratic, maintains order, and provides a tightly controlled setting; distance is maintained between teacher and student, and students are perceived as irresponsible and undisciplined individuals; the teacher is the sole information agent and the guardian of discipline and order.

As opposed to the authoritarian attitude found in the Soviet Union, Israeli school ideology is identified as humanistic and naturalistic. It supports flexible status roles, encourages learning through experience and self-discovery, strives to assist students to develop their potential, and encourages self-expression (Willower, 1965; Oliver and Butcher, 1962). This disparity between opposite approaches to education could seriously harm the immigrants' successful absorption into the Israeli school system because teaching does require more than knowledge of the subject matter and methodological techniques (Lacey, 1977; Horowitz, 1990). In fact, effective teaching behaviors also depend on an understanding of attitudes, values, norms, and beliefs (Berliner, 1986), especially in a new social environment. It is evident that if a teacher is not sensitive to acceptable cultural behaviors, he or she is likely to be alienated from the students (Silberman, 1970). Studies by Ryan (1960) and Morrison and McIntyre (1980) regard this type of sensitivity as a prerequisite for effective teaching and higher student achievement.

Since socialization is usually a long and complex process, and firmly established socialization patterns are difficult to change, this variable is a major criterion in the evaluation of the success of the retraining policy. When this particular retraining policy was initiated it was not clear to what extent adults in mid-life would be able to develop gestalt sensitivity, and to what extent the entire enterprise would be affected by this factor.

Professional Skill Acquisition

We assumed that professional skill acquisition and mastery were important variables in any professional retraining context and that their attainment would be a central factor in establishing the technical feasibility of the retraining programs. In the case of the retraining of scientists for the teaching profession, the related counteracting variables were teacher training considerations and teaching performance — mainly in view of the possible discrepancy between the scientists' subject matter knowledge and their ability to use that knowledge in the classroom.

It has always been considered a problem to teach science efficiently (Henry, 1947; Helgeson, Blosser and Howe, 1977; Shulman, 1986). It is well known that to teach science subjects efficiently, one needs to have substantial knowledge of the subject matter. Subject matter mastery is a crucial component of pedagogical knowledge because conceptual and procedural understanding is the foundation of an adequate transformation and translation of content to teaching (Shulman, 1986). This entails the ability to organize, to be coherent, and to present the subject matter with appropriate examples and application to make it understandable to the students (Anderson and Smith, 1985; Shulman and Richert, 1987; Hawkins, n.d.). Studies in this domain indicate that in a majority of cases teachers cannot transfer knowledge adequately owing to their inability to expand on the subject matter; this results in the discussion span and activities being limited, together with misleading explanations being given for phenomena (Dobey and Schofer, 1984; Smith and Sendelbach, 1982). In addition, students learn factual content and terminology rather than how to develop analytic tools

(Eaton, Anderson and Smith, 1984; Schmidt and Buchmann, 1983; Strike and Posner, 1982; Champagne et al., 1980). In the case of immigrant scientists, their knowledge of the subject matter is far beyond that usually expected of high school teachers, and in this respect their retraining could be viewed as a wise policy decision.

Moreover, regardless of subject matter mastery, any novice teacher confronts methodological and procedural problems when starting to teach, mainly because of lack of "classroom knowledge" (Berliner, 1986). Like any new teacher, the immigrant scientist was still at the "novice" stage after finishing the retraining course, still lacking "reflection in action" or "artistry": the core of experienced professionalism, in Schon's view (1983), or ability to "translate knowledge into teaching" (Schwab, 1978; Shulman, 1986). At this stage the novice teacher is regarded as someone not yet capable of articulating educational or methodological theories, beliefs, and values about his or her roles in the dynamics of teaching and learning (Clark and Peterson, 1986), or "of reflection leading to...meta-cognitive awareness that distinguishes the craftsman from the architect, bookkeeper from auditor" (Shulman, 1986). Novice immigrant-scientist teachers are not likely to possess any of these skills, and at the classroom level this condition will express itself in lack of mastery in teaching techniques and in lack of internalization of methodological theories, beliefs, and roles (Clandinin, 1986; Peterson, Carpenter, Fennema and Loef, 1987; Clark and Peterson, 1986). This often results in classroom management dilemmas and/or problems in discipline, and may interfere with the teacher's successful professional integration.

This study did not assess the impact of the retraining program beyond the first two years of teaching, namely, beyond the novice stage, so its findings may not accurately predict the possible long-term achievements. In this respect our findings should be viewed only as predictions, and as such cannot be used to evaluate the long-term impact of the retraining policy on professional integration and on its benefit to the Israeli school system.

The Evaluation Study

This study was based on evaluation research procedures (Geva-May, 1992; 1993). The evaluation model followed the general pattern set up by the Phi-Delta-Kappa Committee (Stufflebeam et al., 1971) and included the stages of identification of information needs, collection of data, and provision of analyzed data to decision-makers. The information needs dictated a Tylerian evaluation function (Tyler, 1951; Nevo, 1983) by which the study investigated the attainment of three main policy goals: the social impact of the policy as an immediate absorption solution, the impact of the retraining offered by universities on possible employment and professional performance, and the benefit to the host education system.

First Stage

The study was carried out over a period of three years in five out of six universities taking part in the project, and involved participants in retraining programs. During the first year, 1991-1992, the evaluation offered formative process information (Scriven, 1967; Nevo, 1983; Chelimsky, 1985) which provided extensive technical feedback and facilitated primary inter-institutional information. It studied the profile of 193 immigrant scientists and the design of the retraining models. It also examined the ratio of certification and employment perspectives on completion of the course.

The main evaluation tool devised at this stage was questionnaires designed to gather information and assess the attitudes of program directors, lecturers, and immigrant trainees to each other and to the suitability of the retraining programs. The questionnaires included closed- and open-ended questions concerning, for instance, academic degree, years of research experience, or recommendations for future training courses. The attitude statements were rated on a Likert scale ranging from 1 to 4 so as to identify definite tendencies. Consideration was given to language that the immigrants were likely to understand without oversimplifying the message implied. In addition, in order to expand on the quantitative data we conducted a series of semi-structured interviews with all five program directors, and with a random sample population of 30 lecturers and 44 immigrant scientists.

Second Stage

The second part of the study, held during 1992-1993, was devoted to the impact of the retraining project in enabling the immigrant scientists to obtain a teaching position and cope with the requirements of the new profession. It focused on the first year of employment and examined mainly the attainment of two major goals of the retraining policy, namely, professional and social integration. It also examined the immigrants' contribution to the host school system — the third goal of the retraining policy.

At this stage and the next, we employed case study research methodology and followed closely a random sample population of 34 scientists (which represented a third of the currently employed scientists) and their 22 school principals. We conducted 34 separate observation series which provided feedback concerning expressions of professional and social integration for each of the immigrant scientists. The scientists were observed in each school for several days, and their interaction with peers, school employees, and students both in and out of the classroom were noted. This information also reinforced the quantitative and qualitative data gathered from the attitude questionnaires distributed to our target population, whose statements were designed to identify attitudes to the contribution of the retraining models to the actual teaching in schools and to the integration of the respondents in the school system. To assess the validity of the findings, a majority of parallel statements were presented in both questionnaires. The responses were rated on a four-point Likert scale. For the purpose of data validation, we carried out interviews with the target population in three stages — at the beginning, during, and at the end of the school year.

Third Stage

The third part of the study took place at the beginning of the immigrants' second year of teaching, in 1993-1994. To trace developments in professional and social integration, the target population consisted of the same respondents. The evaluation focused on long-term impacts: the percentage of scientists still employed after the first year of teaching, the reasons for dropout, if any, or for continuing employment, and the effect on the school system. The third major goal of the retraining policy, contribution to the school system, could be traced more accurately than in the previous year of study. The evaluation tools used were feedback and attitude questionnaires, interviews and observation sessions, similar to those employed in the second phase of the study.

Goals Attainment and Degree of Policy Feasibility

How reasonable this retraining policy was could be gauged by observing its execution and by detecting attitudes towards its implementation. The first stage of the test of plausibility began at the meeting point between the immigrant population and the retraining enterprise and was dependent on the content, design, and approach of the retraining models and the way they answered the professional and socialization needs of the particular trainee population. Further, to ascertain the causes affecting the extent of feasibility, it was important to note the profile of the actors in this undertaking, namely, the target immigrant population and the nature of individual retraining programs. In fact, the profile of our study population was determined by the acceptance criteria set by each of the retraining institutions and, in turn, the retraining programs' profile was determined by the conceived needs of the trainees.

The main variables affecting trainees' performance in schools were assumed to be age, linguistic mastery, and subject matter mastery. Therefore, the criteria regarding the suitability of the retraining courses considered factors such as the extent of exposure to language learning, level of subject matter presentation, subject matter updating, exposure to theories, methods, and tools used in the West, and exposure to practicum periods facilitating an understanding of the new school system's administration, procedures, approaches, mentality, and methodology in science teaching.

The second and third stages of the study related to the counteracting variables affecting actual social and professional absorption. The reasonableness of the retraining policy was assessed in accordance with ways of coping with the problematics of this stage. We therefore traced aspects related to socio-occupational implications: adult learning, socio-psychological concerns, in-job mastery, and socialization ability. These aspects included: willingness to learn and master the various aspects of the new occupation; acceptance of the new socio-occupational status; ability to cope in the new professional network; attachment to the new career and willingness to continue in the profession; relationship between the immigrant teachers and their peers and students; peers and students' behavior toward the scientist teacher, namely, expressions of lack of trust, jealousy, or rejection, as opposed to professional and personal assistance; classroom performance; custodial or naturalistic orientation; understanding of students' mentality; ability to translate content matter knowledge into suitable methodological practice; mastering professional and everyday language.

Findings

Immigrant Profile

The profile of the immigrant trainees in the program was expected to be one of the principal factors in determining the degree of success of the retraining policy. The qualifications of the participants varied — from scientists holding a Ph.D. with renowned research experience and without any teaching experience, to M.Sc. researchers with publications in the field of expertise — and each institution had its own demands for acceptance into the program. Despite the academic level and research experience in the former USSR, some of the trainees needed to be updated in content areas that had to be adapted to the knowledge acquired in the West and in complementary areas of expertise, such as use of computers.

All participants were required to master the Hebrew language; this was usually assessed in interviews with the candidates. Some institutions required that participants had been in the country for a minimum of two years, based on the rationale that length of time spent in the country would ensure better linguistic mastery as well as better understanding of the mentality of the new society, which, in turn, was expected to facilitate integration.

The age of the participants ranged from 30 to 55. This criterion was the only controversial issue in the institutions, and was, in fact, a major moral and professional dilemma. For example, Hebrew University and Ben-Gurion University of Beer-Sheva were of the

TABLE 7.1
Participant Profile According to Consensus Acceptance Criteria
(n = 174)

Institution	Degree		Teaching Experience (in years)			
	M.Sc.	Ph.D	1-5	6-10	11-15	16-20
Beer-Sheva	43	18	between 11-15			
Bar-Ilan		39	over 10			
Hebrew University	24	7	15	8	3	1
Technion	9	14	no teaching experience			
Tel Aviv	32	7	8	9	4	18
Total	108	85				
	62%	38%				

opinion that after the age of 45 or 50, respectively, the immigrant trainees would be unable to sufficiently master the language, and that the generation gap would be too wide to permit adoption of new professional habits combined with an understanding of clients' (students') mentality. The Technion and Tel Aviv University, on the other hand, assumed that retraining success depended on personality factors and was not age-related, and that scientists holding a Ph.D. with a wide research and publication background could indeed have reached this status only at a more mature age. Moreover, since the stated goal was absorption, they believed that the older scientists needed more assistance in finding employment because they were less likely to be accepted in research institutions. In our study we found that professional adaptation and socialization were personality- and motivation-related, and age was unimportant.

Retraining Program Profile

In all departments the program ran parallel to the academic year, from October to July. This enabled employment of faculty staff and allowed easy access to the institution's facilities. Most of the lecturers were staff members in the department and held Ph.D. degrees. The methodology courses were given by experienced school teachers holding M.Sc. degrees, although the majority had no previous experience with retraining immigrants. Although weekly staff meetings were held, the evaluation findings recommended that tutors in such enterprises be offered special preparation courses prior to and during the program in order to develop empathy for and understanding of the mentality, culture, and habits of the immigrant trainees.

The acceptance criteria limited the number of participants in each program and the accepted candidates generally had additional qualifications such as previous teacher retraining. Initially, only the Technion and Ben-Gurion University required exams for language and subject matter mastery — if only for diagnostic purposes. In most institutions competition for entrance was very high. Tel Aviv University, for instance, accepted only 40 out of 287 applicants for their two classes. Only in rare cases, such as in the mechanics track at the Technion, did institutions make their entrance requirements more flexible because of few enrollment applications. It was understood that the number of participants in the program should be limited to small groups of no more than 20 so as to offer the trainees individual attention. In the pilot program observed in this study, this was not the case, and studying in large groups could have affected retraining instruction and hence subsequent performance in the first year of teaching. Our feasibility evaluation findings might have been affected by this factor.

In retrospect, actual in-service performance during the scientists' first year of teaching indicated that the programs had offered the right components for teacher retraining. In each of the universities' education departments the profile of the retraining courses was almost identical to the training model offered to the Israeli students. The academic requirements concerned content matter and teaching performance. The only demand imposed by the Ministry of Education and Culture was several additional weekly hours for subjects such as language, culture, tradition, history, literature, and the geography of Israel. The degree of emphasis on these additional subjects varied in each institution owing to their ideological or related concepts of effective social absorption.

In each university the final assessment of the immigrant scientists was predetermined by the standards set for Israeli students and also included teaching performance assessments following the practical sessions in order to give uniform certification to both populations of future teachers. Neither the financing agency nor the Ministry of Education demanded any additional uniform exams.

The major subjects which the immigrant scientists were exposed to in all institutions, albeit at different levels of prominence, were discipline-oriented and general education subjects. The discipline subjects included methodology, the use of computers for teaching, and basic subject matter review and content matter updating in mathematics, physics, chemistry, mechanics, or electronics. Only one institution allocated 360 hours to subject matter updating. The feedback evaluation provided in the present study appraised all the retraining institutions that this component should be an important part of such retraining programs because the scientists, having specialized in a narrow field of expertise, do not always master the basic aspects necessary for teaching in high schools.

The general education subjects offered were: introduction to teaching, an insight into the education system of Israel, social and cognitive psychology, and the psychology of the child. Primary recommendations suggested that the psychology classes offered to immigrant teachers should emphasize the mentality and social behavior of the absorbing country to enable them to develop more appropriate tools for social interaction and communication. The case studies showed that in many instances retraining success was sometimes jeopardized owing to insufficient preparation — especially with regard to how to relate to students and parents. The immigrant scientists were also exposed to books and materials on teaching approaches for different learning levels and for different student populations, as well as for evaluation and assessment methods and practices. Deductive and inductive learning, cooperative versus individual learning, group work procedures — all were new issues for the scientist teachers.

On the practical professional level the above topics were further stressed in the practicum sessions. The prerequisites for these were the same as those required of the Israeli students, namely, 50-80 annual hours over a period of one to two months, during which time each immigrant teacher was affiliated to a school under the supervision of an experienced teacher-tutor who assisted in analyzing class situations, and in providing advice for lesson planning and involvement in school activities. The feedback obtained in the case studies supported the view that the practicum sessions were of major importance for future professional integration and that such programs should allow for considerably longer units of such exposure. However, this study found that the short practicum periods could not adequately prepare new teachers for their teaching jobs in Israel. If the new teachers had had longer practicum periods, this would have given them more accurate understanding of the mentality of Israeli children, together with better tools for more appropriate ways of approaching student difficulties; reinforcement of professional, everyday, and school language, including an understanding of children's slang; and an encounter with the school hierarchy, activities and experiences, requirements and procedures, including methods of cooperating with parents. These technical factors, although seemingly minor in the overall retraining project, could significantly influence the success of the policy's implementation.

The participants in the various programs suggested that professional language, children's slang, and listening comprehension should be important features of any retraining program for immigrant teachers. The trainees had no fear of not being understood in class (they could prepare thoroughly at home, search for words in the dictionary, etc.), but they were concerned at not being able to understand their students. The case studies reinforced the assumption that mastery of language is a primary and important tool for both teaching and professional integration, and many hours should be dedicated to learning the language. The social and cultural integration of the immigrants, and their orientation and identification, were helped by lessons in history and geography. The trainee teachers were taken on several organized tours of Israel and provided with an opportunity to get to know the new country, its landscapes, population, tradition, and historical and political background. These tours left a remarkable impression.

The effectiveness of the project and its impact on the retraining policy could only be assessed in the second and third stages of this study, namely, during the first and second years of actual teaching in schools. Surprisingly, after just a few months of teaching, 54 percent of immigrant scientists and 56 percent of school principals expressed positive attitudes towards the general contribution of the retraining courses to scientists' performance in school. Although this attitude gradually changed, the relatively moderate assessment was caused mainly by socialization factors which led to feelings of lack of sufficient preparation for dealing with discipline problems,

TABLE 7.2

Course Models During the First Pilot Retraining Years (no. of hours)

Institution	Technion		Beer–Sheva			Bar-Ilan		Hebrew University		Tel Aviv
	Electronics	Mechanics	Math	Physics	Chemistry	Math	Physics	Math	Physics	Math
In the discipline	360	360				240	240	112	112	112
Computers	80	80			84	60	60	28	28	56
Education subject	140	140	84	84	84	100	100	56	56	56
Psychology	84	84	56	56	56	90	90			56
First language	450	450	112	112	112	128	128	654	654	168
History, literature, geography										
Citizenship, Bible	200	200	168	168	168	180	180	112	112	140
Educational systems	24	24	56	56	56					56
Field teacher training	80	80	280	280	280	50	50	224	224	56
Visits	24	24	28	28	28	16	16	56	56	14
Total	1,442	1,442	784	784	784	864	864	1,242	1,242	714

or for understanding students' problems and being able to deal with them. Conversely, at the same time, the immigrant teachers and their school principals expressed positive attitudes towards the contribution of the teacher training courses to professional knowledge. These attitudes were related, for instance, to dimensions of teaching such as lesson planning (73 percent of principals and 72 percent of scientist teachers), use of professional materials (70 percent of scientist teachers), and teaching at different student ability levels (71 percent of principals and 70 percent of scientist teachers). Seventy-one percent of the immigrant teachers expressed positive attitudes towards the contribution of the retraining courses to "speaking and explaining in good Hebrew," but 56 percent of the scientists and 59 percent of their school principals were of the opinion that the language mastery of the immigrant teachers was inadequate, especially as regards their understanding of "student language."

The observations held during the second and third stage of the study identified the same characteristics in the immigrants as those of native novice teachers and were not connected to the feasibility of the policy. At most, they could hint at the fact that an evaluation held at this phase of professional integration cannot give definite answers. The main problems encountered by the immigrant teachers were generally related to classroom management and were characteristic of this first period of adjustment and transition. To cater to these problems, assist teachers, and prevent dropouts, recent literature has proposed extended connections with the teacher training institution during the first year of teaching (Odell, 1988; Armstrong, 1983; Farber, 1984; Hulling-Austine and Emmer, 1986; Goodman, 1987; French et al., 1993; Geva-May, 1995; Geva-May and Dori, 1997). Such connections, if built into the retraining project, may assist in speeding the transition period and in bridging the gap between the scientists' expertise in content matter and their novice professional status.

Conclusions: Were the Policy Goals Accomplished?

First Policy Goal — Professional Integration

The data regarding professional and social integration point to the fact that a majority (89 percent) of the immigrant scientists obtained a teaching certificate — 174 out of 193 participants in the five teacher retraining programs evaluated in this study. In September 1993, the first month of the academic year in schools, 90 scientists, representing 52 percent of the graduates, were working in schools. Two months later the findings showed an employment rate of 68 percent, and 30 percent of the school principals were certain that they would extend the scientists' position for an additional year. Ninety-one percent of the scientists employed obtained part-time work, and some worked part-time in more than one school, while 32 percent held full-time jobs in one school.

According to the findings obtained in the third phase of the study, the second year of actual in-service teaching, 91 percent of the scientists continued to hold a teaching position. Only 3 out of 34 teachers dropped out. In two cases the problem was mainly connected with socialization patterns, specifically, discipline problems and lack of understanding of the Israeli mentality. In the third case the cause was mainly socio-occupational: the person involved still hoped to find a research position. Despite the fact that most of the respondents had to change the school in which they had taught in the first year, no significant differences in employment percentage or in job status were observed in the second year of teaching.

Interviews with school principals revealed that in all cases it was the scientists' devotion and motivation that persuaded them to extend their employment, even in instances where the immigrant teachers faced socialization problems. The principals believed that socialization is a time-dependent factor and that the contribution made by the immigrant scientists to their schools surpassed the short-term problem.

Second Goal — Social Absorption and Integration

A review of the findings related to social absorption and integration shows that a surprisingly high percentage of immigrant scientists continued to be employed in the following year of teaching. Since employment is an imperative prerequisite in social integration, the stability of a permanent position may imply a first successful step in that direction. Moreover, the observation sessions showed unusual motivation on the part of the immigrant teachers both in their everyday preparations for their classes and in their relations with peers and students. Generally, they felt free to talk about professional matters or consult with the principal, the subject supervisor, or peer teachers.

Unfortunately, they were rarely approached by their peers, either on the professional or on the personal level. The data received in our questionnaires, interviews, and observations show a low degree of awareness on the part of the host society: schools had no internal guidelines as to how to treat the immigrant teachers socially. If existent, any personal relations were very much on an individual cordial level. The communication efforts seemed to be made mainly by the immigrants: very few subject teachers shared

TABLE 7.3
Employment According to Type of Teaching Institution

Institution	Beer-Sheva	Bar-Ilan	Hebrew University	Technion	Tel Aviv	Total receipients of teaching certificates
Number	53	34	30	23	27	174
			In percentage			
Junior High	8	10	17	0	33	11
High	54	10	58	47	67	48
13th Grade	0	10	0	11	0	4
College	5	10	0	15	0	7
Adult	5	0	0	5	0	4
University research/ teaching	0	20	8	11	0	3
Factories	3	0	0	11	0	17
Both Jr. High and High	25	40	17	0	0	18

their lesson materials with the immigrant teachers in their school, and less than 25 percent of the scientist teachers were invited to a native teacher's home or to join a class party or field trip. Moreover, 79 percent of the school principles noted parents' reluctance to have their children taught by an immigrant teacher. This was so even though as many as 73 percent of the immigrant teachers and their school principals identified positive patterns of communication between teachers and students. Future studies might investigate the matrix of parental attitude in depth. The data obtained in this study can attribute this attitude to discipline problems, mentality, language barriers, and other general socio-psychological patterns caused by the immigrants' foreign looks and social weakness.

One of the potential socio-psychological obstacles thought to be highly disruptive was that other school teachers might feel inferior to their scientist peers. This manifestation was not observed. The immigrant scientist teachers did not feel rejected, and the majority of school principals considered their work in the school and their help to peer teachers an asset to their institution.

From the socio-occupational point of view it was found that the majority of scientists employed in the school system expressed positive attitudes toward their integration. Eighty-two percent of our case study population expressed the wish to continue working as teachers. The scientists who expressed this view were those who embarked on the retraining program willingly and were committed to their decision. Interviews with scientist teachers working at a minimal part-time job after graduation and with some of the unemployed scientists (who were not part of our sample population in the second and third year of the study) showed that they were still hoping to follow a research career rather than teach in schools. The occupational commitment to their former academic career was stronger than that of those who possibly compromised, but viewed their future vocation in the new school system.

Third Policy Goal — The Contribution of Immigrant Scientists to the Host Educational System

As regards the third policy goal, the contribution of immigrant scientists to high school teaching, the findings show that as early as the beginning of the first year of teaching, 95 percent of the school principals had already expressed particular regard for the scientist teachers' contribution to their school. The scientist teachers were ready to work in any geographical or socio-economic area, and not necessarily in high schools but also in junior high and primary schools. For instance, three scientist teachers (10 percent of our random sample population) taught at elementary schools in the central Tel Aviv region, and 36 percent at junior high schools. At least 30 percent were reported to teach in the science tracks and to prepare advanced students for their final matriculation exams; 30 percent were reported to teach classes of weak students. Usually in Israel neither primary school children nor junior high school students, or weak classes for that matter, are taught by such highly qualified teachers. Also, only in very rare cases do teachers holding high academic degrees teach in development or low socio-economic areas. The factual data above indicated positive tendencies regarding the contribution of the retraining to the education system.

According to the findings of the first year, approximately a third of our sample scientist teachers were also teaching in gifted learners' classes, 20 percent were participating in the writing up of school curricula, and 50 percent were giving tutorial lessons to weak students. Approximately 80 percent of the scientist teachers shared the materials they prepared for their classes with their peer subject teachers. In so doing they contributed to the teaching level in the school.

This tendency continued in the second year of teaching. The immigrant scientists were reported to be involved in the design and preparation of school-based curricula, and in extra-curricular enrichment classes. In one case, two immigrant mathematics and physics teachers opened a Science Center in one of the remote minority Druze villages of Israel. All science teaching in that minority area depended on these two teachers, while hardly any qualified teacher had taught there before. In another case, all three scientists retrained in the mechanics track at the Technion were offered teaching positions in one of the new technology colleges in the far north of the country which serve mainly development towns.

Summary

Following the massive immigration during 1989-1991, the retraining of immigrant Soviet scientists for the teaching profession
was initiated by the Israeli government owing to its commitment to
immigration. The purpose of this study was to find out whether, or
to what extent, this retraining policy could be considered a pertinent absorption proposition according to the degree to which its
goals had been reached. A number of implementation-interfering
factors could facilitate or jeopardize its execution.

The evaluation study probed the capacity of the retraining
program to attain the three main goals of this policy, namely,
professional integration and social absorption as immediate solutions, and the contribution of immigrant scientists to high school
science teaching in Israel. The summative results of this evaluation
were meant to assist in either changing the goals of the policy (in
view of the relationship between the program's feasibility and the
policy goals) or proposing ways that would facilitate application (if
it was concluded that the obstacles identified could be overcome).

This study showed that the general retraining policy goals have
been accomplished, that the feasibility of the retraining policy has
been proved, and that, with minor alterations, the project can be
continued. First and foremost, social absorption was given a positive boost once the immigrant scientists were offered employment.
In this respect the majority of scientists followed a promising track:
insofar as professional integration is concerned, they were employed immediately after finishing the retraining courses, continued to work in the school system in the next school year, and were
willing to persist in their new occupation. The majority of school
principals stated a willingness to continue employing the immigrant scientists in their schools in subsequent years. Although a
third of the immigrant scientists who finished the course remained
unemployed, most of them admitted not really wanting to change
their occupational identity and were not really interested in obtaining a teaching position.

The third goal of the retraining policy, contribution to science
teaching, has been fully accomplished. This relates to assistance in
schools and to employment in socio-economic areas where highly
qualified teachers do not usually teach. The expertise, motivation,
and personality of the immigrant scientists were viewed as a

valuable pedagogical asset to the educational system. In general, the retraining models presented a feasible profile and contributed to teaching performance. The similar courses, and the similar assessment and certification to all teachers trained in the same university, whether native Israeli or immigrant, warranted that immigrant teachers would not be discriminated against when applying for a teaching position.

The rapid employment possibilities following the retraining program, the contribution offered by immigrant scientists to the school system, together with the formative solutions provided by this study and taken up by the decision-makers, have established the plausibility of this absorption policy. Inasmuch as this study can shed light on similar immigration contexts, the findings obtained show that this retraining approach can certainly be considered a feasible proposition. Nevertheless, it must be noted that the validity of this retraining policy was investigated in a specific social and political climate. In different contexts, this absorption policy should be tested and adapted according to the social and political setting within which the retraining program is proposed.

References

Aaronson, E. 1972. *The Social Animal.* San Francisco: Freeman.

Amir, N. and T. Tamir. 1992. *Beginning Teachers Induction Project: An Evaluation Report.* Tel Aviv: College of Education-Seminar Hakibbutzim (Hebrew).

Anderson, C. and E. Smith. 1985. "Teaching Science." *The Educator's Handbook: A Research Perspective.* Ed. V. Koehler. NY: Longman.

Armstrong, D.G. 1983. "Evaluation of Teacher Induction Processes Associated with the Conditions of Practice." *Eric,* no. ed. 231799.

Averch, H.A. 1987. "Measuring Cost-Efficiency of Basic Research Investment: Input-Output Approaches." *Public Policy Analysis and Management* 6(3):342-361.

Berliner, D. 1986. "In Pursuit of the Expert Pedagogue." *Educational Researcher* 15(7):5-13.

Braybrooke, D. and C.E. Lindblom. 1963. *A Strategy of Decision.* New York: Free Press.

Carpenter, T., P. Peterson, E. Fennema and D. Carey. 1987. "Teacher's Pedagogical Content Knowledge in Mathematics." Paper presented at the Annual Meeting of the American Educational Research Association, Washington, DC.

Champange, A., L. Kloper and J. Anderson. 1980. "Factors Influencing the Learning of Classical Mechanics." *American Journal of Physics* 48(12):1074-1079.

Chelimsky, E. 1985. "Old Patterns and New Directions in Program Evaluation." *Program Evaluation: Patterns and Directions*. Washington, DC: APSA.

Clandinin, J. 1986. *Classroom Practice*. Philadelphia: Palmer Press.

Clark, C.M. and P. Peterson, 1986. "Teacher's Thought Processes." *Handbook of Research on Teaching*. Ed. M. Wittrock. 3rd ed. New York: Macmillan, pp. 255-296.

Committee of Teacher Credentials. 1992. "California New Teacher Project: Evaluation Report." Sacramento: Office of Education.

Cummings A.L. and H.G. Murray. 1989. "Ego Development and Its Relation to Teachers' Education." *Teaching and Teachers' Education* 5:21-32.

Dobey, D. and L. Schofer. 1984. "The Effects of Knowledge on Elementary Science Inquiry Teaching." *Science Education* 68(1):39-51.

Eaton, J., C. Anderson and E. Smith. 1984. "Students' Misconceptions Interfere with Science Learning: Case Studies of Fifth Grade Students." *Elementary School Journal* 84:365-379.

Epstein, H.V. 1986. "The Older College Student. A Changing American Tradition." *International Journal of Lifelong Education* 5:33-34.

Espenshade, T.J. 1994. "Can Immigration Slow U.S. Aging?" *Public Policy Analysis and Management* 13(4):759-768.

Eyal, B. 1990. Internal Protocol of Meeting with Retraining Program Directors. Jerusalem: Ministry of Science and Technology.

Farber, B.A. 1984. "Stress and Burnout in Suburban Teachers." *Journal of Educational Research* 77:325-331.

French, D., B.K. Nichols, J.R. Wiggins and R.B. Calvert. 1993. "The Mentoring Role in a Science Model: Internal Mentor." Paper presented at the 66th Annual Conference of the National Association for Research in Science Teaching, Atlanta, Georgia.

Form, W.H. and D.C. Miller. 1962. *Man, Work and Society*. Ed. Sigmud Nosow and William H. Form. New York: Basic Books.

Geva-May, I. 1992. *An Evaluation Report Concerning New Immigrant Retraining Courses for High School Teaching*. Jerusalem: Ministry of Science and Technology.

Geva-May, I. 1993. *Interim Report on Retraining Programs for Immigrant Scientists*. Jerusalem: Ministry of Science and Technology, and Berkeley: CSHE, UC.

Geva-May, I. 1995. "An Analysis of Induction Models in the State of California: Transfer and Adoption Possibilities for a Teacher Support Policy in Israel." *Support Programs: From Piloting to Adoption*. Ed.

D. Shahor. Jerusalem: Research Center, Ministry of Education and Culture.

Geva-May, I. and Y. Dori. 1993. "An Analysis of an Induction/Support Model for Beginning Science and Technology Teachers." Unpublished. Haifa: Technion, Department of Science Education.

Geva-May, I. and Y. Dori. 1997. "An Analysis of an Induction/Support Model for Beginning Science and Technology Teachers." *British Journal of In-Service Education* 22(3):336-356.

Goodman, J. 1987. "Key Factors in Becoming (or Not Becoming) an Empowered Elementary School Teacher: A Preliminary Study of Selected Novices." *Eric,* no. ed. 280808.

Gregory, R., R. Keeney and D. von Winterfeldt. 1992. "Adapting the Environmental Impact Statement Process to Inform Decisionmakers." *Journal of Policy Analysis and Management* 11(1):58-75.

Hawkins, D. (n.d.) "Conceptual Barriers Encountered in Teaching Science to Adults: An Outline of Theory and a Summary of Some Supporting Evidence." *A Report of Research on Critical Barriers to Learning and Understanding of Elementary Science.* Ed. M. Apelman, R. Colton, A. Flexer and D. Hawkins. Boulder, Co: University of Colorado.

Helgeson, S., P. Blosser and R. Howe, R. 1977. "The Status of Pre-college Science, Math, and Social Science Education 1955-1977." *Science Education* 1. Washington, DC: US Government Printing Office.

Henry, N.B., ed. 1947. "Science Education in American Schools." *The Forty-Sixth Yearbook of the National Society for the Study of Education.* Chicago: University of Chicago Press.

Horowitz, T.R. 1990. *Attitudes of Soviet and Immigrant Teachers in Israel.* Jerusalem: Szold Institute for Behavioral Science.

Hulling-Austine, I. and E.T. Emmer. 1986. "First Days of Schools: A Good Beginning." *Eric,* no. ed. 262031.

Lacey, C. 1977. *The Socialization of Teachers.* London: Methuen.

Lasker, H.M. and C. de Windt. 1976. "Implications of Ego Stage for Adult Development." Mimeographed. Cambridge: Harvard Graduate School of Education.

Leinhardt, G. 1985. "The Development of an Expert Explanation: An Analysis of a Sequence of Subtraction Lessons." Manuscript. Pittsburg: University of Pittsburgh, Learning Research and Development Center.

Lipset, S.M., B. Reinhard and F. Theodore. 1962. "Job Plans and Entry into Labor Market." *Man, Work and Society.* Ed. Sigmud Nosow and William H. Farm. New York: Basic Books.

Loevinger, J. 1976. *Ego Development.* San Francisco: Jossey-Bass.

Morrison, A. and R. McIntyre, R. 1980. *Teachers and Teaching.* Middlesex: Penguin, Education.

Nevo, D. 1983. "The Conceptualization of Educational Evaluation: An Analytical Review of Literature." *Review of Educational Research* 53(1):117-128.

Odell, S.J. 1988. "Characteristics of Beginning Teachers on Educational Contact." *Eric,* no. ed. 290752.

Oliver B. and J.J. Butcher. 1962. "Teachers' Attitudes to Education." *British Journal of Social and Clinical Psychology* 1:56-69.

Peterson, P., T. Carpenter, E. Fennema and M. Loef. 1987. "Teacher's Pedagogical Content Beliefs in Mathematics." Paper presented at the Annual Meeting of the American Educational Research Association, Washington, DC.

Reiss, J. 1962. *Man, Work and Society.* Ed. Sigmud Nosow and William H. Form. New York: Basic Books.

Ryan, P.G. 1960. *Characteristics of Teachers.* Washington, DC: American Council of Education.

Schmidt, W., and M. Buchmann. 1983. "Six Teachers' Beliefs and Attitudes and Their Curriculum Time Allocations." *Elementary School Journal* 84:162-171.

Schon, D. 1983. *The Reflective Practitioner.* London: Temple.

Schwab, J. 1978. *Science, Curriculum, and Liberal Education. Selected Essays.* Chicago: University of Chicago Press.

Scriven, M. 1967. "The Methodology of Evaluation." *AERA Monograph Series on Curriculum Evaluation.* Ed. R.E. Stake. No. 1. Chicago: Rand McNally.

Shulman, C.S. and A. Richert. 1987. "Knowledge and Teaching: Foundation of the New Reform." *Harvard Educational Review* 57(1):1-22.

Shulman, L.S. 1986. "Those Who Understand: Knowledge Growth in Teaching." *Educational Research* 15(2):4-14.

Silberman, C.D. 1970. *Crisis in the Classroom.* New York: Random House.

Smith, D.C. and D.C. Neale. 1989. "The Construction of Subject Matter Knowledge in Primary Science Teaching." *Teaching and Teachers Education* 5:1-20.

Smith, E. and N. Sendelbach. 1982. "The Program, the Plans and the Activities of the Classroom: The Demands of Activity-Based Science." *Innovations in the Science Curriculum: Classroom Knowledge and Curriculum Change.* Ed. J.K. Olson. London: Croom Helm.

Starhovski, R. and R. Hertz-Lazarowitz. 1992. "The Professional Growth of the Beginning Teacher Through Clinical Supervision and Peer Coaching." *Dapim.* Israel Ministry of Education and Culture 15:66-75 (Hebrew).

Strike, K. and G. Posner. 1982. "Epistemological Assumptions of College Students." Paper presented at the Annual Meeting of the Northwestern Educational Research Association, Ellenville, NY.

Stufflebeam, D.L. et al. 1971. *Educational Evaluation and Decision Making*. Itaska, IL: F.E. Peacock.

Tyler, R.W. 1951. *Basic Principles for Curriculum and Instruction*. Chicago: University of Chicago Press.

Verduin, J.R., H.G. Miller and C.E. Greer. 1986. *The Life Long Learning Experience*. Springfield, IL: Charles C. Thomas.

Weathersky, R.P. 1981. "Ego Development." *The Modern American College*. Ed. A. Chickering. San Francisco: Jossey-Bass.

Wilensky, H.L. 1962. "Careers, Lifestyle, and Social Integration." *Man, Work and Society*. Ed. Sigmund Nosow and William H. Farm. New York: Basic Books.

Willower, D.J. 1965. *The School and Pupil Control Ideology*. Philadelphia: Pennsylvania State University.

8

Internal Migration in Israel: From Periphery to Center — From Rural to Urban

David Newman

Introduction

Studies of internal migration within Israel are closely linked to the nature of settlement planning and population distribution. Geographers, sociologists, and economists have tended to emphasize the unique features of the settlement landscape in Israel as bearing little, if any, comparison with settlement patterns in other Western societies. Traditional academic discourse has relegated the role of social and economic forces in forming the country's human landscape, as compared with the dominant role played by government intervention and management of planning policies, at national, regional, and local levels. Zionism, as the driving ideology behind state intervention in the planning process, has, according to many commentators, constituted the only framework within which internal migration, settlement planning, and population distribution can be understood (Kellerman, 1994).

However, the realities of population distribution within Israel would suggest that, while government intervention has been a major theme within planning policy since the early days of statehood, it has not necessarily achieved the type of population redistribution that it has set for itself in an attempt to achieve political and ideological goals. Three major themes served as the focus for government planning: population decentralization to the peripheral regions; the establishment of new settlements in locations deemed to be of political importance, and the creation of rural utopias based around unique forms of agricultural cooperative communities (Newman, 1986).

In this chapter, we will argue that these objectives have only ever been achieved partially, and that the extent to which they have been achieved does not necessarily justify the amount of resources — both human and financial — which have been invested in these planning models. It will be argued that there is an inherent contradiction between government intervention in planning, on the one hand, and the realities of internal migration and population distribution in Israel, on the other. This is partly due to the lack of attention paid to the impact of global social and economic processes, on the one hand, and to the changing social structure and aspirations of second and third generation Israelis, on the other. Questions are raised concerning the future role of government in its attempt to determine settlement policy as contrasted with the growing force of the market in determining where people choose to reside. A willingness to learn from the migration processes which operate in other Western post-industrial societies, rather than dismissing them as being irrelevant to the "unique" Israeli experience, would, it is argued, better serve the long-term policies of regional and settlement planners in Israel.

Processes of Internal Migration

The evolving human and settlement landscapes of the Western world are a function of the dynamic processes of migration — both international and internal — which have been experienced by these societies during the past 150 years (Clark, 1986; Greenwood, 1985; Jones, 1990; de Blij, 1993, pp. 111-133). While natural growth and international migration are the two factors accounting for demographic growth, any understanding of the internal spatial distribution of state populations also has to take into account the major influences of internal migration. These processes tend to be influenced by a variety of geographic, social, and economic factors favoring the location of employment opportunities, socially desirable neighborhoods, "quality of life" considerations, and/or lower living costs.

Three major types of internal migration have taken place during the past 150-200 years: 1. rural-urban/periphery-center migration, 2. suburbanization and exurbanization, and 3. gentrification.

While these different processes have taken place in a clear chronological frame, they have not been equal in either time or size. Neither are they mutually exclusive of each other. Western societies of today are experiencing all three processes at one and the same time, indicating the varied demands and social stratification of increasingly heterogeneous and mobile populations.

Rural-Urban/Periphery-Center Migration

The industrial revolution heralded the beginning of modern mass migrations. The structural move from agriculture to industry and the increased mobilization brought about by the coming of the railroads and, much later, the automobile resulted in large-scale movement from rural to urban areas. The new modes of production, most notably the industrial factory, constituted alternative pull factors to that of the village which, in turn, experienced the transition from a labor-intensive to a mechanized agricultural economy. Rural-urban migration brought about the demographic depletion of many rural and peripheral regions, on the one hand, and the growth of towns and metropolitan areas, on the other. Population became increasingly centralized both geographically and economically. Third world countries undergoing modernization during the past fifty years are experiencing similar mass internal migration trends. However, the rapid rate at which this movement takes place, coupled with the fact that the alternative sources of industrial and urban employment are not available, as was indeed the case in Western Europe during the industrial revolution period, has resulted in the creation of an urban under-class, unemployed and residing in shanty towns on the metropolitan periphery.

Suburbanization and Exurbanization

As towns became more densely populated, urban residents sought to increase their personal and family quality of life by moving away from the metropolitan core areas. Socially, this was perceived as a way of moving into less densely populated surroundings, while economically the availability of cheaper land on the city periphery enabled residents to exchange small inner city apartments for detached housing in new suburban estates. As the city fabric continued to grow, urban residents, especially the middle classes, moved out of the towns altogether into the exurban communities in the metropolitan hinterland. These communities were of two types: either agricultural villages which were slowly being sucked into the urban hinterland and which were undergoing functional and structural change, or new exurban dormitory communities established on agricultural land. Both types of community are characterized by their economic dependence on the metropolitan centers. Residents commute into the towns for employment and other social consumption activities, preferring the distance and cost of commuting to the perceived ills of residing within the heart of the urban fabric.

Gentrification

The most recent phase in the internal migration process has been the commencement of a gentrification process, through which some groups of middle class residents are opting to return to the inner city and core areas of the cities. These populations are characterized by young, professional couples, who desire to move closer to their places of employment and sources of social consumption. Inner city areas, which remained undeveloped and run down, have undergone social and physical face lifts. Much housing rehabilitation has been accompanied by the sharp rise in attractivity and resulting housing prices, slowly forcing the original residents out of the prohibitive housing market. While the gentrification process cannot be compared, numerically, to the rural-urban and exurban movements, it is, nevertheless, an important new phase in the changing balance of internal mobility within post-industrial states.

Regional Planning as Mediation in the Migration Process

Despite the obvious impact of the social and economic pull factors in influencing internal migration, governments often attempt to mediate in the process. Governments intervene in the migration process through the operation of regional planning policies. These policies are intended to create the necessary infrastructural, residential, or economic conditions which will induce people to move (or in some cases not to move) in accordance with national and state ideologies concerning the preferred distribution of population and, in some cases, perceived notions of social equality. Such ideologies may emphasize the need for population decentralization, the settling of the peripheral regions, retaining a rural presence, the creation of socially stratified or socially mixed neighborhoods, and so on.

The first indications of centrally organized regional planning was the publication of the Barlow and Abercrombie reports in Britain during the 1940s (Hall, 1987). The Barlow Commission proposed the intervention of post-war governments in the planning process as a means of slowing down the continued movement of migrants to the south-east and London metropolitan regions. This was seen as a necessary form of intervention which would allow for decentralization and redistribution of population away from a single center which, at that time, was vulnerable to the strategic threat emanating from Germany and the firing of missiles into an over-populated urban center.

The Abercrombie report laid the grounds for post-war regional planning. In the mass reconstruction which took place during the late 1940s and early 1950s, densely populated inner city slum areas were demolished. Much of the population was relocated to new towns in the metropolitan periphery and, in some cases, further afield. Limited population redistribution was achieved by a government which controlled the housing and fiscal resources on which the poorer socio-economic sectors of the population were dependent, and to which they had no direct private access. The improvement of the physical fabric of the new towns, their larger housing units and local social and commercial facilities, was viewed in a deterministic fashion. Better living conditions would, so it was argued, bring about a healthier economic and social fabric, an argument which has not necessarily proved its worth during the ensuing fifty years.

Overall, policies aimed at encouraging population redistribution have not always proved to be entirely successful. At best, they have mediated, or slowed down, the processes of internal periphery-core migration, but they have not brought about a turnaround in the general patterns of mobility. Western societies have continued to experience rapid processes of centralization into a smaller number of urban agglomerations, accompanied by a parallel growth in the spatial extent of the functional area of the metropolitan hinterland as a result of intense processes of suburbanization and exurbanization. These latter processes may have weakened the inner city cores, but have served to strengthen the overall processes of centralization and metropolitanization at the expense of the periphery. The provision of economic incentives for cheaper housing, factory relocation, and the creation of employment opportunities in the periphery have had short term effects. The centralization of both national and global economic activity have proved to be strong counter forces, influencing population mobility and residential desirability in locations of greatest economic and social benefit.

The Ideology of Settlement Planning in Israel

Concerning Israel, the unique experience of "the ingathering of the exiles" has meant that the focus for study has remained on the international aspect of the migration process. The choice of residential location and patterns of internal migration have always been viewed as constituting the immigrant absorption part of this international process, one which is directed and controlled by government rather than possessing independent internal dynamics of its own, especially as it relates and contrasts with similar processes which have been present in other Western societies during the past century.

Notwithstanding, all three dimensions of the internal migration process are present in Israel. Migration from the periphery to the core has continually taken place, especially with respect to the Jewish inhabitants of the country (Kipnis, 1996; Lipshitz, 1991; Shachar and Lipshitz, 1981). The past two decades have also witnessed a strong counter-urbanization movement out of the city centers and into the suburban and exurban landscapes of the metropolitan hinterland (Gonen, 1996, 1997; Kipnis, 1989; Newman and Applebaum, 1989, 1995), while more recently inner city neighborhoods in both Tel Aviv and Jerusalem have been affected by the initial processes of gentrification (Shnell and Graicer, 1991). These processes contrast with the stated planning objectives and ideology of the public sector ministries charged with controlling the spatial distribution of Israel's population.

Settlement planning in Israel has always been a highly centralized activity, controlled and implemented by government (Housing and Interior Ministries) and quasi-government (Rural Settlement Department of the Jewish Agency) institutions (Hill, 1986; Newman, 1986). The establishment of "settlement" is closely associated with the ideological underpinnings of Zionism and state formation (Troen, 1988; Kellerman, 1994). Settlement is perceived as a means by which three major state objectives can be achieved: 1. The absorption of immigrants through the provision of state-subsidized housing, 2. redistribution and decentralization of the Jewish population in the peripheral regions of the country, and 3. creating a political presence in regions of ethno-national conflict.

The Absorption of Immigrants Through the Provision of State-Subsidized Housing

The construction of urban neighborhoods and rural settlements by the state is an important tool for immigrant absorption. The role of the state in providing housing for immigrants was highlighted in the wake of the mass Russian immigration when, following a period during the 1980s during which the private sector became more involved in the provision of housing, the public sector, namely, the state, undertook the major construction schemes necessary for the immediate housing needs of the newly arrived immigrant population (Newman, Gradus and Levinson, 1994; Lipshitz, 1996c).

Redistribution and Decentralization of the Jewish Population in the Peripheral Regions of the Country

For both economic and political reasons, it has traditionally been perceived as undesirable to allow the continued centralization and concentration of the Israeli population in a metropolitan belt in the coastal plain and along the Jerusalem corridor (Lipshitz, 1991). Government has provided housing, mortgage, and tax incentives in an attempt to induce people to reside in the Galilee and Negev regions. In the Galilee, population redistribution is also seen as a means of achieving ethno-demographic balance between residents — Jewish and Arab citizens of the region (Kipnis, 1984, 1996), while in the Negev redistributive policies are seen as a means by which the "empty" desert can be populated as part of state ideology which focusses on the desert as the future, and perhaps only, region for future development (Gradus, 1996). Only the public sector is able to undertake the necessary infrastructural investment during periods of mass immigration. This is as true of the early 1950s as it was in the early 1990s.

Creating a Political Presence in Regions of Ethno-National Conflict

The establishment of settlements along the border regions of Israel, the creation of rural communities throughout the upland regions of Arab-populated Galilee, as well as the establishment of development towns throughout the periphery, were all policies whose objective was to create a Jewish territorial and demographic presence and numerical majority in regions over which there were alternative and conflicting national and territorial claims. Settlement, particularly rural settlement, has traditionally been perceived as a means by which territory is controlled through the creation of a civilian presence which strikes roots and develops an attachment to the land (Kimmerling, 1983; Newman, 1989). Territory which is settled by Jewish residents becomes, according to this perception, part of the Jewish ecumene and will not be given up as part of the political struggle between Jews and Arabs.

The state control of key resources, most notably land and finance, enabled government to intervene in the housing market to a far greater degree than in any other Western society (Gonen and Hasson, 1983; Kipnis, 1987). Government, through the Israel Lands Authority, is the "owner" of over 90 percent of the land in Israel. Development policies and land zoning had to be authorized by government. Planning officials took on the role of ideological and social gatekeepers, through which the urban and rural landscapes were developed according to national objectives. Preference was given to the development of the rural and agricultural sectors, often at the expense of town planning (Cohen, 1970; Troen, 1988). Vast amounts of resources were poured into the creation and geographical dispersion of many small communities, mostly kibbutzim and moshavim, throughout the periphery (Shachar and Razin, 1988). These communities were perceived as being at the heart of the process of state formation and as contributing to the creation of a "unique" social fabric representing the aspirations of the state founders.

Urban development was also guided by national and political objectives. Some thirty development towns were established throughout the country, most of them in the Galilee and Negev regions, as a means of providing housing for the mass immigration of the early 1950s (Shachar, 1971; Troen, 1995). The location of many of these towns in the geographic periphery of the country enabled the state to create a Jewish demographic presence in areas (such as the Galilee) in which there was a large Arab presence, as well as forcefully decentralizing population away from the metropolitan center. Immigrants were often sent to these new towns immediately on arrival in Israel, without any prior knowledge of where they were going, or what, if any, locational alternatives were available. The development towns were transformed into social ghettos of the underprivileged, continually displaying higher unemployment, lower education, and generally weaker socio-economic indicators (Efrat, 1987). They experienced conditions of double peripherality, through which their peripheral geographical location coupled with the socio-economic characteristics of their resident populations resulted in the social construction of segregated spaces inhabited by ethnic groups who saw, and in many cases continue to see, themselves as excluded from the benefits enjoyed by other sectors of society.

Paradoxically, it is in the settlements and townships created by government intervention in the planning process, in which these poorer socio-economic conditions apply. The metropolitan center of the country continues to enjoy relative economic success, as displayed by its attractivity for internal migration, despite the fact that it was largely neglected by the institutionalized planning framework. Regional patterns of inequality have, ironically, partially resulted from government intervention, rather than neglect (Shachar and Lipshitz, 1981; Lipshitz, 1996a, 1996b). This was also partially due to the fact that it was clearly not possible to meet all of the conflicting objectives at one and the same time. Kark (1995) notes that:

> In practice, the political and strategic aims of population dispersal were given priority over the social consequences of immigrant absorption. Mass immigration, for example, created core and peripheral regions that perpetuated differences of ethnic origin, seniority in the country, levels of development and access to economic and cultural resources (p. 487).

Population Distribution:
The Failure of Settlement Planning?

To what extent has government intervention in the planning process achieved the goals set by the national planning ideology? Examination of the population data for 1995 would suggest that while the state has been influential in determining settlement location, the net effect of this heavy intervention has only partially met the objectives set by the planners. This is apparent with respect to both the relative distribution of population between rural and urban communities, as well as the inter-regional distribution of the Jewish population.

Rural-Urban Population Balance

Despite the emphasis on the unique rural experimentation of the social utopias of both the kibbutz and the moshav (Weintraub, Lissak and Atzmon, 1969), the entire rural sector in Israel has never accounted for more than 15 percent of the population. The peak was reached in the late 1950s, following a decade of intense government sponsored settlement activity, particularly the establishment of moshavim for newly arrived immigrants. Since the early 1960s, the proportion of the rural population has undergone continual decline, the absolute growth of the rural sector always lagging behind the national population growth (Table 8.1).

Paradoxically, this situation is partially due to the operation of institutional intervention within the planning process itself. The rural utopias, in general, and the kibbutz, in particular, were perceived as being for the select few. Rural planners operating within the framework of the Settlement Department of the Jewish Agency acted as social gatekeepers who closely screened the social "compatibility" of potential rural settlers. In many cases, they were deemed as unsuitable and, as such, prevented from joining existing communities or establishing new communities. Moreover, in an effort to maintain the utopian vision of rural lifestyles as perceived by the planners, government planning agencies denied access to all forms of alternative community forms other than those which conformed to the moshav/kibbutz organizational models. As controllers of land, government-authorized agencies were in a unique position to zone land according to the ideological dictates of planning policy. Government agencies acted as social gatekeepers, restricting rural lifestyles to the few (Newman, 1986; Applebaum and Newman, 1989; Applebaum, Newman and Margulies, 1989).

Even the small percentage of the population defined as "rural" in official statistics is questionable. Most of the increase in the rural population since the late 1970s consists of the residents of the many new exurban communities which have been created throughout the country, on both sides of the "green line," and which are exurban in nature (Kipnis, 1989; Newman and Applebaum, 1989; Gonen, 1996, 1997). These rurban communities, containing nearly one percent of the total population and continuing to grow at a rapid rate (Table 8.1), continue to be defined as "rural communities" in the census data. But these communities are only rural inasmuch as they are located within non-metropolitan areas and consist of low density, detached housing units. In all other functional respects, they are urban communities, made up of town dwellers seeking to improve their "quality of life" by migrating to the outer parts of the metropolitan hinterland.

TABLE 8.1
Rural and Urban Populations in Israel, 1961-1995
(Total population figures in thousands)

	1961		1972			1983			1995		
	Total	% of Total	Total	% of total	% change 1961-72	Total	% of total	% change 1972-83	Total	% of total	% change 1983-95
Total	2,179.5	100.0	3,147.7	100.0	44.4	4,037.6	100.0	28.3	5,643.5	100.0	39.8
Urban	1,837.6	84.3	2,789.1	88.6	51.8	3,616.0	89.6	29.6	5,130.1	90.9	41.9
Towns over 200,000	736.6	33.8	897.2	28.5	21.8	981.7	24.3	9.4	1,227.2	21.7	25.0
Rural	341.9	15.7	358.5	11.4	4.9	421.6	10.4	17.6	513.4	9.1	21.8
Kibbutz	77.1	3.5	89.7	2.8	16.3	115.5	2.9	28.8	125.4	2.2	8.5
Moshav	120.6	5.5	125.1	4.0	3.7	140.7	3.5	12.4	171.0	3.0	21.5
Dormitory Communities							7.8	0.2	51.8	0.9	566.1

Source: Israel Central Bureau of Statistics, 1995

The statistical definition used for rural communities is becoming increasingly problematic even for the kibbutz and moshav villages. Many of these communities are undergoing structural change. Agricultural production has long been replaced by industrial and quaternary sources of employment for many. As the collective and cooperative frameworks are gradually broken up, many of these villages are becoming transformed into dormitory communities, similar in nature to the new exurban settlements. The fact that they continue to live in communities which, by formal definition, are designated as "rural" no longer reflects the functional realities of their lifestyles.

While the contribution of the rural cooperative sector to the state formation process should not be dismissed, normative historiographies and geographies of the country have tended to overemphasize the disproportionate role played by the rural vis-a-vis the urban. The Jewish population of Israel is, and notwithstanding government intervention in the planning process has always been, a predominantly urban one. This is reflected not only in the 90 percent of the population defined as "urban," but also in the social and economic production and consumption patterns of the remaining 10 percent, defined as "rural." The attempt to introduce rural utopias which were perceived as reflecting the Zionist ideal only ever appealed to the minority. This minority has shrunk even further as second and third generation residents have become transformed into rurban dwellers of the countryside or, in many cases, left the village communities altogether. Just as the shtetl of Eastern Europe was a township rather than the idealized semi-agricultural community, so, too, the advanced stage of rural development in Israel is indicative of the urbanization process experienced by a landscape undergoing transformation.

Center-Periphery Regional Balance

For administrative purposes, Israel is divided into six districts, each of which is, in turn, divided into sub-districts (Table 8.2). All statistical and decennial census data is collected and organized according to these sub-divisions, allowing us to compare and contrast the spatial distribution of the Israeli population over time, as well as examining inter-regional migration trends and balances.

TABLE 8.2
Distribution of Israeli Population According to Major Administrative Regions, 1961-1995
(Total population figures in thousands)

	1961 Total	1961 % of Total	1972 Total	1972 % of total	% change 1961-72	1983 Total	1983 % of total	% change 1972-83	1995 Total	1995 % of total	% change 1983-95
Total	2,179.5	100.0	3,147.7	100.0	44.4	4,037.6	100.0	28.3	5,643.5	100.0	39.8
Northern	337.1	15.5	473.9	15.1	40.6	656.0	16.2	38.4	946.8	16.8	44.3
Haifa	370.3	17.0	483.8	15.4	30.7	575.3	14.2	18.9	746.8	13.2	29.8
Jerusalem	191.9	8.8	347.4	11.0	81.1	472.9	11.7	36.1	682.5	12.1	44.3
Central	407.1	18.7	579.7	18.4	42.4	830.7	20.6	43.3	1,222.5	21.7	47.2
Tel Aviv	699.3	32.1	907.2	28.8	29.7	1,000.3	24.8	10.2	1,158.0	20.5	15.8
Southern	173.9	8.0	354.2	11.3	103.7	478.8	11.9	35.2	753.5	13.4	57.4
West Bank/ Gaza			1.5	0.1		23.8	0.6	1,485.9	133.5	2.4	461.2

Source: Israel Central Bureau of Statistics, 1995

In 1961, just over 50 percent of the population resided in the Central and Tel Aviv districts, as compared with only 20 percent of the population in the Northern and Southern regions of the country. By 1995, these figures had changed to 42 and 30 percent respectively (Table 8.2). An initial assessment of this change would indicate that the internal migration process during the preceding thirty years had resulted in a redistribution of population away from the overcrowded center of the country in favor of the peripheral regions.

A detailed look at the data indicates, however, some contradictory trends. Within the central metropolitan regions, there has been significant growth of population, partially countered by an outmigration from within the urban centers themselves. Thus, while the towns of Tel Aviv and Haifa have experienced a decline in the percentage of the national population residing within them, the wider metropolitan region has experienced significant growth. This indicates the geographic growth of the metropolitan center as a result of processes of suburbanization, exurbanization and the growth and coalescence of the second order towns (such as Herzliya, Petah Tikva and Rehovot, located to the immediate north, east and south of Tel Aviv respectively). The statistical definition of what constitutes the "metropolitan area" has changed in each census. This takes account of continued urban expansion within a highly densely populated coastal belt of towns, with approximately 65 percent of the population residing within 10 percent of the country's land surface. With the easing of land zoning controls in the early 1990s, partly due to the mass construction activity which has taken place throughout the country as the impact of the mass Russian immigration has been felt, the few remaining areas of agricultural land within the central metropolitan region are gradually becoming transformed into urban housing and construction projects.

Within the peripheral Northern and Southern statistical regions, the overall increase in the percentage of the population hides the internal distribution of the inhabitants. The increase in the Southern region from 8 to 13 percent from 1961 to 1995 hides the fact that this population is almost entirely concentrated in and around the two urban centers of Ashkelon and Beer Sheva, both of which are located in the northern margins of this region. Moreover, the Southern region, as statistically defined, covers approximately 60 percent of the country's land surface, while containing less than 15 percent of the population (Yiftachel, 1992). South of Beer Sheva, the Negev remains sparsely populated and less developed by comparison with the rest of the country.

Both the Negev and the Northern Galilee regions have always been designated as priority regions for development and population redistribution. The Negev has played an important part in the creation of a collective spatial imagination, the ultimate realization of the Zionist dream of making the desert bloom and develop. Developing and populating the desert was spearheaded by Ben-Gurion as a central part of his state-building ideology. In the case of the Galilee, the desire to promote Jewish settlement of this region was spurred on by the perceived political need to create demographic parity between Jewish and Arab citizens of the region, and to transform this parity into a Jewish demographic majority.

Neither of these two regional objectives has been fulfilled. While most of the Negev remains unpopulated, so, too, the demographic ratio within the Galilee has not achieved the desired political situation. Within the entire Northern and Haifa statistical districts, there is a tenuous parity between Arab and Jewish populations. However, even this figure is misleading in that it includes the Haifa metropolitan belt along the northern coastal plain as well as the Jewish settlement belt in the east running from Kiryat Shmona south to Tiberias. If taken by itself, the interior sub-districts of the Lower and Upper Galilee display clear Arab demographic majorities, in some cases reaching 75-80 percent of the local population.

This is viewed by Israeli governments as harmful, not least because of the contesting claims to land ownership and territorial control. This has been reflected in continuous government policies aimed at changing this demographic balance in favor of the Jewish population. The creation of development towns during the 1950s was used as a means of bringing large groups of immigrants to the Galilee, while the establishment of moshav communities throughout the mountain interior, despite the lack of cultivable land, was an attempt to preserve territorial control at the micro level. Later projects, such as the creation of industrial villages in the 1970s (Applebaum, Newman and Margulies, 1989) and the *"mitzpim"* (outpost) communities in the late 1970s and early 1980s (Soffer and Finkel, 1988) were further attempts, largely unsuccessful, to achieve similar politico-demographic objectives.

Discussion

The establishment of development towns in the peripheral regions is an important indication of the nature of government intervention in the planning and implementation process. During periods of mass immigration, such as that of the North African immigrants in the 1950s and the more recent Russian aliya, government has been able to "replenish" the slowly dwindling Jewish population of the regions of out-migration through short-term mass operations. Only the public sector is able to undertake the immediate mass construction activity necessary for settling hundreds of thousands of immigrants in such a short time period. As such, it is also able to control the available residential locations and direct the immigrants to preferred locations.

Notwithstanding, the use of such heavy state intervention in the recent period has resulted in a heated debate concerning the effectiveness of such a tool. Proponents of population dispersal and decentralization argued that the government should only construct houses and provide financial assistance for immigrants who opted for the preferred peripheral locations. It was alternately argued that such policies were out of line with the economic realities of the country and that immigrants should be allowed to settle wherever they chose, according to the market realities of available housing and employment opportunities. The result of the huge numbers of immigrants who arrived during this period was that both policies were allowed to operate at one and the same time. Government was active in the construction of new neighborhoods in nearly all of the development towns in both the Galilee and Negev regions, in some cases resulting in short-term increases of nearly 50 percent in the local population (Newman, Gradus and Levinson, 1994). Equally, those who so desired were able to rent housing in the center of the country, often at a far higher cost than that available in the development towns, but with closer proximity to available employment opportunities.

Internal migration balances show a long-term outflow of the population from the peripheral regions to the expanding metropolitan center. In the case of the Galilee, the Jewish residents of the development towns perceive the region as constituting a social and economic periphery, while the Arab residents of the region see this as their political and social center. Thus, not only do differential rates of natural growth favor the Arab population, regional migration demonstrates a trend for out-migration by Jews alone. The large government plans aimed at increasing the Jewish population of the region have done little in the way of achieving their political objectives. At the most, large scale government intervention during periods of mass immigration results in the long-term demographic balance between the Arab and Jewish populations of the region undergoing short-term jumps in favor of the Jewish population, followed by long-term out-migration in favor of the expanding metropolitan center.

Of particular interest has been the paradoxical result of government settlement policies which have promoted Jewish settlement of the administered territories. Despite their self-portrayal as constituting the modern incarnation of the pioneer settlers of the periphery, the region in question is located within the geographical center of the country, part of the expanding exurban belt of the Tel Aviv and Jerusalem metropolitan regions. At the same time, government policies, especially during the 1980s, in favor of this region have meant that the economic incentives normally used to induce settlement of the periphery have also been provided for settlers in these areas. Residents of this region thus enjoy the benefits of "double centrality," namely, the ability to obtain government assistance and subsidies while residing within the center of the country (Newman, 1996b). This largely explains the relative success of the settler movement in attracting over 150,000 settlers, the majority of whom are to be found in the optimal geographic locations hugging the former green line boundary, just a few minutes drive from the urban centers within pre-1967 Israel.

Despite the changed social and economic conditions of Israel, government continues to view itself as the coordinator of national settlement policy. Shachar (1996) notes that the number of new national plans prepared between 1990 and 1995 is only equalled by the number of planning blueprints drawn up during the first decade of statehood. At the same time, the new national plans, partially drawn up in an attempt to absorb the large number of Russian immigrants who arrived during this period, were different than those of the past, with an emphasis on metropolitan development, the partial recognition that Israel, as a small country, is becoming transformed into a single integrated metropolitan area, and that the economic pressure for land in the metropolitan core must enable an easing of the restrictions which have governed the preservation of rural land during the past 50 years (Shachar, 1996). In a similar vein, Kellerman (1996) notes that notions such as settlement challenges and frontier regions no longer have prominence in government policy statements and that attention is now being focussed on the metropolitan centers. Notwithstanding, government policy is to encourage this changing planning doctrine through the same forms of intervention and control which governed the promotion of the population redistribution policies of the past.

The implicit recognition that the formation of the Israeli human landscape is affected by the operation of social and economic processes common to other Western societies is an important paradigmatic change in the thinking of government planners. It marks the transition from a highly ideological and unique interpretation of landscape formation to one which gives due account to processes of metropolitanization and exurbanization. In some senses, it marks a transition from a Zionist to a post-Zionist landscape which fits the socio-economic realities of a post-industrial country entering a new millennium.

References

Applebaum, L. and D. Newman. 1989. *Between Village and Suburb: New Settlement Forms in Israel.* Jerusalem: Bialik Publishers (Hebrew).

Applebaum, L., D. Newman and J. Margulies. 1989. "Institutions and Settlers as Reluctant Partners: Changing Power Relations and the Development of New Settlement Patterns in Israel." *Journal of Rural Studies,* 5(1):99-109.

Cohen, E. 1970. *The City in the Zionist Ideology.* Jerusalem: Institute of Urban and Regional Studies, Hebrew University of Jerusalem.

Clark, W. 1986. *Human Migration.* London: Sage Publications.

de Blij, H. 1993. *Human Geography: Culture, Society and Space.* New York: Wiley.

Efrat, E. 1987. *Development Towns in Israel: Past or Future?* Tel Aviv: Achiasaf Press (Hebrew).

Gonen, A. 1996. *Between City and Suburb: Urban Residential Patterns and Processes in Israel.* England: Avebury Press.

Gonen, A. 1997. "From City to Suburb: Changing Residential Preferences Amongst the Jewish Middle Class in Israel." *Geography and Jewish Studies.* Ed. H. Brodsky and R. Mitchell. College Park: University of Maryland Press.

Gonen, A. and S. Hasson. 1983. "The Use of Housing as a Spatio-political Measure: The Israeli Case." *Geoforum,* 14:103-109.

Gradus, Y. 1996. "The Negev Desert: The Transformation of a Frontier into a Periphery." *The Mosaic of Israeli Geography.* Ed. Y. Gradus and G. Lipshitz. Beer Sheva: Ben-Gurion University Press, pp. 321-334.

Greenwood, M.J. 1985. "Human Migration: Theory, Models and Empirical Studies." *Journal of Regional Science,* vol. 25.

Hall, P. 1987. *Urban and Regional Planning.* 2nd ed. London: Allen & Unwin.

Hill, M. 1986. "Israeli Planning in an Age of Turbulence." *Planning in Turbulence.* Ed. D. Morley and A. Shachar. Jerusalem: Magnes Press, pp. 57-68.

Israel Central Bureau of Statistics. 1996. *Census of Population and Housing, 1995: Provisional Results.* Publication no. 1. Jerusalem: Government Printer.

Jones, H. 1990. *Population Geography.* London: Paul Chapman.

Kark, R. 1995. "Planning, Housing and Land Policy 1948-1952: The Formation of Concepts and Governmental Frameworks." *Israel: The First Decade of Independence.* Ed. I. Troen and N. Lucas. Albany: SUNY Press, pp. 461-494.

Kellerman, A. 1994. *Society and Settlement: Jewish Land of Israel in the Twentieth Century.* Albany: SUNY Press.

Kellerman, A. 1996. "Settlement Myth and Settlement Activity: Interrelationships in the Zionist Land of Israel. *Transactions of the Institute of British Geographers,* 21:363-378.

Kimmerling, B. 1983. *Zionism and Territory.* Berkeley: University of California Press.

Kipnis, B.A. 1984. "Role and Timing of Complementary Objectives of a Regional Policy; the Case of Northern Israel." *Geoforum,* 15:191-200.

Kipnis, B.A. 1987. "Geopolitical Ideologies and Regional Strategies in Israel." *Tijdschrift voor Economische en Sociale Geografie* (TESG), 78:125-138.

Kipnis, B.A. 1989. "Untimely Metropolitan Field 'Rurban' Development — Rural Renaissance as a Geopolitical Process in Israel. *Geography Research Forum,* 9:45-65.

Kipnis, B.A. 1996. "From Dispersal to Concentration: Alternating Spatial Strategies in Israel." *The Mosaic of Israeli Geography.* Ed. Y. Gradus and G. Lipshitz. Beer Sheva: Ben-Gurion University Press, pp. 29-36.

Lipshitz, G. 1991. "Immigration and Internal Migration as a Mechanism of Polarization and Dispersion of Population and Development: The Israeli Example." *Economic Development and Cultural Change,* 39:391-408.

Lipshitz, G. 1996a. "Core vs. Periphery in Israel Over Time: Inequality, Internal Migration and Immigration." *The Mosaic of Israeli Geography*. Ed. Y. Gradus and G. Lipshitz. Beer Sheva: Ben-Gurion University Press, pp. 13-28.

Lipshitz, G. 1996b. Regional Disparities in Israel Over Time." *European Spatial Research and Policy*, vol. 3 (2):95-108.

Lipshitz, G. 1996c. "Integration of Immigrants from the Former Soviet Union in the Israeli Housing and Job Markets: Regional Perspectives." *International Migration: Regional and Urban Economic Impacts and Policies*. Ed. P. Nijkamp and C. Gorter. Aldershot, UK: Avebury Press.

Newman, D. 1986. "Functional Change and the Settlement Structure in Israel: A Study of Political Control, Response and Adaptation." *Journal of Rural Studies*, 2:127-137.

Newman, D. 1989. "Civilian and Military Presence as Strategies of Territorial Control: The Arab-Israel Conflict." *Political Geography Quarterly*, 8 (3):215-227.

Newman, D. 1996a. "Efficiency, Functionality and the Social Construction of Municipal Space: Reforming Rural Local Government in Israel. Working Paper No. 7, Negev Center for Regional Development. Beer Sheva: Ben-Gurion University of the Negev.

Newman, D. 1996b. "The Territorial Politics of Exurbanisation: Reflections on Thirty Years of Jewish Settlement in the West Bank." *Israel Affairs*.

Newman, D. and L. Applebaum. 1989. "Defining the Rurban Settlement: Planning Models and Functional Realities in Israel." *Urban Geography*, 10:281-295.

Newman, D. and L. Applebaum. 1995. "Conflicting Objectives for Rural Local Government: Service Provision to Exurban Communities in Israel." *Government & Policy*, 13:253-271.

Newman, D., Y. Gradus and E. Levinson. 1994. *The Impact of Mass Immigration on Urban Settlements in the Negev, 1989-1991*. Occasional Paper No. 3, Negev Center for Regional Development. Beer Sheva: Ben-Gurion University of the Negev.

Shachar, A. 1971. "Israel's Development Towns: Evaluation of National Urbanization Policy." *Journal of the American Institute of Planners*, 17:271-291.

Shachar, A. 1996. "National Planning at a Crossroads: The Evolution of a New Planning Doctrine for Israel." *The Mosaic of Israeli Geography*. Ed. Y. Gradus and G. Lipshitz. Beer Sheva: Ben-Gurion University Press, pp. 3-12.

Shachar, A. and G. Lipshitz. 1981. "Regional Inequalities in Israel." *Environment and Planning A*, 13:463-473.

Shachar, A. and E. Razin. 1988. "The Development of the Settlement Map of Israel, 1948-1982." *The Transformation of Israeli Society.* Ed. S. Eisenstadt. London: Weidenfeld & Nicholson, pp. 198-208.

Shnell, Y. and I. Graicer. 1991. "Population Return to Tel Aviv, 1979-1989. *Merhavim,* 4:35-56 (Hebrew).

Soffer, A. and R. Finkel. 1988. *The Mitzpim in the Galilee.* Studies in Regional Development, no. 43. Rehovot: Settlement Study Center.

Troen, I. 1988. "The Transformation of Zionist Planning Policy: From Rural Settlements to an Urban Network." *Planning Perspectives,* 3:3-23.

Troen, I. 1995. "New Departures in Zionist Planning: The Development Town." *Israel: The First Decade of Independence.* Ed. I. Troen and N. Lucas. Albany: SUNY Press, pp. 441-460.

Weintraub, D., M. Lissak and Y. Atzmon. 1969. *Moshava, Kibbutz and Moshav: Patterns of Jewish Rural Development in Palestine.* Ithaca: Cornell University Press.

Yiftachel, O. 1992. *Planning a Mixed Region in Israel: The Political Geography of Arab-Jewish Relations in the Galilee.* Aldershot, UK: Avebury Press.

III

Migration to the Diaspora — The Canadian and U.S. Cases

9

With Our Young and With Our Old: Multi-Generational Family Migration and Ethnic/Religious Identity

Allen Glicksman

Introduction

This chapter has two rather ambitious goals. The first is to examine the recent wave of migration from the former Soviet Union (FSU) to the United States (U.S.) and to ask what type of formal ethnic/religious identity these migrants bring with them and how does this identity relate to their lives in the U.S. The second goal is to examine the impact of migration on two- and three-generation families arriving together, a new phenomenon, on their daily lives and on their self-definitions in terms of ethnicity and religion.

Let us begin with a question that comes from the Jewish experience. Why did Joseph Karo write the *Shulhan Aruch*? This is not a question one would expect in a discussion on Soviet immigrants, but one that points to the situation in American Jewry today. Karo wrote the *Shulhan Aruch* in part because the expulsion from Spain had created (in one sense) not a single Sephardic diaspora but multiple diasporas. Jews from each town in Spain set up their own synagogues in the cities of the Spanish diaspora so that a single town could have a Cordoba synagogue, a Barcelona synagogue, etc.

The *Shulhan Aruch* was designed to bring conformity of ritual to this somewhat chaotic situation (Werblowsky, 1977, p. 7).

This model of the Spanish diaspora is perhaps a better model for the current situation in the U.S. than the traditional American model. In the model, a wave of immigrants arrives and establishes an ethnic community. Sometimes this wave is followed by further waves of immigrants from the same ethnic heritage, with each new wave being absorbed by previous waves of migrants. In this second model, persons of similar geographic origin combined to form a single group, such as the creation of an "Italian" immigrant group from the various localities on the Italian peninsula and Sicily. This group then absorbed other immigrants from what became Italy. The majority of Jews in the U.S. today are descended from the same East European Jewish community as the majority of Jews from the former Soviet Union (FSU). However, for the past seventy years one group has been adjusting to an Anglo-Protestant culture while the other has grown in an East European and Soviet culture. The first group has also been allowed to maintain its own institutions and educate its youth while the second has been forbidden to do so. For these reasons the new immigrants are establishing a new diaspora connected to but independent from the old. Whether the two will become one is yet to be seen, but at the present time there are two diasporas living side by side in uneasy alliance.

The data presented here comes primarily from a project funded by the National Institutes of Health designed to determine if minority status has an effect on access to health and social services for elderly refugees. The project was funded to the University of Pennsylvania with a sub-contract to the Philadelphia Geriatric Center. The project collected data from middle-aged women and from some of the elders they care for. Research subjects were recruited from among Vietnamese, Cambodian (minority), Soviet Jewish, and Soviet Ukrainian (non-minority) refugees. We interviewed women because they are the ones most likely to be caring for an older relative. This older relative in turn is more likely to be female because women live longer than men. Women are also more often the "kin keepers," that is, the person in the family who is keeping the family together. We selected Soviet Jewish and Soviet Ukrainian refugees because the Jewish community maintains an extensive network of social and health agencies while the Ukrainian community does not. We wanted to know whether the existence or absence of a network sponsored by the same ethnic group as the refugees made a difference in their use of services. The author of this chapter was responsible for the data gathering in the two Soviet refugee communities. In addition, data from other research projects conducted by the author involving Jewish and Ukrainian respondents will also be presented. These include a study of use of social services by women who immigrated to the U.S. in the 1940s and 1950s, interviews with older women in small villages in Ukraine, and an ongoing study designed to examine the role of ethnic and religious background in the manner older persons construct and express their sense of personal well-being (Glicksman et al., 1994).

All the projects mentioned above shared four common characteristics. Each survey instrument combined open-ended and closed-ended questions so that we could collect some material that allows for comparison with other studies and other material that allows the respondents to speak for themselves. Each of the studies contained certain common questions. This allowed for comparison across subject groups on that question. Third, each of the interviews was done in the native (or most commonly used) language of the respondent (including Russian, two dialects of Ukrainian, and English, depending on the study and the respondent). Finally, almost all the subjects in these studies were born in, or were the children of people born in, what is today Ukraine. Therefore, we can examine similar issues across immigration cohorts and ethnic groups. In this chapter we will restrict our discussion to the Jewish respondents in these studies.

The general themes to emerge from the study of recent Soviet Jewish immigrants are as follows:

1. Both the American Jews and the Soviet Jews have complex identities, constructed from their self-definitions of what it means to be Jewish, their Jewish knowledge, the political cultures in which they were socialized (the U.S. and the FSU), and their socioeconomic status (for the Soviets both in the FSU and in the U.S.). At this point, belief and experience separate the two communities and this gulf is not easily breached.

2. The differences in culture and life experience mean that even common experience, such as having lived through World War II or getting old, has vastly different meanings for the two groups. For the Soviets, World War II is a defining moment in the lives of all the

elders in a way it is not for the American elderly. And the American elderly, who expect to live for many years after age 65, are very different from the Soviet elderly who do not expect long lives after age 60.

3. The arrival of families with three generations has an effect on the relations between the generations. The children are often the ones with the best understanding of American culture (in earlier generations the father came first and taught the family about the new land). On the other hand, the traditional role of the elder, to transmit tradition, becomes more complex when it is unclear what culture is to be transmitted — Soviet, Russian, or Jewish?

Brief History of Soviet Jews

Prior to discussing Soviet Jews, let us note two seemingly contradictory themes in East European Jewish life before the Soviet Revolution: diversity and commonalties. The commonalties here refer not only to commonalties among East European Jews but between the Jews and the other peoples they lived among. Although the difference in cultures between the groups was vast, there were still shared affective styles (often very expressive), general world views (including mistrust of government officials), and influence from the same political and social movements (for example, scouting, fascism, and communism). The Jews of East Europe, like the Jews of other regions, were influenced by and participated in the political culture of their lands of residence. At the same time, there were significant differences among the Jews. Aside from the well-known (at least in the last generation) conflicts between Galicianers and Litvaks, there were strong negative images among East European Jews of certain East and Central European groups (the Hungarians, for example). One also must take into account the impact of the local political structure in explaining diversity among East European Jews. In many ways the lives of the Jews under the Hapsburgs was different than the lives of the Jews under the Romanovs (and the Romanovs were perhaps the only subject that the Ukrainians and the Jews completely agreed on). Later in the century there was a real cultural gap between the Jews who entered the Soviet Union in the 1940s (Baltic, Western Ukraine) and those who were in the FSU from the beginning.

This diversity among Jews continued in the Communist era, albeit in different forms. There were still secular and religious Jews, but these terms took on new significance as to be religious meant opposing the authority of the state and secular came less to mean the cultural/nationalist identities of the Bund and the Zionist movement and more an affiliation, if not an affinity, to the Soviet regime. Russian culture and Soviet assumptions came to be part of the lives of almost all the citizens of the FSU, even those Jews (and others) who opposed Soviet communism. At the same time, life in the non-European republics was very different from the lives of persons in the European republics and especially in urban areas. Rural-urban differences, which were so important in earlier periods, became less important for the Jews after World War II when Jewish life in the small villages almost (but never entirely) ceased to exist.

There are two sides to the story of the experience of Jews under Soviet rule. The better known side is the attempt by the Soviet government to eradicate Jewish identity and assimilate the Jews into the larger society. This process eventually was transformed into a formal anti-Semitic policy by the state. However, at the beginning of Soviet rule Jews experienced educational opportunities never before seen in East Europe. The Jews took to the New World with some gusto and succeeded in it. In both a formal and informal sense they formed a vanguard (as in the area of fertility where Jewish fertility declined first, followed by the rest of Soviet society, a trend [decline] that is now growing stronger). Although the Jewish Section of the Communist Party played a role in the assimilation of Jews into Soviet society, many Jews willingly "Russified" and modernized with enthusiasm (much of the discussion of Jewish life in the former Soviet Union is taken from Ro'i, 1995).

Soviet anti-Semitism is a complex topic and although we cannot explore all of its dimensions here, it is important to understand it because the self-identities of the Soviet emigres cannot be understood without it. Most Soviet Jews were never active refuseniks or members of dissident Jewish groups. The Soviet Union under Lenin took a two-sided approach to the Jews. On the one hand, they attempted to eliminate anti-Semitism as a state-sponsored activity. They allowed Jews access to education and employment opportunities never before offered. At the same time, again following Lenin's insistence that the Jews were not a nation because they did not have a land of their own, the hope was that the Jews would assimilate and disappear. This meant that as individuals the Jews were no longer disabled because of their origin, but at the same time there was no desire on the part of the government for them to continue to identify as members of a separate group. However, early on it was clear that nationality would not wither away and, in fact, the nationality question became the central issue in Soviet politics. In this atmosphere many Jews enthusiastically took on the role of supporters of Soviet (i.e., Russian) culture. Both Lenin and Stalin attempted to deal with demands for recognition of Jewish nationality. Lenin instituted the Jewish Section of the CP-USSR, and Stalin established Birobijan. These were of course seen as tactical moves, with no real desire on the part of either leader for a sustained Jewish national movement. Stalin's personal feelings toward the Jews surfaced after World War II with more and more paranoid feelings directed at Jews. His death in 1953 prevented a large-scale attack on Jews throughout the FSU. Most Jews were not directly affected by Stalin's activity (any more or less than other people living under his rule). However, the anomalous position of the Jews in the FSU as well as continued anti-Semitism on the part of Soviet leaders would not allow the issue of the Jews to die.

By the mid-1960s, before the emergence of a Soviet Jewry movement in the United States, it seems that the leadership of the FSU concluded that the economic role of the Jews in the USSR was completed and that some change, perhaps emigration, had to be made to reduce the role of the Jews in Soviet life. This change, first voiced by Kosygin, lead to two major changes in Soviet policy towards the Jews. The first was that Jews were allowed to leave the country and soon after the first quotas for Jews were imposed in Soviet higher education. It is difficult to determine what role American foreign policy or Jewish activism played in the changes in Soviet policy toward the Jews from the early 1970s to the end of the USSR. Certainly internal considerations as well as foreign policy concerns in terms of the Middle East played a role. For the purpose of our study, the question of why the Soviet Union made certain decisions is less important than the fact that such decisions were made and affected not only the day-to-day lives of Jews living in the FSU but also their attitudes and basic beliefs. The same system that had promised them so much was now turning on them.

For those persons old enough to remember the days before World War II, this was a heavy blow. These attitudes also allowed a resurgence (to some extent) in public anti-Semitism. The same system they had supported and which had promised them unlimited opportunity was now denying them, their children, and grandchildren a role in society. As with all other things, this varied from republic to republic. It also became enmeshed in the issue of anti-Russian feelings on the part of some non-Russian republics, as the Jews were seen as agents of Russification.

The turning point in the history of Soviet Jews is World War II. There are six reasons the war was so pivotal for this generation. The first was the impact of the Holocaust on the Jewish community, as the extermination of so many Soviet Jews meant the end of Jewish life in most of the small villages in the FSU. Further, traditional Jewish life, which had somehow remained in some of the more isolated villages, was now completely destroyed. This is especially true in Belarus. At the same time, the Soviet Union absorbed many Polish Jews escaping the Nazis as well as absorbing the Jews of the Baltics and Western Ukraine, who formally were living in other countries now annexed, partially or completely, to the USSR. The second key point is that many Jewish veterans of the Red Army remember being treated as equals in the combat units and being Jewish did not matter. This memory of a time of complete equality between Jews and non-Jews is very important to many older Soviet Jews. Third, the image of the heroic Red Army, and even of Marshall Stalin as victor and hero, had significant meaning to this generation of Jews. Many older Soviet Jews say today that the anniversary of the end of the war is the only real holiday they have, although they may observe others. Fourth, some Jews found a need to reexpress their identity as Jews as a response to Hitler's attempt to eradicate them from the earth. There are records in Communist Party and Secret Police files of meetings to establish synagogues and Hebrew schools, meetings sometimes attended by active-duty Red Army officers (Kagedan, 1995). This need to express a Jewish identity is also a part of the lives of many older Soviet Jews. The Soviet government, on the other hand, systematically denied that there was any specific issue related to the Jews during the war. This formal silence on the experience of Jews during the war, coupled with a continuing expression of emotion and remembrance of the war itself, is an important element in the lives of many older Soviet

Jews. Finally, the location and distribution of Jews in the FSU is very much a product of the war. After the war there were enormous population shifts for a number of reasons, one of which had to do with the desire to place urbanized and Russified persons in the newly acquired Western Ukraine, a center of Ukrainian nationalism. Most of the Jews living in Western Ukraine at the beginning of the Soviet Jewry movement had come there after the war.

Together, all these items forged a new and somewhat uncomfortable identity upon Soviet Jews. While there were differences primarily based on region (the cosmopolitan, Western Ukraine versus the Moslem republics), the real problem was often that Jews in the FSU considered themselves to have four identities: Russian by culture, Jewish by nationality (the term used instead of ethnicity), Ukrainian (or whatever other republic they lived in) by citizenship, and Soviet by personality. They were all of these, and yet not fully any of these.

If Soviet Jews did not know who they were, American Jews had even less of an idea of who was coming. American Jews were, by and large, totally unprepared for what happened next for a variety of reasons. They had become American enough that they did not remember what East Europe (and East Europeans) were like in terms of cultural style and outlook. They had come to idealize their own past, and attempted to interpret the Soviet Jewry movement as a second attempt to save European Jewry from the Nazis. They assumed that Soviet Jews would be as anti-Soviet as Cold War America. They had adapted the world view and rules of American social service and had little sense that they needed training in cultural diversity.

The last major migration of Jews to the U.S. had ended in 1922. When the Soviet immigrants began arriving in the mid-1970s, fifty years had passed between immigrant cohorts, and most of what people knew concerning immigrants was based on impressions of their parents and grandparents as well as the stories their ancestors told. This past had come to be more and more idealized, first by the immigrants and then by their children. After the Holocaust this process of idealization only increased, with nostalgia expressed in the popular culture of American Jews, which could already be seen among the immigrants themselves (for instance in songs such as "Romania" and "Belz"). With the publication of books such as *Life is With People*, the romanticization became idealization (Zborowski and Herzog, 1952). Perhaps this achieved its height in the Broadway production, "Fiddler on the Roof." Here Tevye was completely transformed from Sholom Aleichem's original character to someone understood and appreciated by American Jews who created a likeness unto themselves (Halkin in Sholom Aleichem, 1987). Nowhere is this more apparent than in the last scene when Tevye does something unthinkable in the original stories — he accepts Fietka, Havah's non-Jewish husband. American Jews were therefore expecting not only East European Jews of another era, but idealized versions of those Jews — idealized and Americanized.

The mid-1960s saw another major change in American Jewry — a reevaluation of the role of Franklin Roosevelt in regard to the Jews. The image of Roosevelt as a father figure was challenged by authors who argued that he could have done more to save European Jewry and instead chose to do nothing. The implication of all this was that the Jewish community, in its ignorance and idealization of FDR, went along. For many Jews the cry "Never Again!" was less about the behavior of the Nazis and more about the behavior of the Jews in regard to FDR. The Soviet Jewry movement was seen as an opportunity to make up for past mistakes. Portraying the Soviet Union as a second Nazi Germany also fit into the anti-Communist American world view and made the movement much less risky than it seemed to be. This led to the belief on the part of many American Jews that all Soviet Jews would hate the Soviet Union and want to shed its memory (and culture) quickly. Finally, we must also understand that Jews, taking up careers in the professions of social work and psychology, were influenced by American notions of the need for people to help themselves and to take responsibility for their own lives and destinies. Jews were in the vanguard of movements to promote these new ideas, just as they were in the vanguard of new ideas in the FSU.

The reasons for immigration among Jews in the FSU are varied and complex. While the West only saw a desire to escape persecution and live a Jewish life, the reasons any individual migrated are much more complex. There were three main reasons for migration from the FSU before its collapse in 1991 and an additional three, not in place of but in addition to, after 1991. The three pre-1991 reasons were: 1) a desire to escape anti-Semitism, 2) a desire for economic betterment, and 3) a desire to live a Jewish life (and Zionism). The three which were added after 1992 were: 1) a desire to escape environmental pollution (including the disaster at Chernobyl), 2) a desire to escape political and economic uncertainty, and 3) family reunification (the ostensible reason for allowing migration in the FSU was now real).

Preparation for the influx of Soviet Jews was done with the assumptions made above, as well as the argument as to whether they should be welcomed to the United States at all. There was an argument that all such emigrants from the FSU should go to Israel, and from the first there was conflict over this group. Soviet immigrants were to be handled within the standard organizations that had handled such immigrants before, especially the Hebrew Immigrant Aid Society (Levin, 1986). Attempts were made to divide the immigrants between cities, and other methods were developed without real attention to the previous history of immigrants to the United States. They were expected to adjust to American life quickly, and this meant not only a home and a job, but to the American and American Jewish way of life as well. The ideological tone of the Soviet Jewry movement was that the Soviet Union was attempting to destroy Jewish life (if not the Jews) and so the desire to be free (American) and Jewish (American Jewish) should be a part of the experience of every Soviet Jew.

The departure to the United States was for many Jews hasty and last minute. Many had relatives who did not leave, or who settled in Canada. More importantly, many had relatives in Israel. Sometimes relatives and contacts in other cities, such as New York, became a basis for comparison of services with those in Philadelphia.

Absorption of Soviet Immigrants

From the beginning, the new arrivals were identified as a single distinct immigration cohort. These Jews were called "Russians," a misnomer in two ways: first, because they were Jews, and second, because they did not all come from the Russian Republic. But attitudes toward the definition of nationality, their speaking Russian, and ignorance of the realities of East Europe all contributed to the fact that they began to call themselves Russians, acquiring a new identity in a new land. Differences in the waves of Soviet migration (1976-1982, 1989-) are also poorly understood.

The Soviet Jews did not know what to expect in the United States. Their only source of information was the government, which they did not trust and which they knew wanted to put America in the worst possible light. At the same time, since their only experience was in the Soviet Union, they used that experience as a base to interpret what happened to them in the U.S. Again, there was and is diversity in the knowledge of America and attitudes. This diversity can come from having relatives already living in the U.S., previous contact with Americans, and the age of the immigrant. Younger immigrants, more open to change and less socialized in the Soviet system, were better able to adapt to the world view and thinking of Americans. This age difference will become more important as we discuss the family. Nevertheless, at the beginning of their lives in the U.S., the FSU was and is the only model they have for understanding the events taking place in their lives. Further, as English language materials are translated into Russian, the full Russian connotation of the word is carried to the reader. For example, the word "help" can be differently understood by Americans and by people from the FSU. When an American says that he will help find someone a job, he means that he will assist the person with looking through job ads, advice on interviewing, etc. What a Soviet immigrant hears when an American says they will "help" is that the American will find a job and make all the arrangements for the Soviet immigrant. The same thing happens with explaining the formal system. For example, SSI, supplementary social security income for the very poor, is sometimes understood by older Soviet immigrants as their Soviet military pension being paid in America.

The rising proportion of older persons immigrating to the United States is one of the major changes in immigration to the U.S. in this century (U.S. INS, 1997). Many of our older respondents said they only left the FSU because they would have been alone otherwise. This is, in part, a result of the low fertility of Soviet Jews where there are one or two children rather than several, as in past generations. Arriving with children and grandchildren means that the older person is now dependent on the younger generations for everything, and can no longer live independently or help the family in the same ways he or she could in the old country. As the role of the elder becomes one of dependency, the experience of old age in the new land becomes one of loneliness and lack of purpose for many of these older migrants. Beyond this, many of the middle-aged and older Soviet Jews are better educated (on the whole) than their American counterparts, a reflection of earlier Soviet policy. This feeling that they are somehow smarter but treated as dumber by the Americans also adds to their frustration. It also enhances the feeling of being part of a separate Jewish community.

The health status of immigrants from the FSU must, like so many other things, be divided into pre- and post-Chernobyl periods for three reasons. First, the disaster affected an area which included significant numbers of Jews (Kiev, for example). Second, the change in attitudes toward health care and health care practitioners was very important. Because of the lies told to the people (such as that drinking red wine with dinner would obviate the effects of the radiation), a more generalized suspicion and mistrust was created that extends to all health care practitioners. Third, it is a convenient, if somewhat erroneous, date for the decline and disintegration of the Soviet health system. Dating it here rather than at the fall of the Soviet Union is a reminder that the decline in the formal health system began long before the collapse of the Soviet Union.

Most of our respondents were post-Chernobyl immigrants and so carry the concerns and experiences of a population that has been lied to and which, in turn, does not trust people in authority. But there is another, more profound issue that affects the lives of these people. In previous migrations, if the migration was in part or in whole because of fear of a disaster that might befall the refugees if they remained in their home country, arriving in a country of refuge gave them safety from whatever caused them to flee in the first place. However, in the case of radiation sickness, these refugees are well aware that the thing they fear the most, and a main reason for their departure, may have traveled with them and appear at any moment. This concern creates issues among these immigrants that are new and a shared fear which also separates them from Soviet immigrants who came before Chernobyl, as well as from their cousins who arrived generations before.

The mental health issues mentioned above are very important to understand the Soviet refugees. It should also be noted that our own notions of "good mental health" are shaped in large part by our Anglo-Protestant culture. Positive outlook and feelings are often taken as signs of good mental health. Jews (and others) from the FSU often have a hard time expressing positive attitudes. While they may not have negative feelings or depression, they prefer the word "satisfied" to the word "happy." In this contrast of Slavic culture with Anglo-Protestant culture we have the American Jewish clinician evaluating the Soviet Jewish person and trying to make decisions concerning the health status of the Soviet Jew. Two Jewish diasporas, from two different political cultures, are attempting to find a common language.

Perhaps the most poignant concern expressed by some of the subjects of this study is their question — is it too late to be Jewish? Is it too late to understand what this means and find a way to express these feelings? Have their lives been stolen from them, so that there is no more time to form a Jewish identity? What is the identity of the grandchildren of these elders? The grandmothers speak of their desire for their grandchildren to lead Jewish lives, to succeed in America, and to read Pushkin, in other words, to understand the world of their ancestors and to fulfill their ancestors' dreams. In many ways this dual desire is reflective of a more universal urge — to preserve the past as one builds a future. The elders are living longer as well, and in a more frail state than they ever expected. This is also part of the general contemporary experience of aging in the United States, but the stresses are exacerbated by the experience of migration. What does the elder do to assist the process of settlement in a new land? If the elder feels that he or she is only a burden, with nothing to contribute, then the last years of that person's life can be empty of meaning and positive experience. If, on the other hand, the elder feels that he or she is contributing to the process of resettlement, from watching the small children to contributing their modest payments from the federal government to the family's rent, then the process can be the final adventure in what has been a life full of challenges. For some of these elders, the thing they most want to pass on is their own story of struggle and triumph, a heritage that future generations can also call their own.

Conclusions

The recent migration of Jews from the former Soviet Union is unusual in two respects. First, entire families are arriving together, which means that the process of settlement in the United States is very different from that of previous generations of immigrants,

Jewish and other. Second, these immigrants arrive in the U.S. in part seeking access to a culture denied to them (Jewish) and at the same time trying to come to terms with the Russian/Soviet culture of their entire lives up to the point of migration. These two issues come together most poignantly in the struggle of the oldest members of the family to find some role to play in their adjustment to life in the United States, when they discover that the traditional role of the elder as expert has been taken from them because they do not know the culture of their new land and feel betrayed by the heritage of their old land.

The problem is further exacerbated by the fact that these new Jewish migrants do not have much in common with the descendants of the last generation of Jewish migrants. Both groups, in the United States and the Soviet Union, enthusiastically embraced the culture and opportunities that they were offered so that by the end of the century the Jews of the United States were as American as the Jews of the Soviet Union were Soviet. No common way of life, as *halakhah* was to the exiles of Karo's day, exists to work as a bridge between the communities. Ultimately, it will probably be American culture itself that becomes the bridge between these diasporas — a bridge that at the same time will be a barrier between the new American Jewish community and Jews who do not share that common heritage.

Bibliography

Aleichem, Sholom. 1987. *Tevye the Dairyman and The Railroad Stories*. Translated and with an introduction by Hillel Halkin. New York: Schocken Books.

Glicksman, Allen, Tanya Koropeckyj-Cox, Svetlana Shevchenko, Marina Mistetsky, Elena Mitnik, and Leanna Kantarovich. 1994. "Asking Questions of Older East European Immigrants: Issues of Translation and Interpretation." 47th Annual Scientific Meeting of the Gerontological Society of America. Atlanta, Georgia.

Kagedan, Allan L. 1995. "Revival, Reconstruction or Rejection: Soviet Jewry in the Postwar Years, 1944-48," *Jews and Jewish Life in Russia and the Soviet Union*. Ed. Yaacov Ro'i. Portland, Oregon: Frank Cass.

Levin, Nora. 1986. "Home and Haven: Soviet Jewish Immigration to Philadelphia, 1972-1982," *Philadelphia Jewish Life: 1940-1985*. Ed. Murray Friedman. Ardmore, PA: Seth Press.

Ro'i, Yaacov, ed. 1995. *Jews and Jewish Life in Russia and the Soviet Union*. Portland, Oregon: Frank Cass.

U.S. Immigration and Naturalization Service. 1997. *Statistical Yearbook of the Immigration and Naturalization Service, 1995*. Washington, D.C.: U.S. Government Printing Office.

Werblowsky, R.J. Zwi. 1977. *Joseph Karo: Lawyer and Mystic*. Philadelphia: Jewish Publication Society of America.

Zborowski, Mark and Elizabeth Herzog. 1952. *Life is With People: The Culture of the Shtetl*. New York: Schocken Books.

10

The Economic Performance of Jewish Immigrants to Canada: A Case of Double Jeopardy?

James W. Dean
Don J. DeVoretz

Introduction

Our purpose here is to ask whether Jewish immigrants to Canada are doubly different: first by virtue of being Jewish, and second by virtue of being foreign-born. More precisely, we will ask whether their wages and several other economically pertinent characteristics differ significantly from the Canadian-born population, circa 1991.

First, we provide some context. The absolute numbers of immigrants moving to Canada has fluctuated widely over the last 30 years, ranging from 222,000 in 1967 down to 84,000 in 1985, and back up to 251,000 in 1993. At their peak, these numbers represented more than 1 percent of the base population. Moreover, this immigration is large enough to have provoked loud and contentious debate that has reached a crescendo in recent years.

In Canada the immigration debate reflects several concerns. One concern is economic. Simply put, do immigrants contribute in terms of earnings and contributions to the public purse? Or do their earnings rise at the expense of the native-born (Laryea, 1997)? And do they, perhaps, draw more from the public purse than they pay into it (Akbari, 1989, 1991)? Finally, do immigrants subsitute for Canadians in the labor force (Akbari and DeVoretz, 1992)?

A second concern is social: do immigrants in any sense "disrupt" the prevailing culture? This concern is voiced somewhat *soto voce,* since Canada is a country constituted on principles of tolerance and multiculturalism (Grubel, 1992). But it is much more a part of Canada's current popular consciousness than it has been in the recent past because the ethnic composition of recent immigration has shifted. Whereas in the late 1960s the majority of immigrants arrived from traditional developed areas, mostly Europe and the United States, by the 1980s most were arriving from developing countries, mostly Asia and the Caribbean. Because of their visibility, ethnic groups have been the subject of extensive economic research in Canada (Pendakur and Pendakur, 1996; and Hiebert, 1996).

This chapter will not address social and cultural concerns. We are, however, asking whether ethnicity or religion (i.e., Jewish or non-Jewish as self-defined by census responses) is related to economic performance in Canada.

Barometers of Immigrant Success

Research on the economic performance of recent immigrants to Canada has focused on such characteristics as age, education, marital status, language, entry category, and intended occupation. *Ceteris paribus,* earnings increase with age, with years since landing in Canada, and with education. Married immigrants earn more than unmarried, as do their counterparts in the general population (Fagnan, 1995). Moreover, immigrants entering Canada who can speak either English or French have a dramatic head start over others.

"Entry category" refers to categories defined by Canada's Immigration Act of 1976, which specifies that potential entrants may apply under an "economic" class, a "family" (unification) class, or as refugees (Akbar and DeVoretz, 1993). Modifications to the Act during the 1980s added to these a "business investor" class. Comparative research on 1981 and 1991 census data (Prescott and

Wandschneider, 1995; Bloom et al., 1995; and Abbot and Beach, 1993) shows that the economic performance of more recent immigrants has deteriorated.

More recent research (Cobey, 1996) notes that when economic-class immigrants are divided into those who entered with pre-arranged employment and those who did not, the former turn out to have fared much better. Even ten years later, immigrants who landed with pre-arranged employment earned almost 40 percent more than those who landed without pre-arranged employment. Moreover, among the latter, the proportion of economic immigrants declaring unemployment insurance income is over 50 percent higher.

Finally, the "intended occupation" declared by economic class applicants without pre-arranged employment proved a powerful predictor of post-entry earned income (Green, 1995). Managers and/or administrators and engineer/mathematicians earn almost double the incomes of other occupations, and the gap seems wider by the end of their first decade in Canada.

These results suggest that much of the economic performance of recent immigrants can be predicted by "human capital" characteristics such as age, education, marital status, language, entry status, and intended occupation, without resorting to "cultural" characteristics such as religion, ethnicity, or country of origin (Coulson and DeVoretz, 1993). The further implication is that immigration policy can effectively pre-select immigrants who will perform well by requiring positive measures of these characteristics, and can therefore afford to be "culture-blind" (Akbar and DeVoretz, 1993).

But what if all or most of these income-enhancing non-cultural characteristics are correlated with cultural characteristics? If so, would it be politically or even morally acceptable for immigration policy to incorporate cultural selection criteria? This is an extremely sensitive question. The closest Canada comes to such a policy is to delegate some control over immigration criteria to the Province of Quebec, which is culturally distinct from the rest of Canada. Suffice it to say that our preliminary findings in this chapter are that immigrants to Canada who declared themselves in the 1991 census to be religiously "Jewish" display much higher earned incomes as well as much higher values for each and every income-enhancing characteristic than other immigrants display.

Data

Our preliminary results are based on samples drawn from 1991 Canadian census data. The populations we chose to sample are all males and females from central and western Canada aged 25-65 who reported wage and salary incomes on the census survey. The populations thus exclude persons who solely reported other sources of income such as self-employment, transfers from government, and investments. They also exclude persons who are unemployed, either voluntarily or involuntarily.

We then divided these populations into four unrelated groups, reflecting census respondents' answers to a query about their religious status: Non-Jewish Canadian-born (NJCB), Jewish Canadian-born (JCB), Non-Jewish Immigrants (NJI), and Jewish Immigrants (JI). We were forced to exclude all persons residing east of the Province of Quebec because the census response for religious status does not distinguish between Jews and a wide variety of unrelated religious groups, reflecting the small size of the Jewish population in Canada's Maritime provinces.

Our sample sizes are one thirty-third of the population in each case. Thus our sample size of 147,334 for NJCB males is drawn from a population thirty three times larger: that is, a population of 4,862,022. Added to the NJCB female population of 4,306,731, this constitutes 9,168,753 persons. Adding in turn the male and female populations for each of the other three categories brings our total population to 11,717,673, or about one third of the total Canadian population of 30 million.

Excluded from our populations are 1) all persons under 25 or over 65; 2) all persons who did not report wage or salary income; (3) all persons residing east of the Province of Quebec; and 4) all persons who failed to complete the 1991 census survey.

Results

We begin with analysis of the male sample. Non-Jewish men, both Canadian- and foreign-born, report average annual wage and salary incomes of just over $30,000 (Canadian) per year. In striking contrast, both analogous Jewish groups report incomes almost 50 percent higher, about $44,000 per year (Table 10.1 Row 1). Note

TABLE 10.1
Characteristics of Jewish and Non-Jewish Male Immigrants

	NJCB	JCB	NJI	JI
Average annual wage	30,946	43,921	31,880	44,056
Number of weeks worked by working men				
25 or less	13.9	11.5	13.6	10.3
25 to 45	15.3	12.1	15.2	12.9
Over 45	69.8	75.8	70.7	74.3
Not working as % of total	0.2	0.2	0.2	0.3
Average age of working men	36.9	38.6	41.4	43.5
Total years of schooling of working men				
12 or less	51.3	17.3	42.5	22.2
Undergraduate	40.7	51.7	44.3	50.6
Graduate	8.0	31.0	13.2	27.2
Status of working men as % of total				
Married	55.9	59.0	71.6	71.7
Never married	34.5	35.2	20.8	18.0
Other	9.6	5.8	7.6	10.3
Language spoken at home by working men				
English	68.5	98.3	57.9	64.2
French	29.8	.7	4.0	12.4
Other	1.7	1.0	38.1	23.4
Language spoken by working men				
English	62.4	62.8	81.1	58.8
English and French	22.3	37.2	13.0	38.3
Other	15.3	0	5.9	2.9
Occupation of working men				
Professional	23.8	55.4	27.1	53.5
Skilled	32.9	18.0	31.9	19.1
Unskilled	42.7	25.8	40.0	25.8

NCJB - Non-Jewish Canadian-Born; JCB - Jewish Canadian-Born; NJI - Non-Jewish Immigrant; JI - Jewish Immigrant
Wages in Canadian dollars.

that all the proceeding rows will refer to Table 10.1. Part of the difference between Jews and non-Jews can be attributed to weeks worked. Thus only 70 percent of non-Jewish men worked full time (over 45 weeks per year), whereas some 75 percent of Jewish men did so (Row 2). Somewhat surprisingly, the average incomes of native- and foreign-born non-Jewish men are virtually the same, as are the corresponding incomes for native- and foreign-born Jewish men.

Row 3 shows the percentages of men "not working." Recall that this category includes any male who did not report wage or salary income, and therefore includes those who are self-employed as well as the voluntarily and involuntarily unemployed. Of course the unemployed may nevertheless receive incomes, from government, family or other transfers, or from their investments. It is interesting to note that both native- and foreign-born Jewish males measured higher on this "not working" scale, which may reflect a higher percentage of Jews than non-Jews who are self-employed, although this is just speculation.

Turning now to human capital characteristics that are typically correlated with income, we note first that the average age of Jewish Canadian-born men is substantially higher than that of their non-Jewish counterparts (38.5 years of age versus 37.0) (Row 4). We note further that the same relationship holds for immigrant men (43.5 years of age versus 41.4). Although age at this stage of the life cycle is generally positively correlated with income, we doubt that age can account for the bulk of the Jewish/non-Jewish income differentials just noted. Below we estimate age-earnings profiles for Jews to detect the effect of age on earnings with other factors held constant.

A second human capital characteristic that is typically correlated with income is education (Coulson and DeVoretz, 1993). Row 5 displays dramatic differences in years of schooling between our four groups. Whereas about 51 percent of non-Jewish Canadian-born men have 12 years or less schooling, only 17 percent of their Jewish counterparts have 12 years or less. For graduate education (17 years or more) the differences are equally dramatic: only 8 percent of the non-Jewish native-born have received graduate education, versus about 31 percent of Jewish native-born. Turning to the two immigrant populations, foreign-born non-Jews have more years of education than native-born non-Jews, but the relationship is reversed for Jews (although Jewish immigrants nevertheless have more education than either of the two non-Jewish groups). Recall from Row 1 that the incomes of native-born and foreign-born populations (both non-Jewish and Jewish) are roughly similar. Thus, at first pass it would appear that non-Jews compensate for the disadvantage of being immigrants by means of more education, whereas Jewish immigrants earn incomes similar to Jewish native-born despite having less education. In other words, Jews apparently overcome the "jeopardy" inherent in being immigrants by virtue of other income-correlates.

A third potential income-correlate is marital status. Typically, married men earn more because of a greater attachment to the labor market. Row 6 shows that Jewish Canadian-born men are slightly more likely to be married than their non-Jewish counterparts (59 percent versus 56 percent). However, the substantial difference appears in the immigrant category. About 72 percent of both Jewish and non-Jewish immigrants are married. This phenomenon may help to explain why Jewish immigrants earn as much as non-Jewish immigrants despite their lower levels of education.

In Canada, a fourth income-correlate is language. We capture this characteristic in two ways. First, in Row 7 we depict the language spoken at home. Some 69 percent of non-Jewish Canadian-born men speak English at home, versus almost 100 percent of their Jewish counterparts. Immigrants, while less likely in general to speak French at home, are relatively more likely to do so if they are Jewish: about 4 percent of non-Jewish immigrants versus about 12 percent of Jewish immigrants speak French at home. Immigrants are also much more likely to speak a language other than English or French at home: about 38 percent of non-Jewish immigrants and 23 percent of Jewish immigrants. Speaking a third language at home is probably a disadvantage in the labor force as it often means less-than-perfect ability in English or French. A second way of capturing language characteristics is in terms of ability to speak. On this score, both native- and foreign-born Jews rank higher than non-Jews in the sense that nearly all speak either English, French, or both, Canada's two official languages (Row 8). By contrast, some 15 percent of non-Jewish native-born men and about 6 percent of non-Jewish foreign-born men speak neither official language. This latter fact constitutes a severe disadvantage in labor markets.

Finally, we examine occupation levels. We classified our census data into three classes of occupations: "professional," "skilled," and "unskilled."[1] Here we observe the most dramatic differences yet between non-Jews and Jews. Whereas only 24 percent of non-Jewish native-born men are employed professionally versus 43 percent as unskilled workers, about 55 percent of their Jewish counterparts are professionals versus only 26 percent unskilled. Among immigrants, the proportions of professionally employed are strikingly similar, as are the proportions of skilled and unskilled. Thus, occupation accounts for some differences in income between non-Jews and Jews. It may also be that occupation helps to explain why foreign-born Jewish men earn incomes comparable to those of native-born Jewish men despite their lower levels of education. However, the similar proportions in each occupational class seems superficially inconsistent with markedly different levels of education. The following section, which controls for the effect of all other relevant variables through regression analysis, may detect the relative importance of occupational choice on Jewish earnings.

Annual wages and salaries for women are reported in Table 10.2 Row 1 (note that all the proceeding rows will refer to Table 10.2). Although the pattern of relative earnings across our four groups is very similar to that for men, absolute levels are substantially lower, ranging from 61 percent of the male level for NJCB, through 58 percent for JCB, 59 percent for NJI, and only 54 percent for JI. In short, women earn 39-42 percent less than men, with the exception of Jewish immigrant women, who earn a full 46 percent less. These lower earnings are partly accounted for by fewer work weeks (Row 2). Weeks worked by women as a percentage of weeks worked by men range from 90 percent for NJCB, through 83 percent for JCB, through 87 percent for NJI, through 82 percent for JI. What is notable about these figures is that both native- and foreign-born Jewish women work fewer hours as compared to their male counterparts than do non-Jewish women. This may account for their lower earnings relative to Jewish males when compared to their non-Jewish counterparts relative to non-Jewish males.

Row 3 shows the percentages of women not working for wages or salaries. The pattern of these percentages across our four groups is virtually the mirror image of that for men. However, significantly higher percentages of non-Jewish women than men, both native- and foreign-born, did not report wage or salary income. By con-

TABLE 10.2
Characteristics of Jewish and Non-Jewish Female Immigrants

	NJCB	JCB	NJI	JI
Average annual wage	18,827	25,564	18,883	23,759
Number of weeks worked by working women				
25 or less	18.5	19.1	17.8	16.4
25 to 45	15.7	16.0	16.2	19.6
Over 45	64.2	63.4	63.9	61.0
Not working as % of total	.3	.2	.3	.3
Average age of working women	36.2	37.8	39.9	41.9
Total years of schooling of working women				
12 or less	47.7	20.8	45.0	22.0
Undergraduate	45.8	58.3	46.3	56.9
Graduate	6.5	20.9	8.7	21.1
Status of working women as % of total				
Married	54.5	58.3	66.5	71.8
Never married	30.9	29.9	20.3	14.0
Other	14.6	11.8	13.2	14.2
Language spoken at home by working women				
English	69.5	98.2	60.1	65.7
French	28.8	.8	3.4	9.8
Other	1.7	1.0	36.5	24.5
Language spoken by working women				
English	62.0	64.2	81.5	62.4
English and French	21.6	35.7	11.4	34.0
Other	16.4	0.1	7.1	3.6
Occupation of working women				
Professional	22.2	36.4	19.3	34.8
Skilled	26.4	28.6	22.6	25.0
Unskilled	50.0	33.2	56.0	37.9

NCJB - Non-Jewish Canadian-Born; JCB - Jewish Canadian-Born; NJI - Non-Jewish Immigrant; JI - Jewish Immigrant
Wages in Canadian dollars.

trast, significantly lower percentages of native-born Jewish women (and about the same percentage of foreign-born Jewish women) did not report such income. In short, given that Jewish women are already in the labor market, they are more likely to work (at least for wages or salaries) than are Jewish men.

Row 4 reports the average ages of our four groups of working women. We note the same monotonically ascending pattern of age, ranging from about 36 for NJCB to 42 for JI. Recall from Table 10.1 Row 4 that the average age of men was one to two years higher. This would account for some but certainly not all of the earnings premium of men over women. To be more precise, we await the analysis of Jewish age-earnings profiles in the following section.

Row 5 depicts education levels for women. Comparisons to the male populations differ across the four groups. Whereas the ratio of high-school-or-less education for women to men for NJCB is only 0.93 — that is, women are better educated — the same ratio for JCB is 1.20, for NJI is 1.06, and for JI is 0.99. In other words, Jewish native-born women, as well as all immigrants, are less well or no better educated than their male counterparts, whereas non-Jewish native-born women are better educated than their male counterparts. A tentative explanation for this is that both Jewish and immigrant cultures are more traditional than the Canadian mainstream, placing less relative emphasis (though in the case of Jewish women, more absolute emphasis than in either non-Jewish case) upon education for women than for men. It is interesting to note that whereas native-born Jewish working women are less well educated than their male counterparts, foreign-born Jewish working women are equally well educated. A final observation is that the female/male differentials in education are not conceivably large enough to account for the huge earnings differentials between genders.[2]

Row 6 reports marital status and language. Marital status shows the following gender difference: women are more likely than men to fall into the "other" category: that is, neither "married" nor "never married." Thus, some 15 percent of women NJCB report an "other" marital status, versus only 10 percent for males. This pattern holds across all four groups. It would appear that divorced women are disproportionately represented in the population of working women, as opposed to the total population of women.

Row 7 shows the languages that working women speak at home. The percentages of English, French, and "other" are almost identical to those for men. Row 8 shows ability to speak languages. Here again, the percentages are almost identical to those for men, except that a slightly higher percentage of Jewish immigrant males speak French in addition to English than do Jewish immigrant females.

Row 9 depicts occupational categories for women. The striking feature here is that the proportions of "unskilled" women are much higher, ranging from 50 percent for NJCB (versus 43 percent for men), through 33 percent for JCB (versus 26 percent for men), through 56 percent for NJI (versus 40 percent for men), and 38 percent for JI (versus 28 percent for men). The corresponding ratios are 1.16 for NJCB, 1.27 for JCB, 1.45 for NJI, and 1.46 for JI, suggesting that immigrant working women are less skilled relative to their male counterparts than are native-born working women.

Regression Results: Jewish Immigrants versus Jewish Canadian-Born

In this section we briefly report the results of testing a human capital model for the Jewish Canadian-born and Jewish immigrant earnings experiences. The purpose of this section is twofold. First, the following regression analysis allows us to isolate the effects of age, etc. on Jewish income while controlling for the influence of the remaining variables. Second, we test whether the Jewish earnings experience in Canada conforms to the traditional investment/demographic model which has held for other immigrants in Canada. In this context, a human capital model argues that after arrival, Jewish immigrants accumulate, via education, experience and greater language facility, human capital which gradually makes them more competitive in the Canadian labor market. Thus, in the absence of discrimination and other imperfections in the labor market the model argues that Jewish immigrants are at first at an earnings disadvantage relative to their Canadian-born Jewish cohort, and then after some years "catch up" and overtake the earnings of the Jewish Canadian-born.

Table 10.3 reports the mean values for the data set, which is drawn from the same source (PUST, 1991 Canadian Census) used in earlier sections.[3] Our sample of all Jewish Canadian households includes males and females who were in the labor force circa 1991. Some salient features of this sample set are that the average person

TABLE 10.3
Statistics for Regression Analysis

Name	N	Mean	St. Deviation
Age	3822	42.5	10.7
Female	3822	.53	.49
Weeks	3822	51.8	21.5
Wages	3822	33408	3223
Single	3822	.17	.37
Foreign-born	3822	.37	.48
No official language	3822	.003	.06
Language spoken at home	3822	.09	.29
SL1	3822	.02	.14
SL2	3822	.21	.40
SL3	3822	.20	.40
SL4	3822	.44	.49
No skill	3822	.12	.33
School	3822	14.9	3.1
Family size	3822	3.17	1.44

Source: Authors' tabulations from 1991 PUST Canadian Census

in the sample was 42.5 years old with an educational attainment of 14.9 years and lived in a household with 3.17 members. Only 14 percent of the Jewish households had labor force members working in unskilled (NOskill) occupations while 44 percent were working in professional and technical trades (SL4). Finally, the average employment was full-time (weeks = 51.8) with 53 percent of the sample being female (female =.53).

We estimated the basic human capital model in two stages to recognize that earnings depend on the prior decision to enter the labor market. Thus, in the first stage we offer:

Equation 10.1:

Prob = g (age, age squared, marital status, years of schooling, foreign birth status, and family size), which argues that the probability of entering the labor market (Prob ranges between 0 and 1) is a function of the arguments on the right-hand side of the equation.

Next, given entry into the labor market, we argue that Jewish wages should be a function of the human capital (schooling, occupation, language) and demographic variables (age, marital status, family size, and gender) conditioned on weeks worked and occupational choice. This is expressed in:

> *Equation 10.2:*
> Ln wages = f (age, age squared, marital status, weeks worked, gender, years of schooling, occupation, language status, marital status and family size).

Anticipating our results, we omitted the traditional and often cited variable of "years in Canada" since this variable proved insignificant when the age of the immigrant appeared in the earnings equation.[4] Estimating Equations 10.1 and 10.2 leads to the results reported in Tables 10.4 and 10.5, which in general support the human capital model of wage determination for Jews in Canada. In the first stage of the modeling we attempt to predict the probability ("Probit") of Jews entering the Canadian labor market. The coefficients reported in Table 10.4 support the hypothesis that Jews who are either single, or foreign-born, or part of a smaller family size are statistically less likely to be in the labor market. These results are consistent with evidence reported for Canadian-born workers in several recent studies (Fagnan, 1995).[5] Thus Jews are less likely to join the Canadian labor force for similar reasons as other Canadians, with the exception that if Jews are foreign born this has a slight extra deterrent.[6]

Turning now to Table 10.5, we report the results of estimating Equation 10.1 for Jews in Canada. The central question is whether, controlling for religious status, the human capital model explains the age-earnings profiles of all Jews in Canada. In short, the answer is "Yes." The traditional human capital model with demographic variables (age, age squared, marital status, single), conditioned on occupational choice, yields the predicted effect on earnings. Moreover, given a positive age coefficient (.007) and a negative age squared coefficient (-.0008), the model predicts concave age-earn-

TABLE 10.4
Estimated Coefficients from Probit Analysis

Variable	coefficient	t-ratio	elasticity
Age	.07	3.6	.74
Age squared	-.001	-4.4	-.45
Single	-.21	-2.5	-.0085
School	.10	12.0	.35
Foreign-born	-.18	-3.4	-.01
Family size	-.06	-2.8	-.04
Constant	-1.37	-2.9	-.31

Source: Authors' tabulations from 1991 PUST Canadian Census

TABLE 10.5
Estimated Coefficients of Jewish Earnings Profiles

Variable	coefficient	t-ratio	elasticity
Age	.007	3.9	3.1
Age squared	-.0008	-3.24	-.1.41
Single	-.104	-2.2	-.02
Years of schooling	.006	.41	.10
Foreign-born	-.108	-0.236	-.04
Female	.67	1.65	.034
Family size	-.018	-1.4	-.06
Constant	6.93	12.09	6.93
Lambda	-.0.25	-.61	-.06
Years of schooling, foreign-born	.01	1.09	.06
Years of schooling, females	.009	1.08	.07
Skill level 2	.14	1.7	.03
Skill level 3	.31	3.9	.07
Skill level 4	.55	7.0	.28
Language spoken at home	-.27	-5.67	-.02
Does not speak either official language	-.16	-.5	-.0002
Female age	-.05	-2.58	-1.00
Foreign age squared	-.0002	-.44	-.11
Weeks	.032	29.32	1.48

Source: Authors' tabulations from 1991 PUST Canadian Census

ings profiles for all Jewish Canadians and Jewish immigrants, male and female respectively. Given the mean values reported in Table 10.3 and the coefficients estimated in Equation 10.2, we generated concave age earnings profiles confirming that a human capital theory is capable of generating the earnings performance for Jews in Canada.

For the representative Jew in Canada income rises from $22,184 (1990 Canadian dollars) at age 19 to a peak at age 49 of $43,958 (1990 Canadian dollars). After age 49, the earnings of the representative Jew in Canada decline steadily to $36,000 (1990 Canadian dollars) at age 65.

Jewish females have a dramatically weaker earnings performance. Female Jews in Canada enter the Canadian labor force at age 19 with earnings of $11,669 (1990 Canadian dollars) or only 52 percent of the predicted total for all Jews in Canada regardless of gender. By age 46 the earnings of Jewish females have peaked at $22,983, declining by age 65 to $19,054.

In sum, these estimated age earnings profiles for Jews in Canada are consistent with the uncontrolled, descriptive analysis discussed earlier. It was shown that economic jeopardy in Canada is associated simply with being female, and not with being Jewish or being foreign-born. The controlled statistical analysis of this section confirms that Jewish females earn lower incomes even after human capital characteristics are controlled for, irrespective of whether they are foreign-born.

Conclusion

Are Jewish immigrants to Canada subject to double jeopardy as other foreign-born immigrant groups? In terms of the wages and salaries they earn, the answer is "No." In fact the reverse is true: Jewish immigrants earn substantially more than do non-Jewish non-immigrants: men earn almost 50 percent more, and women over 40 percent more. This is substantially above the Jewish earnings advantage reported circa 1981.[7] Moreover, among non-immigrants, Jews earn much more than non-Jews, and among immigrants Jews again earn much more than non-Jewish immigrants. The evidence from other countries, namely the U.S.A. by Chiswick (1983), is that Jews earned 70 percent more than their non-Jewish native-born cohort circa 1970.[8]

A more subtle question is whether Jews do better or worse economically once a variety of income-enhancing characteristics are controlled for. Our regression analysis indicates that the standard human capital model holds for Jews in Canada. Given the set of observed facts that working Jews in Canada are better educated, are more likely to be married, are more likely to speak English, are more likely to work as managers or in a profession, and work longer hours, all combine to yield them higher age-earnings profiles. These findings were partially confirmed with 1981 data by Stelcner and Kyriazis (1995) who found that: "The observed large earnings advantages of Jews...can be attributed mainly to their greater educational attainments" (p. 65). In addition, they argue that Jews in Canada in 1981 were differentially rewarded for education, greater than the reference group of British ethnics in Canada.[9]

Immigrant Jews share these characteristics with the larger population of Jews, with the anomaly that they are relatively less well educated. The fact that they nevertheless earn as high incomes as native-born Jews suggests that Jews, unlike other Canadian immigrants, may not experience earnings penalties upon entry into Canada which they must make up for later via further education.

The most dramatic difference between men and women is that the latter's wages are only 54-61 percent of men's, with Jewish immigrant women's at the lower end of the range. At most, one-quarter of these differences can be accounted for by fewer weeks worked. Several other characteristics are not different enough to account for women's lower earnings. Women are only one or two years younger and almost as well educated — in fact, better educated in the case of native-born non-Jewish women. While working women are more likely to be divorced (and probably more likely to be responsible for child-care), and while they are possibly less likely to be self-employed, neither of these factors seems likely to explain much of their wage disadvantage.

What *is* markedly different about women is that they are more likely to be working at unskilled jobs. But given women's similar educational attainment, this merely suggests that they are underpaid because they are under-employed relative to their abilities, compounding the suspicion that the real "jeopardy" in the Canadian labor force lies in being a woman. This is consistent with a considerable volume of evidence — for example, see Beach and Worswick (1993).

References

Abbott, M.G. and C.M. Beach, "Immigrant Earnings Differentials and Cohort Effects in Canada," *Canadian Journal of Economics,* vol. XXVI, no. 3 (August 1993):505-524.

Akbari, A. and D.J. DeVoretz, "The Substitutability of Foreign Born Labour in Canadian Production circa 1980," *Canadian Journal of Economics,* vol. XXV, no. 3 (August 1992):604-614.

Akbari, A., "The Benefits of Immigrants to Canada: Evidence on Tax and Public Services, *Canadian Public Policy,* vol. XV (1989):424-435.

——, "The Public Finance Impact of Immigrant Populations on Host Nations: Some Canadian Evidence," *Social Science Quarterly,* vol. 72, no. 2 (June 1991):334-346.

Akbar, S. and D.J. DeVoretz, "Canada's Demand for Third World Highly Trained Immigrants: 1976-1986," *World Development* (January 1993):177-187.

Beach, C.M. and C. Worswick, "Is There a Double Negative Effect on the Earnings of Immigrant Women?," *Canadian Public Policy,* vol. XIX, no. 1 (1993):36-53.

Bloom, D.E., G. Grenier and M. Gunderson, "The Changing Labour Market Position of Canadian Immigrants," *Canadian Journal of Economics,* vol. XXVIII, no. 4b (November 1995):987-1005.

Chiswick, B. "The Earnings and Human Capital of American Jews," *Journal of Human Resources* (1983):313-335.

——, "The Skills and Economic Status of American Jewry: Trends over the Last Half-Century," *Journal of Labour Economics,* vol. 11, no. 1, pt. 1 (1993):229-242.

Cobey, "Barometers of Immigrant Success," *Applied Research Bulletin,* 1996.

Coulson, R.G. and D. DeVoretz, "Human Capital Content of Canadian Immigration 1966-1987," *Canadian Public Policy,* vol. XIX (December 1993):357-366.

DeVoretz, D.J., ed., *Diminishing Returns: Economics of Canada's Immigration Policy* (Toronto: C.D. Howe Institute, 1995).

——, "Economic Impacts of Immigration Flows in Canada's Labor Market," in *Issues in Canadian Immigration Policy,* S. Globerman, ed. (Vancouver: Fraser Institute, 1993).

Fagnan, S., "Canadian Immigrant Earnings: 1971-86," in *Diminishing Returns: Economics of Canada's Immigration Policy,* D.J. DeVoretz, ed. (Toronto: C.D. Howe Institute, 1995), pp. 166-208.

Green, Alan G. and David A. Green, "Canadian Immigration Policy: The Effectiveness of the Point System and Other Instruments," *Canadian Journal of Economics,* vol. XXVIII, no. 4b (November 1995):1006-1041.

Green, D., "Intended and Actual Occupations of Immigrants," in *Emerging Immigration Issues in Canada*, D.J. DeVoretz, ed. (Toronto: C.D. Howe, 1995).

Grubel, H., "The Economic and Social Effects of Immigration," in S. Globerman, *Immigration Dilemma* (Fraser Institute, 1992), pp. 99-127.

Heibert, D., *The Colour of Work Labour Market Segmentation in Montreal, Toronto and Vancouver, 1991*, RIIM Discussion Paper #97-02.

Pendakur, K. and Ravi Pendakur, *The Colour of Money: Earnings Differentials among Ethnic Groups in Canada*, RIIM Discussion Paper #96-03.

Prescott, D. and B. Wandschneider, "The Assimilation of Immigrants in the Canadian Labour Market: 1981-1990." Paper presented at the Canadian Economics Association Meetings, Montreal, June 1995.

Stelcner, M. and N. Kyriazis, "An Empirical Analysis of Earnings among Ethnic Groups in Canada," *International Journal of Contemporary Sociology*, vol. 32, no.1 (1995):41-79.

Notes

* We would like to note with appreciation the programming assistance of P. Sheldon and J. Heinrichs. In addition, incisive comments by S. Globerman improved the essay. The authors, of course, are solely responsible for the contents.

1. The User Documentation for Public Use Microdata File on Individuals for the 1991 Census provides the following definitions of occupations: Professional = senior, middle and other managers, professionals and semi-professionals and technicians. Skilled = supervisors, foreman/women, skilled crafts and trades. Unskilled = sales and service, manual workers.

2. In fact, the NJCB group, which has more education than men, should on this score be earning more than men, not less.

3. PUST is the Public Use Sample Tape on Individuals for the 1991 Census from Statistics Canada. For further information, see the 1991 Census Dictionary, Statistics Canada, No. 92-301E or F.

4. The problem is that one year of aging is exactly equivalent as one calendar year of residence in Canada and hence with both variables in one equation multicolinearity was present.

5. Jews, however, differ in one further aspect from the rest of the foreign-born Canadian labor force. While many ethnic groups have a secondary or interactive effect on the key arguments, Jews do not. For example, many ethnic groups have a special ethnic-education effect in their earnings or labor force participation equation. In other words,

being Chinese and obtaining education in Canada gives Chinese an extra bonus as they interact with education. No interactions occur when we test for them in the Jewish earnings equations in this chapter.

6. First and foremost it should be noted that being a Jewish immigrant relative to being a Canadian-born Jew has only a small negative impact upon entry in Canada's labor market since the calculated elasticity is close to zero (-.01).

7. Stelcner and Kyriazis (p. 46) find that Jews had the highest average earnings in Canada circa 1981 with $26,820 (males) and $16,240 for females. Their all-Canadian male average was $21,340 and female $13,700.

8. Chiswick (1993), when controlling for all the standard human capital variables, finds a 16 percent premium in favor of Jewish males circa 1972-87 in the U.S.A. Our corresponding value is only a 7 percent premium.

9. Jews regardless of birth place had an 8.3 percent return on education while British ethnics in Canada received slightly less of 7.5 percent.

11

Refugees, Human Rights, and the Making of Israeli Foreign Policy: The Conferral of Refugee Status on Israelis as a Case-Study

Irwin Cotler

Questions of refugee rights and political asylum have emerged as watershed issues on the human rights agenda;[1] "refugee-producing countries" — or countries from which refugees claim they have a "well-founded fear of persecution" were they to be returned to their country of origin — are regarded as "major human rights violators"; countries granting political asylum to these prospective refugee claimants are generally seen as "rights protecting" countries.

It is not surprising that in the eyes of Israel — and world Jewry generally — Israel was regarded as a prototype of a "refugee accepting" country; indeed, the very existence of the State of Israel was deemed to have revolutionized the status of the Jewish people; while the Israeli Law of Return[2] — intended to provide haven and sanctuary to Jews fleeing persecution — was deemed to have made the notion of a "Jewish refugee" obsolete.

Accordingly, it is not surprising that Soviet Jewry — or Jews from the former Soviet Union — emerged as a metaphor for the Israeli *raison d'etre* in the 1980s and 1990s. The emigration — or liberation — of Soviet Jewry had been a clarion call of both Israel

and world Jewry in the 1970s and 1980s; indeed, it was characterized as the single most compelling, if not unifying, issue on the
Jewish public agenda apart from the existence of the State of Israel
itself. More particularly, the very compellability of the right to
leave as a human rights issue — the right to leave having been held
out as tantamount to the "right to liberty if not the right to life itself"
— secured for Soviet Jewish emigrants a prominent place on the
East-West human rights agenda, if not also a priority on the human
rights foreign policy agenda of Western nations as exemplified by
the Jackson-Vanick Amendment; while Western countries — including, and in particular, Canada — enacted and refined their
immigration laws so as to facilitate the entry of prospective Soviet
refugees and immigrants.

It is perhaps ironic — even tragic — that an issue of such
profound Jewish and human rights dimensions, and common cause,
should have emerged as such a divisive issue between Canada and
Israel. But however disturbing this may be, the divisiveness, on
reflection, may not be all that surprising. For the initial emigration
of Soviet Jews in the 1980s had already engendered a certain
tension between Israel and Western countries prepared to accept
Soviet Jews as immigrants, or in particular, to grant them political
asylum as refugees. More particularly, as most Soviet Jews had
claimed refugee status in the West on the grounds that they had been
persecuted against as Jews, and as they had only been allowed to
leave the Soviet Union on condition that their final destination was
Israel, it appeared only appropriate — from a "Jewish/human
rights" perspective, that Israel be seen as the natural, if not "moral-
juridical," home for these Soviet Jewish emigrants. At the same
time, and from a "Western/human rights" perspective, the issue of
the right to leave — and the conferral of refugee status — was
regarded as being "unlinked" to the refugee's prospective country
of destination, and was to be addressed on the merits of the refugee
claim alone pursuant to the criteria for the conferral of refugee
status under international law[3] (i.e., whether the claimant is entitled
to refugee status by reason of a well-founded fear of persecution
owing to inadequate state protection in their country of origin).
Accordingly, Jewish human rights activists in the West — who had
traditionally been at the forefront of support for immigration and
political asylum generally — as they had been at the forefront of the
struggle for the emigration of Soviet Jews in particular — some-

times found themselves between the "human rights" rock and the "Jewish" hard place.

In the early stages of Soviet Jewry emigration in the 1980s there was considerable debate among Jewish communities in the West as to how to relate to the issue of "drop-outs" — those Soviet Jews who once outside the Soviet Union opted to settle in a Western country rather than Israel. Indeed, in these early stages, such "drop-outs," as they were called, sometimes accounted for up to 90 percent of those leaving the Soviet Union. For the most part, Jewish leadership expressed a preference that these prospective Soviet Jewish immigrants settle in Israel; at the same time, they equally felt that they could not forsake those who decided to settle elsewhere.

With the advent of direct immigration to Israel (not via third countries), and the liberalization of Soviet and successor CIS emigration policies, the historic "exodus" of Soviet Jews began, with some 700,000 Jews from the Soviet Union and its successor states emigrating since 1989 to Israel. While the large majority of these immigrants were regarded as Jews under Jewish law (i.e., born of a Jewish mother or who had converted to Judaism), a not insignificant number were non-Jewish family members — husbands and wives of Jews and their children or grandchildren — who were granted equal status and citizenship under the Israeli Law of Return, and received similar "benefit packages" (valued at some $15,000 per annum).

For Israel, the immigration from the former Soviet Union and successor CIS was a vindication of the Israeli *raison d'etre* of the "ingathering of the exiles." But it should not be surprising that among an immigration or ingathering of some 700,000 in some seven years, equivalent to the immigration of some 4,000,000 Soviet Jews to Canada or 40,000,000 to the United States during the same period, there would be hundreds, even thousands, of frustrated, unhappy immigrants, some of whom had been the victims of discrimination in Israel; nor should it be surprising that the unhappiness and felt discrimination, if not persecution, should be greatest among those immigrants for whom the very "Jewishness" of Israel, while the basis for their immigration under the Law of Return, should be a ground for their alienation.

That some of these immigrants — Jewish and non-Jewish — should subsequently seek to emigrate from Israel to third countries is surely understandable, albeit regrettable, from a "Jewish" point of view; and it is certainly understandable, and legitimate, from a human rights perspective, anchored as it is in the "right to leave." But that some of those emigrating should also seek refugee status in a third country seems not only regrettable from a Jewish point of view, but invites serious inquiry from a human rights perspective. For here the emigrant is not so much exercising the right to leave as he or she is seeking the protection of a third country, in this instance, Canada, because of an alleged well-founded fear of persecution were they to be returned to their country of origin, now Israel, the country whose citizenship they voluntarily sought and secured to begin with. Admittedly, from a "human rights perspective," the fact that the number of immigrants from the former Soviet Union seeking to leave Israel is less that 5 percent of those who initially immigrated to Israel would tend to vindicate Israel as a "rights protecting" state; but the conferral of refugee status on such Israelis seeking political asylum in the West, however limited the numbers, has the effect of converting Israel from an "immigrant-accepting, rights protecting state" to a "refugee-producing, human rights violator country."

Accordingly, the convergence of Soviet emigrants from Israel seeking not only immigration but "refugee" status in Canada — and the presence in Canada of not only a liberalized but quasi-judicial refugee status determination process — has transformed what ought to have been a marginal issue even in Canada-Israel terms into a major question of refugees, human rights, and the making of foreign policy. Indeed, the Canada-Israel *contretemps* described in this chapter is less an instructive case-study of Canada-Israel relations than it is a case-study raising not only serious issues of refugee law, human rights, and foreign policy, but profound existential questions about the rights of non-Jewish minorities in Israel, the meaning of Israel as a "Jewish state," the complementarity, or contradiction, in the notion of Israel as a "Jewish and democratic state," the legitimacy of ethnically or religiously based states, and the like.

Accordingly, with this in mind, this chapter will organize itself around the following themes or headings:

1. The demographics of Soviet Jewish emigration to Canada: a snapshot.

2. The chronology of a crisis: how it all began.
3. What does this crisis tell us about the making of Israeli foreign policy?
4. Refugee status, human rights, and the rights of the non-Jewish minority in Israel.
5. The perception of Israel in the culture of human rights NGOs.
6. Refugee status, human rights, and Israel as a "Jewish and democratic state."
7. The status of Jewish emigration and the Palestinization of the Soviet refugee issue.

The Conferral of Refugee Status on Soviet Jews in Canada: A Demographic Snapshot

If *yerida*, or out-migration of Israeli Jews, is an underrepresented subject of demographic inquiry, as Professor DellaPergola has put it, it is largely because Israeli demographics have yet to fully internalize the reality, or normativity, of *yerida*. Indeed, the very discourse is revealing here, as Israeli sociologists still speak of Israelis "travelling about"; while the notion that *yordim* — itself a self-conscious discourse — would now be seeking refugee status is as unprecedented a phenomenon sociologically for Israelis as it is unpalatable normatively.

If the notion of Soviet Jewish *yordim* seeking refugee status is an unprecedented phenomenon both sociologically and juridically, the demographic composition of these *yordim* — many of whom are non-Jews — is itself unprecedented, and raises hitherto unaddressed societal and legal questions concerning the status of non-Jews in Israel.

While the percentage of Soviet Jewish emigrants from Israel seeking refugee status is minuscule in relation to the overall number of Soviet Jews having immigrated to Israel, the percentage of non-Jews among the emigrating group is relatively high.

Those former Soviet immigrants now seeking refugee status have little in the way of a "folk" connection to Israel and the Jewish people; indeed, while they asserted their "Jewishness" as a ground to immigrate from the Soviet Union to Israel, they now assert their non-Jewishness as a ground to secure refugee status in Canada. And so it is, then, that from a "Jewish" perspective, their refugee claim is resented by Israel, but from a human rights perspective, their non-Jewishness is asserted to buttress their refugee claim in Canada.

While this class of emigrants seeking refugee status may not be able to demonstrate a "well-founded fear of persecution" normally required of prospective applicants for refugee status, this distinct class of emigrants may well have endured discrimination as a result of their "outgroup" status, thereby presaging a cluster of issues surrounding the status of non-Jews in Israel, including the status of non-Jewish foreign workers and the particular status of Russian women as a "persecuted social group."

The number of Israeli applicants for refugee status in Canada — some 1,200 per year rising to peaks of 2,050 in 1992 and 1993 — and with an overall refugee acceptance rate of 43 percent — has resulted in Israel being included in the top tier of "refugee producing" countries, together with "other" human rights violator countries like Iran, Sri Lanka, Somalia, India, and Bangladesh.

The discrepancy rates in the conferral of refugee status between Quebec and Ontario from 1992 to 1994 is alarming, raising some serious questions not only about the disturbing disparity — 90 percent of Soviet Jewish applicants for refugee status are accepted in Quebec, yet only 10 percent are accepted in Ontario — but raising some serious questions about the legitimacy of a Canadian refugee status determination system whose criteria include, *inter alia*, uniformity in the application of standards across the country.

It is instructive and revealing to note that if Jews from the former Soviet Union seek to emigrate directly to Canada and claim refugee status on the grounds that they have a well-founded fear of persecution were they to be returned to the former Soviet Union, they are likely to have their application for refugee status denied; but if these same Soviet Jews immigrate to Israel and then leave Israel to seek refugee status in Quebec, they are very likely to have their refugee claim accepted.

Indeed, the seeming perversity — let alone discrepancy — in the refugee status determination system was dramatized recently when an applicant from the former Soviet Union was denied refugee status in Canada on the grounds, *inter alia*, that this applicant could have gone to Israel — a strangely "Zionist" decision, though a questionable "human rights" decision:[4] yet, if the applicant had gone to Israel first, and then applied in Quebec for refugee status, the application for refugee status might well have succeeded.

It is interesting to note that while Canadian Jewish leaders were indignant when this Soviet Jewish applicant was told she could not qualify for refugee status in Canada because she could emigrate under the Law of the Return to Israel, Israeli leaders did not protest this "Zionist" decision by the Canadian courts; but when the Canadian refugee determination process determined that Soviet Jewish applicants from Israel could secure refugee status in Canada, Israelis protested loudly while the Canadian Jewish leadership were initially rather mute in their response.

The Conferral of Refugee Status: Chronology of a Crisis — How It All Began

The public disclosure in the Israeli media in the summer of 1994 of decisions by Canada's Immigration and Refugee Board (IRB) conferring refugee status on Israelis who had immigrated to Israel from the former Soviet Union — and the reaction through the Israeli press by the then Deputy Foreign Minister Yossi Beilin to this disclosure — triggered what veteran Canada-Israel watchers characterized as an "unprecedented diplomatic and media storm" between the two countries.

More particularly, then Deputy Foreign Minister Beilin, reacting to a front page disclosure in the Israeli daily *Ha'aretz* of 31 July 1994 that Canada had granted refugee status to some 160 Israelis in 1993, responded that "the situation in which the Canadian government grants refugee status to Israeli citizens is really ridiculous," and added: "It is our role to ensure that such a crazy thing does not happen. Israel will mobilize a public campaign in Canada, against this absurd situation."

The Beilin riposte triggered what a veteran Israeli journalist called "the sharpest response ever heard from any Canadian Minister in the 46 years of Israel's existence." Replying to Beilin's comments, the then Canadian Minister of Immigration Sergio Marchi declared: "I don't think it's appropriate for another government...(to be) dictating to us who is a refugee and who is not."[5] Moreover, the Beilin reaction not only triggered a sharp diplomatic rebuke from Marchi about unwarranted interference by Israel in Canadian refu-

gee policy, it also provoked an intemperate outburst from Marchi
for which he himself was to publicly apologize. Marchi declared
that Canada would not let Israel tell it what refugees to accept any
more than it would let Saddam Hussein dictate refugee policy.[6]

The "official" Israeli demarche — and response also to the
offensive analogy made by Marchi of Israel with Iraq — was not
long in coming. On 3 August, the former Deputy-Director — and
now Director-General — of the Israeli Foreign Ministry, Eitan Ben-
Tsur, summoned the then Canadian Ambassador to Israel, Norman
Spector, to express the Israeli government's displeasure at Canada
granting refugee status to Israeli citizens, let alone the intemperate
remarks of Marchi. Indeed, the comparison of Israel with Saddam
Hussain — coming as it did from a Canadian minister friendly to
Israel — dramatized and amplified the diplomatic storm which sent
shock waves across the antennae of Canadian Jews. That the
rayonnement from Marchi's comments was not greater or more
enduring was due only to the timing of his remarks. On 2 August,
right after a mid-summer holiday weekend, not many were listening, and of those that were, not many were remembering.

In what was described in the Israeli press as a "difficult"
meeting, Ben-Tsur reminded Ambassador Spector that Israel had
absorbed over half a million immigrants from the former Soviet
Union; that it was inconceivable that one democratic country would
grant refugee status to the citizens of another democratic country,
particularly as these citizens were themselves the beneficiaries of
Israel's "open door" immigration policy; that the very existence of
the State of Israel had made the term "Jewish refugee" obsolete; and
that while one may speak of Soviet Jewish immigrants and emigrants, the Israeli Law of Return grants — and has granted —
automatic entry, and even citizenship, to these would-be "refugee"
claimants.

Ambassador Spector responded that it was not "Canada" or the
"Canadian government" which was conferring refugee status, but
the conferral of refugee status was the result of decisions by an
independent body — the Immigration and Refugee Board — in the
context of an independent inquiry, and with a further appellate
review procedure through the Federal Court of Canada.[7] Indeed,
said Ambassador Spector, the Canadian Refugee Status Determination process was a most respected one, and Canada had itself
received the Nansen medal from the United Nations in recognition

of its humanitarian refugee policy. The Canadian Ambassador promised, however, to convey the Israeli concern to the Canadian government.

The exchange between Ben-Tsur and Spector — like that between Beilin and Marchi, and not unlike that between the two countries generally — revealed not so much how little the countries knew about each other as how little they realized how much they were hurting each other. For each was assaulting, however inadvertently, the other's "neuralgic" center; each was converting the other's "crown jewel" into its "Achilles' heel." For Israel, which had absorbed over half a million refugees from the former Soviet Union and for whom the "ingathering of exiles" — and the Law of Return — was the *raison d'etre* for the Israeli state, the conferral of refugee status was an "absurd," indeed, "intolerable" situation; for Canada, which considered itself as a "nation of immigrants" and which regarded its refugee policy and its refugee status determination system as the most generous and fair of any Western democracy, the attempt by Israel to interfere in, if not determine, the Canadian refugee status determination system was seen as an "unwarranted" and "unacceptable" intervention in Canada.

Admittedly, as of this writing, the Canadian-Israeli diplomatic and media storm appears to have been limited to a summer 1994 *saison*, and the issue appears largely to have abated in both the diplomatic and media arenas in both countries.

This is somewhat surprising, if not ironic, as the diplomatic *contretemps* arose in the light of the disclosure in the Israeli media in late July 1994 that in 1993 the Canadian Immigration and Refugee Board had recognized 157 persons from Israel as refugees, up from some 68 acceptances in 1992. Interestingly enough, however, the Israeli media did not report — or perhaps had not yet known about — the January-July 1994 data which disclosed that the Board had recognized over 150 Israelis as refugees in the first six months of 1994 alone; and that the acceptance rate in the months of March through July 1994 in the Quebec region was over 90 percent, while in the rest of Canada it was less than 10 percent. This raised some serious questions not only about the dramatic disparity in acceptance rates between different regions in Canada, but about why the acceptance rate was so high in Quebec as compared with the rest of Canada.

Regrettably, also, the issue appears to have abated without any attempt to analyze what this unprecedented Israeli-Canadian *contretemps* portends not only for Canadian-Israeli relations — or between Canadian Jews in their relationship to both Canada and Israel — but, more importantly, what does this diplomatic and media "storm" surrounding decisions to confer refugee status on Israeli citizens tell us about the nature of Israeli foreign policy generally speaking? What does it tell us about the perception of Israel in the culture of human rights, and Israel's relationship to non-governmental organizations (NGOs) in that culture? What does it tell us about the status of non-Jewish minorities in Israel, and the "fall-out" from the notion of Israel as a "Jewish" state? What, in a word, are the lessons to be learned from this study — or case-study — that have relevance to larger and more serious and sustained questions such as those relating to Israeli public policy and Israeli relations with other governments, inter-governmental, and non-governmental organizations, let alone the Israel-diaspora agenda? And what do we learn about decision-making in the matter of the conferral of refugee status, the criteria for the determination of refugee status, and, in particular, the meaning of a state's "inability to protect" for refugee status determination purposes.

"Refugee" Status and the Making of Israeli Foreign Policy — What Have We Learned?

As appears from the foregoing, Israeli policy should not be an exercise in "ad/hocracy" or "crisis management" that may itself be self-induced. In a word, the decisions by the Canadian Immigration and Refugee Board to confer refugee status on Israeli citizens — or decisions of Canadian courts reversing adverse decisions of such boards in areas where such refugee status had in fact been denied — did not begin in late July 1994; rather, it was a developing trend which began as early as 1992, which still constitutes the year in which the largest number of applications for refugee status was made, though not the largest number of conferrals of refugee status. If there was a concern to be expressed — or preemptive action to be taken — it should have occurred in 1992 and not in 1994 when it had the appearance of a "crisis"; and where the first official Israeli government response (from Jerusalem) was the "shot across the

Canadian bow" fired by the Deputy Foreign Minister in *Ha'aretz*. One can understand Beilin's consternation at the disclosure of this "absurd" and "extremely ridiculous" situation, as he characterized it. The question is, why the consternation in 1994, and the lack of it in 1992?[8]

Many questions emerge. Even assuming that the matter only became known to the Deputy Foreign Minister in July 1994, why was the riposte made to Canada, in rather undiplomatic language, by way of the Israeli media? Why was there no official protest first launched with Canada through the usual diplomatic channels and then reported in the Israeli media? Why did the Canadian Immigration Minister — or the Canadian government generally — have to learn about the Israeli "shock," if not anger, via the Canadian media, which carried the *Ha'aretz* articles and the Beilin riposte almost verbatim? Why was the Canadian Ambassador to Israel "summoned" after the diplomatic and media storm, and not in preemption of it?

If a foreign policy protest is to be conducted first via the media — or if it is to be conducted at all — why, on such an important matter, or on a matter so important to Israel, did Israel at least not have a better appreciation of the facts or understanding of the matter at issue? More particularly, why was there an indictment of "Canada" or "Canadian policy" respecting the conferral of refugee status when the decisions granting refugee status were those of an independent board, the Immigration and Refugee Appeal Board, or those of an independent court, the Federal Court of Canada, and not that of the Canadian government or its Department of Immigration? How serious will an Israeli government protest be taken, or respected, when the protest appears to misconstrue and mischaracterize the source of the problem — in this instance the decisions of independent boards and courts — and characterize them as decisions of the Canadian government? And what does this fundamental misapprehension by Israeli decision-makers, joined in by the Israeli media, say about the seriousness or sophistication of Israeli foreign policy analysis and decision-making?

What does an Israeli government pronouncement in the Israeli media, that it is going to "mobilize a campaign in Canada against this absurdity," suggest about an understanding of the conduct of foreign policy, let alone about influencing the "court of public opinion?" Is the initiation of such a campaign, even before an official protest is launched, to be announced through the Israeli media? Should the "mobilization" of protest against the Canadian government — as if this were the right "address" to begin with — be received and learned about by Canadian government officials via the media? In a word, can one seek to "intervene" in the Canadian refugee determination process, governed by an independent decision-making tribunal, let alone launch this "intervention" in the pages of the Israeli media? Is this the way to wage a battle in the court of public opinion?

If there was to be a "campaign" against the decisions, why was there no serious critique developed of the decisions themselves? Since the decisions were vulnerable on a number of grounds (e.g., the dramatic disparity in acceptance rates between regions of Canada, the decisions of the Board ignoring or disregarding the principles and presumptions respecting refugee determination status in Canadian refugee law, particularly regarding alleged "refugees" from democracies, the seemingly singling out of Israel — an "immigrants democracy" — for differential treatment among the world's democracies, the questionable "findings of fact," etc.), why was this vulnerability not addressed head-on? In a word, why was the case against Israel, or rather, the conferral of refugee status on Russian claimants from Israel, not confronted on its own terms, as a juridical misapplication of the principles of refugee law and human rights? (See Chapter 3 in this book for an elaboration on this point.)

Why did the Israeli government and media make no mention in its July 1994 comments of the forthcoming "Country Conditions" hearing on Israel that was scheduled for late August, and which was designed, to inquire into and assess the validity of the refugee claimants' allegations against Israel? Indeed, as these hearings had been planned since June 1994, might it not have been more politic to await the outcome of the hearings before firing "shots across the Canadian bow" through the Israeli media, which in turn galvanized the issue in the Canadian media? (The Canadian mainstream media had largely ignored this issue up to August 1994; however, after the Beilin interview in *Ha'aretz*, the Canadian newspapers featured refugee claimant horror stories with such headings as "Israel is Accused of Rape and Torture of New Immigrants.") If Israeli officials had in fact not been aware as of 31 July of the intention of the Canadian board to hold a "Country Conditions" hearing on

Israel in late August — and therefore ignited the issue in *Ha'aretz* in the absence of this knowledge but with adverse media consequences — what does this say about Israeli "intelligence" on these and other matters?

Refugee Status, Human Rights, and the Rights of Non-Jewish Minorities in Israel — Some Additional Lessons

The Israeli protest appeared to assume that the issue was the conferral of refugee status on Jews from the former Soviet Union and their non-Jewish relatives who had immigrated to Israel under the Israeli Law of Return; indeed, this was held out, understandably, as the cornerstone of Israeli immigration policy, if not the "crown jewel" making possible this "ingathering of the exiles." However, it ignored the central thesis in the allegations of Israeli claimants before the Canadian Immigration and Refugee Board, which were about harassment and persecution of non-Jews in Israel; in fact, most Israeli refugee claimants acknowledged that Israel was a "democracy" for Jews, but they commented that Israel practiced discrimination against non-Jews, who were the standing victims of both state and private discrimination and persecution.

Accordingly, while Israel was extolling its herculean effort — and it was — of having absorbed more than 500,000 Jews from the former Soviet Union in five years, the Canadian Immigration and Refugee Appeal Board was being asked to adjudicate on the plight of the thousands of non-Jews who claimed to be the victims of alleged discrimination, harassment, violence, and persecution. In a word, and of particular long-range significance to Israeli public policy and the Israel-diaspora encounter, this Canadian-Israeli *contretemps* on the matter of refugee status determination may well presage a new "front" for Israel — not how it treats Palestinians in the administered territories, but how it treats non-Jews in Israel, or even, as a domestic spin-off, how it treats Jews who are not Orthodox.

It is precisely the alleged Israeli mistreatment of Palestinians in the territories, unaddressed both by Israeli policy-makers and the Israeli media, that underscores, if not supports, the allegations regarding Israeli mistreatment of non-Jews in Israel. In a word, the supporting affidavits by Israeli lawyer Lynda Breyer accompanying the Israeli claims for refugee status concentrated upon — in addition to the allegations of mistreatment of non-Jews — the alleged mistreatment of Palestinians in the administered territories. The inference, if not conclusion, in these affidavits and claims is clear: If you want to understand or assess the validity of the claims of mistreatment of non-Jews from the former Soviet Union in Israel, just look at the "documentary evidence" of the mistreatment of another group of non-Jews, Palestinians in the administered territories. Yet this analogue and its import were ignored, if not dismissed, by Israeli decision-makers and the media.

Refugee Status and the Role of Non-Governmental Organizations: Israel in the Culture of Human Rights

Both the Israeli government and media, as set forth earlier, assumed that the problem was Canada or Canadian government policy; but even allowing for the important clarification that the decisions to confer refugee status were those of independent boards and courts, and not the Canadian government, the Israeli critique completely overlooked or ignored the role of non-governmental organizations as an important documentary source and resource for the work of the Canadian Immigration and Refugee Appeal Board. More particularly, allegations of Israeli mistreatment of non-Jews were advanced, *inter alia*, by the St. Yves Society of Jerusalem, a Catholic NGO which was characterized by representatives from the Canadian NGO network as a "respected human rights NGO working on behalf of Palestinian rights in the Occupied Territories." Moreover, allegations of the violations of Palestinian human rights — including allegations that torture was practiced by Israeli security forces as a matter of policy, and made by respected human rights NGOs such as Human Rights Watch/Middle East, and Amnesty International — only underscored, if not appeared to vindicate, the allegations of refugee claimants.

In a word, if the allegations of Israeli torture of Palestinians were well-founded — so the argument went before the Canadian Immigration and Refugee Board — why should one not believe the allegations of Israeli violence against non-Jews in Israel. After all, in each instance the alleged perpetrators were Israeli authorities and the alleged victims were non-Jews.

As a corollary, Israeli officials, and media officials with whom I spoke, simply regarded the issue of ill-treatment of Palestinians as "irrelevant"; indeed, whenever I raised the issue I was advised, sometimes more subtly than not, that I was "confusing" the issue; that the refugee claimants were immigrants (Jews) from the former Soviet Union and not Palestinians from the administered territories; that the concern was with the Canadian government, not NGOs; and that I was introducing extraneous issues or evidence into the discussion.

But apart from a seemingly analytical failure to appreciate the nexus between allegations of mistreatment of Palestinians that were also used as support for the allegations of mistreatment of refugee claimants from the former Soviet Union, there appears to be an insufficient Israeli understanding of the human rights culture, and of the increasingly important role of human rights NGOs in the formulation of government policy, be it in Canada, the U.S., Europe, or elsewhere. Human rights NGOs, for example, have called on the U.S. government to condition its security and economic assistance to Israel (which of course, is important for Israel as a whole and not just the immigrants in it) on Israeli compliance with human rights norms, which also "feeds" into the refugee status determination system as it does into foreign policy decision-making.

Refugee Status, Human Rights, and Israel as a "Jewish State"

The allegations in the affidavits supporting claimants for refugee status — that Israel as a Jewish state is a racially-based, if not racist, state — may well presage a growing critique of Israel as a "Jewish state," the whole as part of the developing human rights critique of "ethnically or religiously-based states." Indeed, that which Israelis and supporters of Israel have assumed as a given — or accepted uncritically — that Israel is a Jewish state — may well become another "front" with respect to "Israel among the nations."

The general thesis of Lynda Breyer, who was invited to appear before the Immigration and Refugee Appeal Board in its "Country Conditions" hearings into Israel, was that Israel as a Jewish state was not only a racist state, but an "apartheid state"; and while one may regard the allegation of Israel as an "apartheid" state as being as scurrilous as it is absurd, it should be noted that such allegations did receive a responsive hearing from some of the leaders of the non-governmental organizations in Montreal present at the "Country Conditions" hearing into Israel.

The enormity of the indictment of Israel as an "apartheid state," and the relative equanimity with which the indictment was received, appeared to alone merit a response, even leaving aside the main issue at the hearing, Israel's "ability to protect" its citizens as the determinative normative referent for the conferral of refugee status. In fact, it emerged itself as a major issue: for if Israel was indeed a racist, apartheid state, then it was, arguably, a state that did not protect its citizens; or a state whose non-Jewish citizens could indeed argue that they had a "well-founded fear of persecution."

Accordingly, in the course of my testimony as an expert witness in this hearing, I argued, "No one is claiming that there is no incidence or practice of racism or discrimination in Israel, just as no one would claim that any democracy is free from racism or discrimination, particularly against identifiable groups or minorities in their midst. The question, however, and this is crucial to the question of the determination of refugee status of any claimant, is that of the state's 'ability to protect.'" This, I submitted, can only be addressed through the application of a "model" framework of inquiry or "testing criteria" (see Chapter 3 in this volume) to assess the ability of any country, like Israel, to protect its minorities and citizens; and it is this criterion — or criteria — which were set down by the Supreme Court of Canada in the *Ward* case for the determination of refugee status in any given country.[9] In a word, the evaluation of a particular country like Israel under such "testing criteria" would demonstrate that while there are incidences of racism, discrimination, and human rights violations in Israel, there is a basic state "ability to protect," and there is no state support for, or acquiescence in, the alleged persecution of its citizens.

Moreover, the allegation that Israel is an "apartheid" state is not only defamatory to Israel, rather, it has the effect of whitewashing the real "apartheid" of former South Africa. For if Israel is like South Africa, then South Africa (when it was an apartheid state) is like Israel. That means apartheid South Africa met the "testing criteria" of a state's "ability to protect"; more particularly, that South Africa had a universal franchise, one person-one vote, was a parliamentary and constitutional democracy, had an independent judiciary, enjoyed a free press, had a comprehensive legal regime to combat discrimination etc., rather than being what it was — a racist state where racism itself was institutionalized as law. Such a "whitewashing" of apartheid South Africa is no less absurd in its false moral equivalence than saying that Israel is an apartheid state. However unpalatable this may seem, the false moral equivalence — and the notion of Israel as an "apartheid" state — did evoke a certain responsive hearing, and presaged once again, if not also helped to validate, the lesser indictment of Israel as an ethnically or religiously based state.

Even leaving aside the prospective indictment of Israel as a Jewish state on human rights grounds (i.e., that it is an ethnically or religiously based state), the hearings before the Immigration and Refugee Board, which critiqued the restrictive use of the word "Jew" in Israeli law as synonymous with *halakhic* or Orthodox Jew, may well presage and, indeed, already reflects the growing concern with the allegedly monopolistic or preferential jurisdiction given to the Orthodox establishment in Israel in matters relating to the laws of personal status. The allegations respecting the discriminatory treatment accorded non-Jews in Israel are not unrelated to the allegations respecting the definition of "who is a Jew" under Israeli law, and the privileged jurisdiction accorded to the Orthodox rabbinate in that regard.

The allegations by refugee claimants that the Israeli Law of Return is as supportive as it is reflective of an exclusivist and racist immigration and nationality policy may also presage another and more general "front": the indictment of Israel's Law of Return as an example of, or indeed evidence of, the State of Israel itself as an exclusivist and racist state; ironically, also, it may well presage the dual — and converging — attack on the law from both the religious right and secular left groups in Israel and the diaspora — the former concerned that the Law of Return is too indulgent and accessible to non-Jews, while the latter is concerned that it is too narrow in its definitions of "Jew," with some even questioning whether there should be any "Jewish" component at all.

The Status of Jerusalem and the "Palestinization" of the Refugee Issue

Finally, and almost imperceptibly, there is a Jerusalem nexus to this refugee status determination case-study; for if, as the argument goes, the allegations of Israeli ill-treatment of Palestinians are well-founded, and if this lends credence also to the allegations of Israeli ill-treatment of non-Jews, then why should Israeli jurisdiction extend to "east Jerusalem," the home of Palestinian Arabs and non-Jews? If Israel consistently violates the human rights of its non-Jewish minorities, Muslim and Christian, Palestinian and Arab, then perhaps these non-Jewish minorities would be better secured with east Jerusalem as the capital of an independent Palestinian state.

Once again, what appears to be for Israeli policy-makers and diaspora Jews as an issue only of refugee status determination for Jewish immigrants from the former Soviet Union has also been "Palestinized" — with Jerusalem as its core. And what began as a study of the Israeli-Canadian "diplomatic and media storm" surrounding the conferral of refugee status on Israelis — a matter which appears to have abated, if not largely disappeared from the Israeli-Canadian radar screen — may in fact be far more instructive and significant as a case-study of major issues in refugee law, human rights, and Israeli foreign policy; of the perception of Israel in the culture of human rights; of the role of NGOs in the making of foreign policy generally; of the Israeli relationship to these NGOs; and of the conferral of refugee status on emigrants from democracies.

Moreover, it may well portend some new and difficult fronts for Israel and the Israel-diaspora agenda that have been overshadowed by the peace process: the concept of Israel as a Jewish state in a world which increasingly eschews ethnic or religiously based states; the constitutional fall-out from Israel's recent Basic Law on Human Dignity and Freedom whose normative referent is that of Israel as a "Jewish and democratic state"; the status and treatment of Israel's non-Jewish minorities — be they Russian or Arab, or Russian Orthodox, Christian, or Muslim; and the implications of all this for the determination of the status of Jerusalem — as distinct from the status of refugees — the whole arising from this issue. Indeed, this chapter is not so much a Canada-Israel case-study as it is evocative of some profound questions for the refugee-human rights law agenda in general and the Israel-diaspora agenda in particular.

Notes

1. See on this point, for example, G.S. Goodwin-Gill, *The Refugee in International Law,* 2nd ed. (Oxford: Clarendon Press, 1996); James C. Hathaway, "A Reconsideration of the Underlying Premise of Refugee Law," *Harvard International Law Journal* 31 (1990):129; J.C. Hathaway and J.A. Dent, *Refugee Rights: Report of a Comparative Survey* (Toronto: University of Toronto Press, 1995).
2. The Law of Return, 5110-1950, in its inception was a national law, not a religious one, and over the years it was interpreted in a national-secular context. It provides, *inter alia*, that "every Jew has the right to come to this country [Israel] as an immigrant." In 1970, following political pressure by the religious parties, the Knesset changed the law to define the term "Jew" according to principles of *halakhah* (Jewish law), but balanced the "religious" definition with an expanded right for intermarried couples and their children and grandchildren to immigrate to Israel under the Law of Return.
3. Convention Relating to the Status of Refugees, 28 July 1951, 189 U.N.T.S. 150, U.K.T.S. 39 (1954) (entered into force 22 April 1954).
4. See on this point *Grygorien v. Minister of Citizenship*, 1995, where the Federal Court, Trial Division, held that "the basic principle of refugee law is to grant such status only to those requiring surrogate protection and not to those who have ready and automatic right to another country's nationality." The court reasoned that the claimant's right to Israeli citizenship under the Law of Return precluded her from claiming refugee status in Canada.
5. *Toronto Star,* 3 August 1994.
6. *Gazette,* Montreal, 3 August 1994.
7. As it happened, I arrived in Israel from Montreal on 4 August 1994, after witnessing the furor the Beilin riposte had caused in Canadian government circles and the Canadian media. Fortuitously, my first meeting in Israel was a scheduled luncheon with Ambassador Spector, who then provided me with a first-hand account of his meeting with Eitan Ben-Tsur. I subsequently had occasion to meet with Deputy Foreign Minister Beilin, and so was privy to the reactions not only as reported in the media, but as experienced by the main protagonists themselves.

8. None of this, or any of the following, is intended to critique the former Deputy Foreign Minister in particular. Indeed, Yossi Beilin is one of the more astute, and informed, members of the Israeli political elite. If anything, it only dramatizes the somewhat institutionalized — and insular — mind-set of Israeli decision-makers, and their lack of appreciation for the development and discourse of the "culture of human rights."

9. *Canada (A.G.) v. Ward* [1993] 2 S.C.R. 689.

12

The Integration of Jewish Immigrants in Montreal: Models and Dilemmas of Ethnic Match

Morton Weinfeld

The Concept of Immigrant Integration

The experience of the Jewish community of Montreal provides a good example for exploring the various alternative approaches and conceptions of immigrant integration. Here we will look at the issues surrounding the role of ethnic/cultural communities in the integration process and, specifically, in the provision of culturally sensitive services to immigrants. The data for this study are taken from annual reports and other documents of over a dozen Jewish agencies in Montreal, and from interviews with professional staff of the Jewish Immigrant Aid Services (JIAS) of Montreal, as well as other Jewish agencies serving Jewish immigrants.

First, it is important to understand that much of the policy discussion around immigrant integration is based on a flawed assumption. The term "immigrant integration" is an oxymoron to the extent that it refers to a process in which an adult immigrant to a host society, e.g., Canada, the United States, or Israel, actually achieves a high measure of "integration" with that host society. That almost never occurs.

By and large, adult immigrants to Canada — especially if they arrived from a non-English or non-French-speaking society — retain one foot firmly planted in the old country. This simple realization is often overlooked in the mounting concern found in many government circles about the "failures" of immigrant integration. This also impacts on the process of devising and collecting indicators of integration, and, more importantly, on evaluating those indicators. True integration into a host society is usually achieved, if then, by the second generation, and at times the third generation.

This is not necessarily a tragedy. The fact that full integration is a multi-generational process of adjustment does not indicate a failing on the part of the host society, or on the part of the immigrant.

What immigrants go through is best considered as adjustment, or in the now quaint term, settlement, or re-settlement. Moreover, what generally takes place for Jewish immigrants is a three-fold, nested process of immigration: into subcommunity, community, and host society.

The Role of Ethnic and Immigrant Communities

To the extent that immigrants have integrated at all, they have done so mainly within their own pre-existing communities. Historically, when the state supplied little by way of immigrant services, these functions were carried out, formally and informally, by immigrant institutions. As Raymond Breton defined it in Canada, the more "institutionally complete" an ethnic group was, the more likely immigrants would be to integrate first into the ethnic community.[1]

Thus, the process of immigrant integration is in fact one with two or three distinct phases. The first involves the integration of the immigrant, in most cases, into the respective ethnic community. This process should not be seen as problematic, but as a natural response of immigrants to the trauma of the dislocation.

In fact, the range of services provided by ethnic communities has always been large, but of late has increased. They include economic opportunities for workers and employers, schools, churches, media — from newspapers to radio and television, fraternal, recreational, cultural, social, political, and other organizations. Daniel Elazar's typologies, developed for the Jewish polity and its functions, can be applied to ethnic communities in general.[2]

The Jewish Model

Jews have been by far the most institutionally complete ethnic group in North America. The major reason for this tendency towards development of a dense communal infrastructure, which *inter alia* serves to integrate immigrants, is that Jews have a diaspora history of some 2000 years. They have had lots of practice in getting it right and, because of anti-Semitism, have had the need to get it right. This has simply not been the case for other major European groups in North America. For example, the Ukrainian diaspora is only one hundred years old, dating from the 1890s. A second reason is that Jews have generally not thought of their country of origin as a homeland, so their migration would tend to be comparatively permanent, with a resulting need for permanent institutions. Third, the fact that Jews are both a religious and an ethno-cultural group has given them another set of reasons to justify this institutional completeness.

Thus the array of services provided by Jewish communities in affluent liberal democracies such as Canada, including Landsmanschaften, Free Loan Associations, YMHAs, and Jewish Immigrant Aid Services (JIAS), can provide a maximal model for those seeking to likewise maximize the array of services available to groups today.

Ironically, the recent Canadian literature on services for immigrants suggests that the Jewish experience may not be seen as relevant to the case of non-European recent immigrants. The older European immigrant groups have certainly been aware of the Jewish model, and have been inspired by it. Thus the Canadian German Congress and the Canadian Polish Congress have been modeled to an extent on the Canadian Jewish Congress. Perhaps Jews are no longer recognized as a disadvantaged immigrant group within the current "anti-racist" discourse. Perhaps they are seen by newer immigrant groups as an established religious group. Whatever the reason, a 1996 paper, "Immigrant Service Agencies: A Fundamen-

tal Component of Anti-Racist Social Services" makes *no* reference
at all to JIAS.

> It is of course true that some ISAs are associated with service to
> particular ethnic-racial groups. Many OCASI member agencies, par-
> ticularly the recently formed ones, have grown out of the special needs
> of newly arrived immigrant and refugee groups such as the Eritreans,
> Ethiopians, Somalis, Iranians, and Tamils. Other agencies provide
> services to particular groups like the Cambodians, Filipinos, Poles,
> Ukrainians, and Vietnamese."[3]

The New Diaspora Context

There is one sense in which the admittedly ambitious goal of
immigrant integration is even *more* problematic today than in the
past. Immigrants today, thanks to changes in communications
technology and more accessible travel opportunities, are far more
likely to be able, should they wish, to keep one and a half feet firmly
in the old country.

Immigration at the turn of the century often meant, at most, one
return visit to the old country. Letters served as the medium of
communication. Today, immigrants are likely to visit periodically,
and to host old country relatives on periodic visits. Letters have
been supplanted by fax, phone, and e-mail. Movies (videos), re-
cordings, and newspapers from the old country are more readily
available. Ethnic radio and TV stations bring the old country into
the homes of new immigrants. This is true of Israeli or Russian
Jewish immigrants as well as other immigrants.

In this sense, the new migration patterns of Jews are more fluid
than in the past, with greater two-way links with the country of
origin. The example of Israelis who have lived in North America for
twenty years but still see themselves as having left Israel temporarily is a case in point. And many ex-Israelis do in fact re-migrate
to Israel.

This phenomenon, in conjunction with the drive over the past
10-15 years toward the creation of culturally sensitive social services in various policy domains — health, education, criminal
justice — has created a much greater potential for reinforcing
institutional completeness for immigrants. Thus, immigrants are

better able to retain their cultural specificity. In other words, just as the concern is increasing about the failures of integration, we find technological changes and policy directions which may in fact slow down an idealized process of integration.

In the past, the pace of assimilation for the children and grand-children of immigrants has, on the whole, been impressive. It remains to be seen whether the experience of the more recent immigrants and their children will mirror that of earlier generations.

The Concept of Ethnic Match

New concerns for the provision of culturally sensitive services have raised to prominence the option of ethno-specific services or, more generally, the option of "ethnic match." Table 12.1 provides an overview of eight ideal type configurations of ethnic match. JIAS and indeed all the Jewish communal agencies to be described below would represent an example of the case of maximal ethnic match. Moreover, in discussions with their directors, it was learned that in many cases they employ immigrants on staff, particularly for those programs aimed at immigrants. But only a few of these immigrant professionals could be classified as recent immigrants.

The concept of ethnic match can vary along three dimensions. The first of these involves the professional service provider. This consideration refers to the ethnic-cultural congruence between the origin of the service recipient and the service provider: doctor, nurse, therapist, social worker, lawyer, police officer, teacher, or journalist. An assumption is that the recipient of the service will be better off when matched with a service provider of the same group.

In fact, this assumption has not been established through systematic scientific studies. No one knows for certain if minority students are better off being taught geometry by minority teachers; they may or may not. The same uncertainty applies for all the other service domains including immigrant integration services, extending also to children of immigrants.

Even less research has been done on the minority-origin professionals themselves. How do they see work with those of their own group? As a duty, a calling, a niche, an opportunity — or a ghetto? No one knows. One problem not always recognized is that all the

TABLE 12.1

Possible Configuration of Ethnic Match in Public Policy Domains

	Professional	Organization	Practice
Range of Configuration	Is the ethnic origin of the "professional" or "caregiver" the same as the recipient?	Is the "organization" or "institution" providing the service under the auspices or control of the recipient's ethnic community?	Is the actual content of the "practice" of the service reflective of or sensitive to the ethnic culture of the recipient?
1. (maximal match)	yes	yes	yes
2.	yes	yes	yes
3.	yes	no	yes
4.	no	yes	yes
5.	yes	no	no
6.	no	yes	no
7.	no	no	yes
8. (minimal match)	no	no	no

ethnic or cultural categories are extremely heterogeneous. One cannot always assume that a Black, or a Chinese, or a Jewish professional represents the *same* origin and identity as that of a client from the same group. Consider the differences among Sephardic and Ashkenazic Jews, Orthodox and Reform, as well as differences of country of origin, gender, and social class. Matching a Jew with another "Jew" may be no match at all.

A second dimension of ethnic match involves the organization or institution providing the service. Is it under the auspices or control of the recipient's ethnic community? Individuals may receive services from mainstream organizations (e.g., a general hospital or social service agency), or one which is explicitly ethnic. In Montreal, for example, one can find almost cradle to grave ethno-specific service institutions, from day care centers to old age homes. The Jewish community obviously is the most organized, but other groups are catching up. In some cases there can be an ethno-specific unit within a mainstream organization, such as a Black Studies department at a university.

Furthermore, an ethno-specific institution may well employ a mix of professionals, not only those from the given group, while a mainstream agency may also employ, deliberately or not, staff of minority origin. Finally, the funding and to an extent control of an ethno-specific agency may come, to a greater or lesser extent, from the state.

The third and perhaps the key dimension of ethnic match is ethnic practice. How does the role of ethnic culture shape the content of the service — the medical diagnosis, the counselling advice, the teaching style, the punishment meted out to the guilty, the content of the journalism? One can imagine an anti-racist curriculum, or a social worker familiar with the ethnic culture when advising a client.

In theory, culturally sensitive practice can be delivered by a professional of any origin who has been suitably trained, and in any sort of agency. At times it may be difficult for the ethnic practice to gain acceptance within the dominant or mainstream professional culture (e.g., acupuncture, rap music).

It is important for both analysis and policy to distinguish among these three core dimensions of ethnic match. For example, affirmative action programs aimed at hiring minorities in mainstream agencies are not comparable policy responses to the setting up of community-based service delivery agencies. The ethnic match model described here can be applied to any of the policy domains described above, and one can imagine immigrant minorities facing a range of ethnic match, from maximal to minimal. Maximal ethnic match, in theory, might be the case of a Jewish social worker working in a Jewish immigrant service agency and counselling Jewish clients based on Judaic precepts and guidelines.

Jewish Immigrants in Montreal

Montreal has a long history as a pioneer in the reception and resettlement of Jewish immigrants. The estimated number of Jewish immigrants to Montreal, from 1981 to 1993, was just over 6,600, based on JIAS files. As of January 1996, JIAS retained a caseload of 529 family files, totalling 1,250 individuals. (Of course, many Jewish immigrants may arrive without any contact with JIAS at all.)

Historically, JIAS has played a dominant role in immigrant integration and resettlement, but over time there has been a gradual evolution away from meeting all immigrant needs in one agency, toward recognition of a more comprehensive approach. Indeed, it is fair to say that immigrant integration is a major component of the activities of nearly *all* the Jewish communal agencies.

JIAS expenditures totalled $950,000 for 1995-96, while expenditures from other agencies for immigrant services totalled over $528,250. These included special programs for employment at Jewish Vocational Services, and for counselling and support at Jewish Family Services, which includes Le Mercaz, the volunteer food and clothing distribution center, among others.

In Montreal in the mid-1990s, the Jewish Federation established a Council on Immigrant Integration and Acculturation (CIIA), with representation from 28 related communal agencies including JIAS. When the Jewish community approaches the issue of immigrant integration, it clearly does so from the dual perspective suggested above: integration into the mainstream society (finding a job, language acquisition of English or French, meeting immediate basic needs) and, at least as important, integration into the Jewish community.

In 1995 the CIIA set up three specific task forces designed to deal with different elements of the process of immigrant integration, for outreach to immigrant teens, employment, and education. In addition, plans are underway to develop a new multi-agency Welcome Center for Jewish immigrants and refugees. The reports of the three task forces, the proposal for the new Welcome Center, and the general community literature which is available to new immigrants all stress the dual dimensions of integration.

For example, the JIAS Mission Statement states:

> JIAS promotes and advances their well being and integration into the Jewish community and society at large.
> The overall objective of JIAS is to help newly arrived members of the community achieve their full potential as full independent members of the Montreal Jewish community and Quebec and Canadian society as quickly as possible.

Even in the communal organizations devoted to communal subgroups — Ethiopian, Russian, or Israeli — the rationale generally includes the objective of facilitating the integration of these immigrants into the Jewish community.

Integration into the Jewish Community

There has been a renewed focus of late on the development, collection, and analysis of "indicators of integration." Yet there has been little parallel work on defining measures of integration within the Jewish, or any ethnic, community. Possibly these would mean the same array of variables used by social scientists to measure the levels of affiliation and identification of any Jews in North America. One of the problems with such measures of immigrant integration into the host country — reading newspapers, knowledge about the country, political participation, joining voluntary organizations, etc. — is that many of the native born would likely score poorly!

It seems clear, however, that one must make allowances for lower levels of such integration into the host society. Indeed, in fact for some Jewish immigrants we might speak of a third layer of integration, into a specific Jewish subcommunity.

At present, within the Montreal Jewish community there are formal organizations representing Sephardic, Israeli, Ethiopian, and Russian Jews. Thus one can argue that while the formal Jewish community is concerned with the first two levels of integration, in fact, the first level of integration is that which takes place within the subcommunity and may involve both formal organizational and informal networks.

This is not a new story. Earlier waves of Jewish immigrants were likewise segregated into subcommunities, be they German or Russian, Litvaks or Galicianers. More recently, in the postwar period, other multiple subcommunities persisted.

My late father, *alav hashalom,* was a Holocaust survivor who arrived in Montreal in 1948. He was formally integrated into the Canadian community, though not that of Quebec, because he spoke English rather well, read newspapers, and voted regularly. Yet the two jobs he held in Montreal were both within the Jewish community, a bookkeeper first for *Der Kenader Adler*, the Yiddish daily, and later for the Lubavitcher Yeshiva. I attended a Jewish day school, and spent summers at a Jewish summer camp. Informally, his world was circumscribed: specifically, his social circle consisted almost exclusively of Polish Holocaust survivors — a very distinct subcommunity within the Montreal Jewish community. He had nothing to do with Canadian-born Anglo-Jewish Montrealers. The question to be posed here is: What indicators or what measures would we use to assess the degree of integration of my father, and into which community?

This nested process is not limited to Jewish integration. Recently I was in a Toronto cab, with a driver who was clearly of African origin. When I began to chat about issues relating to racism and the Black community in Toronto, he pointed out to me that he was not primarily "Black," nor African, nor Nigerian. Rather he was an Ibo, identified as such, associated mainly with other Ibo, and even belonged to an Ibo organization in Toronto. He also was scathing in his comments about Jamaicans.

These two anecdotes suggest that the process of immigrant integration may proceed from subcommunity, to community, to mainstream society.

Thus the issue of ethnic match becomes even more complex, with our recognition of the complexity *within* the Jewish or any other category. A common Jewishness alone may clearly be insufficient to provide culturally sensitive services between Jewish professionals and Jewish clients. In addition, it is not clear whether those Jewish immigrants who avail themselves more of Jewish communal, i.e., ethno-specific services, fare better in their general processes of integration than those comparable Jewish immigrants who choose not to.

Communal Responsibility and Financial Constraints

Unlike the case of some other communities, the Jewish community, through its own resources, has mounted a parallel system of integration for Jewish immigrants compared to that of the state. This has raised an unusual dilemma. On the one hand, most Jews, and Jewish leaders, have strongly endorsed liberal immigration policies and those which might bring the largest numbers of Jewish immigrants to their communities. On the other hand, the increasing numbers of Jewish immigrants have posed a particular financial burden on local communities, particularly in the case of the Soviet Jewish migration.

As the former leader of the Jewish Federation in Montreal indicated:

> Let's take the issue of refugee admissions. Perhaps there would be benefit for JIAS to consult with representatives from AJCS (the Federation) as to the positions they would take on refugee admissions. This is because even if we put to one side the strictly governmental aspect and the non-sectarian aspect, the positions that they may take in terms of accelerating the admissions do potentially have a local impact on the community which is more responsible in the area of reception and resettlement and absorption in the community. The issue whether the community is prepared to provide the financing is just one issue.[4]

If the Jewish community found it difficult to provide its admittedly wide range of services to increasing numbers of refugees and immigrants, all the more so for less affluent and organized groups.

Three Research and Policy Questions

A generic question is to what extent governments should provide financing for ethno-specific services, which may have as part of their agenda, stated or unstated, the integration of the immigrant into the ethnic community itself. In other terms, to what extent is the process of integration into the ethnic community consistent with the broader governmental objectives of immigrant integration?

For the ethnic community, to what extent is immigrant integration into the ethnic subcommunity a positive or negative development in terms of general communal objectives? What degree of fine-tuning of ethnic match within an ethno-specific agency would optimize services? The Montreal Jewish community developed a specific program to train women from the Hasidic community in basic social work to meet the needs of that particular subcommunity. Does this lead to communal cohesion, or communal fragmentation? Related to this, to what extent must government, and ethnic groups, embrace principles of ethnic match and cultural sensitivity when providing services to immigrants and their families?

Notes

* I would like to thank Mr. Ho Hon Leung for help with the interviews and data collection, and Mr. Joel Moss, executive director of JIAS in Montreal, for his cooperation with this project. Funding for the study reported here came from a grant from the Social Sciences and Humanities Research Council of Canada. Mr. Ho Hon Leung assisted in the research.

1. Raymond Breton, "Institutional Completeness of Ethnic Communities and the Personal Relations of Immigrants," *American Journal of Sociology*, 70 (1964):193-205.
2. Daniel J. Elazar, *Community and Polity: The Organizational Dynamics of American Jewry*, 2nd ed. (Philadelphia: Jewish Publication Society, 1995).
3. Dawit Beyene, Carrie Butcher, Betty Joe, and Ted Richmond, "Immigrant Service Agencies: A Fundamental Component of Anti-Racist Social Services," Carl E. James, ed., *Perspectives on Racism and the Human Services Sector* (Toronto: University of Toronto Press, 1996), p. 178.
4. Anne Kilpatrick, "The Jewish Immigrant Aid Services: An Ethnic Lobby in the Canadian Political System," M.A. Thesis, Department of Sociology, McGill University (1995), p. 77.

IV

Diaspora Experiences

13

Israel-Jewish Diaspora Experience as a Model for Other State-Diaspora Relationships

Manfred Gerstenfeld

Over the past decades Israel has developed sophisticated methods for strengthening its relations with the diaspora, and benefiting from its resources. No other homeland has such a broad and diversified approach towards those whose ancestors once left it.

Together, all these methods of Israel's pro-active policy can be considered as a complex, interwoven system with potential value as well for other countries. Thus it is worth investigating whether this know-how can be marketed abroad and used to improve Israel's good will.

Israeli-diaspora relations have a profound religious and ideological basis. The charity relationship of the Jews resident in what was once Palestine with that of the Jews in the diaspora, precedes both the State of Israel and the Zionist movement.

A Tradition of Millennia

Diaspora philanthropy goes back more than two millennia. Already in the 2nd or 3rd century, the yeshivot in Palestine sent emissaries to diaspora Jews in order to collect funds. And even before that, when the Temple was functioning, Jews from abroad came to Jerusalem to bring their sacrifices. It has been claimed that the reason why the ritual practices of the Babylonian diaspora prevailed throughout history over those of the Jerusalemites was because the latter were mainly interested in paid honor and receiving contributions from abroad, while the Babylonians were pragmatic people.

In pre-Zionist Palestine, the Jewish religious communities in Jerusalem, Tiberias, Hebron, and Safed were supported by Jews from abroad. Over the years the system changed. In order to replace the multiple emissaries knocking on their doors, in 1843 Jews from the Netherlands and Germany created a collection system which institutionally supported the Ashkenazi communities in Palestine.

If we analyze Israel's sophisticated fund collection system of today, and its multiple interaction with the diaspora, we should understand that it has its origins in ancient times as well as in the blue Jewish National Fund box. The latter was not only a tool for collecting money but also a symbol of Jewish identity in a diaspora house. It often meant emotional involvement on top of the financial one. This motive of "philanthropy to Israel as a key element of Jewish identity" abroad still exists today.

Israel's Need to Mobilize All Resources

After the establishment of the State of Israel, Israel-diaspora relations were further enhanced due to Israel's political and economic reality over the past decades as a beleaguered state, surrounded by enemies. Israel thus had to mobilize all possible resources. It developed a variety of methods and instruments in its relations with the diaspora. In the course of time, these have become increasingly sophisticated. This process merits detailed study, not only because it is fascinating, but also because understanding it can be very useful to Israel, as well as to other nations which have a significant diaspora.

One of the characteristics of this process has been continuously improved networking. Fund-raising is the area in which the Israel-diaspora relationship is most capillary. Initially, the biggest potential donors were addressed. However, by now increasingly formalized methods have been developed to reach every willing Jew.

From there, in quite a few countries, it has spread even further and addresses non-Jews sympathetic to Israel. However, we should not focus on philanthropy alone. The development of the Israeli-Jewish relationship covers a large number of areas such as the mobilization of political and financial support, as well as a broad spectrum of economic, educational, cultural, and religious relations.

Assisting Other Diasporas

The analysis and description of this range of economic relations could lead to the development of a know-how package which other nations may be interested in acquiring. With the growth of unemployment problems, more and more nations have discovered the economic importance of diasporas which can help to mitigate these situations.

In this regard, many countries come to mind, such as Ireland and China, with the attraction of diaspora investors. In recent years China has been particularly successful in attracting monies from Taiwan and Hong Kong. An American author coined the term Bamboo Network for the activities of the Chinese. Pakistan, India, and many others have a close connection with their diasporas with respect to unilateral money transfers from expatriates to family members at home.

As unemployment increasingly becomes a worldwide problem, the competition to attract foreign investment will become tougher. In this context, many additional countries are likely to discover the "diaspora as a resource" concept in the future. Spain — and Italy even more so — seem among the more obvious candidates.

Occasionally some foreign authors mention the potential of the diaspora. In his book about the Greeks, James Pettifer addresses the issue: "Generally speaking, it is the same story worldwide. Although within the family there are tight links at every level — and bonds with Greeks stretch across oceans as easily as across a village street — formal business relationships are uncommon. The Greeks of Astoria district in New York, say, obviously provide a ready market for imported Greek food and drink, icons, the travel business, and so on, but there are not many Greek-American businesses of any size in important areas of the economy."[1]

Italy's Diaspora Potential

The Italian diaspora is a particularly large one, compared to the domestic population. It thus merits investigation with regard to possible involvement in the home country in a variety of fields. As far as Italians abroad are concerned, their attachment is more often to their town of origin than to Italy as a whole. This creates a significant collaboration potential. The great majority of the Italian diaspora comes from the southern regions of Italy, where unemployment problems are much greater than in the north. Successful Italo-Americans usually do not speak any Italian, but when they come to Italy, they go and seek out their roots and visit remote relatives in their grandparents' village of origin.

The magnitude of this still unrealized potential becomes clear when we consider the numbers involved. In the 1980 U.S.A census, more than 12 million people (equal to 5.4 percent of the country's population) mentioned Italian origin as one of its ethnic roots; 6.9 million of these were of exclusive Italian origin, while about 830,000 of these were born in Italy.[2]

Thus, the Italian diaspora seems a particularly good example. It has done quite well economically in North America; it has maintained some ethnic identity; its relationship is with the Italian regions most in need of foreign investment. (By comparison, it is much more numerous than the Jewish diaspora.)

The main publicized Italian diaspora connection in the past concerned the Sicilian mafia. This was used by the U.S government in its preparation of the Allied invasion in the latter part of World War II. However, we should be careful not to become prey to stereotypes. Criminals are only a tiny part of society. The big potential lies in the vast majority of honest people.

Israeli experiences and models of interaction with the diaspora can probably find useful applications also outside home country-diaspora relationships. One far-reaching example was the twinning of needy Israeli communities with Jewish communities in the diaspora, called Project Renewal, which could have been useful in a model as to how the West could have helped the Soviet Union on a possible road to stable democracy after the fall of communism. The Western world is likely to pay dearly in the future for its inaction in this matter.

The Main Components of Israel's Pro-Active Policy

Israel's largely pro-active economic policy towards the Jewish community in the world, though never formulated in a systematic manner, has a large number of components, one of which is raising charity funds for Israel for a continuously increasing number of institutions. These include the United Jewish Appeal/Keren HaYesod, Keren Kayemet, municipalities, universities, museums, hospitals, vocational schools like ORT, and yeshivot. The list can be expanded even further.

Few Israelis realize in how many different forms this relationship expresses itself, and how different their day-to-day environment would be had this link not existed. The figures which state that this diaspora contribution to Israel represents only a few points of GNP do not tell the whole story. For instance, many of Jerusalem's public buildings such as the Knesset, the Supreme Court, the Sherover Theater, some community centers, and several of the Hebrew University buildings would not have been built had it not been for diaspora donations. It is also true for the Jerusalem Center for Public Affairs.

The same goes for public parks and playgrounds, as well as the sculptures which we find in so many public places in Jerusalem. How would the Israel and Bible Lands Museums have looked without donations from the diaspora? The country would also have had much fewer forests had it not been for the foreign donors to the Jewish National Fund.

Of all the Israeli institutions raising money, few have as varied a progam around which rituals have also developed, as the JNF. The tree certificate, the inauguration ceremonies in the forest including a specific prayer, the plaques put up there, and the publication of donor names in the newspapers are only a few elements of this.[3]

One may wonder whether philanthropy is an economic activity. To a certain extent, it is. Often one trades honor for money, by naming buildings or institutes after donors. To put it even more clearly: this form of charity can be defined economically as buying a plaque on a building with one's name on it.

Project Renewal

A quantum leap in the sophistication of the giving process, as well as in Israel-diaspora interaction in the field of philanthropy, was made through Project Renewal. This was initiated by the Begin government after the 1977 elections. Part of its uniqueness was due to the scheme's scope. The initial program was to disburse $1.2 billion among 160 distressed neighborhoods throughout Israel. The project affected the lives of over 600,000 people (i.e., one out of every seven Israelis).[3]

The program was also unique in its approach. The classic arms-length donation from the diaspora to a central Zionist fund was supplemented by the earmarking of monies raised from specific communities abroad for specific communities in Israel. Project Renewal implied a significant move towards an interactive partnership between the government of Israel and the diaspora. It created a personal dimension of diaspora involvement through the twinning of the local neighborhoods with individual diaspora communities abroad. The original motivations were not primarily ideological but derived from considerations of having an incremental fund-raising campaign, which needed new channels. As a result, however, Project Renewal has changed some important parameters of philanthropy in the Israel-diaspora connection.

In the framework of Project Renewal also, a significant number of diaspora volunteers came to Israel to try to help the twinned neighborhood. This concept of donating time in addition to, or instead of, money is another institutionalized mode of Israel-diaspora interaction.

Kibbutzim have had diaspora volunteer workers for many decades. There are also a variety of programs for volunteer dentists in various Israeli locations. Many of these volunteer programs address themselves partly to non-Jews from abroad.

Interaction in Other Fields

In addition to fund-raising, there are many other relevant components of the Israel-diaspora relationship with economic aspects which will be referred to here, if only briefly.

Once one reaches a certain saturation in giving, the next obvious step is borrowing money. Over the decades, loan finance (mainly through the Israel Bonds organization) has become another important vehicle for raising foreign currency from Jewish diaspora resources for Israel.

Another instrument in the economic Israel-diaspora relationship has been the raising of investment finance from foreign Jews or corporations controlled by them. This was particularly important because the Arab boycott largely prevented the arrival of the main category of international investors — major multinational corporations. The almost total absence of the latter from the Israeli investment scene was also one of the reasons for the slow transfer of technology and modern management techniques from abroad. Their presence might also have triggered the interaction of Israeli academia and the business world much earlier than has been the case.

The diaspora has played an important role in both the transfer of technology and its diffusion in Israeli society. Studying this, as well as the diaspora's role in the blooming of the innovation process, would probably yield a very interesting document on the history of technological change in Israeli society.

There are many other benefits to Israeli society from Jewish diaspora investments. A single significant investment can make a major contribution to a development town. The Chilean investor Yisrael Polak was persuaded to establish the Polgat factory in Kiryat Gat. Its subsequent expansion gave that town a strong boost in many fields.

1968: Israel's First International Economic Conference

Looking back from the present reality of numerous sophisticated high-tech companies in Israel — and their exports of several billions of dollars per year — to the first international economic conference in 1968, we seem to be reviewing the prehistory of Israeli business. The main result of that conference, initiated by then-Finance Minister Pinhas Sapir, was the establishment of the Israel Corporation. Mainly Jewish investors bought shares in the corporation for tens of millions of dollars. However, it had no specific direction at the time and was an instrument of money investment only. A few years earlier, a similar general-purpose investment corporation had been created: Clal. This group drew mainly South American capital.

Israel has come a long way since then, as there are now a multitude of Jewish diaspora investments which have included not only money but, as said before, also technology transfer. On many occasions these were initiated by a special category of diaspora — Israelis who had gone abroad to study and thereafter to work for foreign firms.

Additional Modes of Interaction

Another element of the economic Israeli-diaspora relationship concerns the promotion of part-time living of diaspora Jews in Israel through the sale of second homes. The borderline between the diaspora and Israel sometimes becomes quite vague as there are quite a few people who live half a year in Israel and half a year abroad.

A further aspect of Israel-diaspora relations concerns the selling of Israeli products specifically to the diaspora market (kosher foods, religious items, entertainment programs, etc.). One example of benchmarking on this is when Christian monasteries sell holy water from the Jordan to Christian pilgrims.

Another facet of the above is the promotion of tourism to Israel on an ethnic/religious basis. In one Jerusalem synagogue, which is close to the hotel area, there is always a surprising influx of North American Jews on the Succoth holiday. They seem to come to Israel as the weather and general environment at home may not be conducive to putting up a Succa there.

An issue on which little information exists, but which should not be underrated, is the use of Jewish diaspora connections as a tool for Israelis entering gentile markets abroad.

Yet another aspect where Jewish connections abroad have often been helpful — particularly because of the Arab boycott — concerns the acquisition of specific technologies which were difficult to come by during the years that the boycott lasted.

On a more individual basis, there is some scouting for Jews abroad who can be enticed to come to Israel to fill specific expert positions which cannot be staffed from within Israel. Examples of this can be found in academia, business, and general management.[4]

In recent years, with the economic strengthening of the Israeli diaspora (i.e., *yordim*), not only do they often transfer money to their families in Israel, but they have also become increasingly involved in the above-mentioned issues.

Sport is another area of Israel-diaspora interaction with many facets to it. It is a means of bringing Jews from abroad to Israel, who otherwise are often difficult to attract. The Maccabiah, the Jewish mini-Olympics, is the most pronounced example. Another stream concerns fund-raising from foreign donors interested in certain sports to foster sports activities in Israel. The tennis centers and tournaments are a good example of this. A third activity is trying, when Israeli sport delegations go abroad, to have them stay, or at least visit, with local Jewish communities.

Using diaspora Jews as a go-between in countries with which Israel has no diplomatic relations is yet another aspect of the multifold relationship between Israel and the diaspora. It is commonly known that prominent Jewish Moroccans played an important role in developing political relations between the two countries. This approach certainly seems to have been more successful than a few ill-conceived attempts by Israel to use Jews abroad as spies. The best known ones have led to the Lavon and Pollard affairs.

In an interview this author conducted with Daniel Elazar a few years ago, Elazar pointed out yet another variation on the long list of Israel-diaspora interactions: "Many diaspora families may settle in Israel and let the breadwinner commute. There will be closer interpersonal communication, by fax and viewphone. This will also involve many non-Jews, because the families in the diaspora will include non-Jews in close relationships."[5]

Sponsoring a Museum in Rome?

The above Israeli experience can be useful to other nations if correctly packaged, as the following shows.

A few years ago, a major Italian state-owned corporation was advised on its business strategy by this author. As a side issue, they mentioned that they had a prestigious building in Rome which they considered donating as a museum. Content was no problem. In the warehouses of the city's art department, there were sufficient unexhibited first class masterpieces to fill it, among which, according to some unverified sources, were a few Raphael paintings. The problem was finding the money to convert the building. They were advised by this author to look for a sponsor for whom to name the building, if he donated the millions of dollars required.

"Italians are not in the habit of doing so" was the immediate reaction. However, most diaspora Italians — some of whom are extremely rich — live in countries where charity in return for public name giving is common. They were told to hire a former Italian ambassador to go to the country where he was posted, where there is a rich Italian diaspora. He then tells the potential donors, the Mrs. Rossi, Bianchi or whatever, that they have a unique chance that, in addition to the Vatican museum and the museum of the Capitol, there will now be a Rossi or Bianchi museum in Rome.

This was considered to be a revolutionary approach. Anybody in Israel, however, who has taken a quick course in fund-raising is familiar with these methods.

Benchmarking Versus Copying

What is proposed here is commonly called benchmarking. This is not identical to copying. In the 1960s, there was an Israeli winery which considered the kiddush wine market abroad to be largely saturated; however, they thought that there might be a market in sacramental wine for churches, for use in communion. Rather than analyzing what was relevant in the kiddush wine experience and what was not, that is, benchmarking, they just copied the concept. The winery approached the monastery at Tabgha, as to whether they would be willing to give their patronage in return for royalties to such wine. This could be exported in distinctive bottles to churches abroad. The monks were very willing and obviously wanted to visit the winery. However, the winery ran into an unexpected problem. The rabbinate's *kashrut* supervisors strongly objected to such a visit, as they were afraid that the monks might bless the wine. To complete the picture — the project still went ahead, but was an economic failure. The religious wine market in the Christian market abroad simply behaves totally differently from that of Jews abroad buying kiddush wine.

Conclusion

In listing the various forms of economic interaction between Israel and the diaspora, an attempt was made to show that we are dealing with a broad area in which specific know-how on interactive relations with the diaspora has been developed. This consists of a number of methodologies and processes which can be formalized. This interaction has helped to shape the Israeli economy and Israeli society in general. This important and relatively unexplored field in diaspora relations merits investigation, not only because of its historic and sociological interest, but also because — once it is available in a systematic form — it has a value which can be transferred to others, either for money or to obtain good will.

In order to market this know-how one would probably have to make a major diplomatic effort to help other countries to understand the value of a diaspora, what to obtain from it, how to do so, and what mistakes to avoid. Most foreign politicians may not want to listen, some will claim that the connection between Israel and its diaspora is very different from that of their own country, which is only partly true.

Still, the idea can be used as an excellent instrument of Israeli image-promotion in some European countries and as a partial counterwieght to the negative propoganda spread by Israel's enemies there, the more so as the risks of failure are very limited. Israel has so much knowhow and these countries start in this field from such low levels of essentially individual approaches, that whatever is achieved will be impressive and the chances of failure are minimal.

Notes

1. James Pettifer, *The Greeks: The Land the People Since the War* (London: Penguin, 1993), p. 219. Petiffer also mentions a speech in Athens by a leader of the Greek community in South Africa: "His speech, widely reported in the business press, expressed disappointment that trade relations with emigre Greeks were not closer and he added that he hoped the 85,000 Greeks in South Africa would be able to play an important role in the economic revival Greece needed" (p. 218).

2. Gli Euroamericani, Fondazione Giovanni Agnelli, 1987, p. 151.

3. The Jewish National Fund has also broadened its appeal to non-Jews abroad. So, for instance, the first trees in the Saint-Exupery Park in the Negev were planted in honor of the French pilot/author in 1998. Among the first groves donated was one by his nephews and nieces. As there are many Saint-Exupery Societies in the world, a link with Israel is created with many non-Jews who will be approached to plant trees there.

4. Paul King, Orli Hacohen, Hillel Frisch, and Daniel Elazar, *Project Renewal in Israel: Urban Revitalization Through Partnership* (Lanham, MD: JCPA and University Press of America, 1987), p. 35ff.

5. Not long after the JCPA conference, the Jerusalem-based Israel Museum made an appointment which illustrates this point well. It decided to hire as its new director an American museum expert with a strong Jewish identity who had never visited Israel before.

6. Manfred Gerstenfeld, *Israel's New Future: Interviews* (Jerusalem: JCPA and Rubin Mass, Ltd., 1994), p. 105.

14

The Loyalties of Ethno-National Diasporas and the Case of the Jewish Diaspora

Gabriel Sheffer

The Main Issues

It is difficult, almost impossible, to disregard the remarkable ethnic renaissance in general, and particularly the revival of specific ethnic groups and communities. It is equally hard to escape the fact that this resurgence of ethnicity and of ethnic groups has been accompanied by a growing societal and political legitimization of the phenomenon. Moreover, it is evident that this old-new phenomenon is further affecting a myriad of current global, regional, and domestic developments.

To use Anthony Smith's terminology, this "ethnic revival" (Smith, 1981) is closely related to regime transformation in various regions and states. Indeed, on certain occasions it has been difficult to determine whether that ethnic revival was a major contributing factor to such regime change, or whether such structural transformation contributed to the re-emergence of ethnicity. Yet, the quest of various ethnic groups for self-determination, and the ensuing social and political unrest and need for adjustment and accommodation, have certainly been contributing factors to the deterioration and the eventual demise of empires and states, such as the Soviet Union and its empire (e.g., Motyl, 1992; Bernstein, 1993).

Here it is almost superfluous to recapitulate that the collapse of the Soviet Union and its empire had far-reaching consequences for the entire global system, as well as for the former "Second World," for domestic politics in the former Soviet Union, and for various ethnic groups in these countries. Similarly, ethnic revolts and conflicts have affected the situation in other continents and regions, such as Africa, the Balkans, the Turkish, Iranian and Iraqi "triangle," and certain parts of the Middle East (Horowitz, 1985; Brown, 1993; Gurr, 1993; Gurr and Harff, 1994). In fact, ethnic revival and upheaval have changed, and are still altering, the history of many other countries such as India, South Africa, Israel, and even Canada and Belgium.

Simultaneously, a remarkable revival of ethno-national diasporas has taken place. Also this renaissance has been closely connected to the general trends in modern ethnicity. This latter outcome of the ethnic revival involves the creation of new diasporas, an increase in the activities of existing diasporas, and the reawakening of older but dormant communities. Thus, for example, new incipient Vietnamese, Korean, Egyptian, and Turkish diasporas have emerged in North America, Europe, and the Persian Gulf states; the Polish community in the U.S., the Greek diaspora in Australia, and the Armenians in the U.S., all have expanded the scope and intensity of their activities; and the Ukrainians, Norwegians, and Croatians in North America are regrouping and becoming socially and politically more assertive and active (Sheffer, 1986, 1994; Esman, 1994; Chaliand and Rageau, 1995; Sowell, 1996). As for ethno-national diasporas' influence on current global, regional, and local political developments, suffice it to mention the destabilizing role of twenty million Russians in the former Soviet republics, the Overseas Chinese involvement in various events in the mainland and in various states of Southeast Asia, and the Palestinians' role in recent developments in the Middle East, Israel, and the administered territories.

Such diasporas influence not only political developments in their homelands and host countries, they are also playing a discernible role in the current processes of cultural, social, and economic change. Primarily, older and newer diasporas are dominant actors in the rapidly emerging multicultural phenomenon. More specifically, these communities contribute to new attitudinal and cultural patterns. Thus, for example, they have helped to change attitudes toward food and fashion; they have contributed to the spreading of multilingualism; and, for example, poets and writers who are members of the Indian, Pakistani, West Indies, and Caribbean diasporas in Britain enrich and reshape the English language, poetry, and literature. Socially, some of these diasporic communities, especially the Jews, have continuously been involved in the unending struggle to legitimize pluralism and multiculturalism. Finally, in the economic sphere, the Greek, Indian, and Chinese diasporas, to mention only a few of these communities, are very active in international trade, shipping, and financial affairs, and have certainly contributed to globalization.

The increasing significance of these entities in current global and local affairs is mainly related to two complementary sets of factors. The first set pertains to the very essence of these groups' identity, needs, and organization. Thus, in view of the spectacular development of transportation and electronic communications, and the various practical means resulting from this process such as the fax, Internet, and interactive television, now more than ever before, ethnic communities can maintain regular intensive contacts with their homelands and with their brethren in other host countries. Usually these contacts are carried out through elaborate transstate networks that are supported by these new technological means. In many cases, however, these easier and closer connections have a potential for triggering or for actually creating tension and conflict between these ethno-national diasporas and both their host countries and homelands. On the other hand, these contacts expedite and amplify new cultural, economic, and political trends.

The second cluster of factors affecting the more conspicuous position and the more assertive posture of such diasporas is related to the greater openness of the social and political systems in most of their host countries with regard to boundaries, sovereignty, and citizenship. This is especially the case in the expanding group of democratic states (e.g., Gottlieb, 1993).

As expected, the growing significance of the old-new ethno-national diaspora phenomenon in recent cultural, economic, and political developments has reopened some significant and interesting theoretical and practical questions. These include questions pertaining to the *identity, identification, status, organization and behavior* of both elites and rank and file in these entities. Hence, politicians, journalists, and academics show an increasing interest in this phenomenon. Consequently, the study of various issues related to these communities and their teaching are occupying a more visible position in campuses around the world and in academic publications. Furthermore, in addition to a special journal which is entirely dedicated to the study of this field (appropriately titled *Diaspora*), more books (e.g., Constas and Platias, 1995; Chaliand and Rageau, 1995; Sowell, 1996) and numerous articles have been published on this subject.

Yet, a very sensitive issue pertaining to these ethno-national diasporas has been almost totally neglected, and that is the issue of diasporas' loyalties. Except for some occasional references and cursory analyses of the issue as it affected diasporas' relations with host countries on the eve of, and during, World War II (e.g., Walzer, et al., 1982), there is only little on this subject in the relevant professional literature or, for that matter, in newspapers and journals. However, as a result of the growing significance of ethno-national diasporas in today's global system as well as in various states, the issue of loyalty has recently resurfaced in a number of host countries. Besides the United States, where both the problem of loyalty and the awareness about its implications loomed large during a long period after World War II, recently it has emerged in other host countries such as Britain, France, and Germany where relatively large diasporas were established after that war and have grown since then.

Here it is worthwhile mentioning the academic literature on the "tangled web of loyalty" (see, for example, Worchel and Coutant, 1995) that deals with the intricate connections between racism, nationalism, ethnocentrism, and patriotism. This literature has been produced mainly by political psychologists (e.g., Bar-Tal, 1993), and the gist of their argument is that the loyalty to a national state, on the one hand, or to an ethnic group, on the other, stems mainly from the psychological need of members of such groups to forge and maintain their identity. These authors argue that consequently ethnic loyalty is bound to clash with loyalty to host states, which claim full sovereignty within the boundaries of the territories they control. A different view can be found in what may be called the *constructivist* literature on ethnicity and ethno-nationalism (e.g., Anderson, 1983). The main argument of the constructivists is that like all other aspects of nationalism, patriotism is an attitude that is artificially inculcated by the state in the citizens regardless of their ethnic origin. The proponents of this approach add that by implication and as part of the creation of modern states, such a sentiment is imposed also on members of ethnic minorities and ethno-national diasporas residing in these states. Consequently, these groups may face a grave dilemma that can lead them to clash with their host country and, in the case of diasporas, this may also lead to a clash with their homelands.

This chapter, however, follows a different approach that might be called the "synthetic ethnicist" approach (see, for example, Meadwell, 1989; Scott, 1990; Kelass, 1991; Smith, 1993). In this vein, we will make an attempt to offer a different conceptualization of ethnic minorities' and ethno-national diasporas' loyalties. Starting from this angle, we will then try to unravel the various analytical and practical aspects of this neglected issue with regard to ethnic groups.

As has already been indicated, for a number of reasons, mainly pertaining to host countries' perceptions about politics and their security, and to host countries' and homelands' interactions, politicians and officials have been far from encouraging the detailed examination of the tangled questions of ethno-national diasporas' loyalties. As part of this cautious attitude, host governments have been inclined to spread heavy veils on security problems that are caused by diasporas and stemming from their equivocal, partial, and conflicting loyalties. These governments have censored information about actual or perceived harmful acts by members of diasporas, such as espionage and sabotage. Similarly, these governments do not publicize diaspora support for guerrilla and terrorist groups laboring on behalf of, or in cooperation with, their homelands. Thus, for example, it is difficult to obtain information about the support that Irish Americans extend to the IRA, or about Palestinian Americans' participation in terrorist activities in the U.S. and aid that this community extends to the PLO and to other Palestinian organizations. Similarly, it is not easy to acquire from the German government information about Kurdish activists' actions in Germany.

It is easy to imagine why governments are suppressing such information. These governments have a number of goals in doing so — to prevent conflicts with the diasporas' homelands; to reduce the

possibility of domestic tension, on the one hand, and of international instability, on the other; to facilitate the activities of host
countries' intelligence agencies; on certain occasions, to conceal
the inefficiency of their intelligence and security agencies in successfully dealing with these sensitive matters; to avoid leaks of
menacing developments that might exacerbate already sensitive
situations; and to prevent damage to other ethnic groups dwelling
in these and other countries.

Only when domestic or international circumstances compel host
governments to disclose details about such events, they may admit
the existence of severe problems in this sphere. In their public
statements, most host governments tend to belittle the significance
of such problems. In addition to the above mentioned factors, such
governmental denial is intended to minimize the possibility of
contagious influences on other similar groups, and to curb any
sense of achievement by the leaders and activists of such ethnic
groups that in turn might spark off additional clashes. In the same
vein, host governments tend to downgrade the political significance of these issues in order to avoid further deterioration of their
legitimacy and control.

Partly because of politicians' and bureaucrats' inherent tendency to conceal the problems involved in such sensitive matters
and developments, partly because of their own late awakening to
the ethno-national diasporas' revival, and partly because of their
unawareness of the actual dimensions of the problem, scholars have
also largely neglected this aspect. In a sense, therefore, this is an
exploratory chapter. It intends to elaborate the few existing references to this topic, examine the various dimensions of this facet of
recent ethnicity and ethno-national diasporas, and draw some wider
analytical and theoretical conclusions.

The Theoretical and Analytical Context

New theoretical and analytical insights into various questions
pertaining to ethnicity in general, and by implication also to
diasporas, may shed additional light on the issue of the loyalties of
ethno-national diasporas which is at the center of this chapter. This
is the case particularly in view of two seemingly contradictory
trends that influence both the internal relations within diaspora

communities and the triangular relations between diasporas, their host countries, and homelands.

The first trend is connected to globalization, which has to do with the new openness of regional and state boundaries, and the liberalization of political and social systems. In Western democracies both aspects encourage greater tolerance toward ethnic groups, including ethno-national diasporas (Watters, 1995). Such newly acquired tolerance facilitates diasporas' integration into host countries' politics, but not necessarily their social assimilation, and eventually their disappearance.

The second trend, which is partly the consequence of the previous trend, is ethnic diasporas' confident adherence to their traditional identity and to their peculiar loyalties. Under such circumstances the loyalty issue gains additional importance since these trends tend to cause instability and conflict in diaspora communities, and between their members and other social and political actors in their host countries.

As has been indicated earlier, this chapter is anchored in what might be termed as the *synthetic approach* to the sources of recent ethnic revival and ascendance. In this context there is no need to provide an in-depth and comprehensive description and analysis of this approach or to compare it to other prevalent approaches to the issue. Here it is sufficient to begin with the observation that none of the three main approaches to the study of the reemergence of modern ethnicity — that is, the *primordial, instrumental,* and *constructionist* approaches — is reductionist in the sense of claiming absolute exclusivity in explaining the phenomenon at hand. In fact, all three approaches have maintained that, except for the variables that each of them emphasizes, there are additional factors influencing the ethnic revival. It seems that according to the same logic there is room for a synthetic approach that will attempt to amalgamate certain features of each of these approaches and give birth to a more comprehensive explanation of the issue.

Thus, the *synthetic approach* attempts to integrate the most salient components of the other approaches in order to form a more comprehensive tool that is capable of dealing with the complexity of the phenomena at hand (the gist of this approach is similar to that presented in Kelass, 1991). In this vein, like the primordial approach, the synthetic approach suggests that genetic and biological factors, combined with notions about a common ancestry, shared

traditions, joint historical experience, and a deep sense of communal solidarity, are consequential elements of any explanation of the
durability of ethnic groups. Like the *instrumental* approach, the
synthetic approach argues that cognitive calculations about possible gains and loses affect the decision to continue to be active
members of the relevant ethnic entity and to act within its various
frameworks and organizations. Finally, like the *constructionist*
approach, the synthetic approach maintains that on the basis of the
primordial and instrumental factors a determined group of people
belonging to the same ethnie (Smith, 1981) can establish a more
closely knit community and reshape or rekindle the identity of its
members. This approach, so it is believed here, may better capture
the complex features of modern ethno-national diasporas and their
loyalties.

The synthetic approach will facilitate a more comprehensive
analysis of the roots, nature, and consequences of the loyalty issue.
Among other things, it will provide a suitable framework for an
inquiry not only of rational choices made by members of these
groups, but also of collective and personal emotive reasons for
developing overlapping loyalties; for an examination of the possibility of homelands to manipulate "their" diasporas; and for a
discussion of the reasons for difficulties in the full integration and
assimilation of these groups into their host societies.

The Demographic and Social Contexts

Since, like all other ethnic groups, diasporas do not act in a
vacuum and they are strongly influenced by their various external
environments (that is, by the domestic social and political systems
in their host countries, and by regional and international factors),
certain demographic and social background factors that recently
have influenced and actually complicated the loyalty issue gain
additional significance.

Most important among these factors is the proliferation of these
entities and the growing size of some of these communities. The
number of such communities is further growing as a result of both
forced flight and voluntary migration of individuals as well as
smaller and larger groups. In the present analysis the relevant fact
is that ultimately most of these migrants permanently settle in host

countries, acquire citizenship, but maintain their ethno-national identity. To the first category of migrants, that is, refugees for various reasons, belong the Bosnians who fled or were driven out of Serbian-held territories, and both the Tutsis and Hutus who moved out of Rwanda. To the second and larger category, that is, of voluntary migrants, belong Moroccans, Filipinos, South Koreans, Vietnamese, and many other ethno-national individuals and groups who have recently emigrated out of their homelands and settled in various host countries.

The ceaseless migration from one country to another is not caused only by sheer economic hardship and needs. Cultural, social, and political reasons also cause these sizable waves of migrants. Thus, for example, Palestinian Christians are leaving the administered territories and joining their brethren in Latin and North America mainly because of cultural and social conflicts with their fellow Palestinian Moslems; Israeli Jews migrate to Anglo-Saxon countries because of anxiety concerning their security, social tensions, and political discrimination (see, for example, Yaar, 1987; Sobel, 1990; Cohen, 1990); and Turkish Kurds have migrated to Germany essentially because of political reasons. The net result of the growing number of such incipient diasporas, whose members, probably more than members of any other diaspora, maintain intimate and continuous relations with their families, clans, and other groups and institutions in their homelands, increases the potential for conflicting loyalties.

The second factor in this set that has contributed to the reemergence of the loyalty issue is the awakening of dormant ethno-national diasporas in their host countries, especially in view of national struggles about or in the homeland. This development is due to long-term processes that began after World War II. Immediately after the war (a period during which the state in both the West and the East reached the apex of its strength, on the one hand, and ethnicity was regarded as an insignificant social and political factor, on the other hand), the "melting pot," integrationist and assimilationist ideas narrowed the incentives to identify as members of ethno-national diasporas as well as the scope of their autonomous activities. With certain exceptions, during that period most of the members of the ethno-national diasporas (e.g., Italians, Jews, and Irish in the U.S., Canada, and Australia) were inclined to adopt integrationist, if not assimilationist, strategies. Hence, during that period, members of these communities invested a lot of their energies in attempts to blur, or even to eradicate, their ethno-national identity so that they would be accepted by the dominant (in these cases Anglo-Saxon) groups in the host society. Whenever such a strategy prevails among members of ethno-national diasporas, their main intention would be to develop and maintain loyalty to the host country. The other side of the same coin is that under these circumstances most members of such diasporas would reject notions of dual or divided loyalties. In other words, though they may be interested in maintaining continuous or sporadic contacts with individuals and small groups back in the homeland, most of the members of such diasporas would demonstrate undivided loyalty to the host country.

More recently, however, when the concepts of sovereignty and citizenship have begun to change, and to an extent erode, and when greater legitimacy and respect for the "other" and for "otherness" have emerged, members of incipient and dormant ethno-national diasporas are more open about their ethno-national origin and identity. Consequently, such members of diasporas are also ready to publicly identify with the nation and its homeland. One of the most immediate consequences of these developments is that the loyalty issue has become more entangled.

Such an awakening of dormant diasporas has been evident in a number of host countries, especially in the U.S. and Canada. In these host countries, for example, simultaneously to the deterioration of the Soviet Union and its empire, American and Canadian Ukrainians, Lithuanians, and Latvians have renewed interest in their old homelands, and have reorganized to help to free these homelands from Soviet domination. Now members of these diasporas are proud in their ethno-national identity, and they do not refrain from expressing their identification with their homelands. Such developments have also created the background for the reemergence of the loyalty issue. When such a reawakening occurs and diasporic communities become more active on behalf of their homelands, the loyalty issue can actually be put on the political agenda either by the host society, the homeland, or the diaspora itself.

Thirdly, the loyalty issue in diasporic politics has been reemphasized by recent tendencies evident among members of some of these entities, including communities that have not been very well organized, to redefine and restate their identity, express their identification with their community and its dreamed of homeland, enhance their social and political status, and become more active in the political arena of their respective homelands. Chief among these groups are the Gypsies. For very different reasons and in a totally different environment, to a degree this has also been the case in regard to certain segments in the African-American community who define themselves and identify as members of an African diaspora.

The Various Modes of Loyalty

Before discussing the intricate issues concerning loyalty patterns practiced by specific ethno-national diasporas in different host countries, it is necessary to suggest certain distinctions between various possible modes of loyalty that are relevant to the exploratory analysis in this chapter. Thus, ethno-national diasporas can demonstrate either *ambiguous, dual,* or *divided* loyalty vis-a-vis their host countries and homelands.

Among these three modes, the easiest to characterize is *dual loyalty*. It refers to situations in which members of diasporic communities feel or think that they owe their allegiance both to their host country and homeland. In other words, these are situations in which members of diasporic communities do not see substantial contradiction between their loyalty to the host country and to the homeland. In these cases, diaspora members feel or think that at the same time they can show not only verbal but also practical loyalty to the host country and to the homeland. Thus, under such circumstances, they accept and behave according to the general norms of their hosts, and they comply with the legal, political, and economic requirements made by the authorities in the host country. Simultaneously, they maintain contacts with individuals, families, and other groups in their homeland, and are willing to promote the homeland's interests in the host country and elsewhere. Although in their host countries they may face disparaging attitudes, discrimination, and even explicit accusations and persecution, the activists in such diaspora communities are ready to cope with such situations and attitudes as long as they can maintain their contacts with their homeland. Most of the members of these diasporas would not confront major difficulties in maintaining this mode of loyalty as long as the relations between their homeland and host country are friendly or, at the least, tolerable. The other side of the same coin is that diaspora members will confront greater difficulties in maintaining this mode when disagreements occur between host country and homeland. And they will encounter even greater difficulties to maintain this posture when actual intense conflicts occur between host country and homeland.

Analytically and practically, the mode of *divided loyalty* is more complex and therefore more difficult to conceptualize. Essentially, divided loyalties denote situations in which members of diasporas demonstrate loyalty to their host country in certain spheres and to their homelands in other domains. Thus, for example, the majority of members of most diasporas would show loyalty to their host country and comply with its norms and principles pertaining to law and order, to the basic rules of the political game, to observance of regulations in the economic and financial spheres; they might even participate in its defense during wars, etc. On the other hand, with regard to a number of other spheres such as voluntary financial contributions, information collection and dissemination, political and diplomatic activities, and cultural connections, diaspora members would show loyalty to their homeland. In these cases, diaspora members would direct a certain, quite often not insubstantial, part of their activities to promote their homeland's interests in either the host country or in international organizations. It is quite obvious that the espousal of this attitude and posture may produce fertile ground for tension and clashes with the host society and its government.

While members of veteran and established diasporas usually adopt one of the two previously mentioned modes of loyalty, members of incipient diasporas, or members of diasporas that are in the midst of reawakening and transformation from a dormant into an active diaspora, may confront difficulties in clearly defining their identity, deciding about their identification, and therefore also determining their actual loyalties. As a way out of such quandaries, members of these diasporas may prefer to adopt a position of "let us wait and see," and maintain a considerable degree of *ambiguity* concerning their loyalties. Only after making their critical decisions concerning permanent settlement, integration or assimilation into the host society, and about the scope and intensity of their contacts with their homeland, would they also clarify the loyalty issue and alter their ambiguous position in this respect. Mainly for political reasons, however, certain diasporas would maintain such an ambiguous posture for longer periods. This may be a result of dissatisfaction with the cultural, social, and political situation prevailing in their homeland, or unfavorable conditions in the host country, or *bona fide* indecision about contacts with the homeland.

The selection and adoption of a particular mode of loyalty is largely, like other aspects of diasporas' daily political behavior, a matter of individual and collective choice. It means that diasporic communities, smaller groups within these communities, and single members thereof, usually make their decisions in this respect after a careful consideration of current conditions in the host countries and of their relations with their homelands. Since older and richer diasporas have substantial political and economic interests at stake, on the one hand, and long traditions and established patterns of behavior, on the other, these communities may encounter visible difficulties in accurately calibrating their attitudes toward host country and homeland at any given time.

The adoption of a certain mode of loyalty, however, is related not only to the stage of historical development of a certain diaspora. That is, the adoption of a certain mode does not depend only on whether these are incipient, established, or older diasporas. As can be expected, there are additional factors that determine the particular mode of loyalty that a particular diaspora community adopts. The first of these factors is the special mix of primordial and instrumental ingredients that determines the identity and identification of each diaspora. In cases in which the *instrumental* or *situational* elements in a community's identity are stronger than the *primordial* components (on these distinctions see, for example, Esman, 1994), the chances are that the diaspora would adopt either ambiguous or divided loyalties. Since, among other things, a diaspora's identity and identification depends on instrumental factors, cost-benefit considerations would be influential in determining communal collective decisions in regard to the preferred strategy in this sphere. It seems that the main rationale for adopting this mode of loyalty would be connected to the diaspora's attempts to avoid clear-cut and continuous commitment to the homeland. In certain cases, diasporas which try to avoid undesirable, unplanned, and unexpected clashes with the host society and its political institutions, and at the same time to maintain close relations with the homeland, may also adopt this posture.

The second factor that influences diasporas' posture in regard to their loyalty is the depth of commitment to the ethno-national identity, as well as the degree of identification with the homeland and with other communities of the same ethno-national origin. The greater the commitment to the ethno-national identity, and the clearer the identification with the homeland, the more a diaspora is ready to adhere to the pattern of dual loyalty. Adopting this posture might implicate these diasporas in clashes with the host societies and governments. On the other hand, lesser commitment to the ethno-national entity would diminish the propensity to identify with the homeland and invest energies in extending help to it.

The third interconnected factor is the main operative strategy that a diasporic community adopts vis-a-vis the host country in regard to daily life in the midst of the host society. This strategy forms a spectrum that includes *assimilation, integration, communalism, corporatism, autonomy, separation, secession,* and *irredentism* (e.g., Weiner, 1990 ; Kelass, 1991; Sheffer, 1994). The closer a diaspora positions itself to the assimilationist pole on the strategy's spectrum, the greater the possibility that the diaspora would adopt an ambiguous posture toward its homeland and try to minimize its identification with it, as well as play down its commitment to the people back in the country of origin. When adopting the communalist or corporatist strategy, these communities may turn to the dual loyalty posture, and when moving toward autonomism or separatism they may adopt the divided loyalty mode.

The fourth factor that influences the loyalty that diaspora communities demonstrate toward their host country and homeland is the degree of their organization. In most cases, the more comprehensive the organization and the activities of communal institutions, the greater the chances that these communities would adopt either the divided or dual-loyalty modes. The rationale of this argument is that members of better organized and more active diasporas maintain closer and continuous connections with their homelands, on the one hand, and feel more secure in their dealing with societal and political forces in their host countries, on the other. Hence, members of such communities are also confident to either split or duplicate their loyalties.

The fifth set of factors that influences diasporas' loyalties includes the structure, scope, and intensity of the activities of the transstate networks that such ethno-national diasporas create and maintain. Again, these networks constitute essential elements in diasporas' life, since through such channels these communities maintain their constant connections with the homeland and other communities of the same flock who reside in other host countries. Since these networks carry various resources from and to diaspora communities, usually they boost the sense of security and self-confidence of individual members and in fact of the entire community. In cases where these networks are effective, often the net result is that the diaspora develops a substantial degree of loyalty to the homeland.

The sixth and final factor that influences the adoption of one of the three modes of loyalty is the impact of both domestic (that is, the prevailing situation in the host countries) and international social and political environments on these diasporas. These sources of influence pertain to the degree of the host government's authority and power, the degree of the host state's sovereignty, the actual meaning and applicability of the concept of citizenship, the existence of regional regimes, and the political trends in the global system.

Among these two sources of influence on the diasporas' decisions concerning their loyalty, the social and political situation in the host countries is the more potent one. Thus, for example, greater openness of borders, substantial tolerance toward "the other" and "otherness," enhanced legitimacy for multiculturalism and pluralism, and societal acquiescence in the establishment of diaspora communities and organizations (including diaspora transstate networks) — all the elements that characterize liberal democracies — are likely to promote diasporas' dual loyalties. On the other hand, political and economic discrimination against diasporas, their premeditated isolation, a substantial degree of intolerance toward these diasporas that is shown by their host societies and governments (especially in non-democratic countries), tensions with other minorities, and regional and world organizations' disregard and disrespect toward such diasporas, are likely to produce ambiguous loyalty.

Though probably less influential than the above mentioned domestic factors, attitudes toward ethnicity and ethnic issues prevailing in the international environment would also have an impact on the loyalties that are shown by diasporas. Similar to the situation on the domestic level, a general atmosphere of openness and tolerance in the international arena would influence the patterns of loyalty that diasporas adopt. It is assumed that such a situation would encourage dual loyalties. This, however, does not mean that under such circumstances diasporas would not comply with the legal norms prevailing in their host countries, or support in all cases and at all costs their homelands.

This discussion leads to the conclusion that the patterns of loyalty which diasporas may show toward their host countries and homelands may depend on the interplay between all the factors mentioned in this section. Therefore, a specific assessment of loyalty patterns of a particular diaspora should take into consideration all of these factors and, in addition, the fact that these patterns are not permanent, that they change with the passage of time, and that they vary in different diaspora communities residing in different host countries. In other words, in this sphere there is a possibility that various diaspora communities would adopt different loyalty patterns during different spans of time.

The Loyalties of the Jewish Diaspora

The discussion in this section is an initial attempt to apply the theoretical and analytical framework and observations suggested above to the Jewish diaspora, and it should be regarded as such. More detailed studies of the Jewish experience in this respect, as well as specific studies of the loyalties of other ethno-national diasporas, are still needed. Such studies will facilitate comparative work, which is essential for a fuller understanding of this important and sensitive aspect of diasporic existence.

Although the following two preliminary points concerning the general situation of the Jewish diaspora are well known, nevertheless, they should be repeated and reemphasized at this stage of the analysis. First, it should be remembered that the Jewish diaspora's strong and continuous primordial attachment to Eretz Israel (the Land of Israel) has created, and still creates, political difficulties and dilemmas for the diaspora in some of its host countries. This observation applies to diaspora communities in both democratic and non-democratic host countries. In this connection, suffice it to recall a number of historical events and affairs, such as the famous Dreyfus affair in France and its various ramifications for the Jewish diasporic communities in France and elsewhere, and in fact for the development of Zionism itself (Marrus, 1980; Lindeman, 1993); the myth of the "Elders of Zion" and the ensuing allegations and accusations about Jewish loyalty to foreign forces that have been made by the Soviets, on the one hand, and by the Nazis, on the other, as well as by many other anti-Semites, especially in various European countries; the plight of Jews, and especially the Zionists among them, in various Arab countries on the eve of, and especially after, the establishment of the State of Israel (and in this context the 1954 "mishap" and the ensuing Lavon affair and its ramifications, the Eli Cohen trial in Syria, the trials in Iraq against Zionists and Israeli agents); and more recently, the Pollard affair in the U.S. and its various ramifications (Bookbinder, 1988; Blitzer, 1988; Hunderson, 1988). There is no doubt that these and other similar experiences have affected diaspora Jews' attitudes and loyalties toward their host countries, the Jewish community in Palestine, and Israel.

The second basic fact that should be remembered and reemphasized here is that past and present patterns of loyalty have not been identical in different Jewish diaspora communities that reside in various host countries. By the same token, during their long history, the intensity of Jewish diaspora communities' loyalty to their host countries was never constant. Rather, it varied during different periods even in regard to the same host country.

When considering actual situations in this respect, it appears that in certain host countries, such as the Soviet Union, in most of the countries in the Eastern Bloc, and in some Arab countries, through an extensive use of these regimes' coercive mechanisms (i.e., the secret and regular police, the courts, etc.) Jews were denied the possibility to translate their personal and collective identity sentiments toward the homeland into meaningful action. Thus, for example, in the Soviet Union they were forbidden to create and maintain relations with the Jewish community in Palestine before the establishment of the Jewish state in 1948 and, during most of the time until the late 1980s, with Israel (Baron, 1964; Pinkus, 1993). Therefore, the issue of operative loyalty and of possible support for the homeland by these communities was either a hypothetical matter, or it had almost no practical meaning. Rather, these Jews were expecting the homeland's support for them, which did not always materialize. In a sense, the cases of the Jewish communities in South Africa and Argentina during the non-democratic phases in their history demonstrated similar characteristics. Although in these cases the freedom of Jews to establish Zionist organizations and parties, as well as express their affinity with the homeland, or keep contacts with Jewish communities in other host countries (especially with such communities in Anglo-Saxon countries), was greater than in the Soviet Union or in Arab countries, nevertheless, the possibility to translate it into full and open pro-Zionist and especially pro-Israeli action was restricted. In all these and in other similar cases, the Jews were compelled to limit their connections (especially in the political, economic, and financial spheres) with Zion, Zionism, and Israel, which might have hampered their formal loyalty to their host countries. Under such circumstances, most of the members of the Jewish communities in these countries had no other way but to develop ambiguous loyalties toward the homeland. This has been demonstrated especially in regard to emigration patterns. Most of those who have emigrated preferred to go to the U.S., Canada, and Australia rather than to Israel (Laikin, 1980; Elazar and Medding, 1983; Sachar, 1987; Sowell, 1996).

In other, especially democratic, countries, Jews were able to maintain their connection with their ancient homeland and to pursue their interests there. Yet, at the same time, they were expected to show full loyalty to the host country. For example, during certain periods of British mandatory rule over Palestine, this was the case with the Jewish community in Great Britain. At the very least, the Jews of Britain were frowned upon when they promoted the Zionist case, or when they rendered assistance to the Zionists, and later to Israel. Yet, in most of these host countries the Jews adopted, and were able to pursue, a cautious strategy of dual loyalty.

In liberal-democratic regimes, most notably in the U.S., Canada, and Australia, Jews were able to maintain open and intensive relations with the Jewish community in Palestine and later with Israel. In host countries where the Jewish communities have enjoyed the privilege to freely and openly form their position toward the homeland, they were divided on the question of the desirable posture and attitude toward the host country and homeland. Certain segments in these communities, especially those who were inclined to assimilate, showed complete loyalty to the host society. Those who preferred social and cultural integration in their host countries developed ambiguous loyalties toward the homeland. Those who openly identified as supporters of the Zionist movement, of the Jewish community in Palestine — the Yishuv, and later of Israel — developed dual loyalties. The staunchest Zionists and other supporters of Israel have adopted the divided loyalty posture, that is, in certain respects they are loyal to their host country and in other respects to the homeland.

As the world is changing, and the concepts of borders, sovereignty, citizenship, and loyalty to any state and to the host country in particular also alter, the Jewish communities in various host countries are modifying their attitudes in this sphere. These developments should mainly be attributed to new trends in the diaspora itself that reflect on its relations with Israel.

"Entrenchment" and "revision" are the two most significant tendencies that have emerged in many Jewish communities all over the world. In fact these are two sides of the same coin. These two trends have been the outcome of a situation in which certain groups in the Jewish diaspora feel an urge to ensure "continuity" (which is a further central concept and catchword in contemporary Jewry), on the one hand, and to revise their views about the centrality of Israel and about the need to limit its involvement and meddling in diaspora affairs, on the other. The first tendency is connected to a recent determination on the part of Jews in various communities to prevent, as far as possible, assimilation that is decimating the number of members of almost all these communities. This determination is translated into attempts to intensify Jewish education, to strengthen communal welfare organizations, to fortify the local federations, and to reorganize the community institutions on the host country level.

As mentioned, the second closely interconnected inclination is to revise the diaspora's view of Israel, of its role in the entire nation, and of relations with it. From this point of view, the most significant new inclination is toward a growing opposition to unquestionably accept Israel's centrality in world Jewry. With some exceptions, such as the Jewish community in Argentina, the challenge to Israel's predominance is coming from both leftist/liberal segments and from rightist/religious and ultra-religious segments in richer and stronger as well as in newer and weaker Jewish communities. This attitude is prevalent in most of the communities in the democratic host countries (for a fuller analysis of this issue and a list of references, see Sheffer, forthcoming).

Israel has contributed more than its fair share to the deterioration of its central position in the entire nation, and thus it has also contributed to the decrease in diaspora Jews' readiness to pledge their full loyalty to Israel. Since it is difficult to assess the accurate relative weight of each of the following inputs to this change, these are not ranked and mentioned in a random manner (for fuller analyses of these issues and lists of references, see Sheffer, 1988, 1993, 1996).

These contributing factors to the changed perceptions, in some quarters, about Israel's position include an image of Israel's social and cultural mediocrity. This image is a result of the fact that while in the 1950s, 1960s, and first part of the 1970s, Israel was perceived as a culturally and socially creative, dynamic society and state, now it is viewed as a mediocre country that is very far from fulfilling the goal of becoming a "light unto the nations."

The second source of the disappointment of certain segments of the diaspora with the Jewish state that has contributed to a discernible diminution in its central position in the entire nation, and hence in the diaspora's readiness to identify with it and show full and continuous loyalty toward it, are laws and policies that alienate various groups, usually the younger and more liberal, which, on the whole, are also the stronger economic and political elements in the diaspora communities. The most relevant Israeli laws and policies pertain to personal status and rights, i.e., to matters such as education, conversion, marriage, divorce, and burial. The disappointment and criticisms are particularly directed at the exaggerated influence of the Orthodox rabbinate and ultra-Orthodox rabbis on Israeli politics in general and on legislation on these matters in particular. According to Reform, Conservative, and Reconstructionist rabbis and lay leaders in the diaspora, the laws and policies that Israel has adopted or intends to adopt, and that are intended to placate Orthodox and ultra-Orthodox leaders in Israel, have been responsible for a marked reduction in immigration of Reform, Conservative, and secular Jews to Israel, for a reduction in donations, for the rerouting of donations, and for the growing alienation from Israel among such diaspora Jews.

The third development in this sphere is the growing dissatisfaction among some with Israel's blatant manipulations of diaspora Jews to push them to actively intervene in host countries' politics and policy-making processes on behalf of the homeland. This reluctance to act as Israeli proxies has already been reflected in the relative freedom of the U.S. government to pursue its own interests in the Middle East and in the peace process, including voting in the UN, without heeding too much to Jewish and Israeli lobbies. The diaspora has been particularly critical of Israel's attempts to recruit Jewish agents and their success in using diaspora Jews for espionage purposes, such as in the Pollard affair. This case has created an unprecedented uproar and extremely negative reactions not only in the American Jewish community, but also in other Jewish diasporic communities. It has been regarded as a clear breach of the Ben-Gurion/Blaustein agreement, "signed" in 1951, concerning Israeli avoidance of any interference in the internal affairs of diaspora Jewry, and to avoid actions that might implicate diaspora Jews in a blatant conflict of loyalties (Liebman, 1977).

The fourth development is the growing negative reactions to the traditional intimate connections between Israeli politicians and bureaucrats, on the one hand, and diaspora lay leaders and professionals, on the other, that enables Israeli officials to meddle in internal diasporic politics. Differently put, the current main tendency in Jewish communities is to gain greater autonomy in the conduct of their affairs. This inclination is already evident in fund-raising for Israel and other financial transfers and investments. Consequently there has been a marked reduction in diaspora financial support for Israel. Income from all communities, other than the U.S., has substantially decreased during the last few years. Moreover, more individuals and communities prefer earmarked donations or special funds, such as the New Israel Fund, which are not connected either to the UJA or Keren Hayesod. A similar reduction is evident in Jews' visits and investments in Israel. As has been indicated, a similar process has happened in the political sphere, where both rightist and leftist Israeli governments find it more difficult to enlist full support for their policies.

Some Initial Theoretical implications

The following are some initial theoretical conclusions based on both comparative glimpses into the patterns of loyalties of ethno-national diasporas, and on the preceding analytical first cut into the situation in the Jewish diaspora as far as its loyalties are concerned. Once again, it should be noted that the following observations are still tentative and not arranged according to any order of importance.

The type of loyalty that an ethno-national diaspora adopts depends, among other things, on the strength of the state in the host country, as well as on liberalization, democratization, multi-culturalism, and pluralism that influence change in traditional concepts of sovereignty and citizenship. Generally, the weakening of the state and the expanding liberalization and democratization (that usually promote pluralism and multiculturalism) encourage ethnic and ethno-national diasporas' revival, augment existing communities and their organizations, and facilitate the emergence of new communities.

Such developments influence change in diasporas' perceptions about the limits of their activities and consequently about their loyalties. Under these new circumstances diasporas feel more secure, and consequently they may upgrade their loyalty and increase their actual support for their homelands. On the other hand, the same trends that produce greater tolerance and acceptance of diasporas may encourage their assimilation and integration in host countries. Whenever this latter scenario occurs, active members of diasporas entrench, and ultimately increase, their loyalty to their host country and reduce their loyalty to their homeland.

The increasing openness of the international and regional systems, the communications revolution, and the greater ease of transportation facilitate the organization, elaboration, and operation of diasporas' transstate networks. As noted earlier, these networks are essential for maintaining regular connections between diasporas and homelands. Even more important is the fact that these networks are indispensable in regard to the operationalization of loyalty to their homelands. The development of these networks makes it easier for ethno-national diasporas to transfer resources worldwide, including to the homeland, to obtain various kinds of support from their homeland or from other ethnic groups, and consequently to diversify their loyalties.

In contrast to certain accepted views, the actual political loyalty of ethno-national diasporas cannot be bought. Hence, an unequal distribution of economic resources is not a reliable predictor for possible ethnic diasporas' revolt against their host society and government, but at the same time, equal access to economic resources does not necessarily moderate ethnic diasporas' actions against their hosts or buy their loyalty. In the same vein, host countries' abilities to obstruct the international ties of diaspora communities, and thus to influence their loyalty, have been considerably limited.

When viewed from the homelands' perspective, it turns out that even when the conditions of their diasporas in host countries are good and they can freely exercise their wishes and inclinations, homeland governments cannot rely on either the "automatic" or total loyalty of their brethren abroad. This is the case since diasporas' loyalty to their homelands depends on various factors pertaining to the global and regional atmosphere and the social, political, and economic situation in host countries. No less important is the fact that to a considerable extent, a diaspora's loyalty to its homeland depends on its homeland society and government behavior. Thus it is clear that when the homeland would disregard the needs and interests of its diaspora and would show disrespect to its sensitivities, the diaspora would reduce its loyalty. Similarly, when the homeland culture and politics are regarded as inferior to those prevailing in the host country or in the diaspora itself, the diaspora might give its full allegiance to the host country.

In conclusion, when all these factors are taken into consideration and empirically examined, it seems that large segments in "stateless diasporas" residing in democratic host countries would tend to develop strong dual loyalties. However, it seems that among "state-based diasporas," well established "classical diasporas" (that is, diasporas that were established in the ancient period, or in the Middle Ages, and survived the vagaries of diasporic existence throughout the last two millennia) develop dual loyalties; large groups in the "new diasporas" (i.e., those that have been established from the mid-nineteenth to the mid-twentieth centuries) develop divided loyalties, and "incipient diasporas" (diasporas that are still in their formative period) show clear patterns of ambiguous loyalties.

As noted, the existence of one of these patterns has not only analytical significance, but it has practical implications, especially in regard to homeland-diaspora relations, mutual reliance, and cooperation. Thus, from the homelands' point of view, as far as their loyalty is concerned, the most reliable are state-based classical diasporas, and the less reliable are incipient diasporas.

Yet, as this author has argued elsewhere (Sheffer, 1994), it would be erroneous to assume that because of their tendency to adopt dual loyalties, classical diasporas pose major threats to their host society and government. Similarly, it would be unwise to dismiss the ability of incipient diasporas to create tension in both the host country and homeland, just because of their precarious situation and lack of political organizations and experience.

References

Anderson, B. 1983. *Imagined Communities: Reflections on the Origins and Spread of Nationalism*. London: Verso.

Baron, S. 1964. *The Russian Jew Under the Tsars and Soviets*. New York: Macmillan.

Bar-Tal, D. 1993. "Patriotism as Fundamental Beliefs of Group Members." *Politics and the Individual*, 3.

Bernstein, A. 1993. "Ethnicity and Imperial Break-Up: Ancient and Modern." *SAIS Review*, 13/1 (Winter-Spring).

Blitzer, W. 1988. *Territory of Lies*. New York: Harper and Row.

Bookbinder, H. 1988. "American Jews and Israel after the Pollard Affair." *Survey of Jewish Affairs*. Ed. J. Frankel. Cranberry, NJ: Associated University Press.

Brown, M., ed. 1993. *Ethnic Conflict and International Security*. Princeton, NJ.: Princeton University Press.

Chaliand, G. and J. Rageau. 1995. *The Penguin Atlas of Diasporas*. NY: Viking.

Cohen, Y. 1990. "The Arab-Israeli Conflict and Emigration from Israel." *Megamot*, 32 (4) (Hebrew).

Constas, D. and A. Platias. 1993. *Diasporas in World Politics, The Greeks in Comparative Perspective*. London: Macmillan.

Elazar, D. and P. Medding. 1983. *Jewish Communities in Frontier Societies: Argentina, Australia and South Africa*. New York: Holms and Meier.

Esman, M. 1994. *Ethnic Politics*. Ithaca: Cornell University Press.

Gottlieb, G. 1993. *Nation Against State: A New Approach to Ethnic Conflicts and the Decline of Sovereignty*. New York: Council on Foreign Relations Press.

Gurr, T. 1993. *Minorities at Risk*. Washington, DC: United States Institute of Peace Press.

Gurr, T. and B. Harff. 1994. *Ethnic Conflict and World Politics*. Boulder, CO: Westview.

Horowitz, D. 1985. *Ethnic Groups in Conflict*. Berkeley, CA: California University Press.

Hunderson, B. 1988. *Pollard: The Spy's Story*. New York: Alpha.

Kelass, J. 1991. *The Politics of Nationalism and Ethnicity*. New York: St. Martin's.

Laikin Elkin, J. 1980. *Jews of the Latin American Republics*. Chapel Hill: University of North Carolina Press.

Liebman, C. 1977. *Pressure Without Sanctions*. New Jersey: Fairleigh Dickinson University Press.

Lindeman, A. 1993. *The Jew Accused: Three Anti-Semitic Affairs*. Cambridge: Cambridge University Press.

Marrus, M. 1980. *The Politics of Assimilation: The French Jewish Community at the Time of the Dreyfus Affair*. Oxford: Oxford University Press.

Meadwell, H. 1989. "Cultural and Instrumental Approaches to Ethnic Nationalism." *Ethnic and Racial Studies*, 12/3 (July).

Motyl, A., ed. 1992. *Thinking Theoretically about Soviet Nationalism*. New York: Columbia University Press.

Pinkus, B. 1993. *National Rebirth and Reestablishment: Zionism and the Zionist Movement in the Soviet Union*. Sde Boker: Ben-Gurion Research Center.

Scott, G. 1990. "A Resynthesis of the Primordial and Circumstantial Approaches to Ethnic Group Solidarity: Towards an Explanatory Model." *Ethnic and Racial Studies*, 13 (April).

Sheffer, G., ed. 1986. *Modern Diasporas in International Politics*. New York: St. Martin's.

Sheffer, G. 1988. "The Illusive Question: Jews and Jewry in Israeli Foreign Policy." *Jerusalem Quarterly*, 46 (Spring).

Sheffer, G. 1993. "Jewry, Jews and Israeli Foreign Policy: A Critical Perspective." *Diasporas in World Politics: The Greeks in Comparative Perspective*. Ed. Constas, D. and A. Platias. London: Macmillan.

Sheffer, G. 1994. "Ethno-national Diasporas and Security." *Survival*, 36/1 (Spring).

Sheffer, G. 1996. "Israel Diaspora Relations in Comparative Perspective." *Israel in Comparative Perspective*. Ed. M. Barnett. Albany: SUNY Press.

Sheffer, G. 1998. "From Israeli Hegemony to Diaspora Full Autonomy: The Current State of Ethno-National Diasporism and the Alternatives Facing World Jewry." *European Jewry: Between America and Israel — Jewish Centers and Peripheries 50 Years after World War II*. Ed. I. Troen. New Brunswick, NJ: Transaction.

Smith, A. 1981. *The Ethnic Revival in the Modern World*. Cambridge: Cambridge University Press.

Smith, A. 1993. "The Ethnic Sources of Nationalism." *Survival*, 35/1 (Spring).

Sobel, Z. 1990. *Migration From the Promised Land*. Tel Aviv: Am Oved (Hebrew).

Sowell, T. 1996. *Migrations and Cultures*. New York: Basic Books.

Yaar, E. 1987. "Emigration from Israel as a Normal Phenomenon." *Politika,* 16 (August) (Hebrew).

Walzer, M., et al. 1982. *The Politics of Ethnicity*. Boston: Harvard University Press.

Watters, M. 1995. *Globalization*. London: Routledge.

Weiner, M. 1990. *Security, Stability and International Migration*. Cambridge, MA: MIT, Center for International Studies.

Worchel, S. and D. Coutant. 1995. "The Tangled Web of Loyalty: Nationalism, Patriotism and Ethnocentrism" (unpublished paper).

15

Have We Learned from History?: Jewish Voluntary Organizations and Israel — Their Attitudes Towards International Migration

Judi Widetzky

One in every 50 people in the world today has recently crossed a border as a migrant or a refugee. This mass population movement can be compared in its possible effect on world order to the invasion of Europe by Attila the Hun in the fifth century when he swept across Asia and Central Europe, uprooting those in his path. The outcome of such a trend can result in a redistribution of the world's population in the next decade.

People are on the move owing to a multitude of reasons: local wars, civil strife, ethnic conflict, and persecution have created political refugees; a general breakdown of economic and social conditions has uprooted people from their traditional communities; natural disasters and an encroaching environmental degradation are destroying the infrastructure and creating economic migrants. Over the past ten years, these circumstances have caused an average of 2,500 people a day to flee their homes. Between 1981 and 1992, the number of refugees more than doubled from 8 million to 18 million and another 20 million persons are displaced in their own lands.

This phenomenon is occurring simultaneously in all parts of the world. Africa, Southeast Asia, the Middle East, Eastern Europe, and South America are the *sending countries*. Western Europe, North America, and, to a lesser degree, Australia and New Zealand are the *receiving countries*. The movement is from south to north, from east to west.

If this migration process continues at the present rate, it will lead to the development of multi-cultural societies in most countries of the world. This is an inevitable trend and ought to be addressed positively and planned for, rather than resisted and later accepted because there is no alternative.

Such a literal deluge of immigrants puts a great strain on the receiving community, and has often escalated into racism and xenophobia. Immigrants often enter an economy already experiencing serious strains, which heightens the host population's resentment towards refugee integration. This occurs especially where minority workers are concerned. It is among these communities that employment, along with housing, medical care, and quality of education, are scarcest, resulting in competition between migrants and minority groups for these basic necessities. The United States is a prime example of such tensions, where both immigration and domestic circumstances are forcing a demographic revolution in a country where non-white "minorities" are quickly becoming the majority.

There are three recognized solutions to this problem: *voluntary repatriation, integration,* and *resettlement.* Israel and Jewish communities around the world have successfully implemented integration and can share their expertise with other countries struggling with similar situations.

As a general rule, however, receiving countries are developing a negative trend. In Europe, even well intentioned government officials or elected parliamentarians are reassessing their policies. Recent meetings with Social Democratic members of Parliament from Holland, Germany, and France revealed a commitment in principle to the moral obligation to keep doors open, but in practice each had his own dilemma. The Dutch MP, for example, represented a constituency of blue collar workers, and the rights of the migrants were in direct conflict with the demands of his voters. Even South Africa has recently developed a growing xenophobia towards migrants from other African countries who are streaming in as a result of the new regime. This has instigated an ongoing reassessment of immigration laws in most countries of the world, and policies are becoming more restrictive.

The European Union is in the midst of a total reassessment of immigration and asylum policies. "Fortress Europe" is slowly closing its doors. As a result of the Maastricht Accords there is a policy to allow asylum seekers to apply only to one member of the Union and, if disqualified, there is no option to apply to another. Such a retrenchment is setting a negative tone for the future.

Great Britain is undergoing a retrenchment of its own. The government has proposed changes to the Asylum and Immigration Bill, which came up for its third reading in February 1996, through which the criteria for asylum have been greatly restricted.

Such trends also extend to North America. U.S. law currently grants asylum to aliens having a well-founded fear of persecution in their country of origin. In fiscal year 1994, 121,000 such persons were admitted to the U.S. Under legislation pending as of January 1996, this number would be reduced to 50,000.

Canada currently places an exorbitant fee on those refugees applying for permanent residence. One type of fee is the "head tax" or "right of landing" fee, set at $975 per adult. This fee is charged both when the person has been determined to be a refugee while already in Canada and applies for permanent resident status, and when a refugee applies to come to Canada at a Canadian visa post abroad. The government does provide loans, but the applicant must demonstrate the capacity to repay. Such practices are proof positive that, "Commitment to refugee protection in principle has often been coupled with denial of refugee protection in practice," as David Matas stated in a report to the UN Human Rights Commission 1995.

There are a few positive developments to offset this tightening stranglehold. In the past two years Australia has developed greater consistency in the refugee determination process. The government has provided limited financial and medical benefits for asylum seekers, has introduced an independent mechanism of review in the determination process, and has initiated improvement of the conditions in detention centers. The Swedish Democratic party in its platform, "Sweden into the 21st Century: A Social Democratic Policy for a New Age," states, "There is a need *for increased respect and understanding between Swedes and immigrants.*" They continue asserting that in a democratic society such as Sweden there is no room for racism towards and/or segregation between immigrants and the native population. Immigrants can be a real asset to Swedish society and, therefore, Sweden must make the best use of immigrants and their unique skills. In its political platform, "Principles, Proposals, Tools, for Italian Foreign Policy," the Italian Socialist Party states: "In a world which is increasingly interdependent there is the need to formulate all of the policies necessary for the rapid transformation of our society into a multiethnic and multicultural one, ensuring secure rights and equal integration of immigrants against any alarming racist and xenophobic upsurges." The government of New Zealand is developing a policy to combat the rising xenophobia that is widely recognized by the government and NGOs as stemming from the massive intake of immigrants and refugees.

NGOs have accepted the challenge of alleviating the tensions and promoting a healthy integration process. This is being implemented on many levels. On the local level, the women's NGOs run the actual programs of teaching language, cultural norms, everyday living, and, most importantly, alerting the newcomers to their basic rights and duties. Here both Israeli and world Jewish women's organizations play an extremely active and creative role.

On the international level, it is the religious organizations which are most visible. In this sphere the public Jewish voice is not strong enough, even virtually non-existent.

A Christian-Muslim Dialogue convened in Malta during April 1991 under the title: "International Seminar on Refugees and Migrants: Christian and Muslim Perspectives and Practices." This conference was the first such interfaith encounter to focus specifically on establishing *practical* cooperation on the global problem of refugees and migrants. An increasing number of asylum-seekers and migrant workers from Muslim countries are living in the secularized but Christian-influenced countries of the Americas, Australia, and Europe. At the same time, there are many Christian migrant workers in the Muslim countries of the Middle East (from the Philippines, as an example). The discussion and tone of the final statement of the conference indicates a clear desire by virtually all participants to build bridges, avoid hostile criticisms, overcome misinterpretation, and explore specific mechanisms for ongoing cooperation, both practical and consultative.

The World Council of Churches has issued the pamphlet, *A Moment to Choose: Risking to be with Uprooted People*, where they state that, "As government policies become more restrictive, and public hostility against foreigners intensifies in every region, churches are challenged as never before to make a choice: will they choose to be the church of the stranger and take the side of the uprooted or will they choose to turn away and ignore the problem?"

In November 1995, "The Global Ecumenical Consultation on Forced Displacement of People" met in Addis Ababa. One hundred and fifty participants from Catholic, Protestant, Orthodox, and Evangelical Christian churches worldwide attended. The "Call to Action" commits the many churches and church-related groups present to "more effective ecumenical and inter-religious collaboration." Objectives agreed to for follow up, evaluation, and action include the support of, and partnership with, the United Nations High Commissioner for Refugees (UNHCR) and governments to promote greater protection for refugees and internally displaced persons. Participants also agreed to develop a strong relationship with the International Organization of Migrants (IOM) and governments to promote ratification of the International Convention on Protecting Migrant Rights.

Women have recently become more active in the formulation of international policy. The program of the NGO forum at the "Fourth World Conference on Women" held in Beijing in September 1995, lists sixty-three migration-related workshops. The most sriking element was that women migrants themselves led most of these initiatives. Plans of action for networking and assistance were formulated and taken back to organizations and countries to be implemented.

A statement that Jews and Jewish organizations are totally uninvolved in the process and unaware of the issue would to an extent be misrepresenting the true picture. However, it is the few, rather than the total community, who are even peripherally aware or interested. Those who are involved have in the past and continue today to maintain a serious commitment to worldwide efforts. For example, the 1942 American Jewish Committee *Report to American Jews on Overseas Relief, Palestine and Refugees in the United States* argues specifically for strong efforts to save Jewish refugees from the destruction of World War II, while calling for "Jewish participation in the organizational work of the International Refugee Organization, particularly in the period of resettlement."

Herbert Lehman was appointed the head of UNRRA (UN Relief and Rehabilitation Agency) when it was set up in 1944 to take care of the survivors, thereby fulfilling the AJC suggestion and establishing Jewish representation in the Agency. JDC, HIAS, and ORT were very active in the immediate post-World War II period to try to find permanent settlement for the DPs, not only in Palestine but also elsewhere. These Jewish organizations, while looking out for the Jewish interest, considered affiliation and cooperation with the wider organizations as important to their work.

On the local level, the Consejo Argentino de Mujeres Israelitas (CAMI) provided aid to many Jewish refugees who had fled to Argentina from persecution in Europe. They opened an employment agency and appointed subcommittees for culture, social services, and foreign relations. The National Council of Jewish Women of Australia saw immigration as one of its top priorities, working with other Australian NGOs to provide services to immigrants in the Jewish and non-Jewish community, and providing assistance to Kibbutz Kfar Hanassi, where many Jewish immigrants from Australia have settled. In 1897, one of the first tasks of the National Council of Jewish Women of Canada was aid to arriving immigrants. They provided English lessons and recreational classes in order to facilitate their integration. The Consejo Chileno de Mujeres Judias cooperated with HIAS towards the integration of Jewish immigrants after World War II, and the Union of Jewish Women's Societies in Switzerland provided aid for needy war refugees. Finally, the Jewish Women's Association of Hong Kong had, as one of its main concerns, aid to Jewish immigrants coming from China, thousands of whom passed through Hong Kong.

Today, the American Jewish Committee has continued its involvement with the issue of refugee integration into the U.S. The authors of the report, *The Newest Americans: Report of the American Jewish Committee's Task Force on the Acculturation of Immigrants to American Life*, argue that despite the problems facing the United States today concerning immigration, the country does have sufficient means for dealing with them. Moreover, immigration is beneficial to the community. America has always prided itself on openness to newcomers, and in the past, this commitment to pluralism has proven to be a source of strength, not weakness. In this same series the American Jewish Committee stresses education as the key to successful integration. They suggest installing programs and workshops aimed at changing the attitudes of teachers, administration, parents, and students to consider new immigrants as a useful asset, rather than as a burden.

The Jewish Community of New Zealand has also been working against prejudice. A recent arrival to this community, American Rabbi Phillip Posner, a 1960s civil rights activist, has joined religious leaders of other denominations in this struggle against escalating racism, which he too insists stems mainly from the "political debate over immigration."

As a reaction to the British government's proposed changes to the Asylum and Immigration Bill, the Board of Deputies of British Jews has taken an extremely strong public line against the British government's harsh legislation affecting asylum seekers. At the same time, the Jewish Council for Racial Equality has devoted its total resources to organizing sustenance for those seeking asylum who have been denied any social security money, are not allowed to work, and consequently find themselves destitute.

The Reform, Liberal, and Masorti communities have also been effective in this work, notably the late Rabbi Hugo Gryn, who was a staunch fighter for the cause of all refugees, and it has been publicly recognized by the British Refugee Council that the major part of the resources provided by the Refugee Hostels over the past months has come from these Jewish organizations.

The Joint Distribution Committee is the founding member of the "Interfaith Hunger Appeal" which includes the Catholic Relief Services, World Church Services, and the Lutheran and Mennonite communities, and which is presently in the process of selecting a Muslim organization to invite to participate.

HIAS, the Hebrew Immigrant Aid Society, has also been very involved in refugee settlement and is committed to cooperating with other groups in representing the interests of all refugees coming to the United States. Since 1972 HIAS has resettled 350,000 people, 3,200 of which have been non-Jews from Iran (especially those of the Bahai faith), Indo-China, Latin America, Haiti, Bosnia, and others. "We work with Catholics on the Cuban issue, they help us with Russians," says Mark Seal, Associate Executive Vice President of HIAS (personal interview, 17 June 1996).

The International Council of Jewish Women, at its Triennial Convention held in Paris in May 1996, formulated a topical statement on refugees which firmly states:

> Present global political conflicts and economic developments show that one person out of fifty on this earth is a migrant or a refugee, 90% of whom are women and children;
>   Integration into the receiving community has become a necessary solution in most cases;
>   Realizing that women play a major role in the process of integration;
>   ICJW urges Affiliates to participate actively, in cooperation with other organizations in local and national programs to,
>   1) facilitate integration into their communities;
>   2) alert these women to their rights.
>   Furthermore, since the magnitude of these waves threatens closing the gates in receiving countries;
>   ICJW urges Affiliates to convince their governments to maintain and/or institute liberal and humane policies of migration.

This is the first public statement on this subject to be issued by an international Jewish organization in recent times. Local ICJW affiliates are also heavily involved on a domestic level. The New Zealand Jewish community has encouraged immigration in order to reinforce their dwindling Jewish numbers, and the Council of Jewish Women is actively involved in this resettlement process. The Swiss Union of Jewish Women's Organizations is represented on this issue by Myrthe Dreyfuss, the president of the Swiss Council of Jewish Refugees. She has been monitoring her government's policies and most recently has been encouraged by the decision *not* to enforce a proposed policy of *refoulement*, where a part of the Bosnian war refugees would have been returned to their destroyed, native country. Members of the GLIF, a women's NGO chaired by Nicole Kahn in Strasbourg, cross over into small Jewish communities in neighboring Germany to educate recent Russian Jewish immigrants in Jewish subjects and practice. The local communities are inundated by the sheer numbers and are unable to cope alone.

The Joint Distribution Committee's recent work in Sarajevo has left quite a mark on this war-torn area of the world. In fact, since 1992, the majority of the JDC's work with refugees has been with non-Jews. At one time during the conflict, the JDC was the only entity able to freely enter and exit Sarajevo. CARITAS, the world-wide Catholic agency, and MEHAMET, a Saudi welfare institution, were able to take advantage of this freedom by sending tons of food and medicines into Sarajevo through JDC convoys. During the height of the conflict, the JDC, through the local Jewish community, became the largest free pharmacy in Sarajevo, *open to all citizens*, and filling a total of 1.5 million free prescriptions in a two-year period.

With funding from the World Bank, U.S. AID, USDA, and the help of the Israeli government, the JDC has participated in a wealth of other non-sectarian programs. It has run eye treatment clinics in Zimbabwe (operated by Israeli opthamologists), built refugee camps for Somalis, and built a 500-bed hospital for Rwandan refugees in Zaire, with Israeli assistance and equipment. In war-ravaged Tuzla, the JDC has built a brick factory which will provide war victims with several hundred homes each month. It has created a field hospital for Kurdish refugees in Turkey, and has, together with UNICEF, trained trauma counselors in Bosnia, Croatia, and Serbia. These efforts are being carried out in partnership with organizations such as the UNHCR, the African-American Institute, U.S. AID, and the Interfaith Hunger Appeal.

Israel should be the prime example that the Jewish people have to offer the world community as a model of immigrant absorption. Twice in the past 50 years we have integrated massive numbers of people into the mainstream society, as well as the ongoing regular influx of people throughout the past five decades.

Israel's basic approach to the absorption of all immigrants has been to integrate the new arrivals as rapidly as possible into the mainstream of Israeli society. This approach has undergone constant revision as new waves of refugees have arrived and new experience is gained. At first the ideal was to take all the different people arriving in the country and turn them into a single homogeneous Israeli type, modeled on the early Zionist pioneers — the melting pot concept. Today we realize that in the 1950s Israel was too eager to change the traditions and ways of refugees coming from varied backgrounds, which resulted in serious social and cultural problems in the second generation. Thus, while Israel's basic approach has remained integrationist, the melting pot ideal has been replaced by that of the "garden of many flowers" — moving towards a multicultural society. For example, the Ethiopian

Jews are being encouraged not to abandon their customs and traditions as they find their way into Israeli society. Our unique experience has endowed us not only with the ability, but with the obligation, to help countries around the world to smooth their own processes of immigrant absorption.

Of the one million people which Israel has absorbed since its establishment, the vast majority have been Jewish. However, as a signer of the 1951 UN convention on refugees, Israel is committed to granting asylum and has done so. A group of Vietnamese boat-people were granted asylum in Israel in June 1977, and Bosnian Muslims escaping from war-torn Croatia were resettled in Israel. Today, there are instances of refugees from all over the Muslim world, Africa, and Eastern Europe who seek asylum in Israel.

Israel has shared knowledge and expertise during times of crisis in other countries and has been active in rescue operations. The experience with the absorption of refugees from Arab countries instigated the development of many new regions in Israel, such as the Lachish region in the south. The basic idea behind the planning of these regions was that a variety of types of rural and agricultural settlements be constructed around a new urban center designed to provide the periphery with varied services. This model was used in Iran in the Ghazvin region, destroyed in 1962 by an earthquake which left hundreds of thousands of people homeless. A large group of Israeli experts, among them Lova Eliav, the founder of Lachish, worked in Ghazvin for over ten years to reconstruct it on the basis of the Lachish model.

Israel was also able to translate experience into action in 1973, after the earthquake in Managua, Nicaragua, which left over half a million people homeless. A large Israeli team went out to Nicaragua to set up transit camps such as those which existed in Israel in the early 1950s to house refugees.

Israel can offer countries absorbing people from many different backgrounds its experience in combatting cultural gaps, and can help train social workers and counselors on how to overcome these differences.

The language barrier is probably one of the greatest challenges with which most receiving countries have to contend. Israel has been extremely successful in overcoming this by providing Hebrew language courses (*ulpan*) to all immigrants. Israel can offer its assistance to other countries in setting up the equivalent of such programs for their immigrants.

This potential was demonstrated to me personally in 1986 at the Third World Conference on Women held in Nairobi, where I presented a paper which dealt with *klita* — the absorption process in Israel, entitled "Refugees: Their Acclimatization into the Mainstream Culture — the Israeli Experience." At the end of the session, I was approached by the American delegation which requested access to expertise on language teaching as they were having specific problems with refugees from Laos. Their interest in the practical programs superseded the political issue of the Palestinians which had pervaded that conference.

Mark Seal of HIAS asserts that wherever possible, they are interested in cooperation with Israel because they absorb similar populations and, therefore, deal with similar problems (personal interview, 17 June 1996).

Israel has recently made more progress in this regard through its work with the IOM (International Organization of Migration) — a service organization with fewer political implications than the UNHCR — a factor which certainly contributed to the election of the Israeli Ambassador in Geneva to the post of Deputy Chairman of the Council. At a meeting of the IOM council in Geneva in November 1995, Israel was among the proposers of the resolution to call a regional convention on "Problems Associated with Population Displacements in the Commonwealth of Independent States (CIS) and Other Relevant Neighboring States." Additionally, the ambassador presented a speech to the Council which dealt with "Long-term Rehabilitation of Migrants and Refugees," in which he offered Israel's involvement in setting up a center of experts to help train professional staff in migrant integration, and an institute for exchange of information on migrants which would utilize Israel's expertise in this issue. Lastly, the Jewish Agency participates in the IOM deliberations and has run counseling seminars for various countries, including a government delegation of top level public administration officials from Armenia which came on a study tour in December 1995.

However, the international community seems unaware of the Jewish and Israeli contribution to the world effort to solve refugee problems. For instance the "Women's Commission for Refugee Women and Children" sent a fact-finding mission to Bosnia and published a report in which they enumerated the work of the organizations cooperating in the field. Nowhere in their report is there mention of the JDC. The report also lists "Women and Women's Groups in Bosnia — Contact Information," which does not include Sonja Elazar, President of "La Benevolencia," the ICJW affiliate in Sarajevo. There should have been a mutual awareness.

Why is Israel not more visible on the scene and why does it not make a more concerted effort for recognition? First of all, in the last 50 years, we have had to contend with rescuing, moving, resettling, and integrating massive numbers of our own people. That saga is in itself phenomenal, but it has also given us the image that we only care for our own people. Additionally, we have complicated the issue by not ideologically recognizing *olim* as refugees. Secondly, the open question of the Palestinian refugees has caused us to keep a low profile in any international discussion. We have not yet been able to confront this question successfully and live with the answer — neither the State of Israel, nor the world Jewish community.

A reflection of our hesitancy is Israel's participation within the framework of the UNHCR. During the past two years Israel has been the only member state of the Executive Committee not to present an official statement. Other member states have black marks tainting their own refugee situation, but they present their statements and deal only with their positive contributions to the world efforts, while avoiding mention of their own problems. In 1995, Israel could have taken credit for giving asylum to Bosnian Moslem refugees, in addition to the government's medical assistance and rescue contingent in Rwanda. The JDC has further created a training program, headed by Margot Pins, to teach social agents in Rwanda how to care for trauma patients. We chose not to make these efforts publicly known.

Third, indifference; other than the defense organizations that deal with the world's refugee problems as one of their objectives, there is a great lack of knowledge and much indifference both in Israeli society and in the world Jewish community. However, it is pleasing to note that NJCRAC, in its 1996 Agenda, devoted a chapter to immigration reform. NJCRAC is a community relations agency and, therefore, this is an important statement, although it deals only with the U.S. and not the international problem.

Jews are not allowed to be indifferent. Elie Wiesel writes:

Indifference is the worst disease that can contaminate a society. I always thought that evil was and is the enemy. I always thought that despair was and is something we must fight. Not so. Despair can be a beginning. Despair can move us to creativity. You may write a beautiful poem, compose a sonata. Despair can give the necessary impetus, the needed impulse to seek a kind of purification of words, of gestures, of encounters. And what are words or gestures if not encounters? Despair can lead you somewhere. Not so indifference. Indifference is the end of the process, not the beginning.

Suggestions to Improve the Situation

A. The UNHCR together with the International Council of Voluntary Agencies (ICVA) launched the PARinAC process which culminated in the global UNHCR-NGO Conference in Oslo in June 1994. The result of this conference was a *Plan of Action* which represents a synthesis of hundreds of local, regional, and international proposals. This document reflects the changing roles of NGOs and UNHCR, which are now becoming more involved not only in strictly humanitarian efforts, but also in efforts related to human rights, early warning, prevention, reconciliation, and peace-keeping and peace-making.

This partnership will forge new mechanisms of implementation in all these areas, in an effort to develop a global agenda for humanitarian action. Israel as a state, and the Jewish NGOs, should become aware of this process and develop their own strategy in order to become relevant to this agenda. Israel has much expertise and experience to contribute in many disciplines, from the humanitarian efforts through the practical implementation to the new aspect of peace-making.

Israeli and Palestinian women's NGOs have been networking for over five years both through dialogues for peace and specific joint projects on women's issues. These groups have been called upon for advice and expertise to set up a similar process among others, most notably concerning a recent meeting between Bosnian and Croat women. They have an important contribution to make in the area of peace and reconciliation as well.

B. Israel and world Jewry must take a public stand on the moral issue of not closing off ways of escape and entry, and see to it that governments act responsibly.

C. World Jewry should become involved in the local communities of every country in projects assisting integration into the community, and educate themselves and the community to be open to accepting newcomers.

D. Jews should join the Christian-Muslim Dialogue, and also cooperate with other NGOs to impact governments and political parties.

If Israel and the Jewish people work for the rights of migration, rescue, resettlement, and integration only of their own and leave the struggle for others to others, they will not be fulfilling their purpose in the international society to be an *"Or l'goyim,"* not only an example, a "light *unto* the nations," but also a participant and guide, a "light *for* the nations." Israel must join the community of nations and demonstrate that its cares about all migrants and refugees while showing the enormous job done in taking care of its own.

References

A Great Tragedy of Our Time. United Nations High Commissioner for Refugees.

A Moment to Choose: Risking to be With Uprooted People. September 1995. Geneva: World Council of Churches, Refugee and Migration Desk.

Banai, Nurit. 1988. *Ethiopian Absorption: The Hidden Challenge.* Trans. Evelyn Abel. New York: United Israel Appeal.

Bradley, Grant. 27 May 1996. "Rabbi Urges Meeting to Tackle Racism Before it Escalates." *New Zealand Herald.*

Christian-Muslim Dialogue on Ministry to Migrants and Refugees. 24 April 1991. Valletta, Malta.

Convention and Protocol Relating to the Status of Refugees. New York: United Nations.

Curtis, Michael, and Susan Aurelia Gitelson, eds. 1976. *Israel in the Third World,* New Brunswick: Transaction Books.

Dreyfuss, Myrthe. Swiss Council of Refugees, President. 26 June 1996 (private correspondence).

Educating the Newest Americans: Report of the Task Force on New Immigrants and American Education. 1989. New York: American Jewish Committee.

Elimination of Racial Discrimination: 10th and 11th Report of the Government of New Zealand. May 1996. Wellington: New Zealand Ministry of Foreign Affairs and Trade.

Focus on Women: Refugee Women. May 1995. New York: Department of Public Information of the United Nations Reproduction Section.

Fuchs, Lawrence. 1988. *American Pluralism and Public Policy: Implications for the Jewish Community.* New York: American Jewish Committee.

Ginzberg, Eli. 1942. *Report to American Jews: On Overseas Relief, Palestine and Refugees in the United States.* New York: Harper and Brothers Publishers.

Gordenker, Leon. 1987. *Refugees in International Politics.* New York: Columbia University Press.

Grange, Mariette. November 1995. *Women Migrants Speak up in Beijing.* Geneva: World Council of Churches, Refugee and Migration Desk.

Harder, Peter. 16 October 1995. "Statement by V. Peter Harder, Deputy Minister Citizenship and Immigration Canada to the Plenary Session of the 46th Executive Committee of the United Nations High Commissioner for Refugees." The Permanent Mission of Canada to the United Nations at Geneva.

Harman, Zena. Honorary Representative for the UNHCR in Israel. 12 June 1996 (interview).

Hyman, Paula E. 1978. "From Paternalism to Cooptation: The French Jewish Consistory and the Immigrants, 1906-1939." *YIVO Annual of Jewish Social Sciences,* vol. xvii. New York: YIVO Institute for Jewish Research.

Iarchy, Nadine. Council of Jewish Women of Belgium. 18 June 1996 (private correspondence).

Immigration Reform: A Position Paper of the American Jewish Committee. January 1996. New York: American Jewish Committee.

International NGO Working Group on Refugee Women. 12 October 1995.

Jones, Tom B. 1989. "Attila." *The Encyclopedia Americana,* vol. ii. Danbury, Connecticut: Grolier.

Las, Nelly. 1996. *Jewish Women in a Changing World: A History of the International Council of Jewish Women (ICJW). 1899-1995.* Jerusalem: Avraham Harman Institute of Contemporary Jewry, Hebrew University.

Mantver, Arnon. Director General, JDC, Israel. 4 July 1996 (interview).

Manor, Uzi. Department of International Organizations, Director, Foreign Ministry. 26 June 1996 (interview); July 1996 (private correspondence).

Matas, David. "Four Horsemen." Acceptance speech on receiving a Canadian award for human rights.

Newest Americans (The): Report of the American Jewish Committee's Task Force on the Acculturation of Immigrants to American Life, 1989. New York: American Jewish Committee.

NGO Statement to the 46th Session of the Executive Committee of the UN High Commissioner for Refugees Programme. 1995. International Council of Voluntary Agencies.

Payes, Shirley. Council of Jewish Women of New Zealand. 18 June 1996 (private correspondence).

Post-War Migrations: Proposals for an International Agency. 1943. Ed. Abraham G. Duker. New York: American Jewish Committee.

Principles, Proposals, Tools for Italian Foreign Policy. November 1995. Partito Democratico Della Sinistra.

Report to the Secretary General of the United Nations on the Situation of Migrant Women Workers in Israel According to General Assembly Resolution 47/96 Entitled "Migrant Women Workers." 26 September 1993. New York: United Nations.

Rubin, Gary E. and Judith Golub. *The Immigration Act of 1990: An American Jewish Committee Analysis*. New York: American Jewish Committee, Institute of Human Relations.

Seal, Mark. Associate Executive Vice President, HIAS. 17 June 1996 (interview).

Seigel, Leila. ICJW Representative at the UN, Geneva. 20 June 1996 (private correspondence).

Schneider, Michael. 1994. *Eighty Years of Global Jewish Service: A Professional Perspective*. Distinguished Service Award from Yeshiva University's Wurzweiler School of Social Work (public address).

———. 17 September 1995. Columbus, Ohio Jewish Federation Annual Meeting (public address).

———. 14 April 1996. *JDC During the Holocaust*. (public address).

———. Executive Vice President, American JDC. 26 June 1996 (interview).

Soble, Lester A., and Doug Grant, eds. 1991. *Refugees: A World Report*. Ann Arbor Michigan: Books On Demand.

Slater, Robert. 1973. *Israel's Aid to Developing Nations*. New York: Friendly House Publishers.

Sweden into the 21st Century: A Social Democratic Policy for a New Age. 15-17 March 1996. Stockholm: Congress of the Swedish Social Democratic Party.

Topical Statement on Refugees. May 1996. International Council of Jewish Women.

Taran, P.A. *Global Forced Migration Conference Strengthens Ecumenical Cooperation*. December 1995. Geneva: World Council of Churches, Refugees and Migration Desk.

Widetzky, Judi. July 12, 1985. *Refugees: Their Acclimatization into the Mainstream Culture — the Israeli Experience*. Nairobi (public address).

———. 18-25 April 1993. *Report to the Executive Meeting. Malta: Standing Committee on Migrants and Refugees*.

———. June 1994. *Report to the ICJW Triennial Convention*. Paris: Ad-hoc Committee on Aliyah and Refugees.

Women's Access to Justice: He Putanga Mo Nga Wahine Ki Te Tika. Law Commission of New Zealand.

Wiesel, Eli. 1993. *Nuremberg Forty Years Later, The Struggle against Injustice in Our Time* (International Human Rights Conference, 1987 — Papers and Proceedings and Retrospective). Ed. Irwin Cotler. Montreal and Kingston: McGill-Queen's University Press, pp. 21-22.

Zolberg, Aristide, Astri Suhrke and Sergio Aguayo. 1989. *Escape From Violence: Conflict and the Refugee Crisis in the Developing World*. Oxford: Oxford University Press.

16

The Dwindling Jewish Communities in the Muslim Countries of the Middle East: Their Current Status and Reasons for Mass Emigration

George E. Gruen

Introduction

While this chapter focusses on developments affecting the Jewish communities of the Middle East and North Africa in the period since the struggle for the creation of the State of Israel, it should always be kept in mind that we are dealing with some of the most ancient and historically significant centers of Jewish life. Indeed, the birthplace of Abraham, and thus the cradle of Jewish history, was in Aram-Naharayim (Aramea between the rivers), later called Mesopotamia by the Greeks, because it was the fertile crescent of land between the two great river valleys of the Tigris and Euphrates. This area is divided today among Iraq, Syria, and Turkey. Significant Jewish settlements date back to the biblical period. King David extended his rule to much of Syria, including Damascus. Following the destruction of the First Temple in 586 BCE, the Jewish exiles made Babylonia the leading Jewish center of life and learning so that even after the restoration of the Jewish Commonwealth in Eretz Israel, the majority of the Jews continued to live in the Middle

Eastern diaspora. Alexandria in Egypt also became a major Jewish center. Scholars now believe that when Obadiah prophesied of the redemption of the "captivity of Jerusalem that is in Sepharad" [verse 20], he was referring not to the Jews of Spain but rather to those of Sardis, a prominent Jewish center in Western Anatolia (Turkey). At Sardis, called Sfard in Lydian and Persian, archaeologists have discovered remnants of a very large synagogue dating to the second century CE.

Whether or not the Jewish community of Yemen actually goes back to those who accompanied the Queen of Sheba back home following her visit to King Solomon, as legend has it, Jewish merchants are known to have been active in the spice trade in Arabia already during the period of the First Temple and large numbers came to Hijaz in northern Arabia even before the destruction of the Temple and many followed afterwards. In a controversy that has a familiar ring in the current debates on Israel-diaspora relations, it is recounted that when the Jews of Yemen ignored Ezra the Scribe's call to return to the Land of Israel, he cursed them; and they reportedly repaid him by refusing to name their sons Ezra. The Jewish communities in North Africa are also quite ancient. During a visit to Morocco in 1980, this author met a gentleman in Marrakesh, the former capital of Morocco, whose family name was Ess-Yemini. He explained that this was their pronunciation of the Hebrew Ish-Yemini, meaning from the Tribe of Benjamin. This is also how the Scroll of Esther refers to Mordechai, the Jewish leader of Persia, who was among the Jewish captives whom Nebuchadnezzar the King of Babylon had carried away (Esther, chapter 2, verses 5-6). Mr. Ess-Yemini said his family had come to North Africa shortly before the destruction of the First Temple. Whatever the accuracy of these traditions, there are inscriptions attesting to Jewish life in Morocco at least as far back as the second century CE. We know that Berber tribes in the Atlas Mountains were converted to Judaism before the Arab conquest. The autochthonous Jewish community was greatly enlarged and eventually overshadowed at the end of the fifteenth century by the flood of Jewish refugees from persecution in Spain and Portugal. The Iberian Jewish exiles were also welcomed into the Ottoman Empire by Sultan Beyazit. Albeit on a smaller scale, in the contemporary period both Turkey and Morocco offered a haven to Jews fleeing Nazi persecution.

This is not the place to assess the great religious and cultural contributions of Middle Eastern Jewry to the evolution of Jewish civilization over the past centuries and even millennia. Although their history of growth and creativity under periods of tolerance has been marked by periods of decline and outright persecution, it is only in this century that the viability of most of these communities has been placed into doubt. While we may rejoice that most have found new lives in Israel and other free democratic societies, this must be tinged with sadness at the ending of once glorious and rich centers of Jewish life.

Exodus from Syria

In April 1995, a few days before the traditional Seder marking *Yitziat Mitzraim*, the exodus from Egypt, this writer attended a special ceremony in New York to mark the last chapter in the long struggle to achieve *Yitziat Suria*, the exodus of the Jews from Syria. Rabbi Abraham Hamra, Chief Rabbi of Syria, was the special guest at a luncheon given by the American Jewish Joint Distribution Committee in New York to honor some of the individuals and institutions who had worked tirelessly for many frustrating years to remove the discriminatory measures imposed upon the Jewish communities in Syria and to lift the ban to their emigration. While Damascus had, since the late 1970s, gradually eased some of the travel restrictions for individuals, Syria continued to forbid entire families to travel abroad together and, like Pharaoh of old, President Hafez al-Assad insisted that if Jewish men were permitted to travel, they had to leave behind their wives and children, in addition to a financial deposit, as security for their prompt return.

The real breakthrough only came in April 1992. Among the major reasons for the change in Syrian policy was that following the opening of direct Arab-Israeli peace talks in Madrid in October 1991, and in the wake of the collapse of the Soviet Union and the American-led victory in the Gulf War, Assad sought improved relations with the United States. Now, for the first time, Damascus indicated that entire Jewish families would be able to travel abroad together "on business and for vacation," just as "all other Syrian citizens." Yet emigration was still technically forbidden and the Jews who left did so on tourist visas. This meant that unlike the biblical exodus from Egypt, when the Israelites left laden with riches, Syrian Jews could not take even their own possessions with them. Moreover, they were still not permitted to travel to Israel, with which Syria still claimed to be technically in a state of war.

Indeed, for many years relatives of Jews who had left illegally were subjected to interrogation and arrest, while Jews suspected of having visited Israel were subjected to torture and faced possible charges of espionage on their return. Those imprisoned longest were Selim Swed, a 51-year old pharmacist and father of seven, and his younger brother, Eli, 31. Eli was arrested in November and Selim in December 1987 on their return from a trip abroad, including an innocent visit to relatives in Israel. After being tortured and held incommunicado for more than two years, they were eventually charged with illegally travelling to "enemy occupied territory" and sentenced to six years and eight months. Following intensive international efforts on their behalf, including a direct appeal to President Assad by Senator Edward M. Kennedy and 68 of his colleagues (more than two-thirds of the Senate) on March 26, 1992, urging him to "free the Sweds and to permit free emigration for all Syrian Jews," the Swed brothers were finally released on April 19, 1992, which was the second day of Passover that year.[1]

The lifting of the ban on the departure of entire Syrian Jewish families was the culmination of decades of effort by the relatives of Syrian Jews in the United States, Europe and Israel, Jewish and general human rights groups in the United States, Canada and Western Europe, as well as by concerned members of Congress and parliaments in the free world and the Israeli Knesset. I had first met Rabbi Hamra when I was invited to his home for lunch on Shabbat following synagogue services in February 1977, which I had attended as co-leader of an interfaith study mission to the Middle East. The rabbi told me of the plight of the unmarried single Jewish women over age 25 who could not readily find eligible husbands since some men had fled and others did not wish to marry and start families unless they could raise the children in freedom. The women were fearful of fleeing after four Jewish women and two men had been brutally murdered in 1974 as they sought to flee to Lebanon. Moreover, the arrest and interrogation by the secret police of relatives of those who had escaped also served to intimidate the community. Also present at the luncheon was Robert Pelletreau, Deputy Chief of Mission at the U.S. Embassy, who had been assigned by Ambassador Richard Murphy to maintain contact with the Jewish community. This served the important dual functions of reassuring the Jewish community that they were not forgotten as well as dramatizing to President Assad that the United States was actively concerned in securing their fundamental human rights. Subsequently, when President Jimmy Carter met with Assad in Geneva, he managed to secure a promise from the Syrian president to permit 14 "Jewish maidens" to come to the United States to seek husbands, as well as a more general promise that the authorities in Damascus would sympathetically consider other requests for travel on humanitarian grounds. While this broke the ice, the removal of the restrictions on the Jewish community was to be an agonizingly slow process. When I chanced to meet him again in May 1996, I thanked Mr. Pelletreau, who was then Assistant Secretary of State for Near East Affairs, for his successful efforts on behalf of Syrian Jewry. He recalled our meeting in Damascus in February 1977 and he indicated that he had kept up with Rabbi Hamra, and during one of his recent trips to Israel to foster the peace process he had visited Rabbi Hamra in his new home and said that they had reminisced over the bad old times.[2]

This story demonstrates the importance of persistent intervention by the United States government on humanitarian grounds on behalf of the Jewish and other minorities in the Middle East and indeed on behalf of human rights around the world.

Nearly all of the 4,000 Jews who left Syria went initially to the United States. A few went to Canada, Latin America, and Western Europe. Chief Rabbi Hamra and his wife and six children came to New York in 1993 after most of his flock had already left the three Syrian cities with a Jewish population: Damascus, the capital, Aleppo, the commercial center, and Qamishli, a town near the Turkish border at Nusaybin. In October 1994 the Hamra family finally made aliya to Israel. They were joined by some 1,800, or nearly half of the other recent arrivals in the United States.

Resettlement of Syrian Jews

When the recent Syrian Jewish emigrants came to New York, they were welcomed by the 30,000 strong and well-established American Jewish community of Syrian origin, dating back to the last decades of the Ottoman Empire. They helped to integrate the new arrivals as did New York's Jewish communal institutions. According to the impressions of some members of the American Syrian community, on the whole, the Aleppo Jews, with their long mercantile traditions, found it somewhat easier to adjust to the American economy than the Jews of Damascus, who were more concentrated among artisans and craftsmen, and reportedly more of the Damascenes went on to Israel, where there was also a Syrian-Jewish community from pre-1948, as well as a few more recent arrivals who had managed to escape from Syria to Turkey or Lebanon and then had gone on to Israel. Further study is necessary to determine to what extent professional and employment opportunities, and to what extent other factors such as Zionist or religious attachment to Israel, location of close family members, and fear of war and reluctance to serve in the army, prompted individual families to choose to settle in Israel or to remain in the United States.

As of February 1997, there were only 180 Jews remaining in Syria, 154 in Damascus, 4 in Aleppo, and 22 in Qamishli. All have valid passports and most are wealthy. Religious services continue. Only a few children still remain to attend the recently renovated Jewish school in Damascus, but circumcisions must usually be delayed beyond the biblically prescribed eighth day, since the community depends on periodic visits of a *mohel* from Istanbul, Turkey.

Assad apparently told the authorities in Damascus to turn a blind eye to the onward movement of Syrian Jews to Israel, belatedly realizing that his policy of keeping the Jewish community hostage had become anachronistic and counterproductive, since by this time Syria was actively engaged in American-mediated peace negotiations with the Israeli government led by Labor party leader Yitzhak Rabin, elected in June 1992, and there were widespread hopes for a formal end to the conflict.

Yemen

In August 1992, Yemen, which for decades had severely restricted any foreign contacts with the roughly 1,000 scattered remnant of its once large Jewish population, announced that they were once again free to emigrate. It will be recalled that nearly all Yemenite Jews had left in the massive "Operation Magic Carpet" that had brought most of Yemen's Jews to Israel in 1949-50.[3]

Syria and Yemen were the last Arab countries to systematically restrict the movement of their Jewish populations. Essentially, virtually all Jews in the Arab countries of the Middle East and North Africa who wished to leave have by now managed to do so. As Table 16.1 indicates, they have in effect voted with their feet. Before going into the various reasons for the massive exodus of Jews from the Middle East over the past five decades, it would be well to briefly survey the current situation and prospects for those who remain.[4]

TABLE 16.1
Population Estimates for Jewish Minorities
in the Middle East and North Africa

Country	Pre-1948	Most recent figures	Year
Algeria	140,000	15	1997
Egypt	75,000	150	1997
Iran	90,000-100,000	14,000-20,000	1994
Iraq	130,000	100	1994
Lebanon	5,000	100	1994
Libya	38,000	2	1996
Morocco	265,000-300,000	5,000-6,000	1995
Syria	30,000 (1943)	180	1997
Tunisia	105,000	1,782	1997
Turkey	80,000	19,000-25,000	1997
Yemen	55,000	250	1995
Approximate Totals	1,013,000-1,058,000	40,579-53,579	

Sources: Data compiled by George E. Gruen from the volumes of the *American Jewish Year Book*, information from the American Jewish Joint Distribution Committee, and interviews with Jewish community leaders and other informants in or maintaining contact with these Jewish communities. Most of these figures are estimates at best and their reliability varies from country to country. The higher estimates for Turkey and Iran are the numbers provided to the authorities by the local Jewish communities.

Factors Affecting the Remaining Jewish Communities

There continues to be a gradual decline in the numbers of the Jewish population living in the Arab and Muslim countries of the Middle East and North Africa. The distinctive demographic, political, and economic situation in each country help account for differences, in the pace of the decline. There are essentially three factors that have contributed to the diminishing numbers:

1. Attrition through death among an aging population.
2. Emigration of young adults and their families seeking better educational and economic opportunities abroad.
3. The lifting of government imposed barriers to emigration.

Throughout the region both governmental policies and popular attitudes have been affected by the momentous global and regional developments. Most notable are the end of the Cold War and the collapse of the Soviet Union, the end of the Iraq-Iran War in 1988, the second Gulf War that liberated Kuwait from Iraqi occupation early in 1991, the opening of direct Arab-Israeli peace talks in Madrid in October of that year and the subsequent Israeli-Palestinian agreements, beginning with Oslo I in 1993, and the Jordanian-Israeli Peace Treaty of 1994. These positive developments have led to some lessening of tension and improvement in the status of the Jewish communities in some Middle Eastern countries and there have even been expressions of utopian hope by some Israeli and Arab leaders that a comprehensive Arab-Israeli peace settlement would eventually usher in a new era of Arab-Jewish coexistence and cooperation in the region. While the improved political climate has resulted in increasing numbers of Israelis of North African origin going back for visits to Morocco and Tunisia, and some may establish joint business ventures, it is highly unlikely that any significant number will choose to return to reestablish themselves in their countries of origin. Moreover, against the optimistic forecasts of a "new Middle East," it should be pointed out that there are still many fundamental outstanding issues between Israel and the Palestinians which can again erupt into violence, that Syria and Lebanon have not yet made peace with Israel, and that most of the regimes in the region are autocratic and face severe challenges from both radical leftists and increasingly militant Islamic political groups that oppose peace with Israel and improved relations with the democratic West. For the most extreme of these groups the distinction between Israeli, Zionist, and Jew is often blurred and in recent years Arab terrorists have gone so far as to target innocent Jews in Lebanon, and isolated Arab terrorist attacks occurred against Jewish worshippers in Djerba, Tunisia in 1985 and in Istanbul, Turkey in September 1986 — two countries whose governments accord full rights to their Jewish communities.

The Fading and Barely Viable Communities

In those Arab countries where the overwhelming majority of the Jewish population emigrated in earlier years and the tiny remnant that remains in each country consists primarily of pensioners over 65, their numbers continue to diminish as the elderly pass on. Another component of the dwindling Jewish population are persons who are intermarried and assimilated, and who for various personal reasons do not wish to leave. In Egypt there are some 150 native-born Jews, nearly all elderly persons, their numbers divided between Cairo and Alexandria. Since the 1979 Egyptian-Israeli Peace Treaty, they have been able to reestablish contact with their families in Israel. (Israeli diplomats and visiting American and Israeli Jewish tourists help to provide a *minyan* for services.)

In Yemen there are only some 250 Jews left, scattered in a few towns and villages in the north. Most of the others have gone to Israel with a few going to the United States.[5] There is still a trickle of emigration. Although officially they did "not sanction their travel to Israel," the Yemenite authorities in 1993 acknowledged that they were aware of the ultimate destination of most of the emigrants and did not try to stop them. Ironically, it was the anti-Zionist ultra-Orthodox Satmar Hasidim, who for many years were the only outside Jewish group permitted to maintain contact with Yemenite Jews, who have continued their efforts to convince these Jews to stay away from the secular, heretic Zionist state and to send their young men to study in American *yeshivot* and then return to Yemen to await the Messianic redemption.[6]

In Algeria, fewer than 20 affiliated Jews remain. As French citizens, they can readily move to France and those who had not left earlier did so recently to escape the continuing conflict between the embattled government and the militant Islamic opposition. In Iraq, there are probably fewer than 100 today, mostly elderly. Since the end of the Iran-Iraq war they have been able to leave, and those who remain are no longer targets of persecution but endure the same hardships as the general population as a result of the United Nations sanctions. In Libya, where fewer than a handful survive in Tripoli, there is no organized community.

Lebanon

In Lebanon there is no longer a fully functioning community or a synagogue with regular services. The few hundred who remained in Beirut despite the Arab-Israel conflict and the years of internecine fighting since 1975 which racked the country, left following the Israeli withdrawal in 1983 and the kidnapping and murder of eight leaders of the Jewish community by the Organization of the Oppressed on Earth, an Iranian-inspired radical Shi'ite group.[7] In October 1991 there were reportedly only two Jews — an elderly brother and sister — still living in the Wadi Abu Jamil section of West Beirut and the main synagogue there closed in 1984. There are reportedly between 50 and 100 Jews living in Christian East Beirut, their average age being around 65. The dozen or so younger Jews are mainly students at the city's universities. Explaining his decision to remain, one young Jew told an Israeli reporter, "There have been Jews here for the past 2,300 years. We're one of the 17 officially recognized sects. We don't want them to become 16 one day."[8] In addition, some Lebanese Jewish businessmen, whose families reside in Europe, make periodic trips to Beirut in hopes of participating in the massive reconstruction effort that is now underway on the assumption that peace will finally come to that troubled country.

Morocco and Tunisia: Still Functioning and Viable

There are two other Arab countries with still viable and well functioning Jewish communities and a more healthy demographic composition. These are Morocco with between 5,000 and 6,000

Jews, and Tunisia with 1,782. At present there are more Jews in Djerba, with its traditionally observant Jewish families, than in the more cosmopolitan and assimilated capital city of Tunis. The regimes in these two North African countries have been protective of their Jewish communities and have, in recent years, expressed increasingly open support for the Madrid peace process and have been gradually moving to establish commercial, tourist, and quasi-diplomatic ties with Israel. They still maintain Jewish schools, synagogues, kosher restaurants, old age homes, and a normal demographic pattern. But younger men go to France, Israel, or Canada for study, and when they find job opportunities their families often follow. Today there are more Moroccan Jews in Montreal than remain in all of Morocco. As a result, there has been a continuing decline in the population. King Hassan II of Morocco officially received Israeli Prime Minister Yitzhak Rabin and Foreign Minister Shimon Peres in Rabat in September 1993 on their return from the Washington signing of the Declaration of Principles with PLO Chairman Yasir Arafat. The king has eagerly encouraged tourism and investment from American Jews and from Moroccan Jews living abroad. It is difficult to obtain a precise figure for the number of Jews living in Morocco since some families divide their time between their North African homes and their residences and businesses in France and other places.

Today, the only Middle Eastern countries — not counting Israel — which still have Jewish populations of more than 10,000 are non-Arab Turkey and Iran.

Turkey

In the case of Turkey, its estimated 20,000 to 25,000 Jews officially enjoy equal rights with all other citizens. It is essentially a thriving and largely affluent community. More than a dozen synagogues operate in Istanbul, where the overwhelming majority of Jews live, and four in Izmir, with a population of around 2,000. Fewer than 100 live in the capital of Ankara. The Jewish community in Istanbul maintains a hospital, an old age home, and charitable services for the fewer than 500 indigent. Jewish schools function in both Istanbul and Izmir, although most children attend state or non-Jewish private schools. In an attempt to keep more middle class Jewish students within the community, a modern new $4 million school, with instruction in English, was opened in 1995. One objective is to stem growing intermarriage, which has risen from 10 to nearly 40 percent as the younger generation of middle and upper class Jews has felt increasingly well integrated and accepted by the Westernized and secularized members of Istanbul's business and professional classes. The younger Jewish generation no longer speaks primarily Ladino or French as did their parents, but speak fluent Turkish instead. They may thus readily meet, fall in love, and marry Muslim fellow students at Turkish universities. Another reason for the new school has been to enable Jewish students to meet the standards for admission to American universities.

Turkish Jews have long been completely free to travel. Since the establishment of the modern Turkish Republic in 1923, except for World War II, the only restriction on travel to Palestine/Israel had been briefly imposed during the period of active hostilities in 1947-49 during Israel's War of Independence. After Arab-Israel armistice negotiations began, Turkey in March 1949 extended de facto recognition to Israel and formal diplomatic relations were established. Israeli immigration officials were permitted to operate in Turkey and direct air and ship routes facilitated the large-scale aliya of nearly half of the 80,000 members of the Jewish population at the time, mostly from outlying towns in Anatolia and from among the poorer elements of the population in Istanbul and Izmir. Many families had been impoverished as a result of the grossly excessive and unfair financial assessments imposed upon the non-Muslim minorities as part of a general nationwide tax, the *Varlik Vergisi*, instituted by the government during World War II. Designed to fight inflation by confiscating the undue wealth of "war-time profiteers," the assessments were made by local committees who often wildly exaggerated the wealth of their minority neighbors. There was no mechanism for appeal and those who could not pay the full assessment within a short time were sentenced to hard labor. Although following American and other foreign diplomatic intervention the law was soon cancelled and the authorities subsequently apologized for the excesses and promised compensation, none was ever paid.[9] At the same time it should be noted that even though Turkey maintained close relations with Nazi Germany during the early years of the war, the Turkish Jewish community was not subjected to any particularly anti-Semitic discrimination. Indeed, in the 1930s Turkey had welcomed Jewish academicians fleeing from Nazi Germany and during the war some diplomats of neutral Turkey in occupied countries helped Jewish refugees to escape to freedom.

Aside from Zionist and religious attraction that had led smaller numbers of Turkish Jews to go to Palestine in the 1920s and 1930s, many of the poorer Jews from Turkey were attracted to Israel after 1948 by the prospect that in the new, socialist, egalitarian Jewish state they would be able to marry off their daughters *parasiz* (without money, i.e., without having to pay a dowry). The number of Jews of Turkish origin in Israel today is estimated at nearly 100,000 and many maintain contact with their relatives back in Turkey and go back on frequent visits. The Jews in Turkey have also been frequent visitors to Israel and have sent large delegations to the Maccabiah games (the Jewish Olympics) in Israel. Turkey has become a popular tourist destination for Israelis in general and some 300,000 visited there in 1996. Turkish-Israeli relations have rapidly developed in all fields of political, economic, and strategic cooperation since December 1991, when Ankara finally raised diplomatic ties to embassy level and began to take an active role in the multilateral working groups of the peace process.[10] Turkish Jewish communal and business leaders have accompanied Turkish officials on their visits to Israel. Moreover, as part of each official visit — by Foreign Minister Hikmet Cetin in 1993, Prime Minister Tansu Cillar in 1994, and President Süleyman Demirel in March 1996 — the high Turkish officials were warmly hosted by the Jews of Turkish origin in the largely Turkish community of Bat Yam. They were profoundly moved and deeply gratified by the continuing attachment shown by the former Turkish Jews. Demirel invited Jefi Kamhi, a member of the ruling True Path Party, to accompany him to Israel. Kamhi was the first member of the Jewish community to run for and be elected to the Grand National Assembly since the 1950s. A prominent businessman, he is the son of Jak Kamhi, a leading Turkish industrialist who headed the Turkish Quincentennial Foundation, established to commemorate the 500th anniversary in 1992 of the Ottoman Sultan's offer of refuge to the Jews expelled from Spain. Israeli President Haim Herzog was invited to participate in the gala celebration in the Dolmabahce Palace. The growing public involvement of Turkish Jews after many years of keeping a low profile reflected both their increasing integration within Turkish society as well as government officials' eagerness to enlist their support in gaining American and Western European support for Turkey in the face of Greek and Armenian anti-Turkish lobbying. Jak Kamhi has also headed the Turkish commission seeking improved relations with the European Union. The value to Turkey of the growing Turkish-Israeli cooperation in recent years was also illustrated by the effective lobbying by then Prime Minister Shimon Peres with his European colleagues in the Socialist International for approval of a customs union between the European Union and Turkey in 1995. Prime Minister Ciller publicly acknowledged the Israeli help.

However, domestic developments within Turkey caused Turkish Jews to feel anxious. In June 1996, the Turkish parliament approved Necmettin Erbakan, leader of the Islamist Refah (Welfare) Party as prime minister and head of a coalition government with Mrs. Ciller's True Path Party. Erbakan had, since the early 1970s, opposed Turkey's entry into the European Economic Community (now the European Union), claiming this to be part of a Zionist plot for world economic domination.[11] In addition to calling for restoration of Islamic values and for Turkey to head an Islamic Common Market, Erbakan has a long record of anti-Israeli and even anti-Semitic statements. The Refah party had opposed the strengthening of Turkish-Israeli relations and especially the strategic defense cooperation between the two countries highlighted by mutual training of air and naval forces and a $650 million contract from the Turkish defense ministry with Israel Aircraft Industries to work together to upgrade Turkey's American-made F-15 fighters. The Refah deputies in parliament had also questioned Demirel's decision to visit Israel and his special invitation to the Jewish deputy Kamhi to accompany him. Erbakan's emphasis on seeking as his first priority to improve ties with Iran, Libya, and other Islamic nations caused concern in Washington as well as in Jerusalem, and among the Westernized Turkish elite who feared that Erbakan would seek to undermine the secularist principles upon which Mustafa Kemal Atatürk had founded the Turkish Republic.[12] Thus far the influential military leadership, who regard themselves as the ultimate guarantors of the Kemalist principles, and the commitments made in the coalition agreement with Ciller's pro-Western and pro-Israeli Foreign Ministry, have prevented Erbakan from scuttling the ties with Israel or weakening the longstanding relations with the United States. Recently Erbakan's chief foreign affairs advisor, Abdullah Gül, has tried to explain that it was only natural for Turkey to seek to improve relations with its regional Arab and Islamic neighbors and sought to reassure Washington that Erbakan's government valued the close relationship with the United States and declared, "We want to maintain it and strengthen it."[13] In Congressional testimony on February 12, 1997, Secretary of State Madeleine Albright emphasized the strategic importance of Turkey to the United States as a NATO ally, but also expressed concern over human rights violations and the Erbakan government's "approaches in foreign policy" that the U.S. did not approve of. She revealed that in a meeting with Erbakan in Turkey in July 1996, when she was still UN ambassador, she "made clear that we feel it vital that Turkey remain a secular state."[14]

While the Jewish community is naturally worried, Refah officials, such as the Refah mayor of Istanbul, have tried to reassure them. Jewish religious, educational, and communal institutions continue to function without interference. Many young Turkish Jews have come to the United States for college and professional training and then have thus far mostly returned home. If the Islamists begin to have a significant impact on public life in Turkey, more young Jews will decide to stay in the U.S. and their parents may choose to join them. Some may choose to go to Israel as others did during earlier periods of economic turmoil and extremist violence in the 1960s and 1970s. Some of them returned to Turkey when economic conditions improved and political stability was restored following the military intervention of 1980.[15]

To summarize, we can say that in Tunisia, Morocco, and in non-Arab Turkey Jews today prosper, enjoy equal rights, and are protected by the authorities. They occasionally even obtain official positions. For example, the Minister of Tourism in Morocco is Serge Berdugo, a prominent businessman and leader of the Jewish community and, as already noted, Jefi Kamhi is a deputy in the Turkish parliament. His father, Jak Kamhi, is a leading industrialist, heads the Turkish commission to negotiate with the European Union, chaired the Quincentennial foundation, and was among the Jewish leaders who accompanied Premier Ciller to the first Middle East economic conference in Morocco and her subsequent visit to Israel.

Fears for the Future

Still, anxiety and concern for the future cast a constant shadow over the daily lives of the small Jewish communities that continue to exist in the Muslim countries of the Middle East and North Africa. For example, three years ago Jak Kamhi narrowly escaped an assassination attempt by Iranian-backed Islamic terrorists. Three men were caught, tried and convicted, and are now serving long prison terms. Fundamentalist groups, believed tied to Iran, also killed a prominent secular journalist in Turkey.

Iran

Although its population is overwhelmingly Shi'ite Muslim, Iran is a non-Arab country and under the Shah pursued a pro-American orientation and avoided direct involvement in the Arab-Israel conflict, although it did support Palestinian nationalism at the United Nations. Iran had granted de facto recognition to Israel in 1950, maintained extensive commercial relations with Israel for whom it was a major oil supplier, and close but discreet political and intelligence ties with the Jewish state. Shared concern with the dangers of Soviet penetration into the region and expansionist Arab nationalism cemented Iranian-Israeli ties until the overthrow of the Shah by Ayatollah Khomeini and the establishment of the Islamic Republic. One of the first acts of the new regime on February 18, 1979, was to sever all formal relations with Israel and the large unofficial Israeli embassy building was ceremoniously handed over to Yasir Arafat to serve as the embassy of the Palestine Liberation Organization. Oil shipments to Israel were cancelled as was the direct air service that El Al Israel Airlines had long maintained between Teheran's Mehrabad Airport and Tel Aviv's Ben-Gurion Airport. This direct link had facilitated the free movement of Iranian Jews to and from the Jewish state. The Islamic Republic of Iran also severely restricted Jewish travel.

While the constitution of the Islamic Republic followed the Quran and recognized Judaism as a revealed religion and the Jews as a protected religious minority (*ahl-al-kitab* or "People of the Book"), the Khomeini regime adopted a virulently anti-Zionist ideology, labelled Israel the "illegitimate offspring" of the "Great

Satan" and the United States as the "godfather" of the "twin evils of Zionism and American imperialism," and called for armed struggle of the Islamic world to eradicate the State of Israel.

Since nearly every Iranian Jew had relatives who had emigrated to Israel and many Iranian Jews had visited Israel or had business connections with Israel or the United States, Iranian Jews felt themselves at risk despite assurances that Jews who were loyal to the Islamic Republic would not be harmed. Indeed, in the turbulent early years of the revolution Jews suffered from a reign of terror marked by the arrest and execution of eleven Jews including wealthy leaders of the community on trumped-up charges, the confiscation of much Jewish property, and the dismissal of Jews from government and university positions.

Many thousands of Jews emigrated in the turbulent period immediately before and after the overthrow of the Shah. From an estimated population of 75,000 to 80,000 in the days of the Shah, Iran's Jewish population has declined to probably less than 15,000 although the community insists it is still above 20,000.[16] Iran not only barred all travel to Israel, but tightened travel restrictions generally following the outbreak of the Iraq-Iran war in 1980, especially banning travel by all young boys and men subject to the draft for military service. In addition to the constant physical danger resulting from the frequent Iraqi aerial bombardment of Teheran and other population centers, for Iranian Jews the climate of insecurity was intensified by personal harassment, beatings, and torture for allegedly violating Islamic restrictions on alcohol or immodest dress, and arbitrary arrests for supporting "Zionism," often used as an excuse to extort money and confiscate property by the local revolutionary Islamic committees and Revolutionary Guards. It became increasingly difficult for Jews to obtain passports after a special passport office for non-Muslims was transferred from the prime minister's office to that of the public prosecutor. The ostensible reason was to bar those who were wanted for a crime, who owed taxes, or had illegally acquired property.

In 1982 a new statute was reportedly adopted making it illegal for children under the age of 12 to leave Iran. Jewish refugees from Iran said that this law was motivated by the desire of the mullahs to indoctrinate the youth in Islamic piety. Although Jewish schools were permitted to function, they were placed under the control of the Islamic committees, required to take in Muslim students, to remain open on the Sabbath, and Islamic religious instruction and anti-Zionist (and indeed anti-Semitic) materials were added to the curriculum. This virulent anti-Israel propaganda campaign continued even after the death of Khomeini. It even made its way into the postage stamps of the Iranian Republic. In 1988 a series of four stamps honoring "The Uprising of the Muslim People of Palestine" showed bearded young Palestinian men standing before a Star of David made of barbed wire, superimposed on a map of Palestine and the Dome of the Rock (the so-called Mosque of Omar). In 1991, to commemorate the United Nations International Year of the Child, the Islamic Republic of Iran issued a stamp showing a young boy in short pants hurling a stone that shatters a Star of David. Another stamp issued that year shows soldiers with bayonets marching into Palestine.

Although Judaism remains an officially recognized religion and synagogues function, there were reportedly attempts by Islamic militants to forcibly convert young Jews to Islam. This added to the fears of the Jewish community, who recalled that in an earlier intolerant period of Iranian history in the nineteenth century the entire Jewish population of Meshed had been forcibly converted under threat of death. (They secretly remained Jews and openly returned to Judaism in the twentieth century when the position of minorities improved under the more secular and pro-Western rule of the Pahlavi dynasty.)

The Exodus from Iran

The combination of physical danger and psychological terror prompted Jews to desperately seek ways of leaving the country. Some managed to circumvent the barriers to Jewish emigration by acquiring Christian or Muslim identity papers and passports. Thousands of other Iranian Jews seeking freedom risked imprisonment if caught and possible death, when they embarked on the arduous and hazardous journey over mountains and deserts to reach safety in neighboring countries. Successful refugees who managed to reach Turkey or Pakistan were permitted to move on to Austria and other destinations where they were aided by the American Jewish Joint Distribution Committee, the Jewish Agency, and other Jewish relief organizations to join their compatriots in the United States,

Europe, and Israel. At a press conference in New York on October 2, 1987, Austrian Foreign Minister Alois Mock revealed that between July 1983 and August 1987 Austria had given temporary asylum to 5,188 Jews fleeing Iran. He stressed that his government was proceeding "without asking too many questions of Iranian refugees and without publicizing individual cases" in order not to jeopardize the flow of refugees in the future or to endanger their relatives who remained behind.

While thousands of Iranian Jews went to Israel, the majority resettled in the United States, primarily in the Los Angeles area in California and on Long Island, New York. Among the early arrivals were relatives of wealthy Iranian Jews who, in the days of the Shah, had already sent their children for advanced education in the United States and had helped them establish professional and business careers. But many of those who followed in later years lacked the wealth or connections that would have facilitated their beginning a new life. Most had been robbed of their possessions and many came only with what little they could carry with them. "The people who are leaving now had really, really tried to stay," Bruce T. Leimsidor, director of the Hebrew Immigrant Aid Society in Vienna, told *New York Times* reporter James M. Markham in an interview on November 13, 1986. He added that about two-thirds of the recent refugees had been tortured or otherwise physically mistreated in Iran. "The people who are coming out now have really suffered," he said.

The *Times* report of increasing Jewish emigration from Iran came at a time that revelations appeared that Israel had served as an intermediary for shipping American weapons to Iran as part of a White House effort to secure the freedom of American hostages being held in Lebanon by pro-Iranian terrorists and to open a channel for improved communication with allegedly "moderate" elements in Teheran. In view of the State of Israel's commitment to protect and, if necessary, to rescue endangered Jewish communities abroad, it was speculated that in addition to the obvious Israeli strategic interest in preventing its avowed enemy Iraq from defeating Iran, the Israeli arms sale was also intended to induce Teheran to end the harassment of the Jewish community and remove the travel restrictions. An unnamed senior Israeli official was quoted by Markham as denying that the increased emigration was tied to the arms deal. "This whole story," the official said, "has nothing to do with all the reports regarding arms and hostages." While some believe the Israeli contacts did help persuade Iranian border guards to turn a blind eye to the "illegal" departure of Jews, others noted that there was in fact an increase in the harassment of the Jewish community in Iran at this time. Some interpret this crackdown on the Jewish community as a calculated response by the Iranian officials implicated in the arms deal to counter the allegations of militant Islamic opponents that they were yielding to American or Zionist pressure.

After a cease-fire brought an end to hostilities with Iraq in 1988, Iran began to ease its travel restrictions. President Ali Akbar Hashemi Rafsanjani, who won reelection to a second four-year term in 1993, sought to rebuild Iran's war-shattered economy and reestablish economic relations with the West, and consequently some Iranian Jewish businessmen were able to travel to the United States and Europe. But entire families are generally not permitted to travel together and there are severe restrictions on how much money departing travellers may take with them. In recent years not only passports but also identity cards and licenses for business have listed the applicant's religion. Jewish businessmen from Iran complain that their identification as Jews combined with a concerted government campaign discouraging Muslims from either buying from or selling to Jews has significantly hurt their businesses and also has made it difficult to dispose of property. This is in addition to the economic hardship that Jews share with the rest of the population because of the country's economic problems. The Iranian government's efforts to attract Western-educated professionals who emigrated to return has generally been unsuccessful, since the political and social climate remains repressive.

Iran's Militant Hostility to Israel

The regime officially maintains its militant Islamic ideology, manifested not only in restrictions on the rights of women and persecution of the Bahai, but also in its foreign policy including support for the Hizbollah (Party of God) in southern Lebanon and other Islamic guerrilla groups that reject Israel's right to exist and actively oppose the current Arab-Israeli peace negotiations. Although Rafsanjani comes from a well-known commercial family, was reputedly a key figure in the American-Israeli arms deal, and is considered to be more pragmatic and realistic than the ideologically-rigid followers of Khomeini, Professor Ruhollah K. Ramazani has noted that when he was Speaker of the Iranian *Majlis*, Hojatolislam Hashemi-Rafsanjani joined with the more radical forces who wished "to extend the struggle against Israel to the entire Muslim world." In one of his speeches to the parliament, Rafsanjani declared: "The means of eradicating the Zionist regime and the establishment of another government to replace it in Palestine lie in massing all powers of the Islamic world, foremost of which will be the capabilities of the Islamic Republic of Iran, Syria, Libya and Algeria."[17] On May 5, 1989, during a national day of support for the Palestinian cause, Rafsanjani publicly called on Palestinians to kill "five Americans, or Britons or Frenchmen" in retaliation for every "Palestinian martyr" in occupied Palestine. He also urged them to blow up factories, hijack airplanes, and harm other American interests. He attacked Arafat for agreeing to Israel's right to exist and for renouncing terrorism. Although Rafsanjani later withdrew his call for killing Western supporters of Israel, the Iranian populace who heard his sermon broadcast on Teheran Radio might have taken it as encouragement for vigilante action against Jews regarded as supporters of Israel.

Reports in 1993 that Iran was actively seeking to obtain a nuclear capability and that both Iran and Syria were purchasing long-range Scud missiles and other advanced weapons from North Korea and China aroused concern in Washington and Jerusalem. They did not share the sanguine view of some Europeans that the Iranian efforts were essentially defensive in nature and prompted by Teheran's concern over the rapid rebuilding of Iraq's military capacity under an unrepentant and unpredictable Saddam Hussein. Israeli Prime Minister Yitzhak Rabin went so far as to declare that Iran, in its vigorous support of Islamic fundamentalism, constituted the main danger to peace and stability in the Middle East. Addressing Israel Bond leaders in Jerusalem on August 15, 1993, Rabin warned that if Iran continued to arm itself at the current rate, it would become the most serious threat to Israel's security within seven to ten years.

Unless there is a significant change in Iranian policy, the present climate of suspicion and animosity between Teheran and Jerusalem does not auger well for the long-term safety and security of the remaining Jewish communities in Iran, which today are concentrated in Teheran, Shiraz, and Isfahan. The Jews in the provincial cities feel even more vulnerable than those in the capital. According to Iranian Jewish emigres, in 1986 a Mrs. Nosrat Goel was executed in Shiraz on charges of Zionism, one day after her arrest. In 1989, a Mr. Shamsa was executed there on the same charge, and in 1991 Yousef Hashimeyreti was tortured to death in Shiraz, under suspicion of Zionism. In May 1992, Feyzollah Mechubad, the 75-year-old shamash of a synagogue in Teheran was arrested and held in Evin prison. The Jewish community reportedly was told that his release could be obtained by a payment of 30 million tuman (approximately $1 million). Before the community could complete raising this extortionate ransom sum, he was charged with illegal contacts with Israel, to which he confessed under extreme torture. He subsequently recanted his confession but was executed on February 25, 1994, on Purim, at the age of 77, even though Iranian law forbids execution of persons over 75. An autopsy revealed extensive signs of torture, including gouging of both his eyes. It is presumed that he was killed in retaliation for the massacre of Muslim worshippers at the Ibrahimi Mosque/Tomb of the Patriarchs in Hebron that had been perpetrated earlier that morning by Dr. Baruch Goldstein. Three other Jews have been executed in recent years for allegedly criminal activities, but it is not clear whether their Jewishness was a factor. These executions, while infrequent, have had the desired effect of terrorizing the Jewish community. Adding to their fears has been the occasional publication of blatantly anti-Semitic articles in the press. On the occasion of the publication of the book "Blood for the Holy Matzoth" by Najib Alkilani, which recounts the infamous blood libel in Damascus in 1840, the major Teheran evening daily *Keyhan* on December 31, 1992, carried a lengthy article by Mohammed Reza Alvand, entitled "Israel Must Be Destroyed." The entire article was filled with vicious anti-Jewish statements, blaming Israel and Zionism for all the world's evils, including the Serbian crimes against the Bosnian Muslims. He concluded with a warning to his readers: "This race and tribe, which is human only in appearance, are so seditious that Allah has ordered us to be constantly on the alert and to ensnare them. The machinations of Zionism in the continuation of Colonialism, Imperialism, Communism and finally in the 'new world order' are still alive and thriving." The Jewish community wrote a rebuttal to this article, which was printed only two weeks later after intervention by the President of the Parliament and the Jewish representative, who feared that fanatic Muslims might see this as justification for a pogrom.

Iran's official anti-Israel militancy has not diminished. During nationwide rallies on February 10, 1997, to mark the 18th anniversary of Iran's Islamic revolution, more than 100,000 men and women marched in Teheran cheering and brandishing posters of Ayatollah Khomeini. They chanted the trademark slogans of the revolution: "Death to America" and "Death to Israel."[18]

Cooperation of Iranian and Turkish Islamists

The increasingly close ties between the Islamist Prime Minister of Turkey and the Iranian regime has also begun to worry the Jews and secularist elite in Turkey. Erbakan warmly embraced President Rafsanjani when he visited him in Teheran in August 1996. When Rafsanjani reciprocated with a visit to Ankara a few months later, he pointedly broke with protocol and refused to lay a wreath at Atatürk's mausoleum. Rafsanjani's daughter, who accompanied him, incensed Turkish secularists when she commented that the popular mood she found in Ankara reminded her of Teheran in the last days before the fall of the Shah. In February 1997, several hundred people jammed a hall in Sinjan, a working class suburb of Ankara, to celebrate "Jerusalem Day," a holiday proclaimed by Khomeini 17 years ago. The host was the local Refah party mayor and the guest of honor was the Iranian Ambassador, Muhammed Reza Bagheri. When Bagheri arrived, the crowd erupted with chants of "Down with Israel! Down with Arafat!" to signify their opposition to any negotiated compromise by the Palestinians with Israel. This was consistent with the fundamental opposition to the existence of Israel on Islamic theological grounds expounded by the late Ayatollah Ruhollah Khomeini. On January 22, 1979, on the eve of his triumphant return to Tehran, Khomeini told a reporter for *Der Spiegel* that his Islamic Republic would break all relations with Israel "because we do not believe there is any legal justification for its existence. Palestine belongs to the Islamic space and must be returned to the Muslims." This reflects the classical Islamic theory that the world is divided into *Dar al-Islam* (the Abode of Islam) and *Dar al-Harb* (the Abode of War). It is the duty of Muslims to extend the frontiers of Islam until it covers the entire world. The more immediate theological imperative is to regain former Muslim territories for Islam, such as Lebanon and Israel, which had come under Christian or Jewish rule. At the February 1997 meeting in the outskirts of Ankara, the Iranian ambassador went on to deliver a fiery speech demanding that all Muslims in the world obey the *Sharia* (Islamic law) and urged his Turkish listeners to "wait no longer" before establishing an Islamic regime. In response, the military ordered tanks to roll through the streets of Sincan.[19]

This was a clear warning to Erbakan and his supporters that their patience was wearing thin. It should be recalled that on September 6, 1980, a demonstration by Erbakan supporters in the Islamic fundamentalist stronghold of Konya, ostensibly to protest Israel's Jerusalem Law, degenerated into calls for the restoration of the *Sharia* and the burning of American and Israeli flags. For the secularist military leaders this was the last straw at a time when Turkey was racked by extremist right and left violence. Six days later the military took control, banned political parties, and arrested their leaders. Erbakan was tried but not convicted of violating the constitutional ban on religious parties. After a new constitution was drafted, the military returned to their barracks and multi-party politics resumed in 1983. Iranian involvement in pro-Palestinian and anti-Israeli demonstrations in Turkey in 1987 and 1988, as well as the distribution of pamphlets by Iranians in Turkey in Turkish and English calling Atatürk an atheistic "scoundrel," led to official protests by the Turkish authorities at the time.[20]

After Erbakan's Welfare Party won major municipal elections in 1994 in Istanbul and Ankara, I asked an elderly Jewish man in Izmir what would happen if the Islamic fundamentalists won the next general election. He whispered to me in Hebrew, "*Nitztarech kullanu livroach*" (We will all have to flee). While the Refah party came in first in the multi-party elections in December 1995, it only won slightly over 21 percent of the vote. A significant majority of Turks continued to support the secular parties. Although recent public opinion polls indicate that as a result of popular disgust with the corruption and incompetence of the existing parties, the Refah support may now be over 30 percent, the Jewish community has not yet fled, although their level of anxiety has increased. However, the increasing influence of the Muslim-oriented Welfare Party and Erbakan's proclaimed efforts to reverse the longstanding Kemalist

Western dress reform, by calling for the lifting of restrictions on women wearing veils or head scarves in the civil service and on public university campuses, have led to a backlash. In mid-February 1997, thousands of Turkish citizens, about two-thirds of them women, marched through the streets of Ankara carrying banners and shouting slogans such as: "Down with Sharia" and "Women's Rights are Human Rights."[21]

Recent Positive Developments in Turkey and Iran

Turkish women and members of the Jewish community were not the only ones growing increasingly concerned by the signs that Prime Minister Erbakan and his Refah Party were seeking to Islamize Turkish society and undermine the secularist principles and pro-Western orientation that were a hallmark of the modern Turkish Republic established by Mustafa Kemal Atatürk. The leaders of the armed forces, who see themselves as guardians of the Kemalist reforms, have also been in the vanguard of the efforts to broaden and deepen Turkey's strategic cooperation with Israel in all areas. It may be more than coincidental that on the day after his return from a precedent-setting visit to Israel on February 28, 1997, General Ismail Hakki Karadayi, Chief of the General Staff, presented a report to Turkey's National Security Council (NSC) stating that Islamist elements were threatening the country's stability and presenting a detailed list of 22 recommendations — read ultimatums — to block the pro-Islamic initiatives that Refah had been advocating.

The NSC communique declared that "destructive and separatist groups" were seeking to weaken Turkish democracy by "blurring the distinction between the secular and the anti-secular." The NSC had therefore decided that "no steps away from the contemporary values of the Turkish Republic" would be permitted, and further asserted that "in Turkey, secularism is not only a form of government but a way of life and the guarantee of democracy and social peace." Referring to the difficulties Turkey faced in its efforts to join the European Union — and no doubt also having in mind the concerns voiced by the United States and Israel — the NSC communique declared: "It is necessary to end all speculation which may lead to suspicions about our democracy and damage Turkey's image and prestige abroad" (*New York Times,* 2 March 1997). In addition to maintaining the ban on religious dress in universities and other public work places, the NSC communique called for the closure of certain Muslim retreats, curbs on the employment of religious fundamentalists in government, mandating eight years of public education and limiting clerical training schools to high school, and putting all Quranic courses under the Ministry of Education. When Erbakan balked at instituting the curbs on religious education, the pressures upon him mounted and he resigned in protest. Erbakan's efforts to form a new coalition failed and in July 1997 the parliament approved a new coalition of three centrist pro-secular parties under the leadership of Mesut Yilmaz of the Motherland Party. As a signal of its determination to expand ties with Israel, one of the first acts of the new government was to give final approval to the free trade agreement with Israel signed the previous year (*New York Times,* 19 July 1997). High ranking reciprocal visits of Turkish and Israeli defense officials have continued, and plans for additional weapons production as well as joint naval maneuvers together with elements of the U.S. Sixth Fleet are also being planned.

The new government and the Turkish courts have also vigorously pursued actions against those involved in Islamist and anti-Israeli excesses. An investigation is under way aimed at outlawing the Refah Party for its pro-Islamist policies, and on October 15, 1997, the Turkish state security court in Ankara sentenced Bekir Yildiz, the mayor of Sincan, who had organized the "Jerusalem Day" anti-Israel protest, to four years and seven months in prison for advocating an Islamic state and "provoking hatred and animosity among people by emphasizing differences of region, class, religion, or race." This was seen as a welcome development by the Turkish Jewish community.

The Turkish government had also declared the Iranian ambassador *persona non grata* and the Turkish ambassador to Tehran was also recalled. In an address at Columbia University on September 30, 1997, Iranian Foreign Minister Kamal Kharrazi declared: "Our relation with Turkey was mended as of last week when I and the Foreign Minister of Turkey met here in New York and decided to send back our ambassadors." Turkish Foreign Minister Ismail Cem agreed following Kharrazi's promise, which he reiterated at Columbia, that Iran believed that "respect for non-interference in domestic affairs should be the basis of bilateral relations."

In Iran itself the surprisingly large popular mandate — some 70 percent of the vote — received by Mohammed Khatami in the presidential election in June 1997 raised hopes that this more pragmatic, intellectually more open, and ideologically less rigid leader might free up the society and reopen contacts with the West. While this might improve the climate for the local Jewish community as well, there were no signs yet of a readiness to resume relations with Israel. In a conversation the author had with Foreign Minister Kharrazi following his address at Columbia University, the Iranian spokesman made it clear that while "promotion of cooperation stands at the heart of President Khatami's foreign policy," this did not extend to Israel, which the Iranians believed had unjustly taken Palestinian land and continued to pursue policies Iran opposed, i.e., "occupation, hegemony, humiliation, and aggression."

Reasons for the Emigration of Middle Eastern Jews

Of the more than one million Jews living in Muslim countries before 1948, fewer than 50,000 remain. If we exclude non-Arab Iran and Turkey, the change is even more stark — of the roughly 850,000 Jews in the Arab countries at the time of the creation of Israel, today fewer than 10,000 remain. In effect, they have voted with their feet. It should be noted that massive emigration has occurred even from Islamic countries where generally moderate and pro-Western rulers have tried to protect the Jewish community.

Why did they leave? One basic reason is that no one can predict when even the most benevolent regime may be overthrown by assassination, coup, or popular uprising. The rise of extremist Arab nationalism has led to several unsuccessful coups against King Hassan of Morocco. The resurgence of militant Islamic political movements in Algeria and the Sudan have greatly troubled their North African neighbors. Occasional local incidents of terrorism and vandalism have filled even these Jewish communities with foreboding. For example, on Simhat Torah in 1985, a Tunisian policeman sent to guard the synagogue in Djerba fired into the worshippers. He killed three and wounded a dozen more, supposedly inspired by Qadhaffi's radio broadcasts calling for the overthrow of pro-Western Tunisian and Moroccan regimes and killing Jews.

Jews have lived in the Arab-speaking countries of the Middle East and North Africa for millennia. Indeed, in certain countries such as Iraq, Yemen, and Morocco, Jewish communities can be traced back to the period of the first exile, following the destruction of the Temple by the Babylonians in 586 BCE.

Why did the overwhelming majority of the Jews in the Arab world "vote with their feet" and leave their homes during the past 50 years? For some there was the positive attraction of political Zionism: the rebuilding of an independent Jewish state in the Land of Israel. For others, such as the Yemenite Jews who were flown to Israel in "Operation Magic Carpet," the return to Zion on "the wings of eagles" appeared as the marvelous fulfillment of biblical prophecy and an age-old Jewish longing.

However, in the great majority of cases it was not so much the positive attraction of Israel or Western Europe — pull factors — but a combination of negative forces in their countries of residence — push factors — that impelled them to leave their homes, sometimes at great personal peril. A variety of historical forces had the cumulative effect of undermining and eroding the position of these communities. These historical forces were:

The Breakdown of the Ottoman Empire and Traditional Islamic Society

In the multi-ethnic and multi-religious Ottoman Empire — a "world state" of 400 years duration — Jews had enjoyed a large measure of autonomy in their communal and religious life. Sovereignty, however, and participation in the ruling elite were traditionally reserved for Muslims. Although Jews and Christians had a second class and inferior position in the Islamic order, they had a clearly defined status. Under benevolent rulers, Jews and other minorities enjoyed affluence and even achieved positions of prominence. Under fanatical or arbitrary rulers they were severely restricted and discriminated against, and at times of political instability suffered murder and pillaging at the hands of Muslim mobs.[22]

During the nineteenth and early twentieth centuries the Ottomans tried to reform their empire. Two attempts at constitutionalism, with Western encouragement, tried to broaden citizenship to include the minorities on an equal footing. But these attempts were resisted by traditional Islamic elements. They succeeded only in undermining the old Islamic basis of political stability and coexistence.[23]

The Domination of the Middle East by Western Colonial Powers and the Rise of Arab Nationalism

With the decay of Ottoman power in the nineteenth century, Britain, France, and Italy seized large areas of the Arab world, a task they completed at the end of World War I. From this time onward, Jews, as well as some of the Christian minorities, played a disproportionately large role in the commercial, professional, and administrative life of these countries. Their knowledge of Western languages, inculcated by the educational efforts of their Occidental co-religionists, and their commercial contacts abroad, facilitated ties between local Jews and the colonial powers.[24]

Local Arab nationalism developed in part as a reaction to foreign rule. Since Jews were visibly associated in trading and administrative relationships with the hated foreign rulers, especially in Iraq, Syria, and Egypt, it was simple for Arab nationalists to scapegoat Jews as tools of the imperialists. As proponents of a new educated, urban class, Arab nationalists were at times jealous of the wealth and position attained by some Jews in administrative and economic life. As they sought wealth and position for themselves through government channels, their policy of "Arabization" became a convenient justification for limiting and ultimately supplanting Jews in these places.

Resentment Over the Development of Jewish Nationalism and its Political Manifestation in the Zionist Movement

With the issuance of the Balfour Declaration on November 2, 1917, the awarding of the Mandate over Palestine to Britain after

World War I, and the subsequent increase in Jewish immigration to Palestine, Arabs within the Mandate and in the surrounding countries felt politically threatened. Zionist efforts increasingly clashed with Palestinian and pan-Arab nationalism. There was rioting in Palestine in 1921, 1929, and throughout the period of 1936-39. Pro-Palestinian sympathy in Arab countries led to demonstrations which sometimes spilled over into attacks on local Jews, as in Syria in 1936.

It should be noted that although a limited amount of Zionist activity — usually clandestine — took place among Middle Eastern Jewries in those years, it was neither widespread nor prevalent enough to warrant being called "Jewish provocation."

The Willingness of Political Movements and Unpopular Regimes to Scapegoat the Local Jews

The new Arab states, politically weak autocracies emerging from imperialist domination, would at times persecute their Jews, or allow others to do so, to divert public attention from their own failings in the political, military, and economic spheres. This trend reached a fever pitch directly after the unexpected defeat of the Arab armies in Palestine during the first Arab-Israeli war, but in some instances it began well before 1948. The chosen governmental methods of persecution were unjust arrests, imprisonment and torture, discriminatory legislation, confiscation of property, and agitation in the press and radio. Members of the Jewish communities were scapegoated as being Communist or Zionist (sometimes both), and imprisoned and despoiled of their property for belonging to these movements that were anathema to Arab regimes. Notorious examples of these practices occurred in Iraq during the 1940s, Egypt during the Nasser era, and Syria since its independence after World War II.

Moreover, pan-Arab and pan-Islamic parties and movements in almost every Arab state have fomented mob violence against Jews, in part to undercut the authority of these very same regimes, as well as in revenge for Israeli victories in the several Arab-Israeli wars. In Aleppo, Syria in 1947, much of the Jewish quarter was set ablaze. In 1948 bombs were found in numerous locations in the Jewish quarter of Damascus; in August 1949 more bombs in the same neighborhood killed and wounded scores. In Cairo in 1945 mobs in the Jewish quarter burned a synagogue, a hospital, and numerous homes and shops; on June 20, 1948, bombs in the Jewish quarter killed 34 and wounded 80. Reportedly 82 died in a riot in Aden in 1947. These are just a few of the examples that can be cited from this notorious and bloody catalogue.[25] As one European observer of these disturbances put it rather bluntly:

> Of all the non-Moslems the Jews are the safest targets. They are considered to be Europeans and as such any 'barefoot' Mohammedan is glad to shoot at them. They are not supported by a powerful empire and attacks on them do not create diplomatic incidents. Moreover, they are 'infidels,' which make them particularly attractive victims of the more fanatical Mohammedans. They are Jews, which satisfies those who are more specifically anti-Semitic.[26]

All these factors combined over the past century to weaken the traditional position of the Jewish communities in Arab lands. But it was the last set of factors, the state-sponsored discrimination and pogrom-like mob violence, that precipitated the rapid dissolution of these ancient Jewish communities. As a result of these events, the Jews of Arab countries in effect became political refugees, that is, persons who have a well-founded fear of persecution and who therefore fled untenable, often life-threatening, political situations in their countries of origin. Within a four-year period from 1948 to 1952, 127,000 Jews escaped from Iraq, almost 50,000 from Yemen and Aden, 36,000 from Libya, and perhaps another 100,000 from French-controlled North Africa. If we examine the events leading up to this mass flight, we can see how violence, discrimination and, in some cases, expulsion effected among these populations what was euphemistically called "whole community transfer." Today it would be called ethnic cleansing.

In Iraq, for example, a large Jewish community having roots dating back to biblical Babylonia was decimated in less than a year. Iraq provides us with a particularly illuminating case study of several of the trends listed above. In this country where a weak, unpopular monarchy installed by the British mandatory power in the 1930s faced subversion by radical pan-Arabist forces, violence and discrimination against Jews were rife from an early period, well before the establishment of the State of Israel. The most notorious example of this violence was the *Farhud* (breakdown of law and order), a two-day pogrom in Baghdad in June 1941. In a spasm of uncontrolled violence, between 170 and 180 Jews were killed, more than 900 others were wounded, and 14,500 Jews sustained material losses through the looting or destruction of their stores and homes.[27]

Although the Iraqi government eventually restored order, the general position of the Jewish community continued to deteriorate as anti-foreign sentiment mounted and Iraq and the states bordering Palestine — Egypt, Syria, Jordan, and Lebanon — became increasingly involved in the Arab-Jewish struggle. The creation of the League of Arab States in Cairo in early 1945 gave a new organizational framework for anti-Jewish measures in some of these states, which were now cloaked under statutes forbidding Zionism and Communism. Jews were squeezed out of government employment, limited in schools, and subjected to imprisonment, heavy fines, or sequestration of their property on the flimsiest charges of being connected to either or both of the two banned movements. Indeed, Communism and Zionism were frequently equated in the statutes.[28] In Iraq the mere receipt of a letter from a Jew in Palestine was sufficient to bring about arrest and loss of property.

In 1945, November 2nd — the anniversary of the Balfour Declaration — became the occasion for widespread rioting, murder, and destruction of synagogues and Jewish property in Aleppo, Syria; Cairo, Egypt; and Tripoli, Libya. It is interesting to note that the same pattern of violence against Jews first exhibited in Iraq had spread to Egypt, Syria, and North Africa. The Libyan Jewish community was particularly hard hit, losing 130 people in the Tripoli area in three days of wanton violence. As in the earlier *Farhud,* the pogrom had been fomented by extreme nationalist elements who were intent on undercutting the British occupation of the country. The British troops in control of Tripoli waited days before restoring order, with an unconcern reminiscent of their conduct in the Iraqi massacre. As in the Iraqi case, the Tripoli massacre inaugurated a train of events that would demoralize and in a relatively short time dissolve the Libyan Jewish community.[29]

The days before and after the adoption by the United Nations General Assembly on November 29, 1947, of a resolution recommending the partition of Palestine into independent Jewish and Arab states, triggered more violent incidents. These were accompanied by threats by Arab delegates from the rostrum of the United Nations itself that any action favorable to the Zionists would, in the words of Egyptian delegate Haykal Pasha, unleash "mob fury" beyond the capacity of the authorities to control. "Unconsciously," he warned, "you are on the verge of lighting a flame of anti-Semitism in the Middle East which would be more difficult to extinguish than it was in Germany."[30] These words were to prove prophetic.

After the first Arab-Israeli war broke out, the belligerent Arab governments lost all incentive to continue what little protection they had afforded their Jewish communities. Egypt, Syria, and Iraq took active measures against Jews under the guise of emergency regulations. Arrests, torture, and sometimes hangings of Jews, severe restrictions on travel, and sequestration or confiscation of Jewish property were imposed when these countries sent armies to prevent the establishment of the Jewish state on May 15, 1948. A climate of fear prevailed in these communities as sporadic attacks against Jews mounted.

After the defeat of the Arab armies and the establishment of Israel, illegal immigration of Jews from these countries increased until it became a flood. In the first years of Israel's existence, its government arranged a variety of rescue operations from these countries either extra-legally or with the Arab governments' tacit agreement. Operations "Ezra and Nehemiah" in Iraq and "Magic Carpet" in Yemen air-lifted many tens of thousands of Jews to their new homes. Jews from other countries fled through ports along the Mediterranean. Whatever their method of escape, Middle Eastern Jews were required to leave behind Jewish communal holdings, and their real property and immovable goods, which were taken over by their home governments. In the case of Iraq, where many Jews had been involved in banking and finance, liquid assets were also frozen.[31] The effect of these measures was that large numbers of Jewish refugees from Arab countries arrived in Israel penniless. The cost of bringing them and resettling them in Israel was estimated in 1987 as having exceeded $11 billion.[32]

It must be noted that certain Arab states or governments refrained from the discriminatory behavior manifested by their more belligerent counterparts and enacted measures to protect their Jewish communities. In these states, notably Morocco, but to a large extent also in Tunisia, the exodus was more gradual. The continued existence of the small but vital Moroccan Jewish community attests to the *modus vivendi* achieved by this state and its

Jews wherein Arab-Israeli problems were held separate from the relation of the state with its indigenous Jews.

The Jews that remained within the confines of other Arab states after the mass exodus of the late 1940s and early 1950s experienced periods of marked hardship, violence, and discrimination interspersed with periods of relative quiet, mirroring the ebb and flow of the Arab-Israeli conflict and the domestic political and economic situations. Iraq and Syria both saw frequent coups d'etat in the late 1950s and throughout the 1960s, which fostered a certain insecurity. Egypt, under the stable dictatorship of the pan-Arabist and Arab Socialist Gamal Abdul Nasser, set about expropriating and nationalizing Jewish property along with that of other Egyptian minorities. In truth, little difference can be discerned between the treatment of Jews in the so-called Socialist states of the period and that of the right-wing dictatorships. In Libya, where Jews had extracted guarantees of protection at the advent of independence under King Idris in 1952, restrictions on Jewish commerce, licenses, and holding of property were gradually imposed under nationalist pressure.

Meanwhile, the propaganda arms of the confrontation states (Syria, Egypt, Jordan, and Iraq), but particularly Nasser's influential *Sawt al-Arab min al-Kahira* (The Voice of the Arabs from Cairo), beamed anti-Israeli and anti-Jewish propaganda on the airwaves all across the Middle East. This inflammatory campaign reached unprecedented proportions in the weeks preceding the June 1967 war. In this poisoned atmosphere, when news came of the unexpected and swift Arab defeat by Israeli forces in the Six-Day War, mob violence broke out with riots against Jews in Libya, Syria, Tunisia, and Yemen. In Morocco and Tunisia the governments struggled to protect the Jews, but in Egypt and Syria the governments themselves unleashed fresh anti-Jewish measures. Cairo arrested some 500 Jewish men and held them for months in terrible conditions. They were told that they would be released only if they forfeited their citizenship and property and agreed to be expelled from Egypt. Riots in Libya were so severe that virtually all of the remaining Jews in the country — slightly more than 4,000 — were evacuated to Italy with the help of concerned Italian and American diplomats.[33] In a 1970 law nationalizing the assets of the Libyan Jews who had left, the Libyan government explicitly committed itself to issue fifteen-year bonds to pay full and fair compensation. Nevertheless, the July 21, 1985, deadline passed without any action by Colonel Muamar Qadhafi to fulfill this pledge. (Some Jews who had Italian citizenship received some compensation in the framework of a Libyan-Italian agreement.) The 1969 public hanging of nine Jews in Baghdad on trumped-up charges of spying for the United States, Israel, and Iran, the kidnapping and killing of nine Jews in Beirut in the mid-1980s by the pro-Iranian Shi'ite militant "Organization of the Oppressed," and the massacre of 22 Jewish worshippers in the Neve Shalom synagogue in Istanbul by Arab terrorists believed to belong to the Abu Nidal group, are three of the worst anti-Jewish acts in the Muslim countries of the Middle East since the 1967 war.

The Claims of Jews from Arab Lands and the Peace Process

At his opening address to the Madrid Peace Conference on October 31, 1991, Israeli Prime Minister Yitzhak Shamir demanded an end to the restrictions on the Jews of Syria and called upon Syria and the other Arab countries to permit their Jews to emigrate freely. In his response, Syrian Foreign Minister Faruk as-Sharaa denied Shamir's charges of discrimination and went on to wax poetic about the idyllic life Jews enjoyed in Arab lands: "The Arabs throughout their long history have always advocated peace, justice and tolerance....The Jews — and Oriental Jews in particular — know better than anyone that they have lived among Muslim Arabs throughout history, wherever they happened to coexist, without ever suffering any form of persecution or discrimination, neither racial nor religious." If there were any problems in recent decades, he contended, they all stemmed from the "Zionist invasion" into the region and its harmful impact upon the Palestinians.[34]

The Jews who have felt impelled to leave Arab countries since 1947 naturally consider themselves victims of the Middle East conflict and seek restitution for their confiscated properties — both personal and communal — from the governments involved. In this quest they have significant basis in international law, the United Nations Charter and conventions dealing with human rights. Indeed, the arbitrary decrees against Jews in many cases run counter to the fine principles enunciated in the much abused constitutions of their countries of origin.

From 1967 they have also received official United Nations recognition of their claims: United Nations Security Council Resolutions 237 and 242. Resolution 237, of 14 June 1967, concerns itself with the safety, welfare, and security of the inhabitants of the areas where military operations had taken place in the 1967 Arab-Israeli war and also with the protection of minorities in the states involved in the conflict. UN Secretary-General U Thant sent his special representative, Nils-Goran Gussing, on a special mission to the Middle East to implement the resolution. The Secretary-General stated expressly that the provisions of the resolution dealing with minorities "might properly be interpreted as having application to the treatment, at the time of the recent war and as a result of that war, of both Arab and Jewish persons in the States which are directly concerned because of their participation in that war."[35] The Israel government had expressed its concern about the treatment of Jewish minorities in the Arab states since the outbreak of hostilities.

Gussing met with officials of the Egyptian government and raised the subject of the treatment of the reported 500 Jewish prisoners and the confiscation of the property of Egyptian Jews. He also met with Syrian authorities to investigate the restrictions placed on the Jews of that country. Moreover, questions concerning Egyptian Jewry were taken up by the Secretary-General with the United Arab Republic's (Egypt) permanent representative to the UN in New York. In Egypt, officials denied that the UN resolution applied to Jews who were Egyptian citizens, while Syrian officials claimed that the Jewish minority was "treated in exactly the same way as other Syrian citizens," and that the special restrictions on movement were for "security reasons."

United Nations Security Council Resolution 242, unanimously adopted on November 22, 1967, was accepted by the parties to the Madrid Peace Conference as the agreed basis for resolving the Arab-Israel conflict. The interpretation and implementation of the provisions calling for withdrawal of Israeli armed forces from territories occupied in the 1967 war in exchange for Arab recognition of Israel's right to exist within secure and recognized borders and a formal end to their belligerence have received most of the public attention. However, Resolution 242 also states that a comprehensive peace should necessarily also include "a just settlement of the refugee problem." Justice Arthur Goldberg, the American delegate who was instrumental in drafting the resolution, publicly declared that the adjective "Palestinian" or "Arab" was deliberately omitted from the resolution to indicate that the claims of the Jewish refugees from Arab lands need also to be addressed. Israel has refrained from calling the Jewish immigrants from Arab lands "refugees," arguing that since they have been welcomed and integrated into their ancestral homeland they are no longer refugees. Indeed, with the exception of two families who returned to Iraq, none of the hundreds of thousands of Jews who left the Arab countries of the Middle East and North Africa are known to have responded to the offers of Colonel Qadhafi of Libya or Saddam Hussein of Iraq to return.

Among the multilateral working groups established under the Madrid framework, one is dealing with the refugee issue. At these meetings the United States delegation has reiterated that the position stated by Ambassador Goldberg continues to be United States policy and has begun to compile data on Jewish financial claims, as has the State of Israel.[36] This issue is also likely to be brought up in the context of the final status talks between Israel and the Palestinian authority where the PLO will press for the repatriation or compensation for Palestinians who became refugees in 1948 or were displaced as a result of the 1967 conflict. Until all the states of the Middle East become full-fledged democracies, the United States, Israel, and other free states must continue their humanitarian efforts to assure the freedom to emigrate as well as protecting basic rights of the small Jewish minorities who may choose to remain in the Muslim countries of the Middle East and North Africa.

Conclusion

What are the lessons from this survey of the decline and exodus of Middle Eastern Jewry? As in other migrations there was usually a combination of negative economic and/or political changes at home and positive opportunities abroad. To leave one's native land is always a wrenching experience and unless persecution or economic privation makes life intolerable, it is unlikely that entire families or communities will voluntarily leave. Where the main stimulus was greater educational and professional opportunity abroad, it was usually the younger males who would first venture abroad. If they were successful and conditions were favorable in the home country, they might return and put their new skills to work in the family business. However, if economic or political conditions deteriorated at home, as they did in Iran after the fall of the Shah, or Algeria at the time of the independence struggle against the French, the educated vanguard overseas, whether in the United States, France, or Canada, served as a magnet for their families, providing them with opportunities and a legal basis for immigration.

It took exceptional pressures and stresses for entire Jewish communities to move all at one time, including the aged and infirm. This was either the result of forced expulsion, as Egypt imposed after the wars of 1956 and 1967, or in official or tacit agreements reached between the Arab states and representatives of Israel, as in the case of Yemen, Iraq, and some North African governments. Depending on the legal and political circumstances, emigrants from the Middle East did not always remain in their first country of asylum. Thus, Syrian Jews were permitted to leave only on the promise that they would not travel to Israel, with which Damascus was still formally at war. Consequently, when permission to leave was finally granted, nearly all first came to the United States, although, as noted above, about half have since moved on to Israel. Conversely, many Jews fleeing from Arab countries and the Islamic Republic of Iran first went to Israel, which was always ready to receive them, and then some went on to the United States or Western European countries, which had more restrictive immigration policies. In some ways this paralleled the experience of Jewish emigrants from the former Soviet Union.

The pattern of migration to Israel from the Turkish Republic was, in some ways, closer to that from the United States than from the Arab countries in that both Turkish and American Jews had, and still have, the option of travelling freely back and forth. Thus, changing factors such as economic boom or recession in Turkey, Israel, and the United States, the political climate, and the likelihood of being drafted into military service have had a bearing on whether Turkish Jewish families have moved to Israel or returned to Turkey or moved on to the United States. During a recent trip to the Museum of Immigration at Ellis Island, this author found the following explanation given by Sarah Asher Crespi, a Jewish girl who came to the United States from Turkey in 1913 at the age of ten: "If I stayed in Europe I wouldn't be married. You had to have a lot of money to give a dowry. Over here my husband didn't want any. Here you work. You work together" (interviewed by the Ellis Island Oral History Project, 1991). This was exactly the same reason I was given in Istanbul in 1960 to explain why poorer Turkish Jews had sent their daughters to Israel after 1948. Both the United States, before the restrictive immigration laws of the 1920s, and the young State of Israel represented progressive, egalitarian societies eager to welcome immigrants to build their nation.

The role of economic factors and the desire to live in a free society were similar to the factors that motivated Irish and Italian non-Jewish migration to the United States. Interestingly, as the economy of the Irish Republic has recently been booming, Irish-Americans are beginning to return to the motherland. To a lesser extent this has also occurred among Italian-Americans. The Moroccan and Tunisian Jews who maintain homes both in their native towns as well as in France or Canada reflect a somewhat similar phenomenon. Yet, as noted above, it is highly unlikely given present circumstances that significant numbers of Jews will return permanently to the Arab world. Bitter experience has taught them that Jewish life will remain precarious in the absence of well-rooted democratic institutions. Those Jews who remain are fearful because of the vulnerability of existing regimes to overthrow, and the ever-present danger of anti-Jewish violence resulting from the outbreak of xenophobic nationalism, social upheaval, or militant Islamic fundamentalism.

Notes

1. For details on the long and ultimately successful struggle to bring about the right for Syrian Jews to leave, see George E. Gruen, *Syria, Syrian Jews, and the Peace Process* (New York: American Jewish Committee, International Perspectives Series, June 1992).
2. Personal conversation, May 9, 1996, in Washington.
3. George E. Gruen, "Jews in the Middle East and North Africa," *American Jewish Year Book 1994*, vol. 94 (New York: American Jewish Committee), pp. 438-464. Developments in Yemen are on pp.

439-442. The May 1994 civil war ended with a victory by the north and the reunification of the country by year's end. Following the end of the fighting, Jewish emigration resumed. There were no Jews in the south, the last having left Aden when the British pulled out in the late 1960s.

4. The following section draws upon the more detailed and comprehensive review of developments over the past decade contained in the author's above-cited 1994 article in the *American Jewish Year Book* [*AJYB*]. For a review of developments from 1977 through 1984, see Lois Gottesman, "Jews in the Middle East," *AJYB, 1985*, pp. 304-323.

5. Latest population estimates on Jews in the Middle East and North Africa provided to the author on February 11, 1997, by Linda Levy of the American Jewish Joint Distribution Committee.

6. Statement by Foreign Minister Abdelkarim al-Iryani to the Associated Press, quoted in Gruen, "Jews in the Middle East," p. 442.

7. For details, see George Gruen, "The 'Oppressed on Earth' and their Jewish Victims, *Jerusalem Post*, 5 September 1989.

8. Joseph Matar, "The 17th Sect: Neither War nor Kidnappings have Driven Out the Last of Lebanon's Jews," *Jerusalem Report*, 24 October 1991, pp. 36-38.

9. Edward C. Clark, "The Turkish *Varlik Vergisi* Reconsidered," *Middle Eastern Studies*, 1972, pp. 205-216. See also the dispatches from Turkey filed by C.L. Sulzberger and published in the *New York Times*, September 9-12, and the editorial in the paper, "The Turkish Minorities," September 17, 1943. Karen Alexandra Leal reviews the literature and assesses the impact of the law on minorities, with special attention to the Greek Orthodox community, in "The *Varlik Vergisi*: An Ottoman Legacy for Republican Turkey and Its Minorities," unpublished term paper for a Columbia University School of International and Public Affairs course on Turkey in World Politics (U6648), December 31, 1996.

10. For details, see George E. Gruen, "Dynamic Progress in Turkish-Israeli Relations," *Israel Affairs*, vol. 1, no. 4 (Summer 1995):40-70.

11. See, for example, the speech by Erbakan, who then headed the National Salvation Party, to the Assembly on December 11, 1970, quoted by Geoffrey Lewis in *Modern Turkey,* 4th ed. (New York: Praeger, 1974), p. 195.

12. Stephen Kinzer, "Secular Turks Alarmed by Resurgence of Religion," dispatch from Sincan, Turkey, *New York Times*, 13 February 1997.

13. Stephen Kinzer, "Turkish Aide Seeks to Shed Image of Islamic Militancy," dispatch from Ankara, *New York Times*, 8 February 1997.

14. Reuters dispatch from Washington, 12 February 1997. She testified before the House Appropriations subcommittee that handles foreign affairs funding.

15. George E. Gruen, "Turkish-Israeli Relations: Crisis or Continued Cooperation?" *Jerusalem Letter*, no. 338 (15 July 1996), Jerusalem Center for Public Affairs.

16. On the longstanding difficulties in obtaining accurate statistics concerning Iranian Jews and the political and security issues involved, see Gruen, "Jews in the Middle East and North Africa," *AJYB, 1994*, p. 443. On the period prior to 1985, see Gottesman, *AJYB, 1985*, pp. 318-320.

17. Cited in Ruhollah K. Ramazani, *Revolutionary Iran: Challenge and Response in the Middle East* (Baltimore and London: Johns Hopkins University Press, 1988), pp. 154-155.

18. Reuters dispatch from Teheran, 10 February 1997.

19. Kinzer, "Secular Turks Alarmed...," *New York Times*, 12 February 1997.

20. George E. Gruen, "Turkey Between the Middle East and the West," *The Middle East from the Iran-Contra Affair to the Intifada*, ed. Robert O. Freedman (Syracuse: Syracuse University Press, 1991), pp. 393-397.

21. Stephen Kinzer, "Turks March in Campaign to Preserve Secularism," dispatch from Ankara, *New York Times*, 16 February 1997.

22. A discussion of Ottoman history vis-s-vis Jews can be found in Bernard Lewis, *The Jews of Islam* (Princeton: Princeton University Press, 1984). Jewish life in the Arab world from the time of Muhammad to the mid-nineteenth century is chronicled by Norman A. Stillman in *The Jews of Arab Lands* (Philadelphia: Jewish Publication Society of America, 1979) and a second volume which chronicles and documents events through the 1967 Six-Day War, *The Jews of Arab Lands in Modern Times* (1991).

23. See Elie Kedourie, "The Failure of Constitutionalism in the Middle East," in *Arabic Political Memoirs and Other Studies* (London: Frank Cass, 1974).

24. See, for instance, Nissim Rejwan, *The Jews of Iraq: 3000 Years of History and Culture* (London: Weidenfeld and Nicolson, 1985). The experience of Iraqi Jews serves as a useful paradigm of these trends. On North African Jewry, see the works of Michael M. Laskier, especially *The Jews of Egypt, 1920-1970: In the Midst of Zionism, Anti-Semitism and the Middle East Conflict* (New York: New York University Press, 1992) and *North African Jewry in the Twentieth Century: The Jews of Morocco, Tunisia, and Algeria* (New York: New York University Press, 1994).

25. In addition to the Stillman volumes cited above, a general history of the treatment of Middle Eastern Jews by Arab states appears in Hayyim J. Cohen, *The Jews of the Middle East, 1860-1972* (Jerusalem: Israel Universities Press, 1973), especially pp. 14-67.

26. Victoria d'Asprea, as quoted in Nehemiah Robinson, *The Arab Countries of the Near East and their Jewish Communities* (New York: World Jewish Congress, 1951), p. 53.

27. For a more detailed discussion of what triggered the outbreak and why the British forces failed to intervene to stop the violence, see George E. Gruen, *The Other Refugees: Impact of Nationalism, Anti-Zionism and the Arab-Israel Conflict on the Jews of the Arab World*, report prepared for the Third International Conference of the World Organization of Jews from Arab Lands, Washington, D.C., October 26-28, 1987 (subsequently referred to as WOJAC Report). A revised version of this report was published as *Jerusalem Letter*, no. 102 (1 June 1988), Jerusalem Center for Public Affairs.

28. Discriminatory legislation against Jews in Arab states is documented by Ya'akov Meron, "The 'Complicating' Element of the Arab-Israeli Conflict," *Indian Socio-Legal Journal* (1977).

29. An excellent history of the Jews of Libya, including the events listed here, is Renzo De Felice, *Jews in an Arab Land: Libya, 1835-1970* (Austin: University of Texas Press, 1985).

30. Statement on November 24, 1947, cited in S. Lanshut, *Jewish Communities in the Muslim Countries of the Middle East* (London: Jewish Chronicle, 1950), p. 33.

31. The details of these confiscations are described in Abbas Shiblak, *The Lure of Zion: The Case of the Iraqi Jews* (London: Al Saqi Books, 1986).

32. See Yehuda Dominitz, *Aliya and Absorption of Jews from Arab Countries* (New York: American Jewish Committee and World Organization of Jews from Arab Countries, 1987) (in Hebrew). Dominitz, who headed the Jewish Agency department dealing with aliya from countries of distress, estimates that Israel spent $11 billion to transport and resettle the Jews from Arab lands.

33. A detailed analysis of the impact of the 1967 war on Jews in Arab countries may be found in Abraham S. Karlikow, "Jews in Arab Countries," *American Jewish Year Book*, 1968.

34. For examples of Jewish counterpolemics, emphasizing the discrimination to which Jewish and Christian minorities in the Arab world were subjected, see the works of Bat Ye'or (pseud. of Egyptian-born Giselle Littman), notably *The Dhimmi: Jews and Christians Under Islam* (Rutherford, N.J.: Fairleigh Dickinson University Press/London: Associated University Presses, 1985) and *The Decline of Eastern Christianity Under Islam: From Jihad to Dhimmitude, Seventh-Twentieth Century* (Madison/Teaneck, N.J.: Fairleigh Dickinson Press/London: Associated University Presses, 1996), as well as Joan Peters, *From Time Immemorial* (New York: Harper & Row, 1984). A more

restrained tone is to be found in the works by Norman Stillman, Bernard Lewis, and other scholars cited above.

35. Report of the Secretary-General under General Assembly Resolution 2252 (ES-V) and Security Council Resolution 237 (1967), p. 59.
36. Before the Ottawa meetings of the refugee working group, the author was contacted by the State Department and requested to furnish its delegation with information on this subject.

17

Jewish on Three Continents: Reflections of a Two-Time Migrant

Ernest Stock

In Jewish history, which is almost by definition group history —
social, religious, and also political — migration has played a
seminal role. Haim Potok has called his historical novel simply
Wanderings. Even though the story of that archetypical wanderer,
Abraham, is that of an individual, his personal fate and experience
merged with the people's fate and, in general, the Scriptures use
personal experience as paradigmatic of the group's experience. The
Tanach is not so much interested in the psychological consequence
of the experience for the individual as such, as in his moral reaction
to the experience, with its implications and consequences for the
group.

In our generation, migration is again a primary factor in the
Jewish experience. On the group level it has been well charted and
documented; on the individual level less so, even though we now
have the tools to understand it, and there is also far more interest in
individual psychology than there was in the past.

There are, however, limits to the relevance of the historical
aspect to more recent experience. Until the Emancipation, the
Jewish migrant, no matter how much on the move, still remained
within the Jewish community where he was rooted far more deeply
than in the surrounding culture. The Torah was his fatherland. Our

migrants in the present, or the recent past, are much more like Abraham, who had to totally uproot himself from his home environment.

I offer here my own experience as a migrant, not only for its anecdotal interest, but also as a possible contribution to the methodology of the study of migration. While the title describes a two-time migrant, perhaps a more cogent term might be multiple, or multi-stage migration. In my case there were actually three stages: intra-Europe (Germany to France); Europe-U.S.A., and ultimately U.S.A.-Israel. In each stage Jewishness was the primary motivating factor.

In Israel, the land of immigration par excellence, the conventional wisdom has it that there are two types of migration depending on the country of origin: one from "lands of distress" and the other from the free countries or, in Jewish Agency parlance, the Western countries. At one time — this just as a gloss, for the historians — the machinery for dealing with the Western immigrants was separate from that handling the mass immigration from the countries of distress (mainly North Africa, the Soviet bloc, and peripheral third world countries, from Libya to India). The latter type was dealt with by the Jewish Agency proper, the former by the World Zionist Organization. The reason for the division had to do with the legal restrictions placed on funds raised by UJA in the U.S.: to be entitled to tax exemption, they had to be used for philanthropic purposes. Migration from "areas of distress" certainly met these criteria, whereas movement from prosperous lands such as the U.S. did not qualify as philanthropy. Therefore, separate Immigration Departments were maintained by the Jewish Agency and the World Zionist Organization.

My two "wanderings" were of both kinds — Germany was then surely a land of distress — indeed, the UJA as we know it was founded in the wake of *Kristallnacht*, which also was the immediate cause for my leaving Germany. The move from the U.S. to Israel did not qualify under that rubric, though the motivation here was hardly less Jewish. In retrospect, it is clear to me that the entire course of my life was determined by those twin, intertwined factors: migration and Jewishness.

Drawing some generally applicable conclusions from that personal experience, I see an important variable in the age at which migration takes place. When leaving the home culture at fourteen, as I did, one's ideas about the world are still half-baked, and they are reformed in the new country as part of one's adjustment there. The young migrant may then go through life with unrealistic notions, such as being in a land of unlimited opportunities. In some cases this may even become self-fulfilling: *vide* the career of Henry Kissinger. Repeating the transition from one culture to another at a later stage may produce somewhat of a mish-mash in the adult personality and keep it from jelling into a coherent whole, perhaps least of all into an Israeli.

If there are pitfalls for the younger migrant, how much more hazardous must be the uprooting for the average adult personality, necessitating a complete changing of gears, culturally, linguistically, and often occupationally. Reading skills in the new language may remain permanently deficient. I myself feel handicapped by my inability to read Hebrew at the same speed as my earlier languages; my Hebrew reading remains limited to newspapers and other "essential" material.

On the asset side, the wider range of experience may make for a broader basis for assessing the nature of Jewishness in its different settings; comparing Jewish communal life and institutions. That in turn may lead to a more objective and possibly more critical perception.

Now for some highlights of my own experience. Concerning the pre-migration period in Germany: the nearly six years I spent there as a youngster during the Hitler period were by no means all negative in the Jewish sense. The Nazi challenge led to a strengthening of Jewish consciousness not only on the individual level, but also on the group and communal levels. Assimilation was no longer an option, as there was no escaping Jewish identity. In many cases this aroused a kind of defiant pride: *"Tragt ihn mit Stolz den gelben Fleck"* ("Wear it with pride, the yellow badge").[1] At the risk of idealizing the period, I would even characterize it as a golden age of German Judaism, especially in institutional and communal development. This includes the press, education (I attended a day school that was extraordinarily effective in both general and Jewish subjects), cultural life (I got my first taste of opera at the performances of the *Kulturbund,* the Jewish Institute for the Performing Arts),[2] as well as outstanding personalities (some of them in the pulpit). Nevertheless, it was all a dangerous delusion if it kept people from drawing the right conclusions and get out while this was still possible — as my own father failed to do. But it is evidence that a doomed community is capable of drawing on unsuspected resources to call forth a final, poignant flowering.

As to the impact of anti-Semitism: there can be no question but that the German variety was the most virulent kind — official policy enacted into racist laws and degenerating into mass murder. (I try to avoid use of the term "Holocaust" because I see in it a euphemism for the most heinous crimes imaginable). But to the German Jews of the period the impact of anti-Semitism was buffered because it was a group libel. Moreover, it was not a new phenomenon. We grew up knowing that anti-Semitism was rife among our neighbors, so that the Nazi use of it was more a matter of degree than a sudden shock. (The term "anti-Semitism" was not part of our vocabulary. German Jews had long used their own codeword for it: they called it *rishes* [Judeo-German for wickedness] and continued to do so under the Nazis.)

My contemporaries and I looked at the *Stuermer,* the current issue of which was posted at strategic street corners, with a kind of prurient curiosity: about half of it was devoted to *Rassenschande* (racial abuse, the Nazis' term for sexual relations between a non-Jewish and Jewish partner). We were also fascinated by the quasi-scientific theories on race the others learned about in school, measuring skulls in accordance with a primitive anthropology and studying about a hierarchy of races in which the Jews were at the bottom.

I cannot recall whether I was hurt more by not being admitted to membership in the Hitler Youth, with their snazzy belts and uniforms, to which all the other boys on the street belonged, or by the fact that my close friend and neighbor informed me somewhat sheepishly that he was not allowed to play with me anymore. Probably the latter, because when he phoned me years later in New York, I curtly told him I was too busy to see him.

But I doubt whether the *rishes* caused any deep psychic hurt, because of the collective aspect that I mentioned. The hurt came, perhaps surprisingly, in the U.S.A., which I had naively believed to be free of such wickedness. I began my American career in Washington Heights, in upper Manhattan, where as a 15-year-old I delivered prescriptions for a pharmacy at twenty cents an hour plus tips. Although it became known as the Fourth Reich because of its attractiveness to German Jewish refugees, the neighborhood was also the turf of other ethnics. To the Irish especially, a Jewish youngster running errands for a drugstore was fair game. It was pretty rough.

I also came across a particularly obnoxious type of anti-Semitism in the U.S. Army, where I had the bad fortune to go through basic training with a group of longshoremen (mostly of Irish and Pennsylvania Dutch origin), one of whom took delight in assuring me that he would "rather kill a Jew than a Jap" any day.

But not to worry; I came through the war unscathed. I owe this perhaps to a Jewish connection in my pre-induction job. My ambition was more limited than that of my fellow student at George Washington Evening High School, Henry Kissinger — I merely wanted to become a Hollywood screenwriter. As a first step I went to work, ca. 1942, as an office boy at MGM. I was assigned to the Legal Department, where I struck up a warm relationship with a lawyer named Weinstein. After my basic training in the infantry at Camp Wheeler, Georgia, I was sent to a so-called replacement depot at Ft. Meade, Maryland, where I was issued tropical gear, such as mosquito netting and anti-malaria pills. The word was that we were being sent to New Guinea, where MacArthur urgently needed replacements for the troops he lost in the jungle warfare against the Japanese. On a last home leave, I called on Weinstein at MGM. I confided to him that New Guinea was not exactly the land of my dreams; that I had hoped to be sent to Europe to fight the Nazis and possibly find my father who was in hiding in Holland.

Weinstein picked up the phone and called an old law school friend who was a staff officer at Ft. Meade. Captain Sharp asked whether I could type; the answer was yes. When I got back to camp, after a tearful farewell from my mother, I found that my name had been taken off the list of those shipping out to Ft. Ord, California, on the way to MacArthur's campaign. Instead, I was reassigned to the unit commanded by Captain Sharp, who had me typing up movement orders for a few months. He eventually saw to it that my name appeared on a shipment destined for England. In August 1944, just over four years after I had left France for Spain, I was back on French soil. No one remembered that in June 1940 the French authorities had stamped my travel document, "*Sans possibilite de retour en France.*"

After the war I had another protracted encounter with anti-Semitism at university. The locale was Princeton, where I transferred under the GI Bill after having completed my freshman year at CCNY evenings before being drafted into the army. City College then had an overwhelmingly Jewish student population, and I felt very much at home there. I was invited to join a group that published a student magazine called *Pulse,* to which I contributed film reviews. Looking back, it was probably a leftist group, very much concerned with social issues of the time, less with politics. The curious thing is that among these socially conscious young Jewish adults I do not recall hearing the slightest concern expressed about the fate of European Jewry. The same was true of MGM, with its mostly Jewish personnel, where I spent my daytime hours. Here there was not even social consciousness; I just missed being fired when my bosses discovered that I had signed up with Local 1702 of the UOPWA (United Office and Professional Workers of America) which was trying to unionize the New York offices of Hollywood. When I realized that my $16-a-week job was in jeopardy, I disaffiliated.

Returning to Princeton, first it should be noted that these are recollections of half a century ago. I was discharged from the army in January 1946 and entered Princeton in the spring semester. I emphasize this to avoid the implication that what I am describing is current reality. A great many things have changed. I recently visited the campus and found there a flourishing Center for Jewish Life such as I would not have dreamed of as a student. But at that period Princeton was the epitome of WASP America. There were all of three black students on campus who were holdovers of a Navy specialized training program, and the 140 or so Jews were roughly five percent of the undergraduate enrollment. There may have been more Jews in the graduate school, but there was hardly any contact between it and the undergraduate college. Ten out of the twelve eating clubs unabashedly refused to admit Jews; of the remaining two, one proved so attractive to Jewish students that it went out of business when Gentiles no longer applied. The whole campus resembled an exclusive club, with most of the Jewish students remaining outsiders. Some tried to crash it by excelling in sports (high grades in courses merely marked you as a grind); thus the cox on the winning crew was a Jew, and so was the quarterback on the team that won the Ivy League football championship in 1947.

When I first arrived on campus I did not know anyone and had no preference as to a roommate. By lottery, I was assigned to room with a sophomore from New Jersey who had also just gotten out of the army. We got along well together, and I would gladly have continued the arrangement in the fall term. But Ed told me that he had to move out — his father would not permit him to room with a Jew. He was obviously embarrassed, but there was nothing he could do. Suddenly I understood why he had never asked me to spend the weekend with him at his home on the Jersey shore, when he asked so many others. I found myself a Jewish roommate.

I was taken aback by the requirement of compulsory chapel attendance twice monthly, which was still in effect at the time, with the Jewish students subject to it like everyone else. True, the service was non-denominational, but it was a Christian service nonetheless. I organized a Friday night Jewish prayer service which the authorities gladly recognized as a substitute. But opposition came from another quarter — quite a few Jewish students opposed the initiative because they did not want to see a separate Jewish group on campus. We called ourselves the SHA or Student Hebrew Association (paralleling the Student Christian Association), which eased the pain a little. Somewhat later, we applied to the national Hillel office for assistance, and they agreed to sponsor a chapter on campus, first staffed by a part-time counselor and, as of 1948, by a full-time rabbi.

Then there was the Palestine Problem, as it was known in the Department of Near Eastern Studies and the Woodrow Wilson School of Public Affairs, which was my major. I found myself pitted against Professor Philip Khouri Hitti, the head of the Department and an eloquent spokesman for the Arab cause, as well as some of his junior colleagues. To the extent that there was interest in the issue at all outside these departments, the student body was almost unanimously pro-Arab; with the Jewish students remaining mostly on the sidelines. I remember Hitti telling a snickering class that American Jews were Zionist because every Jew in Brooklyn saw himself as future ambassador to a Jewish state.

Because of my record as a student activist, I was offered a scholarship to Brandeis Camp Institute, a Zionist leadership training course on an academic level. My stay there in the summer of 1947 was a kind of counterweight to the atmosphere at Princeton, which was beginning to leave its mark.

As a member of his creative writing class, I attended a seminar in world literature given by the poet Richard Blackmur. We spent a whole year analyzing Joyce's *Ulysses*. I found myself blushing every time the hero's Jewish background came up, which was often. To make matters worse, Blackmur playfully called me Leopold Bloom. My embarrassment grew from week to week as Blackmur relentlessly probed into Bloom's Jewishness.

I don't want to give the impression that my Jewish experience at Princeton was all bleak. My venture in community organization, through SHA, and later Hillel, brought me into contact with the Hillel Foundations at other colleges and led me to help organize the Harvard-Yale-Princeton (Hillel) Colloquium, with the editors of *Commentary* as the visiting scholars. Elliott Cohen, Nate Glazer, Clement Greenberg, Irving Kristol (who was then considerably to the left of the *Wall Street Journal*) brought their brand of Jewish intellectual excitement to the discussions. Cohen encouraged me to write for the magazine (also different from its current format), and a friendship resulted which lasted until his tragic death a decade later.

There is no room for further such biographical detail, except to recall that I arrived in Israel for the first time in June 1949 and spent a year. It was an exciting time to be here (a kind of primordial Israel Experience), and my decision to come back to stay ripened then. My early intuition that the main attraction of the Jewish state, for someone of my background, is the psychic freedom it affords, has been borne out. The attractiveness of the scene in Israel and its people then exerted that pull which joined with the push as I have already described it.

Having hopefully established my credentials, I will now focus on my encounters with community institutions in the migratory process.

In my first European period — I later came back as Director of the European Council of Jewish Communities, a post from which I was able to verify, refine, and update some of my early impressions — I found communities and their institutions merging into one another (i.e., they were nearly indistinguishable one from the other). School, synagogue, the kosher butcher, the Jewish hospital where I was born, the Jewish weekly newspaper, were all part of day-to-day existence. There were also fraternal groups such as B'nai B'rith, which in Germany was more of an elite and charitable organization, rather similar to what it is in Israel. My father was an enthusiastic member of the *Reichsbund Jüdischer Frontsoldaten*, the equivalent of the Jewish War Veterans in the U.S., and contributed to its monthly organ. An institution I have not come across anywhere else was the *Erholungsheim* (recuperation home) where school children were sent by the community after recovery from an illness. The home was located in an idyllic rural setting and was operated along Orthodox lines. A three-week stay there after a bout with influenza had a profound effect on me in reinforcing Jewish identity and practice.

Leadership exerted its influence mainly through the press, which reached virtually every household. We received the weekly *Gemeinde Blatt,* to whose youth supplement I contributed my first poem as well as prose pieces; and on the national level, the *CV Zeitung,* which expressed the position of the Central Organization that we were Jewish citizens of the Mosaic persuasion. The paper's rival was the *Jüdische Rundschau,* the organ of the German Zionist Organization.[3]

In retrospect, it is obvious that this leadership was not up to the challenge; it should have sounded the alarm and told people to get out while it was still possible (my father left German soil on September 1, 1939 — just before the outbreak of war; my mother left for the U.S. via Holland in March 1940). Instead, the emphasis on education and culture fostered the illusion that we were witness to a temporary aberration.

My own move — on December 6, 1938 — took place under the aegis of still another institution of the community: the Jewish orphanage, whose eighty wards were being evacuated collectively to Strasbourg, France. The director was a friend of my father's, who knew that he was in a concentration camp, and that my mother was considering an offer by the parents of a former classmate who had moved to France, to have me join them there pending the family's emigration to America. My mother agreed, on condition that my sister Lotte, age ten, could also come along. The director had our names added to the group leaving for France.

Getting off the train in Strasbourg later that day, I learned about the role of volunteers in the community when I saw a group of local women lined up on the platform to welcome the children. My sister and I were taken in charge by Mme. Andree Salomon, a distinguished young leader of Strasbourg Jewry who later saved the lives of hundreds of children by smuggling them across Nazi-infested borders. She soon had me move back to Strasbourg from the small

Alsatian town where my classmate's family was living, to continue my education. She arranged for me to stay in a boarding school run by the community for out-of-town students and apprentices, while opening her home to me on weekends. When I visited the school after the war, it had become part of the ORT network.

In Strasbourg I also came to know the role a community center can perform in informal Jewish education. The city's *Mercaz* was the creation of another charismatic individual, Leo Cohn (brother of retired Israel Supreme Court Justice Haim Cohn), who was executed by the Nazis during the war for being a leading member of the *resistance.* On the premises of the *Mercaz* I was initiated into the E.I.F. *(Eclaireurs Israelites de France),* the Jewish scout movement, another key waystation on my Jewish journey.

One more episode in the chapter on France — my sister and I were among the stream of refugees who clogged the highways leading southward after the Germans entered Paris on June 14, 1940. We were headed for Bordeaux, where I hoped to get on a ship leaving for the United States. We arrived there almost penniless, and there was no ship leaving the port. But Mme. Salomon had supplied us with the address of a Jewish family, formerly of Strasbourg, and they received us warmly. When it turned out that the only way to get to the U.S. was now by way of Spain and Portugal, Dr. Levy-Dreyfus drove us in his car as far as Bayonne, halfway to the Spanish border. Moreover, his wife had been treasurer of the WIZO chapter in Strasbourg, and she insisted on turning over the chapter's entire kitty to us. The 240 francs (about $50) went a long way.

During that same crucial period, my experience with the Jewish bureaucracy was less heart-warming. There was a migration agency in Paris called HICEM, a partnership between HIAS and a French *Comite d'Emigration.* They promised to pay for our passage to the U.S. once we got our visas, but failed to warn me not to mention this at the consulate. When the American consul asked who was paying for our tickets, I naively told the truth — the HICEM office. A week later notice came in the mail that the visas had been denied. If my uncle, who had furnished the required affidavit of support, could not pay for our passage, it could only mean that his means of support were inadequate. What saved the situation was my mother's arrival in New York; she was entitled to have us join her on a "non-quota" visa.

The conduct of the American consul in Paris doubtless reflected the attitude of his superiors in Washington; the published State Department documents contain ample evidence of the indifference toward the Jews' fate of Assistant Secretary Breckinridge Long.[4] But I also encountered a humane and courageous official in the American consul in Biarritz. Even though we were not U.S. citizens, he included us in a group of Americans whom the Germans permitted to cross into Spain after they had sealed the border to other refugees. Unfortunately, I do not remember the good consul's name.

In my initial steps in the United States I had little contact with the organized community. When Lotte and I were taken to Ellis Island upon arrival on July 18, 1940, my mother secured our release without intervention by any Jewish agency. I recall that she visited the offices of the National Council of Jewish Women regularly, possibly receiving financial support. Washington Heights had its branch of the YMHA, but I did not feel the kind of welcoming attitude there as at the *Mercaz* in Strasbourg. Spending most of my evenings at the George Washington High School, I had no time left in any event for "hanging around" outside the Y, which seemed to be a preferred source of entertainment for the local youths.

In the army, I benefitted from the counsel of the Jewish chaplain at Camp Wheeler, without being aware of the involvement of the Jewish Welfare Board (as it was known then) in the chaplaincy. However, I was given a prayer book with the JWB imprint on it, which I still have in my possession. There were no Yom Kippur services at the camp, but Jewish soldiers got the day off. One of the three in my platoon spent it in the barracks playing cards and gave the rest of us a bad name.

A highlight of my army service was my naturalization as an American citizen on October 1, 1943, only three years after my arrival in the country, instead of the usual five. The reason, we were told, was that if we fell into German hands while still German citizens, we might be shot as traitors. In that same context, I was interviewed, toward the end of the training course, by a team from the Office of Strategic Services (OSS), the forerunner of the CIA. They wanted to know if I would volunteer to be dropped behind German lines. I declined, on the ground that I would be easily spotted as a Jew. Another highlight was my return to my native city in American army uniform. Frankfurt, when I came through in April

1945, was 80 percent destroyed; most of it little more than heaps of brick and rubble. I doubt whether there was a single Jew left in it, but I did meet up with Jewish survivors elsewhere in Europe, particularly in Belgium. It is quite likely that the impact of these encounters eventually steered me in the direction of Jewish communal service. But that is another story.

Notes

1. Robert Weltsch's editorial in the *Jüdische Rundschau,* 4 April 1993.
2. For an account of the *Kulturbund*'s brief history, see Ernst Simon, *Aufbau im Untergang* (Tübingen, 1960).
3. The role of the Jewish press during the period is described in Herbert Freeden, *Die Jüdishce Press im Dritten Reich* (Frandfurt, 1987).
4. See also David Wyman's *Paper Walls: America and the Refugee Crisis, 1938-1941* (Amherst, 1968).

V

Freedom of Movement: Should There be a Right of Free International Migration?

18

Freedom of Movement: The International Legal Framework

David Matas

Introduction

International freedom of movement is a fundamental human right. The ultimate test of whether a right is a human right, whether the right belongs to all humanity simply by being human, is whether the respect for the right is essential to the dignity and self-realization of each individual. Is respect for the right necessary for individuals to be free as human beings to live their own lives in the manner in which they would choose to live? Is violation of the right a restriction on the fundamental humanity of individuals? If so, then there is a human right at stake.

Conceptually, freedom of movement is as much a part of what is essential to being human as any of the other fundamental freedoms. It is integrally connected to the other rights and freedoms. Being free means as much being free to go where you want as to say what you want or to associate with whom you want.

There are obvious limitations to the right to go where you want, just as there are obvious limitations to the right to say what you want. However, the limitations are, in themselves, not proof that the freedom does not exist, any more than one can say that the

limitations to freedom of speech prove that there is no such fundamental freedom as freedom as speech.

Regional Standards

The Universal Declaration of Human Rights, when it was first
drafted, was drawn from human rights statements found in constitutions and legislation of states around the world. These constitutions and this legislation can still serve as a source of statement of
rights, even after the Universal Declaration of Human Rights and
the other international instruments have been drafted.

Where rights exist domestically or regionally as human rights,
that is a clear indicator that there is a human right at play, even if
the rights do not exist internationally. Between human rights recognized by governments neither domestically nor regionally nor
internationally and human rights recognized by governments domestically, regionally and internationally, human rights recognized domestically and regionally but not internationally are a halfway point. Such rights are international human rights in the making, *lex ferenda* if not *lex lata*.

One source of international law is the general principles of law
recognized by the community of nations.[1] If a human right is
recognized as such by the community of nations domestically and
regionally, there is a strong argument that it has become an international human right simply because of that widespread domestic
and regional recognition.

It is impossible to break down human rights by borders. If a right
is a human right domestically and regionally, it must be a human
right internationally. It is impossible to say that, for instance, the
right to life exists internally but not internationally. Trans-border
extra-judicial executions are as wrongful as intra-border extra-
judicial executions. Human rights, by their very nature, are universal. Universality is an inevitable consequence of the recognition of
a right as a human right. To deny universality to a right is to deny
its nature as a human right.

Four examples of regional recognition of the principle of freedom of movement are the European Union, the Benelux Union, the
Schengen Community, and the Commonwealth. The Treaty Establishing the European Economic Community[2] provides for freedom

of movement within the European Community in two different ways. For workers, freedom of movement is based on the principle of non-discrimination on the ground of nationality.[3] The Treaty says "Freedom of movement for workers shall be secured."

For non-wage earners, freedom of movement within the Community is expressed by the right of establishment and the right to provide services.[4] The Treaty says "restrictions on the freedom of establishment of nationals of a Member State in the territory of another Member State shall be abolished." Freedom of establishment is defined to include the right to take and pursue activities as self-employed persons and to set up and manage undertakings.

The Treaty says "restrictions on freedom to provide services within the Community shall be progressively abolished." This right concerns nationals of Member States who are established in a state other than that of the person for whom the services are intended. The Treaty goes on further to say that a person providing a service may, in order to do so temporarily, pursue his activity in the state where the service is provided, under the same conditions as are imposed by that State on its own nationals.

In theory, the European Community limits the grant of free movement to movement that is economic. However, the European Court of Justice has held that even the receipt of services as a tourist is considered an economic activity entitled to the right of free movement.[5]

The European Community has, as well, adopted directives on the movement of economically non-active nationals and their families. The directives allow for residence on the grounds of the availability of a set amount of resources.[6]

The Benelux countries — Belgium, Netherlands, and Luxembourg — recognize complete freedom of movement for each other's nationals. The Convention Establishing the Benelux Union provides for free movement of all Benelux nationals.[7]

The Schengen Convention of 1990, which has as signatories many, but not all, of the member states of the European Community, abolishes internal border checks for all persons travelling between the signatory states.[8] Once a person is allowed entry at an external border control, the person is entitled to move without hindrance within the territories of the states contracting to the Schengen Convention.[9] The Convention came into force in 1995.

Although statute law has been legislated to limit the right, the Commonwealth recognizes the right to freedom of movement among subjects of Her Majesty the Queen as part of the common law. Lord Diplock reminded the House of Lords in 1970 that prior to the United Kingdom Commonwealth Immigrants Act of 1962 any British subject had a right at common law to enter the United Kingdom without let or hindrance when and where he pleased and to remain there as long as he liked.[10]

National Standards

Domestic instruments which contain the right to international freedom of movement are Spanish legislation of the sixteenth century[11] and the English Magna Carta of 1215. The Magna Carta asserted the right of anyone, whether English or foreigner, to enter England provided only that the person was not outlawed and that the person was not an enemy national in time of war.[12] However, that expression of the right survived only till 1297. The Magna Carta as legislated in 1297 did not contain this freedom of movement provision.[13]

A survey done in 1978 showed that seventy-eight countries, out of one hundred and forty-two which were examined, protect freedom of movement in their constitutions.[14] For example, the constitution of Argentina provides that all inhabitants of the nation enjoy the right of entering, remaining in, travelling through, and leaving Argentinean territory.[15] The Austrian constitution says that traffic restrictions may not be established within the federation.[16] The Bangladesh constitution provides that, subject to any reasonable restriction imposed by law in the public interest, every citizen shall have the right to move freely throughout Bangladesh, to reside and resettle in any place therein, and to leave and reenter Bangladesh.[17]

The Canadian Charter of Rights and Freedoms provides that every citizen of Canada and every person who has the status of permanent resident of Canada has the right to make and take up residence in any province. The right is subject to any law or practice of general application in force other than those that discriminate among persons primarily on the basis of province of present or previous residence; and any law providing for reasonable residency requirement as a qualification for the right of publicly funded social services.[18] The constitution of Chad provides that every Chadian citizen has the right to establish freely his domicile or residence anywhere in the national territory and to exercise any legal activities.[19]

The Chilean constitution provides that every person has the right to live and remain in any place in the republic, move from one location to another, and enter and leave the national territory on condition that the norms established by law are respected and provided that third parties are not impaired.[20] The constitutions of both Egypt[21] and Jordan[22] provide that no citizen may be prohibited from residency in any place and no citizen may be forced to reside in any place, except in the cases defined by law.

The constitution of India provides that all citizens have the right to move freely throughout the territory of India.[23] It further provides that the right to freedom of movement shall not affect the operation of any existing law insofar as it requires or prevents the state from making any law imposing reasonable restrictions on the exercise of the right, either in the interests of the general public or for the protection of the interests of any scheduled tribe.[24]

The constitution of Japan provides that every person shall have freedom to choose and change his residence. The constitution of the Philippines provides that the liberty of abode and of travel shall not be impaired except on lawful order of the court or when necessary in the interests of national security, public safety, or public health.[25]

The Russian constitution says that everyone who is lawfully staying on the territory of the Russian Federation shall have the right to freedom of movement and to choose the place to stay and residence.[26] The constitution of Tunisia states that every citizen has the right to move freely in the interior of the territory, to leave it, and to establish his domicile within the limits provided by the law.[27] The new constitution of South Africa states that every person shall have the right to freedom of movement anywhere within the national territory.[28]

This is just a partial list of countries that have constitutionally guaranteed rights of freedom of movement. A complete list would be considerably longer.[29] In addition, there are countries like the United States where the right cannot be found in the wording of the constitution, but where the constitution has been interpreted to encompass the right.[30]

United Nations Commission on Human Rights

The right to international freedom of movement as a fundamental human right has been recognized by several governments at the United Nations Commission on Human Rights. At the time the Commission on Human Rights discussed an earlier draft of the International Covenant on Civil and Political Rights, in 1950, many government representatives at the Commission made statements in support of a general right to international freedom of movement. The Lebanese representative, Mr. Malik, said: "although liberty of movement was not a fundamental right, it was nevertheless an essential part of the right to personal liberty."[31]

The representative of the Netherlands proposed a text that proclaimed liberty of movement, albeit subordinating it to "any general law, consistent with the rights defined in this Covenant."[32] The French representative, Mr. Ordonneau, said: "The right to liberty of movement could not be suppressed without infringing upon the physical liberty of the individual."[33]

The representative of Uruguay, Mr. Oribe, elaborated: "the rights of the individual would be very seriously diminished if he were not able to reside at the place most suited to what he considered his needs and to leave his country and settle in any other place, as he deemed fit...the whole of the modern history of the Americas had been the result of international recognition of the basic right to liberty of movement. Had that right not received at least that recognition, America and Australia would still be peopled only by aborigines. The Spanish laws of the sixteenth century recognizing the right of all persons to leave their country and settle in another had been one of the greatest achievements of the fight for freedom."[34]

The United Kingdom representative, Mr. Bowie, noted: "The Commission seemed to agree that liberty of movement was a fundamental right, but was finding great difficulty in adequately defining it."[35] The representative of China, Mr. Chang, contributed this: "the right of liberty of movement was a very important one, particularly for people who had not previously enjoyed it."[36]

The representative of Australia, Mr. Whitlam, offered this: "Failure to state the right to liberty of movement would create a very deplorable effect on public opinion, particularly in the under-developed countries."[37] But, he went on to say: "controls would be necessary in the interest of peace and the maintenance of public order."[38] The representative of India, Mr. Mehta, in continuing discussions of the draft Covenant, two years later, in 1952, said: "if freedom of speech and the right of association were human rights, then the right to liberty of movement was equally a human right."[39]

Academic Commentators

One of the sources of international law, according to the statute of the International Court of Justice, is the writings of academic commentators.[40] A number of authors, both ancient and modern, have accepted freedom of movement as a fundamental human right.[41] The venerable English jurist Blackstone wrote in his commentaries: "The personal liberty consists in the power of locomotion, of changing situation, or moving one's person to whatsoever place one's own inclination may direct, without imprisonment or restraint, unless by due process of law."[42]

Roger Nett of the University of Houston has written: "One other 'right' (the right to free and open movement of people on the surface of the earth) relates directly to opportunity and would go a long way, virtually all the way, to close the existing set of rights and make it functionally much more viable."[43] Ved Nanda of the University of Denver has stated: "(Freedom of movement) is one of those basic human rights, the universal recognition of which is likely to be a major accomplishment in accepting the importance of the individual as a subject of international law."[44] Manfred Nowak of the Austrian Federal Academy of Public Administration has written: "The exact degree of freedom of movement across national frontiers has thus become a touchstone for the respect for human rights *per se*."[45]

The Courts

At least one domestic court, in Canada, has recognized freedom of movement as a fundamental human right. The Refugee Convention provides protection to those with a well-founded fear of persecution for listed reasons. Persecution is any serious violation of a basic human right. It is noteworthy that, for the purposes of the

Refugee Convention, freedom of movement is considered a basic human right, the violation of which amounts to persecution within the meaning of the Refugee Convention.

Shao Mei He claimed in Canada that she was a refugee from China. In China, the authorities, because of her political activity, required her to change her residence to the Sa Woo commune in Yan Ping; she was not permitted to live elsewhere. The Immigration and Refugee Board found her not to be a refugee. Madam Justice Sandra Simpson of the Federal Court Trial Division set aside the decision because of a number of errors the Board had made.[46] One of those errors was a failure to recognize the principle of freedom of movement. The judge wrote: "to permanently deprive the Applicant of her mobility and her freedom to choose where she would live also amounted to persecution."

International Standards

By and large, if we think conceptually of what human rights should be, if we look at national constitutions and legislation on human rights, the rights we come up with are in the international human rights instruments. Although the international instruments are self-imposed restrictions by government, the restrictions are pretty broad. For most rights, the problem is the implementation, not the commitment. The list of accepted rights is long.

There is, however, one notable exception, a right which is a fundamental part of what it means to be human, which is found everywhere in national law as a human right but is found nowhere in international standards: the right to freedom of movement. International instruments have much more limited rights. For freedom of movement at the international level, what we see is a long list of specific rights, rather than a broad general principle with exceptions.

The Universal Declaration of Human Rights and the International Covenant on Civil and Political Rights provide that everyone has the right to liberty of the person.[47] They provide that no one shall be held in slavery or servitude.[48] These instruments state that no one shall be subjected to arbitrary arrest, detention, or exile.[49] The Universal Declaration of Human Rights provides that everyone has the right to seek and to enjoy in other countries asylum from persecution.[50] The International Covenant on Civil and Political Rights provides that no one shall be imprisoned merely on the ground of inability to fulfil a contractual obligation.[51]

The Universal Declaration of Human Rights provides that everyone has the right to freedom of movement within the borders of each state.[52] The Declaration also states that everyone has the right to leave any country, including his own, and return to his country.[53]

The International Covenant on Civil and Political Rights provides that everyone lawfully within the territory of a state shall, within that territory, have the right to liberty of movement and freedom to choose his residence; that everyone shall be free to leave any country, including his own; and that the rights should not be subject to any restrictions except those which are provided by law, are necessary to protect national security, public order, public health or morals or the right and freedoms of others, and are consistent with the rights recognized in that Covenant; and that no one should be arbitrarily deprived of the right to enter his own country.[54]

The Convention relating to the Status of Refugees provides that no contracting state shall expel or return a refugee in any manner whatsoever to the frontier of territories where his life or freedom would be threatened on account of his race, religion, nationality, membership of a particular social group, or political opinion.[55] The Convention also states that contracting states shall not expel a refugee lawfully in their territory save on grounds of national security or public order.[56]

Further, the Convention gives to each refugee lawfully in its territory the right to choose their place of residence and to move freely within its territory, subject to any regulations applicable to aliens generally in the same circumstances.[57] For refugees unlawfully in the country of refuge, the Convention requires contracting states not to apply to their movements restrictions other than those which are necessary; such restrictions should be applied only until their status in the country is regularized or they obtain admission into another country.[58]

I do not propose to go through every provision in international instruments that relates to freedom of movement. To do that would exhaust my energy and the reader's patience. I draw the reader's attention to the United Nations Declaration on Territorial Asylum;[59] the Convention relating to the Status of Stateless Persons;[60]

the Convention on the Reduction of Statelessness;[61] the Geneva Convention relative to the Protection of Civilian Persons in Time of War;[62] Protocol additional to the Geneva Convention relating to the Protection of Victims of International Armed Conflicts;[63] the International Convention on the Elimination of All Forms of Racial Discrimination;[64] the International Convention on the Suppression and Punishment of the Crime of Apartheid;[65] the Slavery Convention of 1926 and its Protocol of 1953; the Convention on the Rights of the Child;[66] and the International Convention on the Protection of the Rights of All Migrant Workers and Their Families.[67]

Even this list of instruments with standards relating to freedom of movement is not comprehensive, but only a sampling. What all the standards have in common is that they are particular aspects of the right to freedom of movement. But, in the international instruments, a general right to freedom of movement is nowhere stated as such. States could not agree on a text, nor even on the principle. Instead what we got was a long list of specific movement rights.

One obvious indicator of whether a right is a human right is whether the right can be found in the international human rights instruments. The rights in the Universal Declaration of Human Rights are, obviously, human rights. But the international instruments do not contain a comprehensive list of human rights.

Human rights existed before 1948, before the Universal Declaration of Human Rights was adopted by the United Nations General Assembly.

As well, the Universal Declaration of Human Rights and other international instruments are what governments are prepared to accept as obligations. However, the starting point for human rights is the individual, not governments. Government acceptance of human rights imposes on governments legal and political obligations. A moral obligation on governments to respect human rights exists even if governments have not accepted them legally or politically.

Freedom of Movement as a Domestic Human Right

It has been argued that the most general human right of movement is the right to move freely within the borders of each state,[68] that there is no broader human right of international freedom of movement. Freedom of movement, so it is argued, is like the right to vote. The right to vote is restricted to citizens of a state. There is no international right to vote in elections in other states.

My response to that argument is that the analogy to the right to vote is false. Citizens have a right to vote in their own country, because the government of their country is a government that governs them. For human beings to be in control of their own destiny they should be able to choose the government that governs them.

There is no comparable linkage between human rights and voting in foreign elections. It is not a meaningful restriction on the humanity of individuals that they cannot vote in foreign elections.

The same cannot be said for freedom of movement. The expression of the right is not exhausted by movement within the borders of the state. Individuals, as human beings, are restricted by not being able to move internationally.

If there were a global government, then respect for human rights would mean that the government would have to be democratically elected. There is no global voting because there is no global government. There is nothing to vote for.

The same cannot be said for territory. Though there is no global government, there is a globe. There are places for people to go to other than the territories of states in which they find themselves, or in which they have lawful status. Prohibiting freedom of movement is a real restriction, not an empty one.

Why do states recognize freedom of movement within their boundaries to their citizens? The reason, I suggest, is that states realize that freedom of movement within the boundaries of the state is an element of what it means to be part of the community of that state.

If we accept that reasoning domestically, we must also accept it internationally. The fundamental basis of human rights is that there is one humanity in which we all share. Freedom of movement internationally is an element of what it means to be part of all humanity.

Freedom of Movement and State Sovereignty

The reason freedom of movement is so little recognized internationally despite its wide recognition domestically and its conceptual connection with human rights is its conflict with the sovereign right of states to control their borders. States would be reluctant to recognize freedom of movement because they would be reluctant to give up control over who enters their territories.

What is at issue here, at least initially, is the formulation of a package of rights and exceptions rather than the acceptance of new substantive rights. In this context, state reluctance is not so much reluctance to admit into their territories new or different people; rather it is reluctance even to admit that there is a higher principle than state control of borders.

States wish to be able to control freedom of movement however they see fit. For states, exceptions to the rule of state control of borders are just that, exceptions to a general rule. The fragments, the list of specific rights involving aspects of freedom of movement, is a list of exceptions to this general rule.

For human rights advocates, there is nothing new in seeing conflicts between assertions of state sovereignty and promotion of human rights. Usually the claim of sovereignty is different — that states have a sovereign right to control their internal affairs — but the conflict is essentially the same.

The international community has come to accept that where there is a conflict between the sovereign right of states to control their internal affairs and the right of individuals to have their human rights respected, human rights must prevail. Respect for human rights is an accepted limitation on state sovereignty. That does not mean that the principle of state sovereignty over internal affairs has ceased to exist. What it does mean is that the principle is subject to an important countervailing principle that, in case of conflict, the right to respect of human rights prevails.

The same can be said of state control over borders. Here, too, is a principle of state sovereignty. This principle is also subject to a countervailing principle, the principle of respect for human rights. Freedom of movement, as one aspect of human rights, is one aspect of the rights that trump state sovereignty over borders.

The question that may arise is this: Is there anything left to the principle of state control over borders if we accept the principle of freedom of movement? The argument may be made that if we endorse the principle of freedom of movement as the exception to the principle of state control over borders, that the exception would swallow the whole. The concern states would undoubtedly raise is that freedom of movement is not an exception to the rule of state control over borders. It is rather the antithesis of state control over borders, its negation.

The answer to this hypothetical objection is that freedom of movement no more negates state control over borders than the general principle of respect for human rights negates state sovereignty over internal affairs. Human rights come first. But human rights do not obliterate the very possibility of state control over internal affairs. Even when human rights are completely respected, there remains a domain of control for states.

This is also true for state control of borders. Freedom of movement as a principle means freedom of movement of people. It does not mean freedom of movement of goods or capital. Border financial or customs control remain beyond the scope of the human rights principle. In these areas the principle of state control over borders would prevail.

There is an irony here. While states have not accepted freedom of movement of people as a principle, they have accepted freedom of movement of goods and capital, free trade, as a principle. There is a treaty regime and a United Nations bureaucracy, the General Agreement on Tariffs and Trade (GATT), which has become the World Trade Organization (WTO), to promote freer trade. There is no comparable treaty, no comparable UN bureaucracy, for freedom of movement of people. The result is that goods and capital have a greater freedom of movement than human beings. The world's freedom of movement priorities are topsy turvy. Goods and capital come first. People come last.

Freedom of movement of people, like any other freedom, is not an absolute. It is subject to exceptions of national security, public order, and public health.[69] These exceptions provide scope for the principle of state control of borders, not as a predominant principle but as a subservient one.

Repressive states use or abuse the principle that states have sovereignty over internal affairs to object to international scrutiny of their human rights behavior. Other states, democratic states, do not. However, no state now asserts the right of international freedom of movement. No instrument, national or international, includes the principle of international freedom of movement.

The principle of state control of borders is not just an evasive device of repressive states. It as well reflects the will of the democratic states. The mere fact that the right to international freedom of movement is asserted by no state, that it is rejected by every state, democratic and repressive alike, is not, in itself, a refutation of the existence of the right. It is nonetheless a phenomenon that calls for explanation. My explanation is threefold, the fear of loss of cultural identity, the fear of mass economic migration, and the fear of correlative obligations that would accompany recognition of the right.

Minority Rights

The Human Rights Committee established under the International Covenant on Civil and Political Rights has recognized that uninhibited internal freedom of movement can lead to violation of the right of a people to preserve its cultural identity, and that it is justifiable to limit movement to allow for cultural self-preservation. It is reasonable to conclude that the principle of international freedom of movement, if it exists, is subject to the same exception.

In the case of Sandra Lovelace,[70] Canada had legislation that prevented Ms. Lovelace from living on her native reserve because she had married a non-native. The Committee ruled that Canada had violated the Covenant. The Committee acknowledged that Canada may be justified in restricting the right to live on a native reserve for such purposes as the protection of resources or the preservation of the identity of the tribe. However, in the circumstance of the Lovelace case, in view of the fact that Ms. Lovelace was divorced, and that her main cultural attachment was to her native band, it did not seem to the Committee that to deny to Ms. Lovelace the right to reside on the reserve was reasonable or necessary to preserve the identity of the tribe.

The Committee found Canada to be in violation not of the right to internal freedom of movement in the Covenant, but the right of persons belonging to minorities to enjoy their own culture in community with other members of their group.[71] The Committee noted but did not apply the limitations to the principle of internal freedom of movement found in the Covenant in order to justify the interpretation it gave to the cultural group right.

The right of each minority to preserve its identity is not recognized as such in the international instruments. But the larger rights, of minorities to enjoy their cultures in community with other members of their group, and of peoples to self-determination, which includes the right of peoples to freely determine their cultural development,[72] are in the international instruments.

The rights of minorities, the right to self-determination of peoples, are rights that have not been fully articulated in international instruments. There is a good deal of confusion about their precise meaning and their applicability in particular contexts. Moreover, the right to international freedom of movement is nowhere to be found in the international instruments.

In the context of a discussion about the limitations on international freedom of movement, the right to self-determination of peoples and rights of minorities amount to much the same thing, since, globally, every people is a minority. International freedom of movement and the right to self-determination of people are two inchoate human rights in mute combat. The evidence of that combat can be found only in the result. International freedom of movement loses hands down. The freedom is blown to smithereens. It becomes, instead, a lot of little specific rights instead of one overarching right.

This state of affairs is unhealthy, of course, for the international right to freedom of movement, but, as well, for human rights generally. Because the global human rights community has not been talking about or thinking about the right to international freedom of movement, the conceptualization of human rights itself has suffered.

Human rights in the international bill of rights have to be read together, as a whole. No one right is allowed to trump all other rights. There is no hierarchy of rights in the international bill of rights. Human rights are indivisible. Each right has to be read and interpreted so as to allow respect for other rights.

Inserting respect for international freedom of movement in the international bill of rights would not, in principle, threaten the right to self-determination of peoples, or the right of persons belonging to minorities to enjoy their culture in community with other members of their group. All these rights, if they are in the same instrument, have to be read together. Each has to be interpreted to allow respect for the other. Each right is limited by the dictates of the other rights.

To sort out in any detail the relationship between freedom of movement, on the one hand, and the right to self-determination of people or the right of persons belonging to minorities to enjoy their own culture in community with other members of their group, on the other hand, is a subject all of its own, worthy of a separate essay. I would say here only that sorting out the relationship does not necessarily mean denying international freedom of movement. It may mean establishing mechanisms to ensure respect for the right of people and/or minorities who, because of the movement of others, shift from being majorities to being minorities in a particular country or region.

Economic Migration

What is the practical consequence of accepting international freedom of movement as a principle? It has been argued that freedom of movement means freedom of movement for economic migrants. If it does, then freedom of movement has enormous consequences, and it is unrealistic to believe that it will ever be accepted.

My answer is that this argument poses a false dichotomy. The notion that there are large numbers of economic migrants is a consequence of the present standards regime. According to present international standards, those fleeing serious human rights violations are entitled to protection. Economic migrants are not entitled to resettlement. States which wish to limit the number of those who enter and stay label many, if not most, of those fleeing human rights violations as economic migrants in order to prevent their theoretical commitment to protecting persons fleeing human rights violations from translating into large numbers of real people arriving in their countries.[73]

The number of economic migrants is nowhere near as large as people who fear mass movement of economic migration would suggest. The bulk of those believed to be economic migrants are in reality people fleeing human rights violations, whether the violations be of political, civil, economic, social, or cultural rights. One advantage of a commitment to a general international right to freedom of movement is that it would get us away from this sham labelling of persons fleeing human rights violations as economic migrants. An assertion and acceptance of a general right of international freedom of movement would be an effective way of confronting and combatting the violations of the specific movement rights that come from an overly narrow application of these rights.

There remains, nonetheless, economic migration, no matter what the international legal regime. Would a generalized right to international freedom of movement mean unrestricted economic migration? The answer is, not necessarily. Economic migration would become the assertion of a fundamental human right. One has only to look at the principle of domestic freedom of movement to see that that is so. It is a violation of the right to domestic freedom of movement to prohibit movement solely on the ground that the motivation of the movement is economic.

There are, however, other valid exceptions to the principle of freedom of movement that come into play, such as prevention of environmental degradation or preservation of cultural identity. A balancing would have to be done between competing rights. The question would become whether the restrictions on freedom of movement are reasonable or necessary. Where the reason for movement is economic, the argument that the restriction is reasonable is more easily made than when the reason for movement is escape from human rights violations. Economic motivation for migration would not, in this context, be a reason in itself to bar the migration. It would be, rather, a factor to be taken into account when deciding whether other circumstances justify restrictions on freedom of movement.

Correlative Obligations

The third reason why states are hesitant to recognize the principle of freedom of movement is the fear of correlative obligations. In a theoretical sense, the recognition of every right or freedom involves correlative obligations. In a practical sense, the fear of freedom of movement is that it allows the entry of large numbers of people who would then have a right to invoke the social service network of the country of destination, at great expense to the taxpayers of that country.

Polling statistics show that this fear is widespread. Economic statistics, however, show that this fear is a myth. Immigrants are producers as well as consumers, sellers as well as buyers, taxpayers as well as users of government services. There is nothing to show that immigrants are a disproportionate drain on the economy of any country.

Statistics for Canada, which has an active immigration program, show that immigrants contribute to economic growth.[74] They create a net tax benefit. Immigrants are self-employed at a higher rate than people born in Canada.[75] The unemployment rate among all immigrants is virtually the same as among the Canadian born.[76] Immigrants save money at a higher rate, hold lower debts, and repay loans faster than the Canadian born.

There is no established link between immigration and unemployment. Immigration has not caused significant job displacement among Canadian-born workers.[77] Wage levels of Canadian-born workers have not been significantly affected by increased immigration levels.

On average, immigrants consume fewer social services than the Canadian born.[78] Newcomers who speak neither of the Canadian official languages, English and French, quickly acquire language skills. At school, foreign-born children perform at the same level as Canadian children.[79]

Immigrants are less likely to commit major crimes than the Canadian born. They are under-represented in the prison population.[80]

Canadian immigration is a mixture of economic immigrants, family reunification, and refugee protection. A study of Indochinese refugees in Canada shows that this population has a considerably lower unemployment rate than the national average, were in better health than the general population, and relied on social assistance less than the general population.[81]

Israel, which has an open immigration policy for persons of Jewish origin, enjoyed significant economic growth while the rest of the world was undergoing a recession. The growth can be attributed to the influx of immigrants following on the collapse of the Soviet Union and the end of the Eastern Bloc exit controls.

There is no linkage between population density and economic prosperity. Among the ten most densely populated countries on Earth are Switzerland, Japan, the Netherlands, and Hong Kong.[82]

Germany in the 1950s took 13 million immigrants and refugees into a pre-war population of 39 million. By the end of the 1950s it had the lowest unemployment rate in Europe and one of the highest per capita gross national products.

The fear that mass migration is somehow bad for the economy of the receiving state, while widespread, is irrational. Unreasoned fear of the uninformed is hardly justification for denial of a right.

Cultural Relativism

Yet another objection that has been raised to the principle of freedom of international movement as a basic human right is the argument that the principle is nothing more than an attempt to apply worldwide a North American model. The principle of freedom of movement, so it is argued, is not universal but just a rationalization and generalization from the North American experience.

In response, I would accept that historically and practically it is true that freedom of movement was crucial for the settlement and development of all the Americas, North, Central, and South. It is also true that territorial boundaries in the Americas led to the creation of nations out of states within those boundaries. In Europe, on the other hand, nations have created states and the boundaries of those states.

Thirdly, it is true that Canada and the United States are countries of immigration with substantial admissions each year. This immigration allows citizens of Canada and the U.S to contemplate freedom of movement with greater equanimity than citizens of other countries might, since Canada and the U.S. are closer to allowing complete freedom of movement than other countries are. As well, the arbitrary distinctions and self-contradictions in both Canada and the U.S. manifested in the working out of immigration policies which have no overarching organizing principle make freedom of movement as an organizing principle an appealing alternative.

All that being true, it is, nonetheless, false to say that freedom of movement is just a North American fixation on movement issues.

It can be said of many if not all human rights that they have a specific historical or geographical genesis, that they are more important to some people than to others. Yet they remain human rights all the same.

For instance, the Genocide Convention came directly out of the experience of the Holocaust. Yet it would be farfetched to argue that the Convention against Genocide is not a human rights instrument, that it is just a reflection of the European or Jewish experience. The crime of genocide is a universal crime, and that is no less so because it has particularistic roots.

To take another example, the Convention on the Elimination of All Forms of Discrimination against Women is not any less a human rights instrument because it has come out of the female experience. Women's rights are human rights, and not just the expression of feminism. To argue the contrary would be unfair both to women and to human rights.

The argument that support for freedom of movement is a form of North Americanism is in substance an argument for the cultural relativity of human rights, an argument rejecting the universality of human rights principles. Yet, it is basic to the nature of human rights that they are universal. Human rights are founded on the notion that there is a core of human values common to all which must be respected, everywhere at all times. Human rights which vary from place to place or time to time are not human rights at all.[83]

Often we are faced not with the choice between respect for rights and violations of rights, but with the need to balance conflicting rights. How that balancing will be done may vary from situation to situation, from place to place. As indicated earlier, freedom of movement and self-determination of people may be competing principles. When they do enter into conflict, how that conflict will be resolved may be very different in Europe and North America. Because immigration is so much more part of the North American experience — the North American identity — than the European experience — the European identity — a mass influx would have to be of an entirely different and far larger dimension in North America than in Europe to enter into conflict with the notion of self-determination of peoples.

However, application of a principle should not be confused with its validity. Varied applications of a principle do not put into question the universality of the principle. Freedom of movement remains a valid and valuable principle even though its working out in conjunction with other principles will vary over place and time.

Freedom of Movement and Non-Governmental Organizations

It is easy to explain, if not to admire, the reluctance of states to recognize the principle of freedom of movement. Recognition would presage, even where it does not accompany, the weakening of state control over borders. But within the international non-governmental human rights community, the principle of freedom of movement is also endorsed virtually nowhere. There are non-governmental organizations concerned with refugees; with migrant workers; with humanitarian principles, which include aspects of freedom of movement; with slavery; with unjust imprisonment. But there are no non-governmental organizations dedicated to freedom of movement as such.[84] There are no international non-governmental organizations that endorse freedom of movement as a principle. The international non-governmental organizations mirror the fragmentation that exists in the assertion of the rights. Why is this so?

One reason is that for the particular aspects of freedom of movement, there are natural constituencies, but there is no natural constituency for freedom of movement as a whole. There are refugees who generate a focus on refugee rights, migrant workers who create a focus on migrant worker rights, stateless who provide a focus on the need to reduce statelessness, and so on. Each of the groups affected develops an advocacy against the violation of its rights.

Freedom of movement as a whole is an umbrella concept covering many disparate affected groups. Victims of the violation of the right to freedom of movement are not a homogeneous grouping that naturally come together organizationally to express their common concerns.

A second reason is that states have not accepted freedom of movement, but they have accepted many aspects of freedom of movement. It is a lot easier to fight the battle of implementation of principles already accepted than to fight the battle of acceptance of new principles. It is a lot easier to ask governments to keep the promises they have made than to ask governments to make new promises it is clear that they will be reluctant to make.

A third reason is the expanding consciousness of human rights. Sensitization about human rights is not something that happens only outside the human rights community. It is also something that happens within. The human rights consciousness, within the human rights movement itself, starts out by focusing on the most egregious violations of human rights and moves on to a realization that the specific violations are a manifestation of a larger problem. Human rights awareness is like any other awareness, a dialectic evolving from the particular to the general.[85]

Formulations of Human Rights

The non-governmental community may well ask: What difference does it make whether or not international freedom of movement is accepted as a right by states? It might be argued that whether the right is asserted with exceptions, or specific movement rights are listed, the situation remains the same. For those concerned with promoting freedom of movement as a right, so this argument goes, energy is better spent in expanding the list of specific movement rights, rather than attempting to assert the right to freedom of movement as such.

There are two different ways of stating basic human rights and their exceptions. One is to state the right as a broad, sweeping category and carve exceptions out of the general rule. The other is to state the specific elements of the right that are protected. The exceptions are what is not stated. The end result of both formulations is the same, in the sense that both formulations forbid and permit the same practices. Yet, there are important differences between the two.

One difference is that stating the general right and then listing the exceptions is a more comprehensive approach. Everything is stated. Nothing is left to guess work. Stating what is forbidden but omitting what is permitted leaves what is permitted to guess work.

That difference is practical. There is another difference that is one of principle. Where there is a general prohibition, with a list of exceptions, the general prohibition states a general principle. It asserts a fundamental human right. There is the implication that the exception should be construed restrictively, to protect the basic right. Border controls would have to be justified as an exception to the right to freedom of movement,

Endless lists have the opposite effect. They have a constraining effect. They leave the implication that there is no overreaching unifying right. There is no one principle that imbues the whole. Each right is contained within its own specific formulation. There is nothing to push out the boundaries of the specific rights. Aspects of freedom of movement have to be justified as exceptions to the rule that states may control their borders as they see fit.

The reason we state human rights as broad rights with exceptions, rather than as a long list of specific rights, is to emphasize and reinforce their human rights character. In a sense, even to talk of human rights as a list of rights is misplaced. It is more accurate to say that there is only one human right, the right to dignity and self-realization of the individual. The specific human rights are ways in which the general human right to dignity and self-realization is realized.

The generalized statement of a right, although in a way just a mere formulation, is so significant to the awareness of the right that the assertion of the generalized statement is, all on its own, virtually a hallmark of the right. There is, obviously, more to, say, respect for the right to life than stating the right to life. But a reluctance to assert the generalized right amounts to a reluctance to recognize the right. If we were to hesitate to assert the right to life in a generalized way, it is as if we were hesitant to recognize the right to life as such.

Human rights instruments have both a legal value and an educative value. The legal right is diminished if it is not stated in generalized form. If all we have is a list of specific rights, that means, legally, that the list is all that there is. If we have a generalized right, with exceptions, then the unstated is included in the right.

While in a general sense it is true that a list of specific rights covers the same ground as a generalized right with exceptions, the list may not be comprehensive, if for no other reason than that it is impossible to imagine every possible manifestation of the generalized right. A generalized right covers the unimagined as well as the anticipated. A specific list can encompass only the anticipated.

A generalized right has an educational value the specific listed rights do not. Asserting a generalized right promotes the right. It is a tool of advocacy in winning people over to the right. It is a tool that is abandoned when the right is not stated in generalized form.

Although the generalized statement of a right is virtually a hallmark of its being a human right, it is wrong to say that it is a test of whether a right is a human right. Some generalized rights are not human rights. Other specific lists of rights mask an unstated general human right.

The list of specific rights in the international instruments relating to freedom of movement is now so long that, if for no other reason, simplicity should suggest stating the fundamental right. The list of exceptions is bound to be shorter than the list of now accepted components of the right.

One advantage of asserting the right to international freedom of movement is that it would eliminate an illogicality in the current international movement standards. Right now the international instruments have a right to leave any country, but no right to enter any country, except your own. Yet, without a right to enter at least one country besides your own, the right to leave is meaningless. Western countries, historically, protested long and loud about exit controls in what were then Communist countries. Yet, once the exit controls were lifted, the West imposed entry controls to prevent the very same people from entering who earlier were prevented from leaving.

By refusing to accept that the right to leave includes a right to enter, states have made the right to leave meaningless. Protests against violations of the right to leave are seen as exercises in hypocrisy.

The same can be said of all the various components of the present piecemeal international regime of standards for movement. Because there is no overarching principle, because it is accepted that states can prevent entry, the working of the specific movement rights is continually frustrated. Respecting the general principle of the right to international freedom of movement would mean that the rights that are already there would be respected in a meaningful way.

With the recognition of the right to international freedom of movement, the stage is set for the expansion of the right. Without the recognition of the right, with the acceptance of state control of borders as predominant, recognition of every aspect of freedom of movement becomes a struggle with the notion of state control over borders.

Notes

1. Statute of the International Court of Justice, section 38 (1) (c).
2. Rome, 25 March 1957.
3. Article 48-51.
4. Articles 52-58 and 59-66.
5. CoJ EC 286/82 and 26/83, Luisi and Carbone, SEW, pp.750-759.
6. EC Directives 90/364, 90/365, and 90/366 of June 28, 1990.
7. Article 2.
8. See J.D.M. Steenbergen, "Schengen and the Movement of Persons," in *Schengen* (Utrecht, The Netherlands: W.E.J. Tjeenk Willink — Kluwer Law and Taxation, 1991), at page 74.
9. Articles 19-21.
10. *D.P.P. v. Bhagwan* (1970), 3 All E.R. 97 at 99; see also *R. v. Governor of Pentonville Prison ex parte Azam* (1973), 2 All E.R. 741 at 747 (C.A.) per Lord Denning M.R.
11. See United Nations Document E/CN.4/SR.151, page 3, paragraph 1.
12. Clause 42, reprinted in J.C. Holt, *Magna Carta*, 2nd ed. (New York: Cambridge University Press, 1992), Appendix 6.
13. 25 Edw 1, reprinted in *The Roots of Liberty*, Ellis Sandoz, ed. (Columbia, Missouri: University of Missouri Press, 1993), Appendix.
14. H. van Caarseveen and B. van der Tan, *Written Constitutions: A Computerized Comparative Study* (Dobbs Ferry, N.Y.: Oceana Publications, 1978), at 107.
15. Article 14.
16. Article 4 (2).
17. Article 36.
18. Article 6 (2).
19. Article 46.
20. Article 19 (7) (a).
21. Article 50.
22. Article 9 (ii).
23. Article 19 (1) (d).
24. Article 19 (5).
25. Article IV (5).
26. Article 27 (1).
27. Article 10.
28. Section 18.

29. See *Constitutions of the Countries of the World*, A.P. Blaustein and G.H. Flanz, eds. (Dobbs Ferry, New York: Oceana Publications, June 1994).
30. See *Aptheker v. Sec. State*, 378 U.S. 500.
31. E/CN.4/SR.150, page 12, paragraph 51.
32. At paragraph 52.
33. Page 14, paragraph 16.
34. E/CN.4/SR.151, page 3, paragraph 1.
35. Page 5, paragraph 12.
36. Page 6, paragraph 14.
37. Page 6, paragraph 17.
38. Page 7, paragraph 18.
39. E/CN.4/SR.315, page 5.
40. Article 38 (d).
41. See Alan Ladyka "Freedom of Movement — The Newest Human Right?" Unpublished essay submitted in 1994 for course in immigration and refugee law at the Faculty of Law, University of Manitoba.
42. William Blackstone, 1 *Blackstone's Commentaries* 134 (Boston: Beacon Press, 1962).
43. Roger Nett, "The Civil Right We Are Not Ready For: The Right of Free Movement of People on the Face of the Earth," 81 *Ethics* (1971): 212.
44. Ved Nanda, "The Right to Movement and Travel Abroad: Some Observations on the U.N. Deliberation," 1 *Denver J. Int'l L. & Policy* (1971):109.
45. Manfred Nowak, *CCPR Commentary* (Kehl/Strasbourg/Arlington: Engel), p. 199.
46. *He v. M.E.I.*, IMM-3024-93, June 1, 1994.
47. UDHR article 3; ICCPR article 9 (1).
48. UDHR article 4; ICCPR article 8.
49. UDHR article 9; ICCPR article 9 (1).
50. Article 14 (1).
51. Article 11.
52. Article 13 (1).
53. Article 13 (2).
54. Article 12.
55. Article 33 (1).
56. Article 32 (1).
57. Article 26.
58. Article 31 (2).
59. 14 December 1967.
60. 28 September 1954.
61. 30 August 1961.
62. 12 August 1949, articles 26, 44, and 70.

63. Articles 73, 74, 85 (4).
64. Article 5 (d) (i) and (ii).
65. 30 November 1973.
66. Article 9.
67. Article 8, 11, 16 (1), and 20.
68. ICCPR article 25 (b); UDHR article 21 (1).
69. See ICCPR article 12 (3).
70. Case 24/1977, 30 July 1981, paragraphs 15 and 16.
71. Article 27.
72. ICCPR Article 1 (1); International Covenant on Economic, Social and Cultural Rights, Article 1 (1).
73. See David Matas and Ilana Simon, *Closing the Doors: The Failure of Refugee Protection* (Toronto: Summerhill Press, 1989).
74. Ather Akbari, "The Benefits of Immigrants to Canada: Evidence on Tax and Public Services," 15:4 *Canadian Public Policy* (1989):424; Don DeVoretz, *Immigrant Asset Performance* (Ottawa: Employment and Immigration Canada, March 1989); Economic Council of Canada, *New Faces in the Crowd: The Economic and Social Impacts of Immigration* (Ottawa: Supply and Services Canada, 1991); Carl Sonnen, *Medium and Long Term Macroeconomic Implications of Increased Immigration* (Ottawa: Informetrica, September 1989).
75. Elliot Tepper, *Self-Employment in Canada among Immigrants of Different Ethno-cultural Backgrounds* (Ottawa: Policy Analysis, Directorate of Immigration, Policy Branch, Employment and Immigration Canada, May 1989).
76. Derrick Thomas, *Trends in the "Quality" of Canada's Immigrants* (Ottawa: Strategic Policy and Planning Branch, Department of Immigration, 1994).
77. Don DeVoretz, *Immigration and Employment Effects* (Ottawa: Institute for Research on Public Policy, November 1989).
78. Derrick Thomas, *Immigrant Immigration and the Canadian Identity* (Ottawa: Department of Immigration, 19 November 1990); T. John Samuel, *Family Class Immigration to Canada, 1981 to 1984: Labour Activity Aspects* (Ottawa: Department of Employment and Immigration, 1987).
79. Monique Richer "Les nouveaux arrivants reussissent a l'ecole," *Le Journal de Montreal* (15 March 1994), sec. A22.
80. Derrick Thomas, "The Foreign Born in the Federal Prison Population." Paper presented at the Canadian Law and Society Association Conference, Carleton University, 8 June 1993.
81. *Former Strangers in our Midst: Refugee Resettlement in Canada* (Toronto: Clarke Institute of Psychiatry and University of Toronto, September 1994).

82. Andrew Coyne, "How Do We Know Canada Couldn't Take in a Million People a Year?" *Globe and Mail,* 1 August 1994.
83. See David Matas, *No More: The Battle against Human Rights Violations* (Toronto: Dundurn Press, 1994), Conclusions.
84. The Greater Manchester Immigration Aid Unit, in their newsletter *No One is Illegal*, has published a series of articles arguing against immigration controls of every sort.
85. See David Matas, *No More: The Battle against Human Rights Violations*, Conclusions.

19

Freedom of Migration:
Legal Standards and State Practice

Justus R. Weiner

Introduction

Few topics relating to international law and practice have generated the amount of scholarly and popular attention that the migration of persons across sovereign boundaries has engendered. This focus has been all the more intense following the 1975 Helsinki Final Act,[1] the Schengen Supplementary Agreement in June 1990,[2] and the 1992 Maastricht Treaty on European Union,[3] each of which extended, in a *de jure* or *de facto* manner, freedom of movement across certain national borders. Yet despite these and other milestones on the long road toward greater freedom of international migration, various practical issues have made even nations that traditionally receive large numbers of immigrants such as the United States, refrain from embracing open borders in practice. Some scholars, citing economic theory[4] and/or libertarian concepts of human rights,[5] advocate virtually unrestricted international movement. Perhaps coincidentally, a popular misconception has emerged which views total freedom of migration as, *a priori*, *the* moral and practical approach. This misperception may have been caused by the media's highlighting the suffering and privation that exists in many countries, or by the transparently racist motivations of some who oppose immigration to their countries.

This chapter questions the legal and practical validity of the position that open borders and unrestricted migration are a prudent course of action. In this context the author will examine the legal and practical limitations on international migration with a particular emphasis on the circumstances in the United States and Israel.[6]

Recent Trends of Mobile Populations

Trends worldwide indicate a growing flood of migrants and refugees. Reasons for the burgeoning numbers of migrants vary. Many seek freedom from violence and discrimination. Others desire family reunification. Economic opportunity is another major reason for migration.[7] Migrants are commonly divided into three categories: legal, illegal, and guest workers.[8] According to the United States Population Fund there are currently 100 million migrants in the world,[9] including 15.5 million migrants in Eastern Europe, 20 million migrants in America, 8 million in the Gulf States, and several million in Australia and Canada. Moreover, illegal immigrants are thought to total several million although they do not appear in official census statistics.[10] Refugees represent another category of people not living within the borders of their country of origin. In addition to the migrants, the number of refugees has increased from 2.8 million in 1976 to 8.2 million in 1980, 11.6 million in 1985, 17.2 million in 1992, and 18.9 million in 1993.[11]

This unprecedented flood of migrants has provoked a backlash. Almost everywhere governments and their citizens have become distressed with the problems posed by international migration.[12] Citizens in many countries:

> have become fearful that they are being invaded not by armies and tanks but by migrants who speak other languages, worship other gods, belong to other cultures, and they fear, will take their jobs, occupy their land, live off the welfare system, and threaten their way of life, their environment, and even their polity.[13]

Surveys in the United States and Western Europe reveal growing hostility toward foreigners and support for proposals to restrict further migration.[14] Virtually every country in Western Europe has a right-wing, anti-immigrant political party or movement.[15] In the United States, voters in California recently passed by referendum the controversial Proposition 187.[16] The Proposition denies medical,[17] welfare, and educational benefits to illegal immigrants who are believed to be draining the state's economy.[18] Yet the crisis is not limited to developed countries. Most migrants move from one developing country to another, where they typically place a severe burden on local and international welfare, health, and educational institutions.[19] Violence often erupts as local people fear they will lose their land or jobs to the new arrivals.[20]

Simply permitting unrestricted entry across all borders is a flawed proposition. Following the 1975 Helsinki Final Act and the 1992 Maastricht Treaty on European Union, massive influxes of refugees from the Balkans and Eastern Europe into Bonn, Paris, Bern, Vienna, and Brussels have given rise to a European Union economic crisis. Those requesting political asylum are fleeing, in most cases, "not political persecution or violence but simply economic deprivation."[21] Unregulated entry of refugees of war also places considerable burdens on host countries. Jordan, for example, was overwhelmed by hundreds of thousands of Palestinians who were forced to leave Kuwait after the Gulf War. Similarly, a number of African countries are encountering great difficulties attempting to cope economically and ecologically with the influx of refugees from Rwanda, Angola, Liberia, Ethiopia, Somalia, and Sudan.[22] Not only is unrestricted freedom of movement problematic for most host countries, but immigration also drains the youth, intellectual, and labor resources of donor countries.[23]

Security issues are another component of restricted migration. Immigration can "strain an economy, upset a precarious ethnic balance, generate internal violence, or threaten political upheaval at the national or economic level."[24] Unrestricted migration permits an unknown element into a society, and the results can be disastrous.[25] In a recent New York City survey, residents believed the number of recent immigrants was too high, and presented a terrorist threat. Many felt the bombing of the World Trade Center was the result of uncontrolled immigration.[26] In fact, Northern Irish, Palestinian, Jordanian, Egyptian, Iraqi, Iranian, and Croatian refugees have been responsible for terrorist attacks within their host countries.[27]

Control of Borders: The Core of Sovereignty

At least since the development of the modern state in the fifteenth century, governments have regarded control of their borders as the core of sovereignty.[28] This applies not only to defending those borders against armed aggression by a foreign army, but also relates to such mundane clerical tasks as passport control at international airports. It is therefore axiomatic that states choose which people to admit and which to turn away. Rules concerning who to admit, what rights migrants should have, whether multiculturalism or assimilation should be the goal, and who should be granted citizenship are difficult issues because they touch upon the very essence of the concept of national sovereignty.[29]

Despite various international instruments and decisions which can be understood to auger greater freedom of transnational migration,[30] states everywhere retain the right to restrict entry into their country.[31] This reality finds expression in the Declaration on the Human Rights of Individuals Who are Not Nationals of the Country in Which They Live, approved by the United Nations General Assembly in 1985. The declaration states:

> Nothing in this declaration shall be interpreted as legitimizing any alien's illegal entry into and presence in a State, nor shall any provision be interpreted as restricting the right of any State to promulgate laws and regulations concerning the entry of aliens and the terms and conditions of their stay or to establish differences between nationals and aliens.[32]

Thus, the power to control national borders, and therefore migration, is legally recognized as a principal component of national sovereignty.

Immigration Policies of the United States and Israel

Immigration to the United States

Policies for admission of aliens vary widely from one country to another. Some nations do not admit migrants,[33] some have quotas, some base decisions on labor needs, and others take family reunification into consideration. Some countries, such as the United States, Canada, New Zealand, and Australia are known historically as immigrant-receiving countries. That does not imply, however, that anyone may immigrate to these countries; rather, it means that they have traditionally allowed many people to immigrate. Nevertheless, certain specific criteria limit who may come. Indeed, every nation exercises some control over migration.[34] Significantly, there is no legal basis for claims that individuals possess an international right to unrestricted migration. International agreements and declarations have not taken away the inherent power of states to regulate the flow of immigrants, which, as argued above, is a fundamental tenet of sovereignty.

The United States has accepted more immigrants than any other country. Some 55 million people have immigrated to the United States since English colonists established a settlement in Jamestown, Virginia, in 1607.[35] Until 1960 the large majority of these immigrants came from Europe, but thereafter Central and South America, Canada, and Asia became the leading sources of the newcomers.

Free or even liberal migration, however, has never been a popular position in the United States.[36] Aside from small groups of libertarians, no major American political party or ideology favors unlimited immigration. Even the economists who view immigration as offering economic benefits to the country have the political sense to campaign for expanded immigration rather than open borders.[37]

Jewish Immigration (Aliya) to Israel and the Palestinian Reaction

In Tel Aviv, on 14 May 1948, upon the termination of the British Mandate, the leaders of the new Jewish homeland signed the Declaration of the Establishment of the State of Israel. It states, *inter alia*:

> THE STATE OF ISRAEL will be open for
> Jewish immigration and for the
> Ingathering of Exiles....

According to mainstream Zionism, all Jews in the diaspora are considered exiles since they or their ancestors were forcibly removed from the land in which "their spiritual, religious, and political identity was shaped."[38] Thus, the birth of the nation of Israel created a putative home for all Jewish people.[39] Regardless of their prior citizenship, Israel opened its arms to welcome Jewish immigrants from all nations.

Jewish history recalls the expulsions during the times of the Babylonian and Assyrian kingdoms, the expulsion from England in 1290, the expulsions from France in 1306 and 1394, the expulsion from Spain and Portugal in 1492-1497, the expulsion from Bohemia in 1744, the expulsion from Nazi Germany in the period prior to World War II, as well as numerous other expulsions from cities and regions throughout the world.[40] Also, geographic limitations on settlement, such as the Pale of Settlement in Czarist Russia and the ghettoes of Europe, were often applied to Jews.[41]

In the years preceding World War II, Jews encountered great difficulty migrating from Europe to countries more remote from the looming threat of Nazi Germany. Many countries, even those which had previously received Jewish aliens, forbade substantial further immigration.[42] Books such as *Voyage of the St. Louis,*[43] *None is Too Many,*[44] and *While Six Million Died: A Chronicle of American Apathy*[45] recount the desperation of Jews in their mostly futile efforts to find a sanctuary.

Even after the Holocaust, survivors faced bleak prospects. Few had any desire to return to their pre-war homes in the countries which had betrayed them to the Germans. Migration to America had been sharply curtailed by the Immigration Act of 1924 discussed below.[46] Until the end of the British Mandate in 1948, few Jews were permitted to legally enter Palestine.[47]

In recent decades Jews have continued to suffer restrictive legislation in certain Arab countries. Saudi Arabia, for example, barred the entry of Jews, even as tourists, and absolutely forbids their settling. Other Arab states, most notoriously Syria, for years prevented their Jewish citizens from emigrating.[48]

The founders of Israel sought to remedy the predicament Jews had repeatedly faced in the diaspora — their periodic rejection and exclusion by the gentiles who governed and populated the various countries in which they resided. To this end, Prime Minister David Ben-Gurion defined a central principle of Zionism when, in submitting the draft Law of Return to the Second Knesset, he stated:

> The State is not granting the Jews of the Diaspora the right to return; this right preceded the State of Israel, and was instrumental in building it. The origin of this right lies in the historic link between the people and its homeland, and the Law of Nations has recognized this link in practice. The Law of Return has nothing to do with immigration legislation: it is a law perpetuating Israel's history. This law establishes a principle of statehood, by virtue of which the State of Israel was created.[49]

Even today Israel's national immigration policy is defined by the Law of Return, which in Article I states, "Every Jew has the right to come to this country as an *oleh*."[50] Thus, Israel explicitly defined its immigration policies from the commencement of the state.

Because Israel emerged from the British Mandate of Palestine, the question of citizenship for non-Jewish populations living within the borders of Israel when the state was established needed to be addressed. Apprehensive of being overwhelmed with hundreds of thousands of Palestinians whose allegiance to the state would be doubtful, Israeli immigration and nationality legislation has blocked the mass return to Israel by Palestinian refugees.[51] Pursuant to the Nationality Law of 1952,[52] a person who resided in Palestine immediately prior to the establishment of the state is automatically considered a resident only if he was registered as a resident before March 1, 1952. This legislation was specifically designed to avoid awarding citizenship to Arabs who had left the country during the 1948 war and had returned illegally thereafter.[53] In addition, the

Law of Entry of 1952[54] directly prohibits entry into Israel except for Israeli citizens or those authorized to enter by the Israeli Interior Ministry. In this way, the return of refugees to Israel without approval is rendered illegal under Israeli law which authorizes the deportation of illegal immigrants pursuant to the above-mentioned legislation.

The Israeli legal system has simultaneously addressed the demographic challenge by encouraging the immigration to Israel of Jews from the diaspora, from which approximately two and a half million immigrants have come.[55] In accordance with the Law of Return, 1950,[56] citizenship is acquired automatically upon immigration by a "Jew" as that term is defined within the legislation. These immigrants are entitled to various benefits directed at assisting their absorption into Israeli society. Not surprisingly, Palestinians object strenuously to this enticement for additional Jewish immigration.[57]

Since 1948, the possibility of Palestinian "return" has been viewed by Israelis as both a security[58] and a demographic threat.[59] This fear has translated into a long-standing policy of Israeli rejection of the Palestinians' claims of a "right to return."[60] The favored Israeli solution was to permanently settle refugees in neighboring Arab countries and to offer them compensation for their property losses.[61] Nevertheless, Israeli governments have readmitted over 100,000 refugees and displaced persons as a humanitarian measure, under the framework of family reunification.[62] This "solution," however, has proven impossible to implement due to opposition by the Palestinian leadership and the unwillingness of the Arab countries.

Palestinians and other Arabs object to Israel's Law of Return. The PLO sees the law as effectively denying Palestinians, who consider themselves refugees and displaced persons, entry into Israel.[63] Yet, the security risks of permitting Palestinian Arabs into Israel are considerable.[64] According to the Palestinian National Covenant, the PLO's charter, the central goal of the PLO is to destroy the State of Israel. Although various efforts have been made to repeal this document, which predates and arguably contradicts the peace process, no such repeal has occurred.[65] Moreover, Palestinian Authority Chairman Arafat has repeatedly stated that Palestinians should wage a *jihad* (struggle or holy war) against Israel, despite the six interim peace agreements that have been signed.[66]

Allowing immigration of persons, many of whom would be devoted to the destruction of Israel, is clearly not in the interest of the state. Furthermore, permitting entry of individuals with an ideological justification for terrorist attacks places the general population at risk.

Deleterious Effects of Unfettered Freedom of Migration

Risks to the United States

In the summer of 1996, policy changes concerning immigration in the United States rekindled the long-running debate over the nature of America's status as a "melting pot."[67] Although a nation built by immigrants, recently "natives"[68] have once again been reacting to a large influx of immigrants, mostly from non-European countries of origin. While the volume of people legally immigrating to America in the late twentieth century is historically unprecedented, unfortunately, negative reactions to immigration in the United States are not.[69]

In the period immediately preceding the Civil War, the Know Nothing populist movement, which protested the wave of Irish Catholic immigrants, had as one of its main planks opposition to further immigration to the United States.[70] Although the Know Nothing movement declined, other prominent individuals, groups, organizations,[71] and political parties have expressed anxiety, fear, and other negative reactions at the successive waves of tens of millions of immigrants.[72] The major fears have been that they would deleteriously affect the quality of life, lower the wage levels and standard of living of the wage earners, increase crime, enlarge the illiterate segment of society, augment the indigent, debase the culture, overcrowd the cities, and fragment U.S. values and loyalties.[73]

These reactions, illustrative of public sentiment at the time, led to the enactment of restrictive legislation by Congress beginning in the 1880s.[74] Between 1910 and 1917 three literacy acts were passed by Congress and vetoed by the presidents.[75] Finally, in 1917, an Immigration Act was passed over a presidential veto. This legislation required all aliens over the age of 16 to prove they were literate in some language to be admitted as immigrants.[76] Would-be immigrants who failed this test were sent back. In addition, persons from India, Indochina, Afghanistan, Arabia, and East India were barred regardless of their literacy.[77]

However, these measures failed to stem the volume of immigration, and the process of fine-tuning immigration policy to fit the needs and demands of the nation continued. Hence, the Quota Acts of the 1920s were enacted.[78] They were much more effective with regard to limiting immigration; for example, the 1924 Quota Act limited new immigrants to 2 percent of the foreign-born population from the same country of origin as counted in the 1890 census.[79] Further restrictive quotas were enacted in the 1950s, although refugees fleeing Communism (initially from Hungary in 1956) were admitted under various special legislative enactments.[80]

It was not until 1965 that national origin was eliminated as a basis of selection for immigration visas.[81] In its place a ceiling of 290,000 immigrants a year was established with a seven-point preference list favoring close relatives of U.S. citizens and those with occupational skills.[82] Illegal immigration ballooned during the 1970s and 1980s and as a response the Immigration Reform and Control Act of 1986 was passed. It intended to reduce illegal immigration by punishing employers who hire undocumented immigrants.[83] The most recent major enactment became law in 1990.[84] It raised the number of immigrant visas to close to one million a year.[85]

Certainly, the many changes in U.S. immigration policy reflect the fact that "the attitudes of native-born Americans toward each new wave of immigrants have shifted among tolerance, ambivalence, and outright rejection."[86] The latest trend and the public policy it has inspired leans toward rejection:

> Now, as in earlier periods when patterns of immigration changed visibly, isolationist sentiment seems once again to have become a political force in the United States. The present isolationism is characterized by a turning inward, by attempts to protect one's family, community, and nation from unwanted outside influences. This inward-turning, anti-immigrant mood has found public expression in the demands for restricting legal immigration and in the "English only" movement. Over 20 states have passed legislation making English the only official language of state business, and federal legislation to the same end was introduced into Congress in 1995.[87]

For decades public opinion has remained overwhelmingly negative about the "return" on the government's generosity towards
immigrants.[88] None of the American public opinion polls taken
since the 1960s favored an increase in immigration; one series of
polls revealed that less than 10 percent of the public favors an
increase in immigration levels.[89] Currently, "one survey taken at
the time of the 1996 election found that over two-thirds of all
respondents felt that President Clinton should 'put stricter limits on
legal immigration.'"[90]

In light of this information, the adoption of a policy of "open
borders" by the United States would be calamitous regardless of the
sensitive and complicated issues of the impacts — positive or
negative — that both legal and illegal immigrants make on the
economy and society of the United States. History demonstrates the
vast fluctuations in the attitude of natives towards immigrants —
corresponding both to the actual volume of immigration as well as
to their mostly negative perceptions of immigration and new immigrants — and the exclusive legislation that their concerns have
inspired. In the future, this trend will certainly continue. Thus, an
"open borders" policy, which would inherently preclude any restrictions on immigration into the United States, is fundamentally
undemocratic. Aside from the fact that the option of restricting
immigration has historically functioned as a safety valve, preventing social instability and massive anti-immigrant backlash when
public opinion favored cutbacks, the regulation of immigration is
an expression of national sovereignty. In a representative system
like that of the United States, where sovereignty is ultimately
vested in the nation's citizens, mandating a policy of "open borders" can do nothing but collide with popular sentiment and thereby
dangerously undermine democracy.[91]

Risks to Israel

Zionist ideology requires the admission of Jews from anywhere
in the world regardless of the availability of housing, employment
opportunities, and the potential social dislocations that may follow.
While it is well known that Israel has a preferential policy for
Jewish immigrants, India's preference for Hindus, Nepal's for
people of Nepali origin, Pakistan's for Muslims, Germany's for

people of German origin, and Arab countries for Arabs are less highly publicized.[92] Moreover, no country other than Israel has a strong security argument to support their communitarian preferences. Jews legitimately fear that Israel would cease to be a homeland for Jews if Israel's borders were open to all Arabs and others who wished to immigrate.[93]

Whatever individual Jews may think about the social, economic, and morality issues connected to immigration, it should be recognized that in addition to offering options to individual Jews (i.e., whether to stay in Russia, make *aliya* to Israel, or to move elsewhere), freedom of migration, in the current political environment, could imperil Israel's demographic survival. This flows from the fact that both Palestinians and Israelis are ideologically committed to the return of their brethren from abroad. The Palestinians aspire to the return of their brethren who, for a variety of reasons,[94] emigrated during the period of the 1948 war. While Israel has substantially fulfilled this goal, a similar Palestinian yearning has yet to be realized.

If unrestricted freedom of migration were to be universally applied, the composition of Israel's citizenry could be drastically altered and its future as a predominantly Jewish state placed in jeopardy. If, for example, there were no barriers for Israelis to gain U.S. citizenship, it is to be expected that the 100,000 to 500,000 Israelis who have emigrated,[95] primarily to New York and Los Angeles, would be joined by large numbers of their former compatriots. Their motivations would vary but many would migrate to countries like the United States in search of greater economic opportunities, to obtain a respite from threats of war and terrorism, or to avoid periods of reserve duty in the IDF. Moreover, if millions of Palestinian or other Arabs gained Israeli citizenship, or large numbers of economic migrants moved there for greater opportunity, the demographic foundation of Israel as the Jewish state would disappear. The dream of the rebuilt Jewish homeland, maintained for 50 years with difficulty and against military and political odds, would likely end.

For Palestinians, their claimed "right to return" is the cornerstone of the decades-long struggle against Israel.[96] It is bound up in their yearning for international recognition of a separate Palestinian national identity which they assert is based, in part, on their residence in British Mandatory Palestine prior to the establishment of the State of Israel. To Israel, however, a return of large numbers of Palestinians would pose direct ideological and existential threats to Israel. Zionism, the modern migration for the return of Jews to their ancient homeland, views a Palestinian "right to return" as antithetical to the special, even God-given, historical and religious relationship Jews have with the land. These concerns have been exacerbated by the rhetoric of Palestinian leaders who have traditionally advocated the return of their diaspora as a means or step toward the liquidation of Israel and its replacement by a Palestinian state. According to a reported statement by Yasser Arafat to a closed meeting of Arab ambassadors in Stockholm, 30 January 1996:

> Within five years we will have six to seven million Arabs living on the West Bank and Jerusalem. All Palestinian Arabs will be welcomed by us. If the Jews can import all kinds of Ethiopians, Russians, Uzbekians, and Ukranians as Jews, we can import all kinds of Arabs. We plan to eliminate the State of Israel and establish a Palestinian state. We will make life unbearable for Jews by psychological warfare and population explosion. Jews will not want to live among Arabs.[97]

Moreover, given that globally Arabs outnumber Jews by approximately 20 to 1, and Muslims outnumber Jews by about 80 to 1, it is not hard to envision how, even putting the political motivations of Palestinian nationalism aside, free immigration to Israel by persons looking for economic opportunity or seeking an escape from the political or religious oppression that pervades many states in the Middle East could adversely impact the demographic balance between Jews and Arabs. These immigrants, no less than ardent Palestinian nationalists, or perhaps combined with the nationalists, could radically alter the balance between the Jewish and non-Jewish population in Israel. Moreover, since the birth rate of these groups is higher than that of Jewish Israelis, Israel might become initially *de facto* and eventually through democratic means, *de jure*, a binational state. Thus, Israel's future as the Jewish state could be undermined by an influx of large numbers of non-Jews whose role could be that of a Trojan horse.[97]

Notwithstanding the current stalemate in the peace process over Arafat's "green light" to resume terrorism, construction on Har Homa and the extent of Israeli redeployment, demographic concerns have become increasingly immediate since the onset of the

Oslo peace process. This process, which Israel saw as a means to avoid responsibility for the two million Palestinians in the West Bank and Gaza, has stirred the long dormant political controversy over what to do with the Palestinian refugees from the 1948 war and the Palestinian displaced persons from the 1967 war.

The Palestinian refugees from the 1948 war, their spouses, and offspring pose perhaps the most delicate problem in the entire peace process. This stems from the large number of people involved and the dilemma posed by their aspiration to return to homes and lands within the pre-1967 war frontiers of Israel. Wary of establishing precedents concerning the Palestinian refugees from the 1948 war, during the interim negotiations to date both sides have staunchly adhered to their original positions. As a consequence, neither the Declaration of Principles nor any of the five subsequent interim agreements substantively addresses the issue of the 1948 refugees. Instead, this issue is postponed until the permanent status negotiations.

The Declaration of Principles provides a general structure for approaching the issue of the Palestinians displaced during the 1967 war.[98] It states in Article XVI (2), "The Continuing Committee shall decide on the modalities of admission of persons displaced from the West Bank and the Gaza Strip in 1967, together with necessary measures to prevent disruption and disorder." Its language on the outcome, however, is inexplicit and fails to provide any detail on the resolution of the displaced persons issue.[99] Moreover, the negotiators were unable to reach agreement on even preliminary matters such as the definition of "displaced person" and the modalities for their absorption and repatriation.

Despite the fact that under the present interim agreements Israel has not allowed the Palestinian Authority to adopt its own immigration and repatriation policies,[100] since the signing of the DOP Israel has generally acquiesced to Palestinian demands for repatriation to the Palestinian Authority administered areas.[101] Pursuant to this liberal policy,[102] Israel not only allowed thousands of Palestinians who overstayed their visitor permits to remain in Palestinian Authority-controlled territories, but has permitted numerous displaced persons to reenter, including a number of persons expelled for security offenses.[103] Thus far, over 84,000 Palestinians have been granted residency (including 15,000 who have overstayed their visitor's permit) in the self-governing areas during the interim period.[104]

Even if one disregards the security implications, Israel does have legitimate concerns as regards the prospect for a return of hundreds of thousands of mostly destitute persons from abroad to Palestinian-governed areas. Namely, the returnees would exacerbate the already dangerous shortage of employment and housing. Recent reports from the Palestinian Authority,[105] Israeli,[106] and UN[107] sources indicate that Arafat's administration is teetering on the edge of economic collapse with, in relative terms, a huge budget deficit and high unemployment.[108] Furthermore, the Palestinian Authority currently cannot adequately provide for the existing population in the areas it administers. It follows, therefore, that the peace process can only become more precarious if Israel were to acquiesce in the return of large numbers of additional homeless and indigent people which the Palestinian Authority appears unable to absorb.

Conclusions

While a policy of open borders might strike some as the moral (or economical) approach a country should take, such an approach is not required by international law and no country has adopted this policy. The leading scholar on the law of international migration, Professor Hurst Hannum, has commented, "[I]t must be recognized that at practically no time in history has the freedom of movement across borders, even in the restricted context of the right to leave and return, been unlimited.[109] Hannum continues:

> All commentators agree that some restrictions on such movement are legitimate if imposed for limited purposes in a fair and non-discriminatory manner, *e.g.*, on grounds of securing compliance with valid judicial or administrative decrees; *preventing the spread of contagious diseases*; ensuring fulfillment of certain contractual obligations; and, in time of war, regulating movements that may directly affect legitimate national security concerns.[110]

Clearly, then, it is necessary to address the tension that exists between the individual's preference for open borders and the legitimate interests of the larger community (typically the state) in which he lives or to which he aspires to migrate.

It needs to be reiterated that "there is no internationally recognized right for a non-citizen to enter a country that is not his or her own."[111] On the contrary, as explained above, international law affirms the right of nations to control their borders as an expression of sovereignty. Moreover, the results of totally open immigration would likely be catastrophic for any secure and affluent nation. Such a country, having taken the "moral" path, would quickly be overwhelmed by a massive influx of immigrants from poor and/or violence-plagued countries, bringing with them different political values, economic demands, cultures, and languages. Risks exist as well for less-developed countries if their borders are open. Many of their most energetic, affluent, and educated citizens could emigrate, in a process commonly referred to as the "brain drain."[112] Peasants from a more densely populated neighbor could cross the border in search of land and employment. Furthermore, in a scenario of open borders, a neighboring country could easily expel its ethnic minorities, encourage the emigration of persons carrying infectious diseases,[113] and empty its prison population across the border.

Thus, realistic problems have prevented nations from embracing the principle of freedom of movement. Indeed, nations are faced with a "[c]onflict between moral obligation...to ensure the safety and well-being of their own population and a more universal ethic that values the well-being of all human kind."[114] This dilemma, and the consequent need of fashioning an immigration policy that addresses both the opportunities and the risks, remains a complex challenge facing governments today. There are no easy solutions.

Notes

* The author expresses his indebtedness to Jerry Bien-Willner, Ashley Kushner, and Donyelle Werner for their assistance in this project.
1. The Final Act of the Conference on Security and Cooperation in Europe (the Helsinki Conference) committed virtually all the European states, the U.S., and Canada, *inter alia*, to facilitating "freer movement and contacts, individually and collectively." The signatories also committed their countries to dealing "in a positive and

humanitarian spirit" with applications for family reunification and marriage to a foreigner.

2. Eight European Community member states (France, Germany, Belgium, Luxembourg, Netherlands, Italy, Spain, and Portugal) agreed to dismantle border controls at their internal borders and to follow agreed-upon arrangements concerning asylum seekers.

3. The Maastricht Agreement enabled European Community institutions to assume responsibility for harmonizing immigration and asylum policies for the member states.

4. For example, economist Julian Simon has stated, "the United States would benefit from admitting many more immigrants than it does now — and far more than are conceivable under existing political arrangements." He has also noted the positive contributions of illegal immigrants to the national economy. See Rita J. Simon and Susan H. Alexander, *The Ambivalent Welcome: Print Media, Public Opinion and Immigration* (Westport: Praeger Publishers, 1993), pp. 227-229.

5. See David Matas, "Freedom of Movement," appearing in this volume; see also Geoffrey Erikson, "Immigration: An Open or Closed Door?" (1997), available online at URL <http://www.creative.net/~star/immigrant.htm>.

6. This author will not address the political or economic reasons for the massive increase in the number of migrants. The issue of freedom to move within the borders of a country shall not be considered. Nor will the philosophical and moral considerations of this issue be examined in detail. Finally, this chapter will not consider the practical difficulties arising out of the need for travel documents (i.e., passports and visas), requirements that "travel taxes" be paid, and the non-convertibility of certain currencies.

7. This article will not focus in detail on the complicated economic issues related to international migration. For additional information on these concerns see, for example, Thomas J. Espenshade, Michael Fix, Wendy Zimmermann, and Thomas Corbett, "Immigration and Social Policy: New Interest in an Old Issue," *Focus*, 18 (Fall/Winter 1996-1997):2-10. Also appearing in this issue: Georges Venez, Kevin F. McCarthy, and Julie DaVanzo, "Surveying Immigrant Communities," 19-23 and William H. Frey, "Immigration and the Changing Geography of Poverty," 24-29. See also Guillermina Jamo and Mark R. Rosenzweig, *The New Chosen People: Immigrants in the US Economy* (New York: Russell Sojn Foundation, 1990).

8. Guest workers are employed by a foreign nation to fill particular labor shortages, often seasonal agricultural labor. Their special circumstances will not be discussed in this article.

9. This figure includes legal immigrants and asylum seekers. It does not include refugees. Myron Weiner, *The Global Migration Crisis: Chal-*

lenge to States and to Human Rights (New York: Harper Collins College Publishers, 1995), p. 2.

10. *Ibid.*, at 2.
11. United Nations High Commissioner for Refugees, *The State of the World's Refugees* (Geneva: United Nations, 1994), p. 3.
12. Myron Weiner, *supra* note 10, at x.
13. *Ibid.* at 2.
14. *Ibid.* at 3.
15. *Ibid.*
16. The referendum was approved by a ratio of 3 to 1. School teachers suspicious of a child's residency status are required to report their suspicions to proper immigration authorities. The constitutionality of the proposition is currently being challenged before the courts and it has not, as yet, been implemented.
17. The economic impact of immigrants needing medical care is also a topic of concern in Israel. Concern about HIV infection among immigrants to Israel from Ethiopia, which reportedly is 50 times more likely than among the general population of Israel, has resulted in concern about accepting blood transfusions from the blood they donate to blood banks. Daniel Braunschvig and Judy Siegel Itzkovitch, "Blood Testing," *Jerusalem Post,* 11 February 1996. These same concerns could influence the willingness of Israel to receive additional Ethiopian immigrants, particularly from the Falasha Mura who are currently Christian but whose ancestors were Jewish.
18. Racism plays a very important role in most countries' immigration policies, either implicitly or explicitly. The Irish, who arrived in the United States after the potato famine in the mid-1800s, were the first large wave of non-Protestant immigrants. Their arrival precipitated riots in New York and Philadelphia. Several decades later the wave of Polish, Greek, Italian, and Eastern European Jewish immigrants was greeted with alarm.
19. Myron Weiner, *supra* note 10, at 3-4.
20. *Ibid.* at 4.
21. *Ibid.*
22. *Ibid.* at 1.
23. *Ibid.* at 40.
24. *Ibid.* at 131. See also Faye Fior, "California Braces for 18 Million More People by 2025," *Jerusalem Post,* 28 August 1997, at 7.
25. Legislation, intending to protect against the introduction of a violent element, has been enacted in the United States. For example, the McCarren-Walter Immigration Act in 1952 excluded any aliens "who might engage in activities which would be prejudicial to the public interest, or endanger the welfare, safety, or security of the United States." See *ibid.* at 140. This law was determined to be too broad by

the Immigration and Naturalization Service as the language could conceivably encompass those legitimately expressing concern or opposition. See also Deborah Sontag, "US Deports Felons But Can't Keep Them Out," *New York Times*, 11 August 1997, at 1.

26. Ron Scherer, "Bombing Trial Begins Amid Terrorism Scare," *Christian Science Monitor*, 4 August 1997, at 1. This topic was again in the news when, during August 1997, the FBI arrested three men of Middle Eastern origin who had built bombs, apparently intending to explode them in the New York subway. *Ibid*.

27. Myron Weiner, *supra* note 10, at 139.

28. *Ibid*. at 9.

29. *Ibid*. at 47.

30. See, for example, Guy S. Goodwin-Gill, *International Law and the Movement of Persons Between States* (Oxford: Clarendon Press, 1978), pp. 96-197.

31. Considerable international authority supports the principle that this restriction may not be exercised on the basis of racial, gender, or religious discrimination (see, for example, *International Covenant on Civil and Political Rights*, art. 4 (1); also Myron Weiner, *supra* note 10, at 154) and that refugees may not be returned to their place of persecution. See, for example, Guy S. Goodwin-Gill, *supra* note 31, at 196.

32. Louis Sohn and Thomas Buergenthal, *Movement of Persons Across Borders* (Washington, D.C.: American Society of International Law, 1992). The balancing test is preserved by the Resolution's subsequent proviso that, "[h]owever, such laws and regulations shall not be incompatible with the international legal obligations of that State, including those in the field of human rights."

33. For example, Japan makes it almost impossible for anyone who is not of Japanese background to become a Japanese citizen. Rita J. Simon and James P. Lynch, "A Comparative Assessment of Public Opinion Toward Immigrants and Immigration Policies" (article forthcoming).

34. Myron Weiner, *supra* note 10, p. 83. France and the United States determine citizenship largely on the basis of birth, *jus solis*. Other nations, like Germany and Israel, base citizenship on inheritance or lineage, *jus sangunis*. See Myron Weiner, *supra* note 10, p. 47.

35. Simon and Alexander, *supra* note 5, at 3.

36. Interview: Rita Simon, 31 May 1997, Jerusalem.

37. Simon, *supra* note 37.

38. "Declaration of the Establishment of the State of Israel" in Daniel J. Elazar, *The Constitution of the State of Israel 1996-5756* (1996), at 22-24.

39. Jews are defined in article 4(b) of the Law of Return as those persons born to a Jewish mother. See Law of Return, 4 Laws of the State of Israel 114, art. 4(b) (1950).

40. See *Encyclopaedia Judaica* (Jerusalem: Encyclopaedia Judaica, 1972), vol. 6, pp. 1070-71; Jean-Marie Henckaerts, "Mass Expulsion in Modern International Law and Practice, International Studies in Human Rights," 41 (1995):257.

41. *Ibid.*

42. In March 1938 only 17 percent of Americans polled favored admitting a larger number of Jewish exiles from Germany. See Leonard Dinnerstein, *America and the Survivors of the Holocaust* (New York: Columbia University Press, 1982), p. 1.

43. See generally Thomas Gordon, *Voyage of the Damned* (Barcelona: Plaza and Janes, S.A., 1976).

44. See generally Irving M. Abella and Harold Troper, *None is Too Many: Canada and the Jews of Europe* (Toronto: Lester & Orpen Dennys, 1982).

45. See generally, Arthur D. Morse, *While Six Million Died: A Chronicle of American Apathy* (New York: Ace Publishing Co., 1968).

46. All told, only 137,450 Jewish immigrants arrived in the United States between 1945 and December 1952, most under special programs (the Truman Directive and the Displaced Persons Acts of 1948 and 1950) and only a smaller number pursuant to the regular immigration quotas. See Leonard Dinnerstein, *America and the Survivors of the Holocaust* (New York: Columbia University Press, 1982), p. 287.

47. See Herbert Agar, *The Saving Remnant: An Account of Jewish Survival Since 1914* (London: Rupert Hart-Davis, 1960).

48. Mitchell G. Bard and Joel Himmelfarb, *Myths and Facts* (Washington D.C.: Near East Report, 1992), pp. 179-181.

49. Moshe Zak, "The Rationale of Return," *Jerusalem Post,* 9 September 1994, at 6. The Law of Return was passed by the Knesset on 5 July 1950. *Ibid.*

50. *Oleh* (plural: *olim*; verb: *aliya*) means a Jew immigrating to Israel from the diaspora. Although the Law of Return stipulates that Jewish identity is determined matrilineally (i.e., inherited from one's mother), many of the Russian Jews claim their Judaism through their father's lineage. It is estimated "that some 1,130,000 Jews remain in the CIS, of whom 700,000 are descended from couples in which both partners are Jewish; 100,000 in families where only the mother is Jewish; and 90,000 in families where only the father is Jewish. All the rest are eligible to immigrate under the Law of Return as the grandchildren of a Jewish grandfather, though they are not Jewish." Liat Collins, *Jerusalem Post,* 11 July 1996, at 3.

51. See, for example, Ariel Bin-Nun, *The Law of the State of Israel* (Jerusalem: Rubin Mass, 1992), p. 15. The reasonableness of this statute is analyzed by Professor Ruth Lapidoth. Ruth Lapidoth, "The Right of Return in International Law With Special Reference to the Palestinian Refugees," *Israel Yearbook on Human Rights*, 16 (1986):121-123.
52. Nationality Law, 6 *Laws of the State of Israel* 50 (1952).
53. Bin-Nun, *supra* note, at 41.
54. Entry into Israel Law, 6 *Laws of the State of Israel* 159 (1952).
55. The absorption of 600,000 Jews from the former Soviet Union and Ethiopia in recent years is almost universally regarded as the fulfillment of national destiny.
56. Law of Return, *supra* note 57.
57. Palestinian opposition to Jewish immigration has taken various forms over the decades, including denying the historical authenticity of the Jewish claim to the land, isolating and condemning Israel at the United Nations, pressuring governments to prevent their citizens from emigrating to Israel, staging terrorist attacks against immigrants en route to Israel, and most recently, in February 1995, issuing a paper entitled, "Jewish Immigration to Palestine and its Devastating Effects on the Peace Process." It is significant that this paper, written long after the Declaration of Principles and Cairo Agreement were signed, was issued by the Palestinian Authority's Ministry of Information. Structured around the new organizing idiom of the peace process, the paper repeats the claim that, "This task [*aliya*] cannot be accomplished without the confiscation of more Palestinian land in the West Bank and Gaza." Ministry of Information, Press Office, Palestinian National Authority, *Jewish Immigration to Palestine and its Devastating Effects on the Peace Process*, February 1995; see Joel Bainerman, "Russians, Da, Palestinians, La," *Jerusalem Post,* 12 April 1991, at 16; Jonathan Kuttab, "Why the Immigration of Soviet Jews Must be Opposed," *Middle East International* (March 1990):16.
58. According to one assessment:

> That the Arab refugee chose to cast his lot with the Arab invaders of Israel is a matter of record. The aggression in which he joined in defiance of the partition resolution of the United Nations created new circumstances, and by no rational, legal, or moral standard could the fledgling unexpectedly victorious, be asked to welcome its enemies. There are, after all, some historical comparisons that are worth making.
>   ...[It is] instructive to recall the attitude of the American revolutionaries toward the Tories who fled the thirteen colonies and made cause with the British. The founding fathers,

notably Ben Franklin, objected not only to their return but to
the granting of compensation for their confiscated estates. So
long as the young republic was in danger, Franklin, who conducted the negotiations with the British in regard to the Tory
refugees, refused to countenance their return. In 1789, he wrote
of a group of loyalists who had settled in what was then British
territory: "They have left us to live under the government of
their King in England and Nova Scotia. We do not miss them
nor wish their return." Though the loyalists were of the same
stock as the revolutionaries and there was no scarcity of land
for them to return to, the Americans were not disposed to trust
in their good faith: "I believe the opposition given by many to
their re-establishing among us is owing to a firm persuasion
that there could be no reliance on their oaths" (Benjamin
Franklin, in a letter dated June 26, 1785).

Marie Syrkin, "The Palestinian Refugees: Resettlement, Repatriation or Restoration," appearing in Irving Howe and Carl Gershman,
eds., *Israel, the Arabs and the Middle East* (New York: Bantam
Books, 1972), pp. 167-168.
59. Shlomo Gazit, *The Palestinian Refugee Problem* (Tel Aviv: Tel Aviv
U., Jaffee Center for Strategic Studies, 1995), pp. 8-10. In 1978, in
assessing the validity of the Palestinian right to return under the
Universal Declaration of Human Rights (GA Res. 217A(III), U.N.
Doc A/810, at 71 (1948), Kurt Radley observed:

[I]t can be fairly be stated that the return of potentially some one
and one-half million Palestinians of doubtful allegiance to a state
whose population itself numbers only somewhat more than three
million is as valid a threat to that state's "general welfare" as there
is likely to exist.

Kurt Rene Radley, "The Palestinian Refugees: The Right to Return in International Law," 72 *Am. J. of Int'l L* 611, 613 (1978).
60. *Ibid.* at 9-10.
61. *Ibid.* at 10.
62. Shamai Cahana, *The Claim of a "Right to Return" for Palestinians
and its Meaning for Israel* (Jerusalem: Leonard Davis Institute of
International Relations, Hebrew University, 1993), pp. 13, 20-22, 28,
32 (Hebrew).
63. Even after Egypt signed a peace treaty with Israel, its representative
to the UN Conference on the Prevention of Racism held in Geneva
(1981) claimed that the Law of Return embodied racial discrimination. Moshe Zak, *Jerusalem Post,* 5 September 1994, at 6.

64. An issue connected to freedom of migration is Israel's deportation of Palestinians accused of terrorist activities who reside in the administered territories. During the decades after the 1967 war, individual Palestinians from the territories were subjected to an administrative-legal process inherited from the British Mandatory government and, if unsuccessful in pressing their appeals, expelled from the West Bank and Gaza. In addition, in 1992 Israel temporarily expelled more then 400 Palestinians affiliated with the extremist Islamic Hamas and Islamic Jihad organizations. Faced with overwhelming international criticism, Israel permitted the expellees to return after spending only half of the period originally intended abroad. Although arguably legal, it is unlikely this method of mass expulsion will be used by Israel in the future. See Justus R. Weiner, "Israel's Expulsion of Islamic Militants to Southern Lebanon," 26 *Columbia Human Rights Law Review* 357 (1995).

65. See Press Bulletin, Israel Government Press Office, State of Israel, *Amending the PLO Covenant: An Unfulfilled Commitment*, 26 January 1997, no. 21; see also Justus R. Weiner, *The Hebron Protocol: The End of the Beginning or the Beginning of the End of the Israeli-Palestinian Peace Process* (forthcoming, *Boston University Int'l L J.,* available from the author).

66. After signing the Declaration of Principles on September 13, 1993, Arafat was taped during a speech at a mosque in Johannesburg, calling upon the Muslim people to wage a *jihad*, generally interpreted to mean a holy war, for Jerusalem, and likened the DOP to the peace agreement signed by the Prophet Mohammed with the Quraysh tribe, and then abrogated ten years later. David Makovsky, *Making Peace with the PLO* (Boulder: Westview Press, 1996), pp. 147-148.

67. Espenshade et al., *supra* note 8, at 1.

68. Oddly, this term is used in studies on U.S. immigration to describe those citizens who were born in the United States, themselves typically descendants of Western European immigrants to America.

69. Over 50 percent of all immigrants in the U.S. have arrived since 1980, with approximately 20 percent of the foreign-born population having arrived within the last five years. Espenshade et al., *supra* note 8, at 3, 5.

70. Simon and Alexander, *supra* note 5.

71. Today, the scope of groups and organizations that take an anti-immigration or "zero population growth" stance is substantial; among them are FAIR (the Federation for American Immigration Reform) and even the Sierra Club. See Simon and Alexander, *supra* note 5, Appendix B.

72. Professor Francis Walker, a prominent opponent of immigration around the turn of the century, described the Poles, Bohemians, Hungarians, Russian Jews, and South Italians in the *Yale Review* as:

> Ignorant, unskilled, inert, accustomed to the beastliest conditions, with little social aspirations, with none of the desire for air and light and room, for decent dress and home comfort, which our native people possess and which our earlier immigrants so speedily acquired, the presence of hundreds of thousands of these laborers constitutes a menace to the rate of wages and the American standard of living, which to my mind is absolutely appalling....Taking whatever they can get in the way of wages, living like swine, crowded into filthy tenement houses, piecing out their miserable existence by begging and by picking over garbage barrels, the arrival on our shores of such masses of degraded peasantry brings the greatest danger that American labor has ever known.

Francis Walker, *Literary Digest*, 17 September 1892.
73. Simon and Alexander, *supra* note 5.
74. The Chinese Exclusion Act of 1882 suspended the entry of Chinese workers for ten years and barred all foreign-born Chinese from acquiring citizenship. They were not permitted to enter until 1942 when the United States was engaged in World War II with China as an ally. Simon Interview, *supra* note 37.
75. Simon and Alexander, *supra* note 5, at 13.
76. *Ibid.* at 13-14.
77. *Ibid.* at 14.
78. *Ibid.*
79. *Ibid.*
80. *Ibid.* at 15.
81. *Ibid.*
82. *Ibid.*
83. *Ibid.* at 16.
84. *Ibid.* at 16-17.
85. *Ibid.* at 17.
86. Espenshade et al., *supra* note 8, at 5. See also Celia W. Dugger, "After Crime, She Made a New Life, But Now Faces Deportation," *New York Times,* 11 August 1997, at A8.
87. *Ibid.*
88. Simon and Alexander, *supra* note 5, at 246.
89. *Ibid.* at 246, 257. Simon Interview, *supra* note 37. Free immigration or at least liberal immigration strikes a positive chord for many Jews. This is hardly surprising — many Jewish American families have been

in the country less than 100 years. Their grandparents or great-grandparents may have fled persecution in Eastern Europe to relative safety in the United States. Indeed, the story of the exodus from Egypt by the Hebrew slaves, reiterated yearly in the *Pesah* liturgy and *seder* dinner, tends to highlight the danger that looms for the Jewish minority when exposed to anti-Semitic threats in the diaspora. This awareness has been driven home repeatedly by pogroms, expulsions, massacres and, ultimately, the Holocaust. American polls reveal that Jewish attitudes towards immigration to the United States are typically more positive than any other identifiable group. Nevertheless, most American Jews probably do not favor unrestricted immigration.

90. Espenshade et al., *supra* note 8, at 2.
91. While proponents of unregulated migration may claim that freedom of movement allows immigrants to enjoy human rights that are denied in their home countries, careful analysis of this point reveals that in order to enforce a policy of "open borders," one must subvert the basic right of national self-determination as manifested in popularly-approved immigration policy in the target country. Paradoxically, the civil rights of the citizen population are suspended in order to enhance the human rights of the immigrants.
92. See Myron Weiner, *supra* note 10, at 181.
93. *Ibid.* at 182.
94. Justus R. Weiner, "The Palestinian Refugees' 'Right to Return' and the Peace Process," 20 *Boston College Int'l and Comp. L. Rev.,* XX no. 1 (Winter 1997):15-17, 21-27.
95. From 1948 to 1979, approximately 340,000 people emigrated from Israel. Zvi Sobel, *Migrants from the Promised Land* (New Brunswick: Transaction Books, 1986), p. 13.
96. Syrkin, *supra* note 59, at 157. The Palestinians are unique among groups of refugees in that they have aspired to repatriation while the political conditions that caused them to be refugees persist. Generally refugees have sought asylum rather than repatriation. Radley, *supra* note 60, at 586, 611. Hence it finds little support in the international law on refugees, principally the Convention on the Status of Refugees (189 UNTS 137, July 28, 1951). See *ibid.* at 609-11.
97. Andreas Vistnes, "Arafat Spoke About Eliminating Israel," *Dagen,* 16 February 1996, 1. The report was denied by Arafat's office in Gaza, but was confirmed by Israel Television's Arab Affairs correspondent Ehud Ya'ari. Regardless of its accuracy, both its content and strident rhetoric increased Israeli apprehensions about the direction of the peace process. Justus R. Weiner, "The Peace Process and the Right/Claim to 'Return,'" *Survey of Arab Affairs,* 15 May 1996.
98. See Teddy Preuss, "Refugees: The Real Issue," *Jerusalem Post,* 20 October 1993, 6.

99. Declaration of Principles on Interim Self-Government Arrangements, September 13, 1993, Isr.-Palestine Liberation Organization, 32 I.L.M. 1525, art. XVI (2).

100. *Ibid.*

101. Israeli-Palestinian Interim Agreement on the West Bank and the Gaza Strip, 28 September 1995, Isr.-Palestine Liberation Organization, Annex III, art. 28.11, available online at URL <http://www.israel-mfa.gov.il/peace/interim.html>. Indeed, the Palestinian Authority is forbidden to grant permanent residency in the self-ruled areas without the prior approval of Israel. *Ibid.*

102. *The Silent Migration to 1967 Occupied Palestine*, Article 74, April 1996 (Published by the Alternative Information Center/Project for Palestinian Residency and Refugee Rights). Many Palestinians who fail to obtain Israeli approval for an extension of their visitor's permit choose nonetheless to remain illegally in the West Bank and Gaza Strip. Many of these do so because they are unable to return to the country of their previous domicile, like Libya or Kuwait. Interview with Ingrid Jaradat, Alternative Information Center/Project for Palestinian Residency and Refugee Rights, 18 June 1996.

103. Examples of this policy include Israel's allowance of six hundred Palestinian refugees to immigrate from Lebanon, "Palestinians from Lebanese Refugee Camps are Going to Israel," *Davar Rishon,* 29 January 1996, at 1 (Hebrew original); its incorporation of two hundred Palestinians stranded on the Egyptian-Libyan border by Libyan leader Muhammar Qaddafi in an effort to punish and humiliate the PLO for reaching an agreement with the Jewish state, Miles Crawford, "Qaddafi Expels 30,000 Workers," *Biladi The Jerusalem Times*, 15 September 1995, at 7.

104. Included in this number are several hundred persons expelled for security offenses who now work as Palestinian policemen and Palestinian Authority officials. *Ibid.* Danny Rubinstein, "The Little Return," *Ha'aretz*, 23 September 1994, at B3 (Hebrew original); Eytan Rabin and Gideon Alon, "Security Apparatus Considering Possibility of Evacuating Six Cities in West Bank by End of 1995," *Ha'aretz*, 4 July 1995, at A1 (Hebrew original).

105. Jaradat, *supra* note 101.

106. David Harris, "Palestinian Authority: Closure Will Cost $600m. in 1996," *Jerusalem Post,* 25 August 1996, at 2. According to a report of the Palestinian Economic Council for Development and Reconstruction, unemployment stands at 40 percent in the West Bank and 51 percent in Gaza. This unemployment has caused a reduction in tax revenues for the Palestinian Authority. *Ibid.* at 108.

107. According to an Israeli journalist who visited Gaza to meet with Arafat:

The depressing economic deprivation that we saw — primarily the result of overpopulation, Palestinian Authority fecklessness and corruption, and the six-month-long closure — is a problem that can only be addressed effectively with a large measure of Israeli cooperation and goodwill.

Yosef Goell, "Clueless in Gaza," *Jerusalem Post*, 23 August 1996, at 4.

108. Jon Immanuel, "UN Coordinator: PA Near Financial Collapse," *Jerusalem Post*, 15 August 1996, at 2.
109. See generally Hurst Hannum, *The Right to Leave and Return in International Law and Practice* (Bordrecht: Martinus Nijhoff Publishers, 1988).
110. *Ibid.* at 4. (Emphasis added). In the opinion of the author the AIDS epidemic, which has infected millions of people in certain countries, is likely to become another factor, along with fear of terrorism, which augments the reluctance of certain countries to admit immigrants.
111. Thus, the refusal of many Arab states to admit tourists who had an Israeli stamp (indicating they had visited Israel) in their passport probably does not violate international law. *Ibid.* at 83.
112. See Alan Dowty, *Closed Borders: The Contemporary Assault on Freedom of Movement* (New Haven: Yale University Press, 1987), pp. 184-187. Even in the case of Israel, a developed country, if there were no barriers for Israelis to gain U.S. citizenship it is to be expected that the 100,000 to 500,000 Israelis who have emigrated, primarily to New York and Los Angeles, would be joined by large numbers of their former compatriots. Their motivations would vary but many would migrate to countries like the United States in search of greater economic opportunities, to obtain a respite from threats of war and terrorism, or to avoid periods of reserve duty in the IDF. See Zvi Sobel, *Migrants from the Promised Land, op. cit.,* p. 13.
113. "HIV/AIDS: The Global Epidemic," UNAIDS and World Health Organization, (http://www:us.unaids.org/highband/document/epidemio/situat96.html, 1996). In certain countries in central Africa, the percentage of persons carrying HIV, the precursor to AIDS, is upwards of 40 percent. *Ibid.* at 12. The AIDS epidemic carries with it enormous medical expenses which, in many countries, are borne by the public.
114. Myron Weiner, *supra* note 10, at x.

Appendix

Study of Jewish Community Organization — Publications

(See separate sections for Canadian Jewry, U.S. Jewry, and Jews from the Former Soviet Union)

World Jewry

Books

The Balkan Jewish Communities: Yugoslavia, Bulgaria, Greece and Turkey — Daniel J. Elazar, Harriet Pass Freidenreich, Baruch Hazzan, and Adina Weiss Liberles (1984)

European Jewry: A Handbook — Ernest Stock, ed. (1982)

Jewish Centers and Peripheries: Europe between America and Israel 50 Years After World War II — S. Ilan Troen, ed. (1998)

Jewish Communities in Frontier Societies: Argentina, Australia and South Africa — Daniel J. Elazar with Peter Medding (1983)

The Jewish Communities of Scandinavia: Sweden, Denmark, Norway, and Finland — Daniel J. Elazar, Adina Weiss Liberles, and Simcha Werner (1984)

The Jews of Yugoslavia: A Quest for Community — Harriet Pass Freidenreich (1979)

Ottomans, Turks and the Jewish Polity: A History of the Jews of Turkey — Walter F. Weiker (1992)

People and Polity: The Organizational Dynamics of World Jewry — Daniel J. Elazar (1989)

Monographs

"The Communal Organization of South African Jewry," Steven Aschheim (1977) CS1

"The Democratization of a Community: The Case of French Jewry," Ilan Greilsammer (1979) JWP10

"The Jewish Community of Belgium," Adina Weiss Liberles (1970)

"The Jewish Community of Bulgaria," Baruch Hazzan (1974)

"The Jewish Community of Denmark," Adina Weiss Liberles (1977)

"The Jewish Community of Finland," Adina Weiss Liberles (1977) CS30

"The Jewish Community of Greece," Adina Weiss Liberles (1974) CS8

"The Jewish Community of Iran," Daniel J. Elazar (1975)

"The Jewish Community of Mexico," Seymour B. Liebman (1978)

"The Jewish Community of Sweden," Adina Weiss Liberles (1977)

"The Jewish Community of Turkey," Adina Weiss Liberles (1974)

"The Jewish Community of Yugoslavia," Harriet Pass Freidenreich (1974)

"Jewish Multi-Country Associations," Ernest Stock (1975) CR6

"The Jewries of Scandinavia," Daniel J. Elazar (1977) EJ4

"Jews of France: From Neutrality to Involvement," Ilan Greilsammer (1978) EJ5

"The Jews of Norway," Simcha Werner and Adina Weiss Liberles (1977) CS28

"The State of World Jewry: A Contemporary Agenda," Daniel J. Elazar (1976) JPA8

"The Sunset of Balkan Jewry," Daniel J. Elazar (1977) EJ3

"Trend Report on Jewish Social Research in Britain," Ernest Krausz (1971) EJ1

Jerusalem Letter/Viewpoints

"Are There Really Jews in China?," Daniel J. Elazar (1985) JL82

"Argentine Jewry Between Dictatorship and Democracy," Judith Laikin Elkin (1985) VP45

"Australian Attitudes Toward the Jews," William D. Rubinstein (1987) JL98

"Australian Jewry in the Asian Pacific Region," Isi J. Leibler (1986) VP47

"The Brazilian Jewish Polity in a Democratizing Society: The Israelite Federation of Rio de Janeiro State (IPSRJ)," Marcos Chor Maio (1994) JL302

"The Cuban Jewish Community Today," Margalit Bejarano (1990) JL117

"The German Jewish Community: Between Adjustment and Ambivalence," Alan Mittleman (1997) JL368

"How European Jewish Communities Can Choose and Plan Their Own Futures," Daniel J. Elazar (1995) VP320

"Is There a French Jewish Vote?," Shmuel Trigano and Jacky Akoka (1985) JL81

"The Jewish Community of Cracow," Sonia Misak (1997) JL358

"The Jewish Community of Vienna: Existing Against All the Odds," Sonia Misak (1997) JL356

"Jewish Demography — Realities and Options," Rela Geffen Monson and Daniel J. Elazar (1987) VP68

"Jewish Hungary Today," Geza Komoroczy (1997) JL351

"Jews in Egypt — 1983," Ernest Stock (1983) JL60

"Jews of Sao Paulo, Brazil," Alberto Milkewitz (1991) JL124

"The Last Jews in India and Burma," Nathan Katz and Ellen S. Goldberg (1988) JL101

"The New Agenda of European Jewry," Daniel J. Elazar (1984) VP35

"The New Status of the Italian Jewish Community," Yaakov Lattes (1988) JL103

"New Zealand Jewry in Transition," Stephen Levine (1987) JL92

"The Renewed Jewish Community of Spain," Diana Ayton-Shenker (1993) JL270

"Survivors of the Spanish Exile: The Underground Jews of Ibiza," Gloria Mound (1988) JL99

"Who is a Jew and How? — The Demographics of Jewish Religious Identification," Daniel J. Elazar (1986) VP53

"Zionism as a Strategy for the Diaspora: French Jewry at a Crossroads," Shmuel Trigano (1984) VP32

Canadian Jewry

Books

Maintaining Consensus: The Canadian Jewish Polity in the Postwar World — Daniel J. Elazar and Harold M. Waller (1990; National Jewish Book Award, 1991)

Monographs

"Alive and Well and Living as a Jew: Expressions of Commitment to the Synagogue, the Home, and Israel among Jews in Atlantic Canada," M.M. Lazar and Sheva Medjuck (1979) WP

"The Canadian Jewish Community: A National Perspective," Harold M. Waller (1977) CS26

"The Governance of the Jewish Community of Calgary," Harvey Rich (1974) CS16

"The Governance of the Jewish Community of Edmonton," Jennifer K. Bowerman (1975) CS17

"The Governance of the Jewish Community of Hamilton," Louis Greenspan (1974) CS18

"The Governance of the Jewish Community of London," Alan M. Cohen (1974) CS19

"The Governance of the Jewish Community of Montreal," Harold M. Waller and Sheldon Schreter (1974) CS20

"The Governance of the Jewish Community of Ottawa," Zachariah Kay (1974) CS21

"The Governance of the Jewish Community of Toronto," Yaakov Glickman (1974) CS22

"The Governance of the Jewish Community of Vancouver," Edna Oberman (1974) CS23

"The Governance of the Jewish Community of Windsor," Stephen Mandel and R.H. Wagenberg (1974) CS24

"The Governance of the Jewish Community of Winnipeg," Anna Gordon (1974) CS25

"In the Beginning: A Brief History of Jews in Atlantic Canada," M.M. Lazar and Sheva Medjuck (1979) WP

"Surviving: Various Dimensions of Jewish Identification in Atlantic Canada," M.M. Lazar and Sheva Medjuck (1979) WP

Jerusalem Letters/Viewpoints

"The Canadian Jewish Community and the Politics of Quebec Independence," Jack Silverstone (1997) JL361

"Canadian Jewry: Challenges to a Growing Diaspora Community," Michael Brown (1990) JL113

"Canadian Jewry: A Diaspora Community in Transition," David H. Goldberg (1995) JL322

"The Emerging Generation of Canadian Jewish Leaders," Harold M. Waller (1989) JL108

"The Integration of Jewish Immigrants in Montreal: Models and Dilemmas of Ethnic Match," Morton Weinfeld (1996) JL345

"The Montebello Mystery," Harold M. Waller (1988) VP76

U.S. Jewry

Books

Community and Polity: The Organizational Dynamics of American Jewry — Daniel J. Elazar (1996)

A Double Bond: The Constitutional Documents of American Jewry — Daniel J. Elazar, Jonathan Sarna and Rela Geffen Monson, eds. (1992)

Monographs

"Decision-Making in the American Jewish Community," Daniel J. Elazar (1972) CR3

"The Geography of American Jewish Communal Life," Daniel J. Elazar (1973) AJ3

"In the Absence of Hierarchy: Notes on the Organization of the American Jewish Community," Ernest Stock (1970) AJ1

"The Institutional Life of American Jewry," Daniel J. Elazar (1971) AJ2

"The Jewish Community of Delaware," Adina Weiss and Joseph Aron (1976) CS12

"The Jewish Community of Norristown, Pennsylvania," Adina Weiss and Joseph Aron (1976) CS11

"Jewish Education and American Jewry: What the Community Studies Tell Us," Daniel J. Elazar (1970) AJ7

"The Legal Status of American Jewry," Daniel J. Elazar and Stephen R. Goldstein (1971) CR4

"A Note on the Structural Dynamics of the American Jewish Community," Daniel J. Elazar (1971) AJ8

"Patterns of Jewish Communal Participation," Daniel J. Elazar (1972) AJ5

Jerusalem Letter/Viewpoints

"American Jewish Demography: Inconsistencies that Challenge," Sidney Goldstein (1986) VP54

"The Geo-Politics of the American Jewish Community," Jonathan Woocher (1992) VP124

"Is Momentum Enough? The State of the American Jewish Community Today," Daniel J. Elazar (1991) VP119

"The New Geo-Demographics of American Jewry," Daniel J. Elazar (1993) JL278

Jews from the Former Soviet Union

Books

Jewishness in the Soviet Union: Report of an Empirical Survey — Benjamin Fain and Mervin Verbit (1984)

Jerusalem Letter/Viewpoints

"Biblical Scholarship in the Communist World," Yoel Vainberg (1990) JL114

"Birobidzhan 1990: A Traveler's Report," Joshua Stamp (1991) JL119
"The Changing Face of the USSR: A Traveler's Notebook," David Clayman (1989)
    VP84
"The Changing Fortunes of Baltic Jewry," Yoel Weinberg (1992) JL264
"Jewish Identity in Lithuania," Sidney and Alice Goldstein (1996) JL336
"Operation Exodus: Soviet Jewry Comes Home," David Clayman (1990) JL116
"Post-Soviet Jewry: An Uncertain Future," Betsy Gidwitz (1993) JL280
"Post-Soviet Jewry at Mid-Decade — Part One," Betsy Gidwitz (1995) JL309
"Post-Soviet Jewry at Mid-Decade — Part Two," Betsy Gidwitz (1995) JL310
"Rebuilding Jewish Education in Russia," David Pur (1992) JL257
"Revolutionary Times in the Soviet Union," Irwin Cotler (1989) VP93
"Revolutionary Times in the Soviet Union — 20 Months Later," Irwin Cotler (1991)
    VP115
"Russia's Jews: Extinction or Renaissance?," Theodore H. Friedgut (1993) JL284
"Soviet Jewry: An Update from the Field," Robert O. Freedman (1990) VP109
"Soviet Jewry: Yet Another Turning Point," Isi J. Leibler (1990) VP98
"Ukrainian Jewry: Some Personal Observations," Moshe Tutnauer (1996) JL330
"The USSR after the Summer of 1991," Daniel J. Elazar (1991) VP122
"Uzbekistan: A Traveler's Notebook," Arthur Eidelman (1994) JL287

Contributors

Shmuel Adler has been an official of the Israel Ministry of Immigrant Absorption since 1969 where he has served as Director of the Planning Department, Director of the Publications and Information Department, Economic Advisor to the Minister, and Director of the Center for Absorption in Science. He is currently Director of the Planning and Research Division. He has written numerous internal reports and publications, including "Israel's Absorption Policies since the 1970s," in *Russian Jews on Three Continents — Migration and Resettlement* (London: Frank Cass, 1997).

Irwin Cotler is Professor of Law at McGill University and an international human rights lawyer. A constitutional and comparative law expert, he has litigated every section of the Canadian Charter of Rights and Freedoms, including landmark cases in freedom of speech, minority rights, women's rights, and the application of international law to domestic law. He has testified on human rights matters before parliamentary committees in Canada, the United States, the United Kingdom, Norway, Russia, and Israel, and has served as an expert witness in refugee matters before the Federal Court of Canada and the Refugee Status Determination Board.

Natalia Damian is a former professor at the University of Bucharest and is currently Senior Researcher in the Planning and Research Division at the Israel Ministry of Immigrant Absorption. Her latest publications (with Yehudit Rosenbaum-Tamari) include *The First Five Years in Israel: Immigrants Who Arrived from the FSU in July 1990 and September 1991*, Ministry of Immigrant Absorption, 1997

(Hebrew); and "Identite juive et immigration en Israel," *Revue Europenne des Migrations Internationales,* 1996 (12):123-137.

James W. Dean is a Professor of Economics at Simon Fraser University in Burnaby, BC, Canada, and Kaiser Professor of International Business at Western Washington University in Bellingham, WA, U.S.A. His most recent publications include: "Is the European Common Currency Worth It?" *Challenge,* May/June, 1997; "Has the Market Solved the Sovereign Debt Crisis," *Princeton Studies in International Finance,* August 1997; *Banking and Finance in Islands and Small States* (London: Cassell Publishers, 1997); and "Harvey Leibenstein as a Pioneer in Our Time," *Economic Journal,* November 1997.

Sergio DellaPergola is Professor and Head of the Divsion of Jewish Demography and Statistics of the A. Harman Institute of Contemporary Jewry, Hebrew University of Jerusalem. He has published extensively on Jewish international migrations, and on Jewish population trends in Israel and in major communities in North and Latin America, Europe, and South Africa.

Don J. DeVoretz is a Professor of Economics at Simon Fraser University and Co-Director of RIIM, Vancouver's Centre of Immigration Studies. His latest studies on the economics of immigration can be found in *Diminishing Returns: The Economics of Immigration Policy.*

Daniel J. Elazar is President of the Jerusalem Center for Public Affairs, Senator N.M. Paterson Professor of Intergovernmental Relations at Bar-Ilan University, and Professor of Political Science and Director of the Center for the Study of Federalism at Temple University in Philadelphia. He is the author of numerous books including *Community and Polity: The Organizational Dynamics of American Jewry; Israel: Building a New Society; The Other Jews: The Sephardim Today;* and a 4-volume series on *The Covenant Tradition in Politics,* as well as founder and editor of the *Jewish Political Studies Review.*

Manfred Gerstenfeld is a Fellow of the Jerusalem Center for Public Affairs and an international consultant specializing in business and environmental strategy to the senior ranks of multinational corporations. His books include *Israel's New Future: Interviews, Environment and Confusion, The Future Isn't What It Used To Be,* and *Revaluing Italy* (with Lorenzo Necci).

Iris Geva-May is affiliated with the Department of Political Science at Haifa University and previously was visiting professor and research associate at Carleton University and UC Berkeley. She is editor of the *(International) Journal of Comparative Policy Analysis: Research and Practice,* and co-author with Aaron Wildavsky of *An Operational Approach to Policy Analysis: The Craft* (Boston: Kluver, 1997). In recent years her research has focused on immigration policy and investment of human capital, health care policy, educational policy, and comparative policy studies.

Allen Glicksman is Senior Research Scientist and Blanche Goffman Scholar in Jewish Aging Studies at the Polisher Research Institute, Philadelphia Geriatric Center.

George E. Gruen is currently an Adjunct Professor of International Affairs at Columbia University's School of International and Public Affairs. He is on the Academic Advisory Committee of the National Committee on American Foreign Policy and is an Associate of the Jerusalem Center for Public Affairs. From 1962 to 1990 he was Director of Israel and Middle East Affairs for the American Jewish Committee. Recent publications include *The Water Crisis: The Next Middle East Conflict?* (Los Angeles: Simon Weisenthal Center Report, rev. ed., 1992); "Jews in the Middle East and North Africa," *American Jewish Year Book, 1994;* and "Where is Turkey Heading: Implications for the United States, Israel and the Middle East," *American Foreign Policy Interests* (February 1997).

David Matas is a lawyer in private practice in refugee immigration and human rights in Winnipeg, Manitoba, Canada. He holds many positions in the area of human rights including Director of the International Center for Human Rights and Democratic Development. He is the author of *Canadian Immigration Law*, 1986; *The Sanctuary Trial*, 1989; co-author of *Justice Delayed: Nazi War Criminals in Canada*, 1987; *Closing the Doors: The Failure of*

Refugee Protection, 1989; and *No More: The Battle Against Human Rights Violations,* 1994.

David Newman is Professor of Political Geography and Director of the Humphrey Institute of Social Research at Ben-Gurion University of the Negev in Beer Sheva, Israel. He has published studies of the West Bank settlement process, the green line boundary, and the territorial aspects of the Israel-Palestine conflict. His latest book is *The Dynamics of Territorial Conflict: A Political Geography of the Arab-Israel Conflict* (Westview Press).

Alti Rodal is a policy and management consultant to the Federal Government of Canada where she has worked for the Privy Council (Cabinet) Office, several Commissions of Inquiry, the Treasury Board, and a number of government departments. Her areas of work have included policy relating to immigration, multiculturalism, constitutional development, and public sector reform. She has taught Jewish history at universities in Montreal and Ottawa, and has authored numerous reports for government as well as texts in medieval and modern Jewish history.

Yehudit Rosenbaum-Tamari is currently a doctoral student in sociology at Hebrew University in Jerusalem. She is Director of the Research Department, Planning and Research Division, at the Israel Ministry of Immigrant Absorption. Her latest publications (with Natalia Damian) include *The First Five Years in Israel: Immigrants Who Arrived from the FSU in July 1990 and September 1991,* Ministry of Immigrant Absorption, 1997 (Hebrew); and "Identite juive et immigration en Israel," *Revue Europeenne des Migrations Internationales,* 1996 (12):123-137.

Gabriel (Gabi) Sheffer is a professor in the Department of Political Science at Hebrew University, Jerusalem. He is the author of *Moshe Sharett, A Biography of a Political Moderate* (Oxford: Oxford University Press, 1996), and editor of *US-Israeli Relations at the Crossroads* (London: Frank Cass, 1997).

Ernest Stock was director of Brandeis University's undergraduate program in Israel and taught in the political studies departments of Tel Aviv and Bar-Ilan Universities. He is the author of *Partners* and *Pursestrings: A History of the United Israel Appeal* (1987); *Chosen Instrument: The Jewish Agency in the First Decade of the State of Israel* (1988); and *Beyond Partnership: The Jewish Agency and the Diaspora, 1959-1971* (1992).

Justus R. Weiner is an international human rights lawyer and a member of the Israel and New York Bar Associations. He is currently a Scholar in Residence at the Jerusalem Center for Public Affairs and an adjunct lecturer at Hebrew and Tel Aviv Universities.

Morton Weinfeld, an Associate of the Jerusalem Center for Public Affairs, is Professor of Sociology at McGill University in Montreal. He is co-editor of *The Jews in Canada* (Oxford University Press of Canada, 1993), and co-author of *Old Wounds: Jews, Ukrainians, and the Hunt for Nazi War Criminals in Canada* (Penguin/Viking, 1988).

Judi Widetzky is a graduate of the International Leadership Seminar — School of Foreign Service, Georgetown University, Washington, D.C. She is on the Executive of the International Council of Women as Advisor on Migration and Refugees, is a member of the Executive of the International Council of Jewish Women where she is Co-Chair of the Committee on Aliya and Refugees, and has served as Chairperson of the World Labor Zionist Movement.